DINING WITH AL-QAEDA

ALSO BY HUGH POPE

Sons of the Conquerors

Turkey Unveiled

DINING
WITH AL-QAEDA

Three Decades Exploring

the Many Worlds of the Middle East

HUGH POPE

Thomas Dunne Books ☙ St. Martin's Press

NEW YORK

THOMAS DUNNE BOOKS.
An imprint of St. Martin's Press.

www.thomasdunnebooks.com
www.stmartins.com

Translations of all poems by Hafez are by the author

Map by Mike Shand

Library of Congress Cataloging-in-Publication Data

Pope, Hugh.
  Dining with al-Qaeda : three decades exploring the many worlds of the Middle East / Hugh Pope.—1st ed.
    p. cm.
  Includes bibliographical references and index.
  ISBN 978-0-312-38313-8 (alk. paper)
  1. Middle East—Description and travel.   2. Middle East—History—1979–   3. Middle East—Politics
and government—1979–   4. Journalists—Middle East—Biography.   5. Pope, Hugh—Travel—Middle
East.   I. Title.
  DS49.7.P67 2010
  956.05—dc22

                                                                            2009040291

First Edition: March 2010

10 9 8 7 6 5 4 3 2 1

For my mother and father,

who showed me the way

CONTENTS

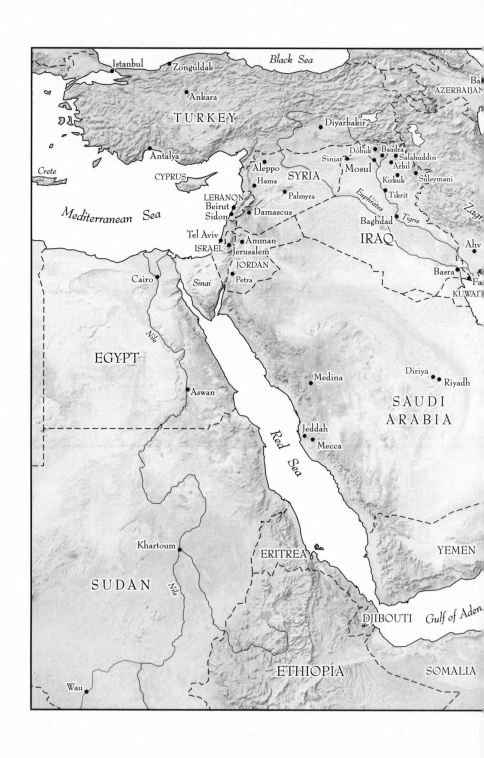

Istanbul
Zonguldak
Black Sea
AZERBAIJAN
Ba
Ankara
TURKEY
Diyarbakir
Dohuk
Baadra
Salahuddin
Sinjar
Mosul
Arbil
Crete
Antalya
Aleppo
Suleymani
CYPRUS
Hama
SYRIA
Kirkuk
Palmyra
Tikrit
Euphrates
Mediterranean Sea
LEBANON
Beirut
Damascus
Sidon
Baghdad
Tigris
Zag
Tel Aviv
IRAQ
Ahv
Amman
ISRAEL
Jerusalem
Basra
JORDAN
Fa
Cairo
Sinai
Petra
KUWAIT
Nile
Diriya
EGYPT
Riyadh
Aswan
Medina
SAUDI
ARABIA
Red Sea
Jeddah
Mecca
Khartoum
ERITREA
YEMEN
SUDAN
Nile
DJIBOUTI
Gulf of Aden
Wau
ETHIOPIA
SOMALIA

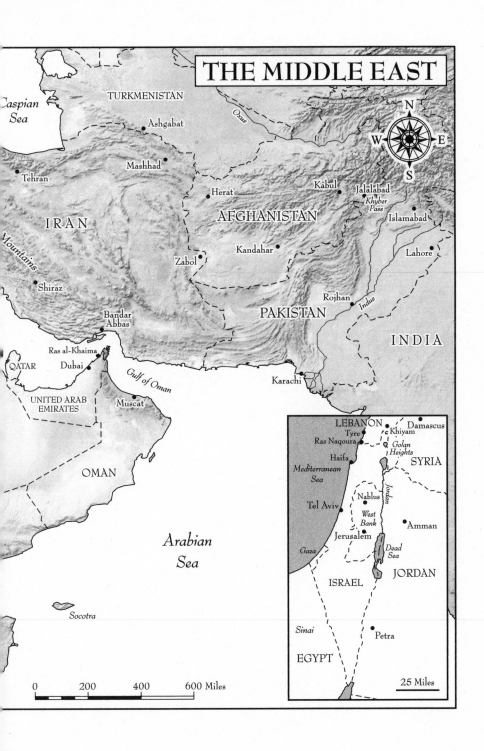

THE MIDDLE EAST

TURKMENISTAN

Caspian Sea

Ashgabat

Mashhad

Tehran

Oxus

Kabul

Jalalabad

Khyber Pass

Islamabad

Herat

IRAN

AFGHANISTAN

Kandahar

Lahore

Zabol

Mountains

Shiraz

Rojhan

Indus

Bandar Abbas

PAKISTAN

INDIA

Ras al-Khaima

QATAR

Dubai

Gulf of Oman

Karachi

UNITED ARAB EMIRATES

Muscat

OMAN

Arabian Sea

Socotra

LEBANON

Damascus

Tyre

Khiyam

Ras Naqoura

Golan Heights

Haifa

SYRIA

Mediterranean Sea

Tel Aviv

Nablus

Jordan

Amman

West Bank

Jerusalem

Dead Sea

Gaza

JORDAN

ISRAEL

Sinai

Petra

EGYPT

0   200   400   600 Miles

25 Miles

PROLOGUE

I have lived and worked in the Middle East for more than three decades, and this book contains what I feel to be my most compelling experiences from journeys and meetings in some two dozen countries. I have visited many of these lands repeatedly, first as a traveler, then as a student of the Arabic, Persian, and Turkish languages, and then as a foreign correspondent, most recently for the *Wall Street Journal*.

I chose the stories to underline what I believe is essential to understanding the people, governments, and social forces at work in the region. They sidestep the ins and outs of theoretical debates, acronyms, and quickly forgotten politicians' names. As I wrote these pages, I imagined an enthusiastic student or well-educated traveler trying to make sense of the Middle East and frustrated with dry and theoretical approaches.

I wanted to share my confusion, insights, and the hilarious moments as I was educated out of my initial bafflement and into an understanding of the absurd paradoxes of dysfunctional states. I met people trapped between ruthless tyrants and an insensitive outside world. I experienced not only cruelty, fear, and war, but also poetry, love, and adventure. Along the way I want to explain how I came to terms with a very muddled East and also suggest new ways that a meddling West can better come to terms with the region.

I believe that the United States and other nations' policy mistakes of the past decades are based on a fundamental blindness toward the people and circumstances of Middle Eastern countries, and an overreadiness to think of the region in terms of simplistic ideological labels like "Arabs," "Islam," or "terror." As President Obama's new American administration took office explicitly promising to listen to and to reassess its approach to the Middle East, I hope my observations can be a source of new ideas, empathy, and change.

Avoiding classic territorial subdivisions, I have made the scope of this book the whole Middle East. This is not to say that the Middle East can usefully be seen as a single political grouping; indeed, every country of the region prioritizes its relations with outside powers over any mutual solidarity, and there can be bewildering differences of ethnicity, language, and religion. There are, however, also continuities and overlaps in Middle Eastern societies, history, and geography. This book ranges therefore from Turkey in the west to Pakistan in the east, from Afghanistan in the north to Sudan in the south. There is a particular focus on Saudi Arabia, Iran, Syria, Lebanon, Israel, and, of course, Iraq.

The first five chapters recount my introduction to the Middle East and how I became a foreign correspondent. The next five chapters follow my deeper explorations, from dodging through the streets of Jeddah with a Saudi businesswoman to the chilling night I sat up until dawn talking with a missionary from the al-Qaeda camps in Afghanistan. Three chapters then take a frank look at state formation, dictatorship, and governance in the region. The final five focus on Iraq—before, during, and after the U.S. invasion.

Above all, however, this is a book of stories, from unexpected hiccups with my Egyptian girlfriend, to reeling from explosions in the Iran-Iraq War, to enduring ten weeks trapped in a forgotten, besieged, and famine-struck Sudanese town. Rather than trying to fit every idea into any single political or economic scheme, the artificial, virtual framework that traditional news reporting uses to explain events, I have allowed myself to go with the flow of the truer and more interesting confusion of everyday life. I have tried to recreate on these pages the sense of plunging into the cumin-heavy vaults of the Aleppo bazaar or the edgy backstreets of Baghdad as if you were at my shoulder, so as to communicate as intensely as possible the Middle Eastern reality and vivacious human contact that make the region so addictive to me.

Along the way, I show why it was so hard to accurately report my developing understanding of the Middle East to a Western, and especially to an American, audience. I was lucky to write for the *Wall Street Journal* in its golden age. Yet even in this most prestigious of American newspapers I found it hard to keep my stories out of the ruts of traditional coverage of good "moderates" versus bad "radicals," a misleading focus on an Arab-Israeli "peace process" that has yet to proceed anywhere, and the way many people overemphasize the role of "Islam" as an analytical tool in assessing the Middle East.

The idiosyncrasies of the region, I believe, are more the product of universal problems of inequality, circumstance, and international politics, not uniquely Middle Eastern religions or ideologies. The lives of Middle Easterners, the majority of them only a generation or two away from an illiterate peasant background, differ greatly from those of Americans and Europeans, especially members of Western elites likely to read newspapers that I wrote for, including the *Wall Street Journal,* the *Los Angeles Times,* and London's *Independent.* This is not because there is some insoluble "clash of civilizations" but because of bridgeable disparities in education, security, prosperity, and expectations.

Outsiders find it hard to see that despite the Middle East's occasional agonies, its people are like any other and can have fun too. The stress and conflict in media reports are only part of a much larger reality, just as Middle Easterners should realize that the normality of Western countries is not all as presented in Hollywood films and TV sitcoms. I hope that this book allows a wide audience to see the countries of the region in a new and less confrontational light, to hear the voices of its peoples, and sometimes to laugh out loud.

—HUGH POPE
Istanbul, April 2009

DINING WITH AL-QAEDA

1. MR. Q, I LOVE YOU

Oriental Studies Meets the Middle East

Two watermelons can't be held in one hand.
—AFGHAN PROVERB

I urged my gaze back down to the book of Arabic grammar that lay open on my lap. However hard I pressed my lips together, the curling script kept dancing away from me. My eyes went back up to the flimsy door of my hotel room, rattling in its frame. The knocking was growing insistent. I prayed that Jean-Pierre Thieck, the exuberant Frenchman who had persuaded me to visit Syria, would soon return.

Over lunch on a faraway houseboat moored to a grassy canal bank near the River Thames south of Oxford, Jean-Pierre's wild stories of Eastern adventures had put me under his spell. Now we lodged on the upper floor of a brothel in the northern Syrian city of Aleppo. He had left on an obscure mission and, as the evening lengthened, he had not returned. From time to time, bursts of machine-gun fire echoed over the rooftops. I was only dimly aware of the cause of the fighting. I was paying more attention to the man banging on the door, a tall, virulent Iraqi truck driver from the next-door room. He was clearly determined to break in: first through the door, and then my own efforts to defend my virtue.

"Mr. Q! Mr. Q!" the Iraqi roared, beating the plywood panels. "Open the door!"

Then came silence. He'd be back, I knew. I gave up on the cartoon images of the grammar's polite get-to-know-you conversations. *Arabic Without Pain* was its title, but the promise was false. I sat staring at the wall, anxiously waiting for

Jean-Pierre. I was a second-year student of Persian and Arabic at Oxford University, and felt as if I was getting nowhere. Back at home, it humiliated me that friends in other faculties were climbing the foothills of scientific achievement or testing the boundaries of philosophical debate, while I spent most of my first year copying the ever-changing curves and dots of the Arabic alphabet chalked up on a blackboard as if I were in primary school. The droning of the lecturers, bored numb by our hours of simplistic drudgery, often left me fighting with sleep. None of it seemed relevant to real life. The narrow historical scope of my Oriental Studies course seemed so disconnected from everything I read in the newspapers about the dramas of the modern Middle East.

Still, those same news stories had made me anxious about traveling to the region alone. Over our houseboat lunch, Jean-Pierre, then visiting Oxford for his research into the administration of Middle Eastern cities in the nineteenth-century Ottoman Empire, had gaily insisted that I fly out on my next vacation to join him in the field. When I eventually tracked him down to the cardamom-coffee-scented corridors of a French institute in the Syrian capital of Damascus, he swept me off to Aleppo, two hundred miles to the north. Guidebook in hand, I begged to stay in the colonial-era Baron Hotel, with its creaky, cavernous iron beds, its skyward-ho airline posters from another age, and its threadbare memories of guests like Agatha Christie. After one night, however, Jean-Pierre declared the atmosphere of genteel decay claustrophobic and demanded that we decamp into a rough-and-ready hotel around the corner. It took me awhile to realize that the reason the floor below us was populated by fleshy, middle-aged ladies was that this was a whorehouse known locally as Madame Olga's.

We spent three weeks in Aleppo. Sometimes Jean-Pierre took me to help with his research, notably in an ancient Aleppo merchant's *khan,* or trading house in the bazaar. Here we dug out everything from nineteenth-century photographs to handwritten Korans to Chinese porcelain, buried deep in a cluttered storeroom behind the colonnaded courtyard, where years earlier camel caravans unloaded their wares. I jostled with donkeys and black-swathed housewives through the narrow souks of the bazaar, drinking in the smell of spices and the elixir of being utterly distant from England. Nearly everyone wore ankle-length gowns, not Western dress. The medieval-looking arched alleys had shops on aged wooden platforms, with a knotted rope suspended above to help the shopkeeper heave himself in. At other times I stayed at home and struggled on with my Arabic catechism, sitting upright on one of the two beds in our bare room of whitewashed cement. My ritual of study kept the chaotic rush of new experiences at bay and offered the distant promise that one day I might be able to comprehend them.

My academic efforts, however, were rapidly being overtaken by a crash course in

Middle Eastern reality. At five A.M. on our first morning in Madame Olga's, we awoke to dozens of large explosions shaking the city. Later that morning we discovered that the Syrian army had ringed and sealed all roads into the city. The shopkeepers had declared a general strike, locking down their metal shutters in what I was to learn was the time-honored but often futile fashion of Middle Eastern urban protest. Now a few keystrokes on a computer can dig out reports on the Aleppo troubles of March–April 1980 as part of the Syrian government's unending quest to crush its domestic opponents. Some commentaries say power-hungry Islamic extremists were fighting to overturn the secular order. Others note that moderate Islamists were finding sympathy among businessmen frustrated with impoverishment and corrupt economic mismanagement. Apparently, conservative Sunni Muslims were chafing at domination by the schismatic Alawite Muslim minority who monopolized the country through their strongman, President Hafez al-Assad. Perhaps all of the above was true. Back then, I couldn't have told these concepts apart, and nobody was framing events in these easy sound bites anyway. News agencies and radio stations in Beirut eventually carried a few confused reports from Aleppo, but they were short, appeared days later, and vaguely quoted "travelers from the city." We did not hear about these. Not even Jean-Pierre's vivacious cross-questioning of everyone we met could explain what was going on.

The populace lived in a swirl of conflicting rumors. The bazaar was nearly empty except for the soldiers. A few tradesmen watched in silence as army platoons smashed the padlocked shop fronts open with sledgehammers, making the stone vaults ring with metal clangs and explosions of glass. The army conducted searches for Islamist dissidents, district by district, house by house. I spent most of the first evening on our tiled balcony, hypnotized by the lines of tracer bullets lacing through the night sky. Armored vehicles clanked along the nearby main road, occasionally passed by columns of open trucks filled with frightened civilian captives in pajamas or flowing nightgowns. I could read stress on the faces of everyone, but the population was not necessarily cowed. One of our ladies at Madame Olga's did her share, emptying a bucket of water over the heads of two soldiers as they left the establishment. That image of a prostitute servicing the oppressors but at the same time supporting supposedly "Islamist" rebels implanted in me a long-lasting suspicion of all ideological interpretations of the Middle East.

The soldiers arrested Jean-Pierre and me several times. They were unpredictable, either extraordinarily friendly or so nervous that they armed their guns and rocket-propelled grenade launchers and rammed them into our bellies. Once, when Jean-Pierre's loose-leaf photocopies of Ottoman texts were mistaken for the flyers calling for shopkeepers to strike, we spent an uncomfortable hour in one of the impromptu torture and interrogation centers set up in construction sites on the edge of the city.

With my donkey outside the ancient city of Petra on the edge of the southern Jordanian desert, age four. My family took me on frequent trips to the eastern Mediterranean as a child, one likely cause of a lifelong addiction to the Middle East. 1964. *(Phyllis Garle)*

Jean-Pierre charmed the officer in charge, teaching me that an ability to make people laugh was an essential survival skill. Protected by Jean-Pierre, the edginess was exhilarating. I soon gave up trying to read the few history textbooks I had taken with me.

We did escape for a while from Aleppo, leaving Madame Olga's and its insatiable Iraqi truck drivers behind. One day, Jean-Pierre suggested we visit nearby Alexandretta, over the border in neighboring Turkey. I brushed off my guidebook to line up the most interesting ancient sites to see along this stretch of the Fertile Crescent, cradle of some of the world's first civilizations. I felt a comfortable surge of familiarity. My father, a scholarly detective in the decipherment of ancient scripts, and my mother, a handsome Englishwoman of the indefatigable school, had marched me through countless eastern Mediterranean classical ruins. This was done with little reference to contemporary peoples around them, rather as my university course in Oriental Studies seemed uninterested in modern Middle Eastern culture. At Oxford, Lawrence of Arabia's exciting epic of desert adventures was considered more part of English literature than the Islamic history we had to study from difficult modern theorists. I had not yet discovered the delights of reading accounts by Victorian adventurers, imperial proconsuls, and romantic travelers who could really communicate their broad and intimate relationships with the Middle East, great writers like Richard Burton in the Arabian deserts, Freya Stark in remote mountain villages, Gertrude Bell as she paced the boundaries of modern Iraq, and John Glubb Pasha, who commanded Jordan's Arab Legion. My era judged such nonacademics as lightweight and unworthy. The fashion was for bookish specialization and, partly thanks to the shaming impact of Edward Said's critique of "Orientalism," there was a scorn for Westerners dabbling in Eastern adventures. "Persian," one British professor warned me sternly, "is not a subject for dilettantes."

My antidote to all this was Jean-Pierre, and a new lesson in how to take in the Middle East came in a nondescript village a few hundred yards after the tortuous formalities of the Turkish border crossing. Just as I was relishing picking up speed again, the beat of a drum and the wail of a reed horn made Jean-Pierre's ears prick up. He pulled his car onto the shoulder and headed over to a small crowd gathered in an uneven space before one of the mud-brick houses. A wedding party was getting under way. With cheerful waves we were ushered into seats of honor next to the bridegroom in a wide circle of chairs. I marveled at Jean-Pierre's unending appetite for conversation but was unable to follow more than the overall cut and thrust of the talk. The afternoon wore on.

"Jean-Pierre, shouldn't we be leaving? It's getting dark."

"Take it easy, Hugues. Don't you see how fascinating this is? A pure Kurdish celebration in the midst of Turkey. They've cast aside all their inhibitions . . ."

"But Jean-Pierre, please. If we're to get to the mosaic museum in Antioch, we have to . . ."

He wasn't listening anymore, dragged away by an invitation to join the line of young men who were dipping and dancing to the music, their leader delicately twitching a white handkerchief high in the air and then sweeping it low over the beaten earth courtyard. Jean-Pierre joined in seamlessly yet outrageously, energizing the line with his extra, laughing pirouettes, a jester who had found his court. His hosts would have been surprised to learn that he was actually half Jewish, brought up in the house of a French banker. His conception was as exotic as his life, being the fruit of a brief affair between his French Marxist mother and an English trade union leader from the northern town of Wigan, both of whom had attended the same Socialist conference in Vienna.

Just being part of his sparkling circle made me feel like I was on a romantic Eastern journey. His boisterous chat and infectious laughter charmed all into believing that they were living a special moment, flattered by his boundless curiosity about their lives and politics and disarmed by his wide-open blue eyes, broad forehead, and bald head. Certainly, our hosts were upholding the Eastern obligation of hospitality. But in this Kurdish village, Jean-Pierre intuitively understood how to unlock the clannishness of the occasion, which, if we had driven straight on past, would have been bound by narrow conventions of a village whose livelihood derived from two wheat harvests scratched out each side of the blazingly hot summer months. However, it was linguistically and culturally impenetrable to me. I had a lot to learn and felt like an outsider.

"Jean-Pierre, let's go," I pleaded again. My Oxford cocktail party training had at least helped me spot a natural break in proceedings as people got up and moved around. "We're not going to find a hotel at all if we don't leave now."

"The party's only just starting. Come on!" He led me into a house where torn limbs of freshly roasted lamb lay heaped on a mound of rice.

I had no choice but to follow my guide. I was forced to set aside my English reserve, which I now realize was actually my anxious determination not to be separated from my long-laid, book-guided plan, from my habits of chairs, tables, and restaurants, and from my control over the company and conversation. Jean-Pierre cheered me up by teaching me to plump rice into a ball with my right hand. He reminded me in a whisper that, in the absence of toilet paper, the left hand was used only with water for personal hygiene. Seeing my nose wrinkle, Jean-Pierre rolled his eyes and insisted that this toilet procedure was actually far more pleasurable.

"Don't be so disgusting," I snorted.

"I've even installed a special tap for the purpose in my flat in Paris, you know," he teased me. "It's much cleaner than our filthy ways."

He turned to discuss an aspect of sheep grazing with our host, and I applied myself to the feast before me, and in the right hands of my neighbors, who would pass choice morsels on to me. When I next ate with a knife and fork, I noticed a hard, metallic coldness that I had never tasted before. Many years later, a new generation of upmarket restaurants in Turkey, after decades of imitating Western manners, would come full circle and make a marketing point of doing away with the cutlery.

Back in the village, I spent the night on a thin mattress on the concrete floor of our hosts' main living room, shared with half a dozen other men snoring and scratching away. Hopes that we would be away at dawn came to naught, as a new host captured Jean-Pierre for a breakfast that took yet another millennium. Twenty-four hours later, my touristic plans were in tatters, but Jean-Pierre had acquired an encyclopedic overview of the villagers' life, hopes, and relationships that no guidebook could ever have captured. I gave up on ancient sites and simply followed him, understanding a little more each day. I learned to enjoy the Middle East for what it was, not what it had been or what the guidebooks told me to expect. Above all, Jean-Pierre taught me how to use a magic cloak of unprejudiced openness that guarded him from all suspicion. It was a gift that would serve me well.

Jean-Pierre was, however, not all innocence. He was an enthusiastic homosexual and, thanks to events in a Chicago bathhouse, HIV positive years before either he or anybody else in the Middle East had heard of AIDS. He spiced his love of people with several sexual contacts a day, and I now shudder to think what a swathe the illness may have cut through the communities in which we stayed. He passed away in 1990, adored by a wide circle of friends and honored by French academia with a collection of his writings titled *Passion d'Orient*.

Before those warning twinkles in Jean-Pierre's eyes forced me to take note of it, I had no idea of the homosexual current that runs through much of the Middle East. Unlike in the West, consorting with another male is usually not a statement of sexual identity but mostly a pragmatic solution to the lack of available women. I bumped against it often. After a visit to a Greek Orthodox church in Aleppo, I was astonished to find one of the junior priests looking me up in my hotel and offering me a "massage," which, he claimed, was his day job. And three weeks after I moved to a Syrian village to try to perfect my Arabic, living cheerfully among families with children, all the men in the extended family of my kind hosts invited me to drink tea after dinner.

The conversation took a familiar turn.

"Who are you, Mr. Q, really?"

All eyes were on me, sympathetic and expectant. I sighed.

"I've told you a hundred times. I'm English! Mohammed here and his sister Ayshe visited me in Oxford."

It was true. Jean-Pierre had introduced me to the village during my first visit to Syria in 1980, and I had subsequently guided this pair of unexpected guests around the colleges for a day.

Everyone smiled indulgently. My denials that I was Israeli or American were never taken very seriously. Clearly, they didn't believe a word I was saying.

"No, no, what are you, Mr. Q? What are you?"

"I'm a student, a student! If I was a spy, they would have trained me a bit better than this, wouldn't they?"

The looks all implied that they had seen through my double act long ago and had forgiven me.

"Mr. Q! What we want to know is this," their spokesman said. "Are you Iraqi? Or are you Lebanese?"

This went beyond the most imaginative accusations hurled at me yet, and I looked around the happily smiling group in absolute incomprehension.

"Relax, Mr. Q! What we mean is, do you like to do it, like an Iraqi, or have it done to you, like a Lebanese?"

I retreated the next morning to a new abode in Damascus, where I learned to limit propositions from all and sundry by growing a mustache. Although unlovely, I wore it as a prophylactic talisman for the next fifteen years.

Men assumed that European men were easy game, just as they did European women. Jean-Pierre showed me how a disproportionate number of my contemporaries embraced the Middle East with their interest in male company in mind. It was an attraction to the East shared by famed Western explorers, painters, and adventurers in the past, from T. E. Lawrence to the legendary photographer of the Arab marshes and deserts, Wilfred Thesiger. Indeed, Peter Avery, the Cambridge academic with whom I first discussed my interest in studying Persian, practically sat me on his knee. The achievements of such men had played a big role in firing my imagination, and I wondered whether my lack of a homosexual drive would doom my small attempt to follow in their footsteps. Perhaps their ability to go with the Middle Eastern sexual flow was the key to the success of their exploits—or at least the route to learning some decent Arabic. Perhaps it would lessen the alienation I felt dragging me down when Jean-Pierre was not on hand to interpret events. I even criticized myself for my confused unwillingness to adopt this lifestyle, fearing that without it I would never be able to commune with the storied inner world of the East. In more desperate moments, I wondered if it was my own primness that was perverted.

It took a long time for me to realize that it was actually the absence of women in the public space that was disorienting me, or, given that I had lived in a brothel, perhaps I should say the lack of educated women. Problematic attitudes burst from a Syrian epic film set in medieval times that I went to see in Aleppo. It quickly taught me more about male perceptions of the lusts of war than all my years of reading short, dry accounts of battles in Oxford's Oriental Institute library. For two hours, the turban-clad costume drama indulged in a merry abandon of nonstop massacre, pillage, merciless executions, and the indelible delusion of a rape scene in which the female victim gave a postrape smile of happy satisfaction.

Seeking entertainment during my introduction to Aleppo under siege, Jean-Pierre took me to a nightclub, open in the afternoon because of the curfew. We watched women strippers work a meager audience of bedouins in checkered kaffiyehs, blowing the proceeds from a market-day sale of sheep or goats on the establishment's bootleg whisky. One lady from Angola danced around a chair as her prop but surprised us with her choice of background photographs as she removed her clothes: huge black-and-white images of Adolf Hitler. The few waiters made a show of rushing up to the stage after each successive act, holding a battered, champagne-shaped bottle in one hand and its cork in the other. The audience had no idea of what real champagne was, I supposed, and the performance may have resembled a nightclub scene from 1950s Egyptian films. But I wasn't ready for the climax. As the lady made her bows, the waiters shouted "pop" and flung the cork of what turned out to be an empty bottle onto the stage. Western ways and images might have been a sexy escape from Middle Eastern reality, but the Middle East had made them all its own.

Back on that early evening at Madame Olga's, much of my education was still ahead of me. It was getting late, Jean-Pierre had not returned, and the Iraqi truck driver was back, knocking and Mr. Q-ing me ever more insistently. None of the several Iraqis had any more money for the ladies downstairs. Jean-Pierre was bored of them. He had seduced the brothel's night porter and left to prowl the dark passageways leading to the many shops in our quarter, which had become impromptu barrack rooms filled with soldiers in uniform. This, he declared, was the kind of dangerous excitement that he liked best, even though one morning he had returned bruised and bleeding like a cat that had been worsted in a fight. So the truck drivers were turning to me as the next best available thing. I was young, beardless, and a foreigner in Jean-Pierre's company, so I must therefore share his sexual tastes. Cooped up by the military operations around us, this matter was a subject of general debate. It amused all but me.

"You can't have him," Jean-Pierre would trill in my defense, explaining that I was a *waqf,* or charitable endowment as ordained by Islamic law, whose assets could not be touched by the state, or rather, in this case, the domineering Iraqis. For a while they followed Jean-Pierre's lead in calling me *waqf,* but it was only a temporary defense. They soon went back to the Arabic mispronunciation of my name that stuck fast over the decades to come. But the beating on my door forced me to an early epiphany in the face of all these competing pressures.

"Mr. Q! Where are you? My friend!" said the Iraqi, returning to the offensive with a series of knocks that approached the strength of a battering ram.

"My friend after one minute he will return!" I slowly articulated through the door in my schoolboy Arabic.

"Mr. Q! Mr. Q!" he bellowed. "Mr. Q, I love you!"

A clear response came to me at last: No. I would not be fresh meat for an Iraqi truck driver. I made a hurried calculation. I put down my grammar and laced up my shoes. I faced a lesser threat outside in the shooting and dark army curfew. Smartly exiting the room, I dodged past the astonished Iraqi and out of the brothel. I made it to a nearby restaurant, one of the few that stubbornly kept their doors open onto the deserted streets.

Safe from immediate harm, I felt elated. Yes, it had seemed dangerous. But I had got away with it. Over a heartwarming bowl of lentil soup, I considered my experiences of the previous few days. I realized that I was tasting history in the making and felt a heady awakening of survival instincts never tested in England.

Brave again, and with no patrols in sight, I slipped around the next corner to the

Baron Hotel. There I could celebrate my new state of mind with a drink at the bar and, just possibly, a conversation with someone of my own kind. As I mounted the wide stone steps, I looked through the deep-set illuminated windows. My luck was holding. A busload of foreign tourists was checking in. The Syrian state was proving its skill at pretending that nothing untoward was happening in the country. Soon enough I was chatting with a young secretary from a coal mine deep in the Australian Outback, discovering the world on a yearlong tour. My head didn't just spin with my sudden change of fortune. As I ordered us a new round of cold Syrian beer, it dawned on me that my few days of Aleppo siege living had made me an insider, glamorous in her eyes. Jean-Pierre's high-wire acts had persuaded me that I could not be his kind of orientalist. My South African childhood and early Mediterranean travels meant I was never likely to be fully comfortable in Britain. That evening, I began laying the foundation of my own future in the Middle East. As I unrolled my new-learned wisdom, the Australian traveler gazed up at me in amazed admiration. I was hooked.

2. IT'S A FINE LINE

Journalism on the Road from Damascus

If skill could be learned by watching,
every dog would be a butcher.
—KURDISH PROVERB

The first memory I have of a newspaper is on an ancient oak table in the wood-paneled bay window at my English boarding school. The front page of the tabloid presented a graphic account of the 1973 war in the Middle East. The thick black arrows, showing great movements of armies, were thrilling in a way far above the dull studies I pursued with pale-faced English boys. The tone of the reporting reincarnated other reading material widespread in the school system: irresistible little cartoon booklets that lay everywhere in changing rooms and day rooms, telling and retelling tales of plucky heroism on the part of outnumbered British soldiers fighting a caricature of Nazi Germany. Our masters and parents had known that war and remained under the spell of its excitement.

That sense that the Middle East would supply the great events of my time was strengthened at home. The *Times* correspondent in the Middle East, Robert Fisk, took up the story in sections of the newspaper passed down the breakfast table by my father once he had moved on to his survey of the letters page, the London Stock Exchange, and the crossword. Unlike my educational texts, Fisk had no time for obscure references and on the one hand this and on the other hand that. I adored his dispatches, so close to the action, so clear in their moral vision, and so much more stirring than the humdrum routines of England.

Perhaps that is why, when I finished my degree in Persian and Arabic, I did not interview well for real jobs. I chatted in Persian with a plutocratic British merchant banker, but three years after the Islamic Revolution, there wasn't much demand for Persian speakers in the City anymore. My efforts to enter the British diplomatic service foundered at an exam in which I took double the time allotted to summarize a set text. Finally, three rounds of interviews with a civil engineering company brought me face-to-face with a man who thought I might be useful on Saudi Arabian construction sites.

"What do you feel about building a hospital? It's pretty tough to get right, you know. The oxygen pipes, the nitrogen . . ."

The interview room was small and stuffy, there was a desk between me and the man, and the light coming from the window behind his head darkened his face. An X-ray of a hospital building shimmered up before me, an impossible spaghetti of pipes. I compared that to chasing around Aleppo after the military curfew with Jean-Pierre. I stayed silent.

"Mr. Pope, if we were to offer you this job, would you take it?"

"You're right. I wouldn't. No."

And that was that. I felt a curious relief, despite weeks sacrificed to filling out job application forms. Yet as my contemporaries began to migrate to London, I began to feel the pressure to move on from champagne parties and to come up with a plan. So when my much-loved English girlfriend challenged me as to my intentions, I said, "I'm going to be a journalist in the Middle East."

That fateful change of direction, I realized later, had long been brewing inside me. Perhaps the seeds were sown in happy childhood months traveling with my parents in the east Mediterranean, riding donkeys every day in Crete, asking my mother to buy me carrot juice from street vendors in Damascus, or becoming addicted to the heady taste of honey and thick-skinned yogurt in Athens. Or it was the memory of early excitements, being left in bedouin tents while my parents explored ruins in Jordan, being allowed to handle a police chief's revolver while he gambled with the town governor at our Bekaa Valley hotel, or feeling the wind in my hair as I clung to the ample belly of a Lebanese man who gave me exhilarating rides on his motorbike. Family legend has it that at the age of four I built a cairn of stones amid the colonnades of Palmyra, an ancient city in the Syrian desert, and announced, "I shall come back here."

I'd already experimented with journalism at my boarding school. Nick Thorpe, later the BBC's Eastern Europe correspondent, and I used to sneak at midnight into the headmaster's office, where we would use an ancient stencil-and-ink copying machine to crank off a scurrilous underground newspaper attacking the school regime. New friends at university founded a high-minded and short-lived international magazine and let me help out with the typesetting. And when I sent myself to Egypt for a year halfway through my Oriental Studies program, I unexpectedly spent two months working for a newspaper in Cairo.

This was the *Egyptian Gazette,* to which I was introduced to by Charles Richards, an Arabist who had left Oxford a few years before me. I had heard there might be a job to be had there, and by chance I bumped into him on my way up the stairs of the century-old building that housed the mother newspaper of the *Gazette, al-Gumhuriya,* or the *Republic.* Charles wore a crumpled off-white linen suit and looked as English and debonair as the decay of central Cairo allowed.

"Ah, Hugh! I heard you were here. How are you, my dear boy?"

"Very well, very well," I lied. In fact, I ached with loneliness in those early days in Cairo, however much I enjoyed losing myself in the cacophony of car horns and overpowering smells of the impossibly overcrowded old city.

"Looking for a job at the *Gazette?*" he asked.

"Well, if there is one, you know."

"You can have mine. I've just resigned."

It was like someone offering the services of an unwanted lover. Before I could consider a retreat, however, Charles turned on his heel and led me back into the

My indomitable parents visit me in Beirut, here taking a walk through old Martyrs' Square during a brief interlude without hostilities along the Green Line no-man's-land that divided the city. 1984. *(Hugh Pope)*

newspaper's offices. Here chipped Formica-and-metal tables covered in loose papers were scattered around what looked like had once been a bourgeois apartment. The Egyptian editor, Ramez, was delighted to fill the vacancy so quickly. Yes, he said, I could start right away.

I soon learned why the editor had not asked me for any credentials beyond Charles's airy introduction. My job, alongside Francis, Tom, and others, was simply to take large coils of international and local agency copy from the teleprinters and shorten it for publication. The main running story was the fallout from the Camp David peace treaty with Israel, signed a year earlier by Egyptian President Anwar Sadat and Israeli Prime Minister Menachem Begin. The Syrian and Libyan regimes were meanwhile in the process of "merging" to form a front against Israel. As far as I could work out, however, this was just a ploy to deceive their peoples that at least some kind of action was being taken against the Jewish state. At Oxford, I had enjoyed impressing people with slick cocktail party clarity about Middle Eastern politics. Here, in the field at last, I became increasingly confused. The volume of rhetoric was so loud, the passions so opaque, the information so unreliable.

The *Gazette*'s editorial line worthily promoted Egypt as a bridge between East and West. Almost every country I was subsequently to report from in the broader Middle East made the same claim. Ultimately, I learned, every country in the region viewed itself as a kind of island uniquely connected to the West, not the East. Politically, the "Middle East" barely existed. Thanks to jealous dictatorships and the geographic variety of a region stretching from the Atlantic to the Hindu Kush, I was to learn that this Western-invented term swept under the carpet a great scramble of ethnicities, languages, and religions.

Every day the *Gazette*'s front page had to laud the leader, at that time Anwar Sadat: a photograph, perhaps, or a headline like SADAT: STEADFASTNESS BEARS FRUIT. We were a nationalized newspaper, and there were none of the subtle divisions like those, say, which divide Britain's BBC and the government, or the supposed Chinese wall between the editorial and news operations of grand U.S. newspapers. Out here, politicians were the actors, we were their chorus line.

I was later to discover that the *Egyptian Gazette* was not alone. The ousting of Saddam Hussein in 2003 revealed long lists of columnists in the Arab world who had been on retainer for the Baghdad regime. Indeed, the joke was on those Arab nationalist stalwarts who supported Iraq without being paid. After the invasion, the Iraqi journalists' union agitated for state land to be given to its members, and the Pentagon—through an American PR firm—paid Iraqi media for favorable coverage. Even in Westernized Turkey, TV announcers often read out sneering character assassinations of their owner's political or commercial rivals. At a reception in Istanbul I once challenged a pretty Turkish TV presenter over this practice. She looked unblinkingly back at me and sincerely replied that, obviously, her duty was to read out whatever she was told to, since the television owner paid her to do so.

I don't think any of us who worked on the *Egyptian Gazette* knew anyone who actually read it. After 101 years in the business, dating back to the days when it catered to the occupation forces of the British Empire, it had drifted away from its potential readers. The machinery was so antique that the lines of print rippled along in little waves. The type was still set in lead, composed on the printing machines by curve-backed Egyptian operators. Perhaps some of these men did technically read the newspaper as they took our texts and picked out each letter by hand. But I never saw any evidence to contradict the legend that they could not understand a word of this mirror writing.

Within a couple of weeks I was judged competent enough to work late nights alone as the "stone editor." Every night the paper was underset, which meant there were too few stories to fill the available columns. I had to retrieve stories from the chief subeditor's wastebasket, or translate new ones from an Egyptian news service. The material was utterly irrelevant to the life of anybody I could think of. The temptation to inject some excitement into the process was strong, especially for someone just twenty years old and still at university. I began to make up stories, filling more empty space each evening with my freelance activities. I first tested the water with slightly facetious headlines. Nobody commented. I then invented the sport of racing up pyramids and reported on it. There were no complaints. So it was true. Nobody read the paper, not even the editors themselves.

Needless to say, I soon overreached myself. A story landed on my desk about a broken sewage pipe causing yet more problems with the creaky Cairo telephone system. I spiced it up with a quote from an imaginary telecommunications ministry official: "Unusual smells from telephone receivers should be disregarded." Two days later, Ramez, the editor, a kindly Egyptian who blushed either at the embarrassment of the situation or at the juvenility of my humor, called me into his office for a mild dressing-down. Perhaps he would have worn a less indulgent smile if he had noticed that elsewhere on the same page I had made Egyptian police dogs "recognize the gangsters in lineups of police." In a nearby column I had further reported that one of my pyramid racers, a supposed Liberian tourist out to beat the sport's seven-minute record for the ascent of the Pyramid of Cheops, had slipped and plunged to his death three-quarters of the way up. PYRAMIDS CLAIM ANOTHER VICTIM ran the headline.

I was so ashamed that I resolved then and there never to make anything up ever again, a pledge to which I have remained true. I soon left the paper, however, tired of correcting spelling in secondary international news and bored with recording the daily rounds of governors of distant Egyptian provinces. The paper seemed to be the palest of reflections of the Middle East. My benchmark was still the talents of a Robert Fisk, who won British and international prizes for the unique genius with which he gave voice to the frustration, pain, injustice, and oppression of the region.

After graduation, I decided to start my journalistic career in Syria, a country with which I was familiar, to which I knew I could get at least a tourist visa, and where I reckoned I would face little competition. A friendly editor of the *Economist* gave me a letter of accreditation, but I was so intimidated by the magazine's grandeur and my inexperience that I didn't actually write anything for it for fifteen more years. More at my level was a promise to take my dispatches from a fortnightly specialist magazine called *Middle East International*. With my newly minted degree in Oriental studies, a backpack, and an Olympia manual typewriter bought for me by my grandmother, I took a one-way flight to Damascus.

I had little to lose, and I gradually found my feet. I was helped by a thick-skinned ability to shuffle sheaves of forms patiently between obscure academic offices, the passport directorate and the Ministry of Information, which won me the unusual and mostly unsought distinction of supposedly being a student with an annual residence permit who could also do media work. Before long, visiting reporters started paying me for talking Arabic and guiding them around the journalistic sights, all things I would have readily done for free, star struck as I was by foreign correspondents. The correspondents, mostly from Beirut, would phone me and I would "fix" meetings for their trip and then translate the interviews. Hungry for work and a diet beyond bread and chickpeas, I learned to time any requested briefing on the turgid daily outpourings of the Syrian press at breakfast. That way I could also go round and round the buffet at the Damascus Sheraton Hotel. One day, I heard that Robert Fisk was in town, and the next morning I brought something I thought might win me a chance to work with him: my collection of black-and-white photographs from an obscure old engineering yard of the Hejaz Railway, the one Lawrence of Arabia kept blowing up. With the Ottoman sultan's carriages, ancient abandoned steam engines, and trees growing out through old cast-iron bogeys, I thought it was a rare treasure of a subject. I dared myself to approach him at the Sheraton check-in desk. He had time for only a cursory glance at my offering, however, even if I could take some satisfaction that he did do his own story on it later. These glamorous encounters made me hope that my lot as a twenty-two-year-old freelance fixer might one day become less lonely, monotonous, and impoverished. And indeed, an American news agency soon offered me a dollar for every line of telexed news I sent. I typed long into the night.

My apprenticeship in the ways of the international press ended after just six months. A new Beirut-based correspondent had called me up and I had eagerly accepted an invitation to dinner. We had been alone in the large, soulless Sheraton restaurant. Alone, that is, save for two Syrian security men, who sat next to our dinner table. Between our orders of steaming steaks and decorative desserts—the agents watched us sourly over their tea, supplied free of charge by the hotel—the correspondent offered me the chance to report occasionally for an American radio network. After my excited agreement, he gave me contact names and telephone numbers to write down. With every piece of paper that passed between us, the Syrian agents glowered harder. The job, my new friend said disingenuously, was previously held by a Syrian news agency man who never sent any dispatches and couldn't possibly mind. Unfortunately for me, however, this Syrian journalist could count on his assiduous reporting to his government to prevent any competition. The next morning I was summoned to the Syrian Ministry of Information and ordered to stop all journalistic work. My world collapsed, and I got a miserable bout of flu on top of it.

A week later, my old black Bakelite telephone began to ring again. Night had fallen over the courtyard of my Damascus home, and I was tending to the slow drip of a kerosene stove as it battled against the icy February drafts. I wasn't expecting a call, and it rubbed salt in my wounds to hear the voice of Jack Redden, one of my previous employers from Beirut. On the line, it turned out, was not one caller but a whole group of international correspondents, all joking around a restaurant table to which Redden said they had summoned the waiter to bring a telephone to call me. I was in awe of them all. I loved their cynicism, their carefree irresponsibility, and their daring throwaway lines about the pettiness of Syrian dictatorship.

I also envied the mere fact that they were in Beirut. Only fifty-five miles distant, it seemed a world away, and not just because of checkpoints manned by Syrians, Israelis, militiamen, and multinational soldiers. Getting to Lebanon as a foreigner was greatly impeded by the fact that Syria did not recognize its neighbor, viewing it (until diplomatic relations were finally established in 2008) as one of the most unjust of the colonial divisions of the Middle East. So there was no Lebanese embassy in Damascus from which to obtain a visa. In one of many previous futile attempts to get there, I had taken a twenty-four-hour bus ride to the dour capital of next-door Turkey, stayed a week in a miserable hotel, and become so depressed upon failing to get a visa that I ate two pounds of treacly baklava in one sitting. To me, struggling to pursue my voyage of discovery through the Middle East, Lebanon symbolized everything I couldn't have in Syria: freedom, glamour, fateful international wars, and imported English tea.

From his restaurant table in Beirut, Redden clearly wanted to talk business. He couldn't know of my growing discomfort at the fact that he had called me, and I dared not tell him. By now I had reason to believe that I was being followed and assumed that the Syrian secret police were tapping my phone. What would they be making of clinking glasses, convivial laughter, and talk of an "offer"? If I wasn't careful, I might get expelled altogether.

"Hugh!" Redden shouted down the crackly line from Beirut. "We've got a job for you!"

"I'm afraid I can't. I'm terribly sorry."

I wondered what the job would have been. I felt that I had impressed Redden on his last trip by smuggling him into a Syrian jail, where he wanted to interview a busted drug runner. I had used the ruse that he was a relative, since both were born in Thunder Bay, Canada.

"No, Hugh, here in Beirut. We're offering you a job, reporter and radio monitor. Full-time!"

The arched windows and dark courtyard of my Damascene lodging seemed to expand. A princely salary was named, at least so it seemed to me. The prospect of regular work was heavenly after sitting for hours on the pavement outside the Reuters office, wondering whether the venerable Edmond Khleif would show up to work that day so that I could punch my telex tapes. I accepted the new offer on the spot. Jubilant, I went to make another pot of tea in a corner of the courtyard, negotiating my way around a lemon tree that grew through the kitchen and out through the roof.

I did not yet comprehend the full extent of my professional luck in being taken on by a happy-go-lucky American news agency, United Press International, nor had I yet realized that the large sum I thought I'd agreed to every month would in fact be paid every fortnight. All I could think of was that I was going to the promised land of Lebanon. My ambition to go there wasn't just that all Middle Eastern reporting seemed to come from Beirut. Unlike Syria, stuck in its dictatorial time warp, Lebanon was said to be on the make, full of new possibilities after the Israeli invasion the year before. Even better, someone else was paying for me to travel, giving the first taste of a lasting addiction. Within a week I landed at Beirut International Airport. A visa was waiting for me, all miraculously arranged by UPI.

Nothing had prepared me for the aftermath of the 1982 Israeli siege of Beirut, which itself followed seven years of Lebanese civil war. Buildings were not just left pockmarked by the battles. They were wind-worn by bullets and shrapnel. Some quarters along the short ride into the town center were so wrecked that the only municipal housekeeping had been to bulldoze the shattered concrete into mounds on both sides of the highway.

Gisele, UPI's bright and glamorous office manager, had met me at the half-rebuilt airport.

"It's nothing! We'll soon have it all fixed up," she cooed, seeing what an impact these scenes of devastation had on a first-time visitor. Her bubbliness symbolized Lebanon's false spring of 1983, when, like so many people in the city, she gave in to the temptation to believe that the nightmare was over.

I too wanted to believe that Beirut was being reborn, helped by my own sense of liberation from east bloc Damascus. When Gisele brought me to a supermarket, blithely paying for my first cart of supplies, giggles of disbelief overcame me in one of the aisles double-stocked with luxuries that I had not seen for eighteen months. The fragrance of Earl Grey tea still takes me back instantly to the luxurious feeling of that balmy spring day.

My enthusiasm was buoyed by my ignorance of the real forces that hobble the Middle East. Peace talks were in progress between Lebanese factions, occupying armies like those of Israel and Syria, and external powers, chiefly the United States. In our busy newsroom, deep reflection about the origins of the Lebanese and other Middle Eastern conflicts was not encouraged. Our job was to bash out stories for instant release on who had just said what and where—as one of the editors put it, snapshots of the "twists of the snake." We didn't spend too much time analyzing the snake itself, or its poisonous fangs. For sure, I endured long lectures about the conflicting views of the various sides. I puzzled at all their complicated scenarios. I felt bad for them, and for myself too. I still thought it was my fault that I didn't understand a thing.

Sometimes, of course, it seemed easy. Each morning I learned to tune the short-wave radios in the back office to the frequencies of the Iraqi News Agency and Iran's Islamic Republic News Agency. The two countries were at war, and so were their agency teleprinters, zip-zipping side by side whenever one of their radio signals burst into life. We kept the door slightly ajar in order not to miss the competitive alarm bells, which every few days would announce a new offensive or missile attack on an oil tanker. We would rip off the paper, translate the bulletin, and rush it onto the wires. We had no hope of getting real details. Nobody in Baghdad talked, Iranian spokespeople never seemed to be on duty, and our dutiful attempts to radio-telephone the captain of a stricken vessel rarely got through. Whatever had really happened, it was easy to write and felt comfortably distant, contained in that back room.

Between times the staff would teach me how to write "Sheikh Mohammed" stories. I resented these tiresome court circulars from the Gulf principalities. Agency lore dictated that these lists of who met whom and in what pecking order were essential for our Arab subscribers, but they symbolized the superficiality of media coverage of the Middle East. Then came my introduction to the Arabic radio stations of Lebanon. The government newscast came on the hour, the main Christian station on the quarter hour, a Druze station on the half hour, and the right-wing Christians at the quarter-to. As American envoys crisscrossed the Levant and issued their upbeat statements about hope and progress, we at UPI were trying to do our bit, watching out for stories of progress and setbacks to peace and recon- struction. We also chronicled the wretched aftermath of the Israeli invasion, which had made all the peace talks and reconstruction necessary in the first place. At the time, Israeli roadblocks could still stop me even on roads north of Beirut.

Soon I was allowed to start real reporting. Julie Flint was an early guide, taking me under her wing as a translator. But I had much to learn.

"Let's try these folk!" she cried as we picked our way through the Palestinian camp of Ain al-Helweh, whose name, Spring of Sweetness, belied the crowded squa- lor of a slum reduced to rubble by Israeli tanks and warplanes during the invasion the year before.

"Are you sure?" I asked, looking cautiously in at the wretched home she indi- cated. Plaintive faces looked back. Some Palestinian children trooped over a nearby pile of blasted concrete in imitation of an Israeli patrol, with wooden guns slung around their necks and a radioman to the rear.

"Of course! Go on, my boy!" Julie replied.

I made an elaborate opening statement to the collected old men, wives, and chil- dren about our British origin, our American news agency, and our need to under- stand their plight in order to change the Western perception of the Palestinian problem.

"Just find out if they've seen the guerrillas coming back to the camp," Julie or- dered impatiently.

I winced at this directness. How could we ask these poor people to betray their own? I opened an elliptical conversation, starting somewhere decades before when their relatives had been forced out of Palestine by the expansion of Israel. We quickly bogged down in the awful details. Julie looked at her watch. When she dragged me out an hour later, I still had no proper answer to the question. Julie was indignant.

"You're going to have to learn this is not all about drinking tea!"

I had let her down and felt miserable. Back in Damascus, it would have been an inconceivable slight to small-town customs to spend just a few minutes as a guest in someone's house. Julie, however, had survived the siege of Beirut. She had a boyfriend who was a militiaman, whose camouflage trousers were hanging on her clothesline, and was steely in her determination to lay bare injustice to oppressed nations. That's what I wanted to do, too. Confronted with the unfortunate peoples themselves, however, I never quite got the steel-clad sense of the journalist's right to probe.

Still, I was feeling my way forward on my chosen Middle Eastern path. When I could shake free of my duties at UPI's radios and telexes, I began to go out in the

Walid Jumblatt *(right)*, hereditary leader of the Lebanese Druze community, being interviewed by me *(center)* and veteran *New York Times* correspondent John Kifner *(left)*. Jumblatt had an irreverent panache, joking: "My grandfather was killed. My father was killed. It's a family tradition." 1984. *(Jack Dabaghian)*

field on my own, sometimes even reporting the same stories as the man whose writing had inspired me, Robert Fisk. He tended to work apart from the rest of us. Once, however, I remember waiting half an hour in a queue of half a dozen reporters, all eager to file our stories from a town's single working telephone line, while we listened to the great man arguing why it was vital that his story be on the front page. I was irritated but accepted that his report was going to be more influential and valuable than ours. Another time, I wondered how he'd managed to get an amazing-sounding story from a dull day we all spent staking out Israeli anti-insurgency troop movements in south Lebanon.

When I asked my colleagues about this, they rolled their eyes. "Fiskery!" one exclaimed with an indulgent smile. For a few dazzling reporters, he explained, the essential thrust of the story, and the political message behind it, might well be true, or, from the author's point of view, illustrate a higher truth. But the details, quotes, witnesses, and even whole battles could be embellished to make the story fly, preferably onto the front page. It was a sobering allegation against our trade, and hard to prove. One might doubt or complain wryly over a drink at a bar, and over the years I was to hear dozens of eye-opening stories. But nobody wanted to look jealous or throw stones in our reporting glass house by publicly challenging somebody else's body of work. One might be found to have glossed over something oneself. It's a fine line. Nobody's memory is infallible.

Indeed, I was proud to join the same newspaper as Fisk in 1990 as a freelance stringer in Turkey for the London *Independent,* as well as sending stories to the *Wall Street Journal* and the *Los Angeles Times.* A year later the Gulf War broke out and my stories and photographs began to appear regularly on the front pages of these great newspapers, a thrilling experience. To have a war break out on one's doorstep is, of course, great luck for a stringer seeking to make a reputation and to win the skittish attention of editors.

It was therefore a shock on many levels to wake up one morning soon afterward to a phone call from the Turkish Foreign Ministry spokesman, regretting to inform me that I was to be expelled from Turkey for something just written by Fisk. I hadn't even known Fisk had arrived in Turkey to report on the agonies of five hundred thousand Iraqi Kurdish refugees pressing against the country's southeastern border. The *Independent* had printed in boldface on the front page his story about a terrible drama playing out far from the eyes of the world under the headline TROOPS STEAL FOOD AND BLANKETS FROM REFUGEES.

According to Fisk's report, British Royal Marines and American Special Forces had "cocked their weapons in a confrontation with Turkish troops" after the "Turkish army went on a rampage of looting." The British and Americans, "heavily outnumbered and with little ammunition . . . were forced to watch impotently as the Turks took blankets, sheets and food from the frightened refugees." Fisk quoted a young British soldier saying that "the Turkish soldiers here are shit . . . One of them said to me, 'It's better to starve the Kurds, that way we can control them.' "[1]

It was guilt by association. I was ordered out on the grounds that I worked for the *Independent* too. The Turks questioned Fisk and expelled him the next day. They also immediately drastically scaled back their cooperation with the allied relief effort, worsening the misery of the Kurds freezing and starving on the mountaintops. The *Independent* printed a series of follow-up reports by Fisk and others, condemning and mocking the Turkish reaction.[2] Since my work and my family's livelihood were in Istanbul, I rang every contact I knew in the Turkish hierarchy to plead for a reprieve. They interceded for me, and I was allowed to stay, on the condition that I suspend my main work for the *Independent* for a period that lasted several months. British diplomats told me at the time that Fisk's claims were greatly exaggerated, and that they were aware only of Turkish troops seizing some loading pallets to use

---

1. *Independent,* April 30, 1991.
2. "Police Arrest Award-Winning British Journalist," *Independent,* May 1, 1991; "What Would Ataturk Have Said About the Expulsion of a British Journalist?" *Independent,* May 4, 1991.

as floors for their tents.[3] Still, that did not seem to contradict Fisk's essential story of confrontation and looting. The newspaper offered me a month's salary as compensation, but I was too proud to accept it. Later that year, Fisk happened to pick up the phone when I called the office. "Hello, old boy," he said, and passed me on to the editor. And that was it. Or so I thought.

Nearly two decades later I was unexpectedly taken back to this near-forgotten episode when I stumbled onto Fisk's account of the Iraqi Kurdish emergency midway through his epic book on the Middle East.[4] My eyes started opening wide as I read about that day in April 1991, when Fisk had been able once again to phone his editor and say he "had a story for the front page."

In the book, Fisk conjures up dramatic new detail about the incident. The alleged British-Turkish weapons-cocked confrontation becomes something Fisk witnesses rather than a one-time incident that is reported to him. He flies in with CIA agents who are somehow also American embassy guards. Such guards, as any frequent visitor to U.S. embassies knows, are in reality almost always either U.S. marines or local contract workers. There is an aside: "Why were British soldiers about to shoot at Turkish soldiers for the first time since Gallipoli?" In fact, the British and Turks fought in Iraq and elsewhere for two years after the end of the Gallipoli campaign in 1916, and signed a final settlement of the British takeover of the formerly Ottoman Middle East only in 1926. Never mind, I said to myself, even if I was taken aback by his misspellings and mistranslations, revealing for instance that he "has never seen let alone tasted . . . an exotic commodity . . . a form of Turkish biscuit" that he calls *helvar,* actually meaning *helva* or *halawa,* the most common honey and sesame sweet in the Middle East, sold by weight in delectable sticky blocks, not as a biscuit. Then I came across a puzzling detail that stirred a long-suppressed sense of betrayal. The demand made on my youthful professional solidarity, and the way my livelihood in Istanbul was turned upside-down and nearly put to an end, was all for this?

I decided to check Fisk's account myself. I contacted a senior diplomat I had known in Ankara at the time, and he was more forthcoming than his embassy had been then. He sent me his diary entry showing that the British Royal Marine captain in the area had told him: "Fisk's story has no basis in fact." I pushed further. In his initial report and in the book, Fisk quotes a Royal Marine doctor on the scene, Peter Davis. A few days' inquiries led me to where Davis now worked, no longer a lieutenant surgeon but a lieutenant colonel in the Royal Army Medical

---

3. Nicole and Hugh Pope, *Turkey Unveiled: A History of Modern Turkey* (Woodstock, NY: Overlook Press, 1998), pp. 236, 360.
4. Robert Fisk, *The Great War for Civilisation: The Conquest of the Middle East* (New York: Knopf, 2005), pp. 668–76.

Corps and a consultant in emergency medicine in a civilian hospital in Glasgow, Scotland. I wrote Davis a letter introducing myself and then telephoned him to find out what really happened up in those Kurdish mountains nearly two decades before.

Davis remembered everything well. He told me that he had already spent a week in the camp before Fisk's arrival. And he had no hesitation in saying that Fisk's account of British-Turkish confrontation, terror among the refugees, and rampant looting displayed "artistic license."

"But was it actually wrong?" I asked.

"The gist of what I said was in my quote in the article," Davis answered. "But the tense armed confrontation was incorrect. I was able to go about my business in the camp, doing sick parades of several hundred people, without being oppressed by the Turkish gendarmes. And he has me say, 'locked and loaded,' an expression I have never used in my life."

For sure, Davis said, Turkish troops had gone to the drop zones onto which aid supplies had been parachuted, and demanded money and valuables from the refugees in exchange for delivering the aid. But no, they had not rampaged or seized goods from refugees' hands. Davis had seen no evidence that this profiteering was state policy and thought it was the local action of conscripts. There was indeed ill feeling between the several hundred Turks who "patrolled with attitude" and the forty to fifty American and British soldiers. But no, there had never been any kind of confrontation, and any cocking of weapons would have been considered "macho posturing" and would have had grave implictations for all the soldiers present.

"There was certainly not any difficulty that I can recall," he said. "There may have been an incident between one or two soldiers. But if there had been an armed confrontation, then there would have been an emergency at the camp and orders given for defensive measures, along with 'rules of engagement' to be obeyed in the event that such a confrontation progressed into actual conflict."

Davis and the others involved in the emergency relief effort had been puzzled when, after Fisk's visit, the Turks suddenly demanded that they pack up and leave. At the time, the British contingent had no access to newspapers or the *Independent*'s story.

"We were given less than twenty-four hours' notice to clear out," he said. "We were frustrated, because there was just starting to be a semblance of order in the camp."[5]

A Fisk trademark is scorn for the oversimplification of Middle Eastern news by

---

5. Telephone and e-mail communications with the author, January 2009.

the "boys" of the American networks and the U.S. media in general, that is, reporters like me. Fisk's writing, more than almost anyone else's, manages to step around the cautious conventions of Middle Eastern reporting and drive home at an emotional level the injustices of the dictators and the cruel side of U.S. policies. But facts are facts, indispensable legitimizing agents of readers' emotional and political responses. That is doubtless why Fisk in his book defends his account of the supposed British-Turkish standoff as "perfectly accurate."

Fisk illustrates his story with sudden focus on detail involving U.S. military equipment, terminology, and procedures. Intoxicatingly communicating adventure on his way to the Iraqi Kurdish refugee camp, he describes how a hook-handed U.S. airfield dispatcher unexpectedly thrusts him through lashing rain toward the passenger compartment of a waiting helicopter. A crew member hauls him on board, telling him he has stumbled onto "one hell of a fucking story." The key detail is his recognition that he is in an Apache helicopter, "a big tank-killer," a "mechanical wasp." He describes the Apache's "astounding ability to 'skid' in the air, to turn corners like a car and to flatten out and swoop like a bird."[6] These are indeed the striking capabilities of this machine. The reader vicariously swoops through the mountains with him, a heady moment of the kind that makes reading Fisk addictive, or, as Fisk puts it while describing another such helicopter ride, provides an "Olympian" perspective.

It was as I contemplated this divine touch that the magic of the penmanship wore off. I have clambered over an Apache at a Turkish airshow and I have reported from Apache forward bases in Albania and Iraq. What was Fisk talking about? An Apache helicopter gunship flies with only one pilot and one gunner, a two-person crew sitting fore and aft in an armored cockpit. I contacted the American manufacturers. They confirmed that since production began in 1980, there has never been an Apache built with a passenger compartment.[7]

Another of my illusions about the writing business was crushed when I sat discussing a book I wanted to write about Turkey with an agent in London, she leaned forward to give her most important piece of advice: Don't let hang-ups about facts get in your way. Seeing me recoil, she sought to encourage me with the success of another of her clients. This travel writer had taken one of her ex-husband's stories, she said, and seamlessly integrated it into his text as if it happened to him on his travels through some distant continent. Sure enough, when the same writer came to interview me while on a new Eastern journey, he exaggerated what I said and invented gory details. The technique spiced up sensationally

---

6. Fisk, *The Great War*, pp. 674–75.
7. Information by e-mail from Hal Klopper, International Rotorcraft Communications, the Boeing Company, April 2, 2009.

the two pages devoted to our lunch together, but left me unable to believe the rest of the book.

Editors are reluctant to challenge established writers, and with reason. I still believe that most writers are committed to accuracy. I admired many who spent their careers in the Middle East and rejected the cavalier infotainment culture spreading from the tabloids—meticulous David Hirst, indefatigable Jonathan Randal, brave Patrick Cockburn, omnipresent Jim Muir, thoughtful Max Rodenbeck, not to mention consummate Arabic-speaking agency reporters like Alistair Lyon and Jonathan Wright. Indeed it is the ground-level and often overlooked dispatches of Reuters and the Associated Press that should anchor the footnotes of history, not newspaper rewrites of agency reports. The next generation of writers already features many more Western-educated Middle Easterners, who will doubtless integrate local narratives even further with a new, more universal reporting culture.

I learned the hard way to keep any real criticism of colleagues dry and private. The one time I decided to let it be known that a fellow reporter was cheating and passing off others' work as his own, it was I who became the odd man out, an informer with a chip on my shoulder, and a standing joke. Even in more transparent Western countries, moments of public self-examination are few and far between. The *New York Times* did force one of its reporters to resign for plagiarism and fabrication in May 2003. But to earn this sanction the reporter had to really ask for trouble, cheating in three dozen stories in just seven months on a high-profile domestic beat. In the Middle East, where facts are hard to get and even harder to check, such a rigorous audit is far more difficult; even so, in 2004, the *New York Times* formally regretted that it had not challenged "insufficiently qualified" information published by its reporters and editors justifying the invasion of Iraq. This relative American rigor always made me prefer working for U.S. media. On the news side of the *Wall Street Journal,* where how we handled market-sensitive news was obviously essential to our credibility, we were drilled in a code of conduct to keep us honest and given apparently bottomless American Express cards to fund our work. Refusing free tickets, hotel stays, or gifts did make me feel freer to tell the truth. This was all backed up by seminars on journalistic ethics with straight-backed senior editors, whose starched white shirts I would conjure up in my mind when a person, government, or company sought information or favorable treatment.

But the stricter American approach could go only so far in helping to communicate what people felt in the Middle East. Fisk's technique, however flawed, did allow him to excel in this. Our readers were too far away, physically and mentally, to grasp the emotional context of careful reporting. There was another problem too.

In Iran in the 1980s, I used to tease the eight Tehran-based Japanese correspondents about their daily meetings to harmonize the interpretation of the news that they would then send to Tokyo. Now I see that reporters and editors in most countries, very much including the United States, are reluctant to stray far from national preconceptions.

3. THE PLOT IN THE CONSPIRACY

Spies in the Syria-Lebanon-Palestine Triangle

Trees full of fruit attract many stones.
—SYRIAN PROVERB

At least four governments have put out feelers to recruit me as a spy in the Middle East. Once was in the Oxford University Careers Office. The man who would put me on my path through life was looking at my forthcoming degree in Persian and Arabic.

"Would you consider . . . hmmm?"

"Sorry?"

I felt like I was being propositioned. He looked out of the window.

"You know, government service."

"I thought of the Foreign Office. I like the idea of working abroad. But I got stuck in the civil service exam."

"No, not that, you know, but like the foreign office. We're in touch with . . . you know."

The penny dropped. Spying: cloaks, daggers, deadly games of intrigue. I did not want to live a life full of deception and rejected the idea out of hand.

Yet within two months I found myself beginning a career of reporting about exactly the things spies care about, at ground zero of many a Middle Eastern trouble spot. So what was the big difference in job description? In the early 1980s, Western governments were ramping up their spying capacity as a defense against the terrorist unknown from the Islamic East. There was a lot of public support for that. Wasn't my attitude a little treacherous?

In some ways, it probably was, and therein lay my problem. My initial contacts with the Middle East had aroused doubts in my mind about who was right and who was wrong. I began to think of Britain as an originator of great injustices, and in particular Britain's secret agents. In the First World War, T. E. Lawrence seemed reprehensible for inciting the Arabs to revolt behind Ottoman lines with promises of independence that London was readying to betray. In the 1950s, British and American secret agents in Iran had engineered the ousting of a popular nationalist leader and then propped up a shah whose eventual tyranny provoked the Islamic Revolution. My early days in Syria were so full of history lessons that I can hardly tell them apart. But one was from a kindly old Syrian on the bench-like seat next to me in the train out of Damascus one day in 1980. I was still a student.

"So why did you do it?" he asked.

The question came gently. Perhaps I had misheard. We were surrounded by the clanking of the train, climbing the slopes of the Anti-Lebanon Mountains. Despite

A century-old Swiss steam engine from the Hejaz Railway passes through Ain al-Fijeh, a village where I lived in the mountains above Damascus. 1982. (*Hugh Pope*)

Lawrence of Arabia's efforts to blow it all up, the century-old Swiss steam engine and wooden carriages of the Hejaz Railway had somehow survived the demise of the Ottoman Empire six decades before.

"Excuse me, why did I do what?"

"What had we done to you to deserve it?" he continued.

I looked into his aging face for a clue, but all I saw were deep mournful lines and big sad eyes. Someone had done something bad to him, it seemed, but I knew it hadn't been me. We had been chatting amicably enough. I had told him I was an English student of Arabic. He had told me of his family house farther up the Barada River valley, a ribbon of green poplars that we were weaving in and out of between the rocky desert mountains.

"We have only just met. God is my witness, I have certainly done you no harm," I said.

"So what about 1917, then?"

"What?"

"The Balfour Declaration."

I was stunned into silence as he quietly ticked through the dates and points by which Britain had conquered the Middle East between 1870 and the First World War, divided parts of it up with France, permitted the formation of the state of Israel, and then waged the 1956 Suez War alongside the new Jewish state. I did have a bookish familiarity with the story, but I had never felt any personal connection to it. My traveling companion, however, was holding me responsible for not just British Foreign Secretary Arthur Balfour's promise of a national home for the Jews but also for the miserable lack of development in Syria, the wars that had killed his countrymen, and the myriad limitations that hemmed in his life.

"Listen, I'm just twenty years old! I had nothing to do with it!" I rebelled.

"You're British, and the British did this to us. That's all there is to it," he replied.

"But the Balfour Declaration said that the rights of non-Jews should be protected. If Zionists went too far in Israel, it's not our fault!"

"But it is!" he replied, smiling at the vindication of his assumption, born of centuries of foreign rule, that everything is a plot by outside powers. "More British deception."

"For goodness' sake, that's in the past!" I remonstrated, trying another tack. "If anything, I'm on your side. Look, why else would I be learning Arabic?"

"We know why you want to learn Arabic," the man went on with a knowing look. "They're training you, aren't they?"

I became upset. But the more I protested, the less he believed me. He gave little credence to the possibility of individual action. I was British; therefore I represented Britain. Britain was a stooge of America and America protected Israel; therefore I was the embodiment of the Zionist conspiracy to rob and humiliate the Arabs.

Buttressing this conspiracy theorist's logic was the universal human weakness that assumes that the rest of the world works just like the way it does at home. Since he knew Syria's Baathist regime would certainly try to force a Syrian in London to be part of its nefarious plots, of course an Englishman in Syria would be serving some British spy network. Americans made the same mistake about Iraqis, assuming that because Americans had a democracy and liked the U.S. army, why, the Iraqis, innately democratic people "just like us," would welcome a U.S. army to liberate them from the dictatorship of Saddam Hussein.

The Syrian on the train was neither the first nor the last Middle Easterner to suspect me. I began to spot the "Why did you do it?" question coming even before I was asked if I'd like some tea. A shadow darkened the eyes of anyone I was talking to as he decided I was a secret agent. The accusation of being a spy cut deep, since it classed me alongside the most despised elements in Middle Eastern societies, the agents and traitors within, those whom one is obliged to kill off. Such turncoats, readily available in any impoverished society, are the reason Israeli agents and warplanes have always been able to assassinate Palestinian officials almost at will.

Suspicions ran deep. Since I'd spent four years at university learning to speak Persian, the first place I had looked for work was in Iran. Somehow I got through by telephone to the editor of the *Tehran Times,* who immediately offered me a job as a subeditor. There was one problem: I'd have to acquire my own visa.

I had little idea what it meant for Iran that the Islamic Revolution was still just three years old and that a war with Iraq was bleeding the country dry. But I did think that for my visa interview I should look sympathetically revolutionary and rode the train up to London wearing army surplus green military-pattern trousers. The Iranian visa officer looked me up and down and let me in no farther than the embassy hall, where he sat me at a table under the stairs. I poured out what was in my heart, still filled with medieval Persian poetry. I wanted to help explain the real Iran to the West, I told him, to show the human face of Islam to the world. The rough-bearded official's shadow of suspicion turned into silent scorn. What an obvious, ridiculous spy. He didn't even accept my visa application papers.

Over the years I learned how justified Middle Easterners were to be paranoid about spies. In 1980, a lonely Soviet agent in Cairo courted me with vodka and propaganda films. Later in the decade, American agents in Ankara asked if I'd like to come in for "conversations." I gradually realized that a number of my Oxford contemporaries were in the secret service, including the best Arabist among them, who took me to a country restaurant to pop the question again. "Help us," he said. "We feel like we're blind in Istanbul." Once I tried consulting work but soon found myself batting away polite requests for innocent-sounding essays for a U.S. defense agency even more secretive than the CIA. A French secret service station chief in

Ankara, an army officer who seduced me with fine lunches and sparkling conversation, offered me cash on the table if I would undertake Balkan reporting trips.

Luckily I had never been financially desperate and was able to turn them all down. Still, people didn't believe me. When I was awarded a place in an American business journalism magazine's "dream team" of correspondents, the headline punned on the introduction always used by James Bond: THE NAME'S POPE . . . HUGH POPE. This made me all the more determined to avoid any collaboration or commercial contact with intelligence agencies, convinced that my cast-iron knowledge that I was no spy was the magic element in my protective cloak of innocence. Without it, I wouldn't have dared go to many places I did as a reporter. Of course, I was careful, too. I made sure that my minders in dictatorial places had all the right things to report back to their bosses. I have always assumed all my communications are read and telephones tapped. I learned never, ever to make a joke about spying, a tar that can quickly tarnish one's name. Or, as in the case of my much missed colleague Danny Pearl, a slur that could get a reporter killed.

For many years, I abhorred spying not just because it symbolized the injustice I felt had been meted out to the Middle East, but also out of a kind of snobbery. Spies, I told myself, must live in a uniquely deceitful world of lies. I now see I was being unjust, that there is no absolute truth, and that secret service people are just one of many kinds of government agents, with similar qualities to the rest of us. Their reports could be hit or miss, just like journalists' stories. And I soon became aware that the two lines of business could at times be closely intertwined.

There was only one story in Syria in 1982, or rather, only one issue whose discussion was much permitted in the public domain: Palestine and the Palestinians. In my naïve early days, it seemed a simple enough story to me. The refugees from Palestine still mostly lived where they had set up camp after fleeing or being expelled by the foundation and expansion of Israel. More arrived with the Israeli siege of Beirut in next-door Lebanon. I watched on a mountain road as motley groups of Palestinian fighters retreated into Syria over the mountains, noisily proclaiming victory in yet another hour of defeat. I felt the injustice of what had happened to the Palestinians and was determined to do what I could to write about their plight.

Soon I was sending reports to United Press International. But as I did my interviews, I became tired of the constant spoken and unspoken accusations that I was a spy, or at best irretrievably biased. I wondered if there was any way to prove myself to be evenhanded. So I teamed up for a day with a chance acquaintance from a press conference, Vassily, the correspondent for the Soviet features agency Novosti.

We headed down into the wintry streets of the Yarmuk camp. The squalor would have upset anyone. Why not at least paint the houses? I thought. Or keep

Having known civil war, bombardment, and massacre, the Palestinian refugee camps of Sabra and Shatila still suffer from poverty and discrimination in Lebanon fifty years after the first refugees fled the war in which Israel established itself. 2000. *(Hugh Pope)*

the filthy mud tracks between the two-story concrete houses clean? I had not yet learned how shock could simply paralyze a refugee population. Or how Syria, like other neighboring states, allowed its rhetoric about Arab solidarity to deliver only so much for the Palestinians on its turf. Of course the Syrian government was poor and didn't want to destabilize the balances in the country. But it also deliberately kept the Palestinians in misery to underline the sins of Israel to the world.

That day I asked my questions as usual "on behalf of our American readers." Just when the blaming of all ills on the West was about to begin, or I could sense that I was about to get a more personal "Why did you do it?" speech, I would introduce my friend Vassily "from the Soviet Union." They would look from one of us to the other, speechless for a while. Vassily would give a smug little bow. I got the impression he rarely went out of his office in the Soviet embassy to get his shoes dirty like this. He certainly didn't take any notes for his story.

"You remember everything and write it out later?" I asked admiringly when we were driving back up to town.

Vassily looked at me indulgently and pointed to a little lapel pin. I still didn't understand. So he opened his jacket to allow me to see his inner pocket. A sleek aluminum case peeped out. He slipped it into the palm of his hand. Inside was a beautiful miniature reel-to-reel tape recorder. The lapel pin was the microphone.

"Made in Switzerland," he said lovingly. "It costs three thousand dollars."

DINING WITH AL-QAEDA   33

It was my turn to be speechless.

If I had wanted to be a spy, there were plenty of opportunities. I still missed England and found some solace in the depressing bar in the British embassy basement. There I would pick up extraordinary tales, but, not wanting to be thought a spy, and lacking real reporting skills, I rarely pursued them. U.S. marines would tell the inside stories about underreported assaults by Syrian mobs on their embassy compound. Their accounts were always more hair-raising than the public versions, with hair-trigger fingers on extreme solutions like hidden heavy machine guns or tear gas bombs to knock out the whole diplomatic quarter, always restrained in the end by Washington, D.C. Other regulars told me tales about the fifteen competing intelligence agencies in Syria. And Israel needn't have been worried about Syria's military capacity. One of my drinking companions worked on the Ministry of Defense computers. Fed up with experiencing electrical shocks from the machines, he went down to the basement to check the cable to earth. In a grimy web of wiring, instead of the necessary thumb-thick line to a copper plate, he found just one light-bulb lead trying and failing to do the job.

Even though I didn't seek spying opportunities, spies found me. I happily accepted occasional invitations to dine at the home of a young couple from the British Embassy, luxurious moments of shared Englishness during which I eagerly poured out my new impressions. My host, John Sawers, flew high in the diplomatic side of his career, but his original affiliation only became clear to me when he was appointed in 2009 to be the chief of MI6, Britain's secret intelligence service.

To keep my visa to stay in Syria, every weekday morning I had to attend an Arabic-language college. I had stopped sharing an apartment with my original mentor, Jean-Pierre. One evening I came home and found him cavorting with a half dozen naked Syrian men, one of whom, when I went to brush my teeth, started chasing me with a whip. At first I took refuge with Olaf, half Iranian and half German, who let me sleep on his terrace overlooking the elegant 1950s villas of the Christian quarter. I then shared an Arab house next to the Hejaz Railway station with other friends from the college. Today there are fifty Americans alone studying Arabic in Damascus, but back in 1982 we were just a handful of Westerners. Most of the student body was from the Eastern bloc and Soviet Union. Among them was an impossibly loud-voiced, irrepressible Yugoslav, Slobodanka, my occasional traveling companion and girlfriend.

Slobodanka sometimes helped me after school, when I usually headed down to the Palestinian Liberation Organization's news agency WAFA to pick up their latest bulletin and laboriously plod through its turgid prose. Learning a language is to my mind always directly linked to unavoidable necessity. My motivation was that one of my reporting outlets, UPI, paid me by the line. I didn't hesitate, in those pre-Internet, prefax days, to translate every half-relevant word that WAFA produced and send it on to my editors in Beirut. I still couldn't decipher Arabic media signaling code, and Slobodanka, who spoke very good Arabic, impatiently tried to explain the facts of life.

"You see here, where it goes on about the 'independence of Palestinian decision making'?"

"Yes, of course. That's obvious. The PLO speaks for the Palestinians. So what?"

"No, no, it's an attack on Syria, don't you see? The Syrians are trying to throttle Arafat, to control the Palestinian question. WAFA is saying, no way. This is what you must report."

"But why would they do that? They're on the same side, aren't they?"

Slobodanka would then look at me in mock amazement, throw her head back, and let loose a crazy laugh that could silence an entire male tea shop.

UPI in Beirut cared about these Palestinian ephemera because Damascus was yet again at the center of the great muddle of the Middle East "peace process." A former foreign minister once explained the Arab side of this insoluble equation: The Arabs could not win a war without Egypt, could not make peace without Syria, and couldn't pay for either without Saudi Arabia. Syria had lost the Golan Heights, a strategic swathe of territory just southwest of Damascus, to Israel in 1967 in the Six-Day War. Since then it had blocked any peace moves that did not return them. Syria had just seen Egypt sign a separate peace with Israel, a huge loss of bargaining power for the Arab side, and it wasn't about to let anything similar happen again. So it played the two cards it still had: an "invited" army of occupation in Lebanon and the Palestinian cause.

One evening, Slobodanka told me she'd heard a rumor that Palestinian leader

Yasser Arafat was coming to the Syrian capital. Excited to catch sight of the grand old man who had for a while managed to unite all the Palestinian factions, and who had heroically survived the recent Israeli siege of west Beirut, we spent a whole evening in a crummy quarter of town sitting on old orange crates outside the office of Fatah, Arafat's faction and

Yasser Arafat, chairman of the Palestine Liberation Organization, reflects in Damascus after hearing news that Israel has allowed Lebanese militiamen to kill eight hundred Palestinians in the Sabra and Shatila refugee camps in Beirut. July 1982. (*Hugh Pope*)

the biggest member of the Palestine Liberation Organization. Suddenly, a motor-cade drew up and there he was. We rushed in, only to be barred at the door. "Pho-tographers only!" went up the cry. I held up my battered old Canon copy of a Leica and was ushered upstairs.

This gave me a chance to take a portrait of Arafat himself. In the frame he still sits there, cornered, depressed, and stubbornly defiant. The world had banished him after the Israeli siege of Beirut to faraway Tunis. He was visiting Damascus to recon-nect with Palestinians in Lebanon and Syria but found the Syrian government blocking his way. Soon there was another flurry of movement and we "photogra-phers" were allowed in to record a meeting of the PLO's Central Committee. My film ran out after two frames. I started trying to change it. The other photographers filed out. Fingers shaking, I fiddled with the negative strip and the infuriating spool. A minute, two minutes passed. Arafat and the PLO high command watched. They were crowded around a table that was too small. They knew they were in trouble, that their organization was crushed, and that the presence of the Syrian vice presi-dent at their table meant the end of their "independence of decision making." One of the burlier PLO leaders began to growl something at me. Finally the film caught, I gratefully clicked off a couple of shots, and fled back to the street where Slobodanka was waiting. I gabbled excitedly about seeing Arafat, and my slapstick attempts at photographing the PLO.

"Look, if you want to be a journalist, I think I can help you. There's someone you should meet," she boomed back.

"Fine," I said. "Where?"

"I'll let you know."

A few days later she took me across town to the compound housing the Soviet embassy. It looked then like many U.S. embassies look today, surrounded by high concrete walls and solid metal gates. The guards were expecting us and ushered us in, deeper and deeper, until we reached a building with a plaque announcing it to be the Soviet-Palestinian Friendship Society. There, waiting for us, was a dignified gentleman with silver hair, a military uniform, and a cravat.

His name was Colonel Mousa Abu Mousa, and he was something in the PLO. I'd never heard of him, but I tried to keep my cool, partly because the embassy had put in a minder to watch over our conversation, and mostly because I didn't want to be mocked afterward by Slobodanka for any ignorance. Abu Mousa soon got my attention, however, shocking me by denouncing Yasser Arafat as a traitor to the Palestinian cause and insisting that Arafat intended to betray the Arabs by doing a separate peace deal with Israel. (Such plans were indeed afoot with Jordan at the time.) He, Abu Mousa, was now raising the flag of rebellion against Arafat. This new defender of the purity of the Palestinian cause would prevent imperialist

America buying off the Palestinians like it had bought off Egypt with the gift of billions of dollars per year.

I didn't think to ask: Why are you doing this in a Soviet embassy building? Why are we doing this in front of a KGB minder? Or even, What's my friend Slobodanka doing here with these people? Everything else about my life in Syria was so strange that this seemed quite normal. In fact, what struck me as pleasantly unusual was that at the Soviet embassy they served chocolates with the tea. I did of course guess that this fuss meant that Abu Mousa was newsworthy and so I wrote down all he said. My notebook fueled an arm-long roll of telex—at a dollar a line, I had no incentive to mince my words—and it turned out to be a scoop. Huddled around the telex machine in Beirut as my dispatch rattled in from Damascus, my UPI editors understood its value. They duly announced to the world that the Syrian-backed civil war against Arafat's long dominance of the PLO had begun.

So it was that the next time I photographed Yasser Arafat, a few months later, he was in a basement in the northern Lebanese port of Tripoli, where he had slipped in to support his men cornered by the Syrian-backed rebels. We were being shelled furiously by Syrian field guns. It was Arafat's last stand as the Syrian army, assorted intelligence services, and the forces of Abu Mousa were driving his men out of Syrian-occupied areas of Lebanon. In my photograph, his beard is obviously graying and his eyes bulge out unnaturally. If he lived off the adrenaline, close calls were certainly taking a toll. I watched later as his faction of the PLO drove their remaining vehicles onto Greek car ferries, expelled by the Syrians from Lebanon in much the same way as the Israelis had forced them out of west Beirut the year before. The retreating fighters showed their disgust by setting off ear-splitting explosions of antitank weapons, fired into the air like massive firework rockets.

For sure, with so many enemies within and without, caught between the vise of Syria and Israel, it was not easy to be a Palestinian. And I learned to moderate my protests whenever a Middle Easterner insists that all the world's spy agencies are out to get him.

4. HUNTING FOR SCAPEGOATS

Foreign Interference and Misrule in Lebanon

The serpent brings forth nothing but the little serpent.
—ARABIC SAYING

The Lebanese civil war began in 1975, before which, as the Lebanese never failed to remind me, Beirut had been a glorious playground, banking center, brain trust, and trading hub of the whole Middle East. Then, too, there was that crazy freedom that attracted Middle Eastern dissidents, international correspondents, and foreign spies. Much blame for the outbreak of that civil war lay with the virtual takeover of parts of the country by the various factions of the Palestine Liberation Organization. So when the PLO was forced out at the end of the Israeli siege of Beirut in 1982, in Lebanese minds it followed that all the good old days would come rushing back.

But cash and a power base are needed to hold up a Middle Eastern state structure. Respect for the idea of a state of law has been lost throughout the region, and in its stead has come fear of the ruler's changing dictates, and sometimes pure fear of the security services. Leaders like Syria's Hafez al-Assad and Iraq's Saddam Hussein had their populations completely cowed into a version of the Stockholm syndrome, a condition when the human defense mechanism tricks hostages into loyalty to their kidnappers. The balance of power had always been more freely negotiated in Lebanon. But the civil war had gravely damaged what passed for Lebanese national infrastructure, of which all that remained seemed to be banking secrecy, the enormous national debt, and the creaky old Casino du Liban.

So as the government picked up the pieces, it decided to make a judicial show of a return to the rule of law. The perfect case was soon found to demonstrate who was boss. It involved a man convicted of a particularly nasty murder who buried his victims in a central park. When the Israelis seized west Beirut, they emptied the jails, as all conquerors seem to do, presumably to terrorize the population and legitimize the need for the occupiers' presence to catch them all again. But this murderer was possibly mentally unstable and certainly unsuited to life on the outside. He soon turned himself back in, even though he had been sentenced to death. The government announced that it would see justice done.

Since the hanging was due at dawn, and seemed gratuitously gruesome for colleagues who had just been through the Israeli siege of Beirut, I was handed the assignment. As we gathered in the park in the thin dawn light, it became clear that there was little public interest in this nation-building exercise. The gallows, however, looked well made, as was often the case when the Lebanese put their minds to something. I wandered up to the gates of the prison, not far away. Here there were more reporters, and we waited quietly for the sun to start rising. Then from the depths of the jail came a dreadful scream in Arabic: "Innocent! I'm innocent!"

The man's time had come and, even if he was deranged, he knew it. The screaming continued through the hallway, into the courtyard, and in the struggle of being pushed into a van. Then we all followed the convoy down to the park. Men in uniform manhandled the hysterical convict toward two hooded hangmen who had appeared by the gallows. There was a superficial resemblance to a scene I remembered of a group bullying and then stripping a boy in the bushes at my preparatory school. I, for one, felt like shouting, "Enough . . . you've made the point now!"

But I kept my silence as the new Lebanese government finished what it had started. The hangmen, wanting to observe the niceties of the occasion, were struggling to put a hood on the murderer's tossing head. His screaming protestations were replaced by a hopeless moan. Suddenly, the climax came. The condemned man refused to step forward. The hangmen seized him and dragged him there bodily with his legs flailing. Somehow they got the noose around his neck, and, almost with a sense of relief, pulled a lever and the trapdoor swung down. Dumbstruck, we watched the life twitch out of him for a minute or two. Then it was over, and a damp patch spread across his groin.

I was numb. I looked around for someone with whom to share my inner horror. But normality was different in Lebanon. My traumatized Lebanese colleagues had developed a thick exterior shield to this kind of brutal scene. They had seen far more bodies during the Israeli invasion of Lebanon and siege of Beirut. They were already talking about where to go for breakfast. I asked one if he remembered the case, and whether there was a chance that the man was innocent.

"Probably not, but the point was not who it was, but what he was," he answered, listing Lebanon's three main communities: the Maronite Christians, on top since the French colonial era; the Sunni Muslims, on top in the preceding Ottoman Empire; and the Shia Muslims, now the most numerous and determined to reach the top in the future. "You see, the government is run by Maronites and some Sunnis, so they had to pick on a Shia."

With this body under its foundations, perhaps the post-1982 Lebanese state was always cursed. Certainly, the government never found its feet, and the country was to go through many more spasms of civil war and foreign intervention. Something had sapped the Lebanese ability to bounce back, not least the departure of most of the middle classes. When I returned to Beirut in 2000 as a Middle East correspondent for the *Wall Street Journal,* few of the Lebanese I had known were left in the country. True, I was able to sit and discuss with Prime Minister Rafik Hariri all his noble plans to re-create the center of Beirut better than it had been. A company even began dismantling the vast rubbish dump in the city center, which everyone had used when it was a front line. But a few years later Hariri himself was blown up, and the long arm of Syria's secret service was suspected. Israel had invaded again. The Persian Gulf had risen to become the undisputed new banking and trading hub of the Middle East. Lebanon remained prostrate, unable to unite at home or to rise above all the foreign forces acting against it from abroad.

Still, the Lebanese did things with élan, or the remains of it, derived partly from a privileged colonial experience including decades of cosseting by France of the formerly dominant Maronite Christians. This endowed that community with the greatest sense of entitlement in the country, and a sense of style rubbed off on the other communities. Compared to many other landlocked, isolated, or poorer peoples of the Middle East, the Lebanese had also been enriched by a long tradition of internationalism, trade, and travel.

But the Lebanese, like the luckless Palestinians, had a tendency to look at a given political outcome and then rearrange actions and motives in the narrative to suit their preexisting political paranoias. Their national state weakness had given rise to a slave-master syndrome with the outside world that induced extravagant extremes of love and hate. In Lebanon, the love could express itself in copies of Western entertainments, restaurants, and hotels that at times of prosperity could rival any in the region. The hate would lead to the invention of the suicidal Islamist driving a truck bomb.

Brought up as I was in an Anglo-Saxon world of self-improvement, opportunity, and entitlement, I tired of hearing outsiders blamed for everything. Usually, it was an excuse never to try. The same defeatism applied to politics all over the Middle East. With the exception of the first centuries of Muhammad's great Arab and

Militiamen relax during a quiet day on the Green Line in Beirut. Front lines mixed boredom and terror, and a clash could start just because a cameraman asked a band of gunmen to fire off a few rounds to record the requisite "bang-bang." 1983. (*Jack Dabaghian*)

Islamic empire based in the Arabian Peninsula, this crossroads between continents has always been a cockpit for battles between the marcher lords of stronger powers elsewhere. From a Middle Eastern perspective, this has bred a sense that since foreigners controlled one's fate, there was no point in trying to cure one's own ills. It was so much easier, and politically much safer, to blame all problems on foreign spies, global conspiracies, and imperialist plots.

Lebanon did have something to complain about. When I arrived in 1983, the country was occupied by six foreign armies. The sloppy checkpoints of the Syrians held corrupt sway over the smuggling haven of the Bekaa Valley in the east. Arrogant Israelis were all over the south, neck-deep in the Middle Eastern delusion that conquerors were keepers. In Beirut itself, a multinational task force symbolized another fantasy, that a bandage of international intervention could cure the endemic ills that crippled the region. Most idiosyncratic was a small, underfunded British unit, led by a military adventurer who terrified his men with nighttime patrols to chase the snipers who took potshots at them from the badlands all around. Perhaps the sheer unpredictability of British actions spared them the disaster that was to strike other multinationals. There were also the Italians, who mystified us all by the way they escaped attack, even though they were posted in a most dangerous area, the Shia Muslim southern suburbs of Beirut. We thought it was because they made such a point of generous, warm, Mediterranean interaction with their neighbors. Only years later was another explanation offered by the then Syrian minister of defense, Mustapha Tlass. He told a Dubai newspaper that he ordered the resistance not to attack the Italians because of his admiration since his youth for actress Gina Lollobrigida, whom he wished to spare a single tear of distress.

No such quarter was granted to the American contingent, or to the French, who tried and failed to keep a low profile at their base in west Beirut, which we always called "mainly Muslim," because a usually non–Maronite Christian middle class still clung on here in the hope that the old days would return. The French were a target since it was clear from the beginning that they were still trying to shore up the power of their colonial-era Maronite allies. The Americans, meanwhile, were hopelessly identified with the Israelis, who had long before convinced them that Israel above all others should be America's Middle Eastern ally.

My position gave me a ringside seat to watch the unraveling of the American engagement in Lebanon in the early 1980s. On one hand, since I worked for an American news agency, I reported exhaustively on what we presented as a U.S.-led peace process. In what was to become a familiar pattern, as a first step the United States was going to save a country with a crisis—in this case, Lebanon—and after that perhaps solve the ills of the whole Middle East. On the other, I became personally involved in a way I had not foreseen. When choosing an apartment, I wanted a view of the Mediterranean Sea, but the only place I could afford was the equivalent of a two-room hut on a roof. I loved it, even though Lebanon's absent infrastructure meant the apartment block rose from rubble-strewn wasteland. By chance, it was right behind the U.S. embassy.

I walked past the mission just before lunch each day to start my shift at UPI, intoxicated by the magical air of Beirut in the springtime and the happy enjoyment of my first proper job. My few days off I spent exploring the ruins of city center buildings along the Green Line between the east and west Beirut sides of the Lebanese civil war. De-mined by the peacekeeping forces, the idea that these would now be reconstructed seemed a natural part of a "good" story, spelled out to us in press releases or by Western spokespeople with neatly pressed clothes.

Even though we reporters often joked cynically that the idealistic-sounding U.S. policy could never work, we could hardly lead our stories with the anti-American side, with all its ill-phrased, pessimistic, and paranoid hostility. It also seemed implausible to highlight anti-American mouthpieces, the unpleasant dictatorships of Syria, Iran, or Libya, or the relatively unattractive, marginal political radicals in Lebanon who echoed their views. Two decades later, the cumulative effect of this natural bias of Western newcomers to the apparent good intentions of their own side, and blindness to anything else, would have disastrous consequences for the United States as it blundered into Iraq.

Fate decreed it would take only a month in Beirut for me to be brought down to earth. I had met a lovely Palestinian woman, and one morning she borrowed her father's car to drive me around outlying areas of Beirut ruined by the Israeli siege the year before. She wanted to show me how Beirut was fixing itself up and I wanted to enjoy her golden-skinned beauty. Thus it was that on April 18, 1983, I was not walking to work past the U.S. embassy at the usual time, just before one o'clock. In fact, I had arrived early for my evening shift in the UPI office. I was standing next to veteran reporter David Zenian when a shock wave of explosive force whomped through the office. We didn't need to run to the window. A column of evil yellowish smoke and debris was spiraling up into the sky from the seafront, then gradually spreading into a general haze.

Zenian had seen all kinds of mayhem before and rushed to his keyboard to be the first out with the news bulletin—preceded in those days of teleprinters with nine bells that would then ring in newsrooms all around the world. I stood rooted to the spot.

"Run! Get down there! Run!" Zenian shouted.

It goes against all natural instincts to run to the site of a disaster. As my legs took me downhill, I could feel my chest seizing up in fear and denial. I was on the scene within minutes. I must have seen what everyone saw: dead bodies, the wrecked and twisted cars on the corniche, the smoking carcass of the high-rise building with the front blown off it, and the dust-blasted figures staggering out of the embassy. Indeed, Zenian's stories quote my accounts of such sights, including a body blown in half, all phoned in when I eventually got a line through to the office from my landlord's phone. My own mind, however, has erased most of what I saw.

My memory of that date restarts as I returned home late that night, just thirty yards behind the stricken ruin of the embassy. I found my way past the new security cordon to reach my building. Up in my apartment, the only damage, perhaps because I had left all the windows open that morning, was that the lock had blown off the lavatory door. Also scored into my brain are the trips I made every day for the next two weeks into the putrid stench of the mortuary at the American University Hospital, where my job was to ask the mortician what the death toll was. One day he turned around in angry frustration and held a clear plastic bag up to my face. It contained a blood-and-concrete-dust porridge of human remains.

"How many people would you like this to be?" he said.

I refused to go to the mortuary after that. But from then on, my natural optimism switched to the cynical outlook of the Middle East. The Lebanese civil war soon reignited along the Green Line. At my news agency, hopeful stories about the Lebanese or Middle Eastern peace process reverted to what Zenian and others called "bang-bang." We went back to talking about the "Christians" and the "Muslims," then Shia, Sunnis, and Druze. This was mendacious in two ways: Most of Lebanon was at peace most days, and using religions to identify the main parties was a misleading oversimplification. But warfare made the news copy glamorous, it got stories into newspapers, and was easier to write because so little needed to be explained. Exhausted during one frightening upsurge of fighting, I too became a hostage to the "bang-bang" routine. When a U.S. radio network commented in awe at a thumping series of explosions in the background to a live interview with me, it somehow seemed silly to let them know that, this time at least, it was just a colleague knocking on the door of the office's soundproof recording booth.

For those not watching their own homes or families go up in smoke, the adrenaline of armed conflict, or proximity to armies on the move, can be exciting, even addictive. I watched in awe on the coastline south of Beirut as the U. S. Sixth Fleet steamed over the horizon. After the attack on the American embassy, the United States was sending its troops back to Lebanon. Dots grew into ships, which then sprouted funnels, superstructures, and guns. Then they spawned a flotilla of landing craft, which either drove directly onto the beach or dropped their bows to let marines lumber out over the lapping wavelets. They had just taken part in subduing a Marxist coup on the Caribbean island of Grenada, but they looked nervous as they took in the less easily definable scene before them.

The marines saw traffic driving insouciantly along the coast road as normal. Kids waited with buckets of cola to sell to them as the new invaders of Lebanon. Of course I was there too with my notebook, pen, and a thirst for names, ages, and event-defining quotes. From the misty barrier of mountains in the middle distance came the booms of an artillery duel in progress between "Christians" and "Druze." I remember the look of disorientation as I tried to explain to a marine with sand stuck to his wet boots that the fighting was nothing directly related to them but part of the background music of the civil war.

Somehow, I had persuaded myself that this violence couldn't touch me. In the weeks when the Syrian army was trying to finish off the independent Palestinian political movement represented by PLO leader Yasser Arafat, I headed without a thought for the northern port of Tripoli, where Arafat had holed up with his men. I'd grab a pita filled with thin slices of *shawarma,* sizzling spit-roasted lamb or chicken meat, in the little shop outside our office door. Then I'd hail one of the taxis from the nearby rank and head north. At a certain point we'd pass the front lines, where Syrian artillery would be noisily firing into the section of Tripoli where Arafat had made his headquarters. Masonry would be falling around our cars and heads as we neared his basement hideout. There we would photograph the great survivor, listen to his latest defiant outburst, and return the same way we had come. Once I even stopped on the way back to visit a crusader castle.

As usual, the Americans were dragged in deeper. They may have persuaded themselves that they were there to keep the peace and to promote Western civilization and Middle Eastern acceptance of Israel. But there were plenty of Lebanese— not to mention the regimes of Syria and Iran—who were ready to oppose the U.S. effort to promote a pro-Israel, pro-American dynamic.

The perimeter of the U.S. base began taking fire from snipers. The death toll mounted. It took awhile for me to get used to my colleagues' jokes about how an unofficial scale of importance in our news judgment equated one American to two Jews or Israelis to three Europeans to five Middle Eastern Christians to ten Muslims. Nobody dictated this. It was just the prism through which we ordered the importance of things, another of those little everyday distortions of which the American misunderstanding of the Middle East is made. Indeed, Iran's Islamic Republic News Agency teleprinter had to claim one hundred dead in their war with Iraq before we'd even discuss writing a story. But we were sensitive to the Americans. I once wrote ten purple paragraphs about the first marine to win a decoration for his injuries. An uncharitable version of the incident would have been that he sustained a scratch while jumping out of his jeep under fire.

The U.S. fleet offshore sometimes opened fire over us in support of the American base around Beirut airport, a rolling thunder that shook the whole of Beirut from its sleep. The shelling never seemed to achieve much, despite frequent U.S. claims of success that we had to write down and recirculate. The gap between American and Middle Eastern reality opened wide for me when I found myself helicoptered out from my Beirut routine to the flagship of the Sixth Fleet for lunch alone with the admiral. I felt like a cat visiting a king. Perhaps the admiral hoped for publicity and an insight into what his gunnery was achieving, but he seemed more bemused than anything else by my youthful outrage about injustice and oppression in the Middle East. Even more revealing was a visit to the USS *New Jersey,* a World War II–vintage battle ship that boasted enormous guns whose barrels were sixteen inches in diameter.

"The shells weigh as much as a small car," said the ship's spokesman with proud confidence. "They can hit a tennis court at fifteen miles."

The trouble was that one night a shell made it only as far as the beach, where it dug an impressive crater in the sand. Another day I raced up into the mountains in a friendly rivalry with my colleague Jonathan Wright from Reuters to see what had been hit during an all-night barrage. I failed to find any new damage. After a hike through a forest, Wright found one dead goat next to a stretch of blasted mountainside. The work of the marine snipers defending their airport camp was far more deadly, but nobody sent us press releases from the teeming southern suburbs of Beirut that surrounded the base perimeter.

When it came, the Middle East's response was devastating: two massive truck bombs that blew up the U.S. marines' barracks and the French base, killing 241 American and 58 French soldiers. I was briefly out of the country and saw it on television, and my emotional response had already become pure journalist: guilty that I had missed the big story. Back in Beirut, I woke up in my apartment not long afterward to the sound of armored vehicles clanking along the seafront corniche. I rushed out with my camera just in time to photograph the last marine amphibious

American helicopters airlift some of the last U.S. troops to pull out of Lebanon from the corniche in Beirut. They had arrived a year before to shore up a pro-Western government but were forced out by suicide bombings and regional hostility toward Washington's pro-Israel stance. July 31, 1984. *(Hugh Pope)*

vehicle as it drove into the tiny fishing harbor nearby and chugged noisily out to sea. The commander waved to me from his turret and was gone.

The charred wreck of the U.S. embassy was unguarded at last. I climbed the stairs, picking up ruined books on Middle Eastern diplomacy from the rubble-strewn floor. Up on the top floor was the apartment where the marines who guarded the embassy lived. They had painted a reproduction of the flag-raising scene from Iwo Jima. But someone, a triumphant Islamist perhaps, had got there before me and daubed black devil's horns onto the American soldiers' helmets.

The pullback of the Americans did not imply any strengthening of Lebanon's capacity to govern itself. In March 1985, a uniformed immigration officer at Beirut International Airport drew his revolver and commandeered a Boeing 707 because he wanted more pay. Passengers scrambled off the plane. Police and militia opened fire. When the hijacker ordered the pilot to start the engines, the jet blast killed an elderly man. The plane took off, trailing an orange escape chute from one of three open doors. Radio stations in Beirut began broadcasting the cockpit–control tower conversations live as the plane shuttled for hours between Lebanon and Cyprus, a twenty-minute flight. Gunmen brandishing Kalashnikovs and pistols brushed aside the government security forces and took over the airport, joining onlookers and a few journalists in the tower. The next day, the hijacker calmly appeared at a press conference, in his immigration officer uniform, next to a top government minister who said he sympathized with the man's demands.

It was the fourth Beirut airport hijacking in seven months, and nobody was the slightest bit surprised. Indeed, the piratical madness of the whole affair just made people laugh and shake their heads in satisfaction—"This is Lebanon." If Beirut might no longer be the jewel of the Middle East—and the Lebanese had trouble admitting that—it could at least claim to be the wildest place on the planet. But the country was sawing off the branch on which it sat. Thieves were stealing the airport's runway lights and electric cabling in broad daylight. The official head of airport security had tendered his resignation four months before, but the cabinet could not decide whether to accept it. The Lebanese army soldiers I spoke to as they played cards in a dilapidated bunker of the abandoned U.S. marine base around the airport perimeter laughed at the idea that they could prevent the entry of animals, let alone guerrillas: They pointed to the cows and goats grazing on spring grass pushing up through the tarmac by the main runway.

This breakdown began to make me feel unsafe. What the Lebanese always referred to as the "situation" worsened. We began to hear more of the name Hezbollah, as Iran and Syria put their weight behind organizing the Shia into an anti-Western stance—not difficult due to the excesses of the Israeli invasion and occupation of Shia-majority south Lebanon. Fighting broke out again along the Green Line, and the quarter-hourly bulletins of my radio monitoring became vital guides to survival. Sometimes when the shelling got bad I would spend the night with my landlord's family huddled in the ground floor stairwell. Then several days might go by of seemingly complete normality.

On one such morning I decided to break out of our routine and go to the famed ski slopes above Beirut. But by the late afternoon, when I drove down from the mountains, the streets had a dark and suspiciously empty feel. Negotiating the jittery checkpoints in the unlit blackness of the front line was scary. I had twisted my ankle badly on the mountain, and when I went to get it X-rayed, I discovered that Lebanon's life had turned upside down once again. The hospital emergency room was filled with bloody casualties streaming in from fighting in the southern suburbs, often encrusted with concrete dust from when shells exploded in buildings. When the doctors saw a limping foreigner, they cleared an examination table immediately.

"What happened?" one asked, full of concern.

I was so ashamed that I told him the truth, my contribution to Lebanon's patchwork of reality. He politely wound a compress around my ankle and dismissed me.

By this time, I had changed employer from UPI to Reuters. I had worked out that UPI would never agree to my request for a spell in the Washington, D.C., head office after the nearly bankrupt agency started sending messages to our teleprinter with twelve-bell alarms demanding that we "immediately transmit funds." Little did they realize that due to an electronic fault, these messages also went to all our dwindling band of subscribers, so we laughed and hoarded our funds even tighter. Then the hostage taking began to get serious.

On at least two occasions at Reuters, I was doing a shift when one of the calls came in from the hostage takers, claiming responsibility.

"This is Islamic Jihad . . ." the voice would begin to say in Arabic, and I would start writing down what he said. Sometimes I'd have to ask him to repeat some obscure Koranic verse with which the group sought to justify its beastly crime. I would politely say "thank you" when he'd finished, even though I knew some of the victims and realized that there was a chance I would be next. Gradually the kidnappers moved from seizing a real American spy to supposed spies to journalists.

One weekend I went to Cyprus for a break; if I had stayed home I would have probably accompanied my friend Jonathan Wright on a trip in which he ended up as a prisoner of Palestinian gangster Abu Nidal's group. He escaped through an air-conditioning vent after a few weeks, only to be taken into custody by another group for another week. Reuters managers made us move into hotels, and then made us move hotels every three nights. We began to be the only guests, and to drink too much at adrenaline-fueled dinners as the empty streets boomed with the echoes of explosions near and far.

Soon two dozen foreigners were being held hostage, and as many again had had near escapes. One of the correspondents I respected most, David Hirst of the London *Guardian*, a slight and utterly unphysical man, evaded his would-be kidnappers in the vital first few minutes by kicking and shouting as they tried to force him from the street into a basement. AP bureau chief Terry Anderson went from gregarious party giver one day to suffering hostage the next. Glamorous ABC newsman Charlie Glass escaped from being chained to a radiator in Beirut's southern suburbs. They were lucky. In April 1986, after U.S. warplanes attacked Libyan leader Muammar Ghadafi's tents from air bases in Britain, two British academic acquaintances, Leigh Douglas and Philip Padfield, were kidnapped walking home from a backstreet Beirut bar where I too sometimes had a drink after work. Abu Nidal's group was believed responsible for shooting them in the head and leaving them dead in a village outside the city, wound in white sheets and with a note accusing them spuriously of being spies.

I began to feel nervous each time I was on the street. When a bearded man followed me around the display cases one day in a shop, I had my first experience of being paralyzed by terror. By the time that Reuters decided to follow the trend and to pull out all its remaining Western staff, I was flitting around town like a spy whose cover had been blown.

5. A PILGRIMAGE TO JERUSALEM

The Israel-Palestine Entanglement

Hardship never lasts forever. Never lasts forever.
—PALESTINIAN LULLABY

It was in the summer of 2000 that an old dream came true. I was working for the *Wall Street Journal,* living in Istanbul with an already romantic remit to report on anything that seemed unusual from Albania to the borders of China. Now the *Journal* began to reorganize its coverage of the Middle East. The Jerusalem correspondent had left two years before and had not been replaced. The Arab world reporter wanted to move on, frustrated after years of trying and failing to interest the newspaper in the Arab-Israeli stalemate. It was then that my foreign editor, John Bussey, chose to telephone me.

"Hugh! We've been thinking about Middle East. Could you expand your beat?" John enthused, rushing to the point as always.

Three years before, John had hired me over a hasty cup of coffee in a Berlin mall where he'd just lunched. I'd had to take a plane all the way from Turkey for the audience. He never visited me in Istanbul, but he did once telephone from an airplane when he noticed that he was flying overhead. He preferred Asia, where things got built and done. Legend had it that in his years posted to Japan as the *Journal*'s bureau chief, he'd worked so hard that he'd never taken the time to completely unpack.

"I'd love to," I replied, thrilled. Becoming the Middle East reporter for a great American newspaper was the closest thing I had to a lifelong ambition.

John had given me a good run in the paper with stories explaining how Turkey and the newly independent states in the south of the former Soviet Union were making their mark. But when I'd reported once about each of these countries, I'd noticed a distinct drop in the editors' appetite for more.

"Obviously you'd stay put in Istanbul and keep an eye on Turkey, the Caucasus, and Central Asia. But could you do Iran for us?"

"Sure. If they ever give me a visa."

"And of course there would be Saudi Arabia and the Gulf. Just a story or two per year. Syria, Jordan, and stuff. Egypt. North Africa."

"Fine," I said, wondering how I would cope. This was already more than thirty countries. Individually they were mostly unimportant and underdeveloped in the great scheme of the globe, but all were awkward, complicated, hard to get into, and veiled by ignorance, disinformation, and authoritarian rule.

"And Hugh," Bussey finished up, "can you also keep an eye on the whole Arab-Israel thing?"

In retrospect, knowing about the September 11 attacks on America and the U.S.-led Middle East wars that followed, such a scaling back of coverage by one of the biggest U.S. newspapers looks ill-advised. But it seemed logical to the *Journal* at the time and wasn't just forced by an advertising crunch after the Internet bubble popped in 2000. Seven years after the signing of the Oslo Accords between Israel and the Palestinians, all seemed quiet, even humdrum on the Middle Eastern front, and Americans had little interest in the complaints of the losing Arab side. Oil prices had been rock-bottom for years. I had enough trouble interesting the *Journal* in stories about Turkey, since its economy was barely as big and arguably less innovative than that of a midsized U.S. city; as for the Middle East and North Africa, all those countries together managed to produce only twice what Turkey did, and were almost entirely disconnected from each other. A new front-page editor had also abandoned the international outlook of his predecessor in favor of an approach that appealed more directly to what he saw as American interests. This ruled out many a potential Middle Eastern story. One reporter was enough, they decided, to inform the two million subscribers of the *Journal* about events in the heartlands of the Muslim world. I felt flattered that they thought I could do it. I didn't even have an assistant.

Inevitably, my status as lone Middle East correspondent didn't last. The illusion that Israeli-Arab quiet meant peace almost immediately blew up in our faces. In late September 2000, Israel's general-turned-politician Ariel Sharon decided to stage a show-of-force walkabout in the precincts of the holy al-Aqsa Mosque in Jerusalem. A new Palestinian rebellion, the Second Intifada, broke out. While Americans had been lulled into passivity by the rhetoric of the so-called peace process, it turned out that Israel had continued its expansion into traditionally Palestinian territories. Jewish settlers had bought Arab land between the 1880s and 1920s, skirmished for more in the 1930s and 1940s, and captured vast new territories in wars in 1948, 1967, and 1982. To be sure, Israel gave back Sinai in exchange for peace with Egypt in 1982, and, under pressure, withdrew from southern Lebanon by 2000 and pulled settlers out of Gaza in 2005. But Israel continued consolidating closer to home. In the 1990s alone, the years of the supposed peace process, it increased its settler population in the Palestinian territories occupied since 1967 by 72 percent.

My predecessor, Stephen Glain, had fought prescient battles to point out trouble brewing due to these uncomfortable facts. Our new front-page editor had shot down the last dozen of Glain's proposals, telling him, in so many words, that it felt like reheated Middle Eastern trivia he had already read in the *New York Times*. The foreign pages ran the stories, but everyone knew that the front page was the one that mattered if you wanted to make an impact on Americans' minds.

Wondering where I should start, I reckoned that learning more about Israel was the best first step to working out what would happen in the region. Within what would soon become known as the "greater Middle East," Israel was the country that had the most coherent national ideology, disciplined state, effective military, and best-functioning economy, not to mention the close embrace it enjoyed with the United States.

Part of me wanted to grow out of my own anti-Israel prejudice from years spent on the Arab side of the front lines. At the same time, I wanted to challenge the American national blind spot for Israel. It seems as alive now as it was then. President Barack Obama initially suggested a new approach, showing unusual compassion in a March 2007 speech in Iowa, saying "nobody's suffering more than the Palestinian people" and that "the Israeli government must make difficult concessions for the peace process to restart." As his campaign progressed, he made sure that he was seen as solidly behind Israel's "security," albeit with hints that he would not do so blindly or support all Israeli settlements. But in President Obama's body language when meeting hard-line Israeli leaders, in his choices for key staff, and in his empathetic approach to the rest of the Middle East, there remains a strong hint of a high-minded ambition to change the status quo and challenge the pro-Israel lobbies that have distorted U.S. national interests so damagingly and for so long.

Beyond Obama, the grip of the old paradigm was made clear in a minor storm over United States–Israel ties stirred up by the briefly famous Joe "the Plumber" Wurzelbacher when he suggested that Obama might not maintain America's absolute

support of Israel. Right-wing Fox News presenter Shepard Smith, who was interviewing Wurzelbacher, was so shocked that he rushed to read out Obama's pro-Israel
pledges. "Man, it just gets frightening sometimes," Smith commented incredulously.
The editorial page of the liberal *New York Times* didn't see the irony, even though there
is significant American intellectual support for a more evenhanded U.S. policy. The
Times seconded Fox News' disbelief under the title SHEPARD THE ANCHOR. Even
after the disasters of September 11 and the Iraq War, in which the United States has
so disastrously adopted hard-line Israeli approaches to the Middle East, a bipartisan
political consensus in America seems unable to conceive a situation where it might
be worth debating alternatives.

The situation was not much different in the 1980s and 1990s, of course, and I
knew from experience that for the unwary reporter, the Israel story was full of traps
in the U.S. media. An avalanche of complaints could fill my editors' mailboxes.
When, for instance, I wrote that Palestinians were "forced to leave" their homes
into exile, the watchdogs of the pro-Israel lobby, who carefully scoured the media
for any perceived anti-Israel bias, triggered a mail campaign to demand the use of
"fled." When I said the three million Palestinians outside pre-1948 Palestine were
"refugees" forced into exile by Israel's expansion and barred from return, the lobbyists wanted our newspaper to split them into original refugees and their descen-

A new Israeli settlement towers over Israeli-bulldozed Palestinian houses north of Jerusalem. About
half a million Jewish settlers now live in the West Bank, east Jerusalem, and the Golan Heights, occupying hilltops, creating a parallel highway system, and dividing Palestinians in an archipelago of
areas between which it is hard for them to travel. 2001. *(Hugh Pope)*

dants. My experience is that all polite letters to the editor about correspondents' work are taken seriously, because genuine reaction from readers is rare. At the *Journal*, we were required to draft explanatory answers to any real objection. Mistakes requiring a correction in print were black marks officially entered into our files. As intended, the tactic of lobby-organized write-ins tempted a busy correspondent to err on the side of caution. This was the first step toward perpetuation of the real error, the acceptance of powerful lobbyspeak as truth. With each omission or white lie, we laid another brick in the great wall of misconception that now separates America and the Middle East.

The Jewish-American community is not the only one in which the most intransigent elements are the best organized and most vocal. Armenian, Cuban, and Greek Americans also tend to be represented by radical parts of the political spectrum. This politically active element in diaspora populations—and this includes, say, the various Muslim diaspora communities in Europe—are free of the need to share in the necessary compromises of living in their original part of the world. National myths are no longer balanced with reality. If a place of origin is important to a diaspora's sense of identity, its members can also overcompensate for the fact that they don't actually live there anymore.

For sure, many Jewish Americans enthusiastically supported Israeli compromise with the Palestinians in the Oslo peace process. Some opposed periods of Israeli government intransigence. But Jewish concerns about security, both historical and current, allow a hard-line organization like the American Israel Public Affairs Committee to become arguably the most powerful lobbying group in the United States. It adopts uncompromising Israeli doctrines, and its campaigning has impact. Debate and self-criticism of Israel's actions are vibrant within Israel itself, but the American media are rarely as frank as even a mainstream liberal Israeli publication like *Ha'aretz*. A measure of U.S. media bias came from a statistical survey of *New York Times* coverage of Israel-Palestine news by the U.S. group If Americans Knew. It found that in 2004, when twenty-one times as many Palestinian as Israeli children were killed (174 compared to 8), the *Times* headlines and lead paragraphs reported the Israeli children's deaths seven times more frequently. In the main text, this rose to ten times more frequently overall. In this period, three times the number of Palestinians of all age groups were being killed compared to Israelis, yet the *Times* reported the Israeli deaths at least three times more often. The same message was repeated by the hundreds of other newspapers that reprint stories from the *Times* wire service. There can be no doubt that this gave readers all over America a totally unbalanced impression of the human costs involved.

Nevertheless, experience had thickened my skin and taught me the pointlessness of being too blunt. When in the early 1980s a U.S. radio host asked me in genuine exasperation why some new attack on U.S. troops in Lebanon had happened,

I took a deep breath. I thought about the ruin, violence, and misery all around, about the U.S. navy guns offshore pounding the mountains behind me, and I let him have my feelings straight and passionate on live rush-hour news. The line soon went dead. To be acceptable, we had to varnish our version of the truth. The problem was that most people mistook the varnish for the truth.

As I planned how to get my version of the truth into the *Journal*, however, I worried that my past really did make me biased against Israel.

From the beginning, I'd avoided reporting on the internal politics of the Jewish state and viewed the impenetrability and immobility of the Middle Eastern "peace process" as evidence that it was at best an artificial cover-up and at worst a great Western injustice. As a Saudi king once asked an American president, if the West felt so bad about the crimes of Germans against Jews in World War II, why didn't they give the Jews part of Germany? When Israel behaved just like an arrogant Middle Eastern dictatorship toward its Arab subjects and neighbors, why did our governments so unquestioningly support it? If in reality Israel controlled most aspects of life in the West Bank and Gaza, shouldn't it accept that it had taken responsibility for a large Palestinian population, and therefore, as a democracy, shouldn't it find some more inclusive identity than that of an exclusively Jewish state? Wasn't embracing the Palestinians actually in Israel's best interest, given that Palestinians will soon be a majority in the whole area Israel effectively controls, and will likely be a majority even in the pre-1967 borders of Israel within a generation or two?

I didn't see Israel, home to about one-third of the Jews of the world, as having a monopoly on Jewishness anyway. For me Jews were an integral and significant part of my school class in Cape Town, my close circle at Oxford, and lifelong friends in America, itself home to more Jews than Israel. I was conscious of their wish for a distinct identity, and how English slang and England's older generation could view Jews with prejudice, but I had moved on, just like my Jewish friends said they struggled with their parents over integration and marriage to non-Jews. Some Israelis would tell me that the Jews were a people, not a religion. I was convinced that political jurisdictions make people and religions what they are, and thus Israel was on weak ground if it made claims for support based on an idea that its state and people represented all Jews. Similarly, I believed it was a delusion to think that Arabs were a "people." Arabness describes certain characteristics shared to a greater or lesser extent by many Middle Eastern peoples, mainly Arabic speakers, but also to some extent by the Jews as well.

Jewishness itself was not an issue for me. If I saw Israel as a problem in the Middle East, it was because I could easily see the parallel with the selfish discrimination of whites against blacks where I'd grown up in South Africa, because in England I had internalized the measured, telling criticism of Israeli injustices by David Hirst in the *Guardian* and in the sensational dispatches of Robert Fisk in the *Times,* and because in Lebanon I had direct experience of Israeli abuse of power.

In the early 1980s, I'd hidden in village houses as Israeli tanks drove past with civilians blindfolded and tied on top in order to deter any attack by Lebanese resistance fighters opposing Israel's occupation of Lebanon. I'd seen indiscriminate roadside destruction of hard-to-grow olive and orange groves when those attacks took place. I'd interviewed victims of Israeli torture and later toured the torture chambers in the Lebanese hill town of Khiyam, where former inmates showed me electric shock torture chambers and a concrete basement where Israelis had hosed them with freezing water. I'd opened a Lebanese morgue door to see the body of a man almost certainly killed and defaced at an Israeli checkpoint—literally, his face and scalp had been skinned off his head. An Israeli once casually shot out the radiator of my office car while I cowered behind a wall a few feet away.

At the same time, I was aware that my early days in the Arab world were spent steeped in radical propaganda, talking to people in Syria and Egypt who either dreamed of driving "the Jews" into the sea, or wishfully described Israel as a latter-day colony or crusader state, bound by its own internal contradictions to collapse, probably soon. But I didn't know what my line should be now that I was supposed to be covering both sides. Everyone knew that the dictatorship in Syria, say, had blood on its hands, and nobody really pretended otherwise. Despite its own poor record, Israel could claim credit for being far more democratic, and I was unsure how far it was fair to criticize it.

I knew, for instance, that Israelis had once decided not to kill me when they  must have been tempted to do so. I was talking to two early Shia resistance leaders in south Lebanon, back in the early days, before the name Hezbollah had really begun to stick. They joked about a strange Israeli raid the day before. The Israelis had just missed finding the men in their usual meeting place, in the side room of a mosque where we were sitting.

Two blindfolded Lebanese captives on top of an Israeli armored personnel carrier, apparently to deter any attack by Lebanese resistance fighters opposing the Israeli occupation of Lebanon. 1985. *(Hugh Pope)*

In fact, the Israelis had loaded the sofas with radio-controlled explosives and listening devices. They could have killed the two resistance leaders right then, along with a pair of reporting colleagues and me. Instead, the Israelis pressed the button the next day, killing the young Shia fighters as they held a private council of war.

The paradox of Israel's Western-style connections coupled with its Middle Eastern ruthlessness had intrigued me long before the *Journal* suggested I start reporting on the country. In fact, in 1983, I had already embarked on a pilgrimage to Jerusalem to see Israel for myself.

The overland trip from Beirut to Jerusalem has rarely been possible in the past few decades. In mid-1983, when Israel still occupied all of south Lebanon, news reached Beirut that the uneasy Israel-Lebanon border had opened to civilian traffic. Against the odds, Israel was trying to show that its invasion of Lebanon the year before could lead one day to normalization with its northern neighbor.

Under an ugly overpass in a suburb of west Beirut, still mauled from the Israeli siege the year before, I squashed up into the backseat of an old Mercedes shared taxi and headed south. This was an odd weekend off work. I was to cross front lines between armies, a war zone, a border zone run by an Israeli-backed Lebanese Christian militia, two no-man's-lands, Israeli territory populated by Arabs, Palestinian territory controlled by Israelis and, of course, Jewish-populated areas ruled by Israel. Within myself, I began a move into new territory too, a journey that has led me to more questions than a final understanding.

We'd been lucky to have no trouble at Israeli checkpoints on the way down through south Lebanon, but I was nervous as we set out over the last few miles of UN-monitored Lebanese no-man's-land to the Israeli border at Naqoura. Empty spaces are dangerous in zones of conflict. My taxi driver shared my anxiety and made me walk the last few hundred yards. The Israelis had set up a tent to handle frontier formalities for the few people crossing the border, mostly Lebanese Christian relatives of those involved in an Israeli-backed militia in the border zone. My few belongings and identity stirred little interest among the Israeli reservists. They waved me through to walk up the rough road to the crest of the hill. Once there, I experienced a sudden shock.

I had spent fifteen unbroken months in Syria and Lebanon, largely deprived of Western comforts, reporting on Palestinian refugees in squalid camps, picking over the debris of Palestinian homes destroyed by Israel—in short, living a life in which Israel was blamed for everything bad. I felt as though I was about to enter enemy territory. But the wealthy infrastructure that welcomed me made me feel as though

I was back in the comfort of my own home country. I looked in wonder at the smooth tarmac and neatly pointed stone walls and parapets.

Then I saw the tourists, standing on a wide, round viewing area at the end of the road from Israel. They wore shorts, fanny packs, and other vacation paraphernalia. I was by then unaccustomed to seeing anyone's knees in public, so they looked half naked to me. They clustered in small groups, chatting excitedly and inspecting Lebanon through binoculars. A rush of rage filled my chest and my head began to spin. I rarely lose my temper, but here I was, barely controlling an animal fury that our Israel-blighted lives in Lebanon should be the object of such prurient Israeli interest. I hailed a taxi and slammed myself down into the backseat.

"Take me to Haifa, please," I said unthinkingly in Arabic to the driver.

"Sure," he said, somewhat puzzled. He turned out to be a Palestinian, and when I launched into an invective-laden diatribe, he sighed and commiserated cautiously at appropriate moments. I took a vow during the drive. My revenge for the tourist outrage would be to speak nothing but Arabic during my whole trip in Israel.

I began to take in the details of the countryside around me. The Israelis had a reputation for making the desert bloom. In my current mood, the memory of Lebanon seemed greener, except of course where the Israelis had massively bulldozed the orange groves by the roadsides as punishment for attacks on them. The Israeli-plated Mercedes taxi was only a bit newer than the ones I was used to in Lebanon, too. Haifa itself was in much better shape than Lebanese ports on the Mediterranean, but I recognized the same old stone streets and pointed archways. When I visited the al-Jazzar Mosque, however, the similarities overcame me.

Here I was, in what I saw as Israeli-occupied Palestine, and the Palestinians there, as if to show their own rejection of what had happened to them, had basically frozen their development in time. Old men walked by in elegant ground-length gowns as if they had stepped straight out of a nineteenth-century engraving. Noon prayers had just concluded, and there was a pious, ageless atmosphere in the mosque and its stone-flagged courtyard as if Israel had never been. It was too much. I sank under the accumulated stress of a year in retarded Syria, another six months in mad Beirut, and my sense of guilt that Britain had caused all this turmoil. I collapsed.

When I regained consciousness on a bench around a sapling on an edge of the courtyard, a group of bearded young men were excitedly discussing me.

"Look, he's coming to!" one of them noticed.

I looked at them, tears streaming down my face.

"You'll be fine, you'll be fine," one of them said, taking my hand.

"Are you one of the Muslim brothers from England?" asked another.

I blabbered out a confused version of my story. I didn't understand clearly myself.

But even at this critical moment, when I had obviously earned the open trust of a community that I deeply sympathized with, my English reserve and stiff upper lip soon rushed back. I declined all offers of help and hospitality. I tottered off alone, leaving the astonished congregation whispering behind me. This Haifa break-down was not a variant of the Jerusalem syndrome, in which afflicted persons don white robes or begin to preach about purity. I just felt crushingly sad about all the people I had seen suffering so much.

My depression deepened when I rode into the West Bank in a taxi driven by a bedouin Arab who kept his Israeli-licensed Kalashnikov under my seat in case of attack by a Palestinian Arab. I was heading to the town of Nablus, where I hoped to visit the family of a friend who was a Palestinian exile in Damascus. He'd given me his parents' address, and I wanted to do them the favor of bringing rare news of their son. I found the middle-class house, and his father and mother politely served me tea on a balcony. Animated to be among friends at last, I told them how their son was enjoying himself and doing well at university, described my trip, and asked questions about Nablus. I gradually realized that they were saying very little. His mother turned her face away to the floor.

"Perhaps you'd better go now," said his father quietly.

It wasn't until I was on the street again that I realized what had happened. They had thought I was an Israeli spy. I felt number than ever.

Arriving in Jerusalem I headed straight for the epicenter of what I supposed being in Israel was all about. My goal was to walk close to the Dome of the Rock, the gilded half globe that has become the symbol of Muslim dreams of winning back their place in Jerusalem. Years later, I hired a guide to try to understand who really owned what and where. He warned me that only madness lay in the details, just as the Christian sects argued over every square inch of the Church of the Holy Sepulcher. It was all down to lack of space, said Ross Culiner, the well-known educator and guide, as we dodged in and out of the millennial back alleys of the city; indeed, the whole country's pre-1967 territory is only as big as Mas-sachusetts and is two-thirds desert. Then there was the geographical imperative. Israel/Palestine straddles the crossroads of three continents: Africa, Asia, and Europe. When King David founded Jerusalem, I also read, it was as an artificial city that aimed to integrate rival tribes, yet belonged to neither. In the subse-quent four thousand years, it was besieged and conquered more than thirty times. Everybody had struggled to control it—Egyptians and Mesopotamians, Romans and Parthians, Ottoman Turks and British, Soviets and Americans. Fi-nally we came to the great stones still holding up the Temple Mount, the foun-dations of the Western Wall of the Jewish Second Temple of Solomon, leveled by the Romans 1,900 years ago, and since A.D. 700 the site of the third-holiest shrine of Islam.

"All three main monotheistic religions put their reference points here, Judaism, Christianity, and Islam. Their holy places are on the same piece of ground. And remember, there are forty different kinds of Christians," said Culiner, neatly defeating my hope that all would be put in an easily accessible framework.

"So there's no one in the right?"

"Possession means sanctity, and that means a lot," he said. "A Western solution based on rational compromise won't work, because you can't divide God. That's why there are so many crazies around here."

Indeed, on my first visit, I was one of those crazies. Determined to live down my sense of rejection by my friend's family in Nablus, I headed for the Muslim gateway to the Dome of the Rock. My appearance caused the bored guard there to stop me and direct me to the tourist entrance. I drew myself up to my full height.

"But I am on a pilgrimage from Beirut!" I protested in Arabic. He was so astonished he did not even ask me if I was a Muslim. I passed through and into the courtyard. At this moment of triumph for my Arabic-language education, I walked straight into the arms of one of my more friendly Arabic tutors from Oxford. He was impressed at last. I awarded myself a twenty-four-hour English break from my Arabic-only vow, and he invited me back to stay at the British School of Archaeology in Jerusalem. I could tell, however, that my stories sounded wild and unsettlingly radical to the company there. And I couldn't identify anymore with the pleasant, rarefied academic atmosphere. After hungrily roaming the ancient streets of the Arab quarters, wondering at Israel's slow swallowing up of the city, I was soon pushing my way into the back of a shared taxi for the journey to Tel Aviv and back to Beirut.

For the first time after two days in the country, I was among Jewish Israelis alone. While some in the long-wheelbase Mercedes taxi bristled as I asked the price of the fare loudly in Arabic, one Israeli in the middle kindly translated for me and passed back my change. It was an ambivalent pattern that was to be repeated often in Tel Aviv. I had long realized that Israel's reflexes were quite in tune with those of the rest of the Middle East: the militaristic political culture, the powerful state machinery, the eye-for-an-eye attitude of public opinion, the overlaps in story lines of the Torah and the Koran, and the vengeful ease with which politicians called for enemies to be killed. Now I became aware of how some words I kept hearing in Hebrew sounded the same as their Arabic equivalents, a Semitic brotherhood especially noticeable in numbers and common expressions, and saw how some letters of the alphabet visibly shared a common root. Middle Eastern influence is strong in the population, too: of Israel's 6.7 million people, about half are native Palestinian Arab Muslims and Christians, or Sephardic Jews who migrated to Israel from Islamic countries and especially the Arab world.

To get anywhere with my Arabic, I learned to aim my questions at middle-aged, darker-skinned Sephardic Jews who could still remember the language from their native lands. In numbers, Sephardic Jews began to outnumber the Europe and American-born Ashkenazi Jews in the 1970s, but they were not very visible from outside Israel since the Ashkenazis tend to dominate Israeli politics. When Ali Salem, an Egyptian playwright, made his own pilgrimage to Israel in 1994, he too felt this unexpected street-level familiarity. Indeed, he believes that the explanation for why Israelis got on so badly with their neighbors was the very Arabness of their country—"Is there any one more cruel to an Arab than another Arab?" he asks in his book *Journey to Israel*.

The constant tension with Arab neighbors also meant that Israel had to keep its entire population mobilized. When I started looking for a northbound taxi to start my journey back from Tel Aviv to Lebanon in 1983, I was astonished at the sheer number of Israeli army reservists crisscrossing the area around the bus station with their rifles strung over one shoulder. I exchanged glances with an old Palestinian standing on a curb and, in one of those live-contact moments that make the Middle East so addictive, I knew that he was on my wavelength of wonder at the unreal scene of civilian-soldiers before us.

"Why," I asked him, "do they all have to have guns here?"

"The thief," he solemnly answered me, "is always frightened."

As I felt my way into my role as the *Journal*'s lone Middle East correspondent in 2000–2001, a new editor was appointed to watch over this and other parts of the world, Bill Spindle. Together with my predecessor Stephen Glain, we all met in Jerusalem to discuss how to cover Israel and the Arab-Israeli "peace process."

Every news organization holds such meetings to discuss upcoming themes, and perhaps they make editors feel that coordinating foreign correspondents is less like herding cats. I attended my fair share of them, and they made little difference to what we did in the field. Spindle was a Japan specialist and sometimes winced at my directness. What fundamentally new could we say, I asked, about the Arab-Israeli conflict that hadn't been said over and over? How could we demonstrate the core problem that the United States, for reasons of sentimental attachment and the lobbying of special interest groups, supported one Middle East side extravagantly and yet tried to present itself to the other as an honest broker to make peace? And how could we reflect the desperation of and injustice done to the Palestinians in a way that would not sound shrill, would be judged fair by Israelis and cautious New York editors, and yet be trenchant enough to be noticed by Americans and maybe change their minds a bit?

The 1990s and the Oslo process had left a trail of glamorous front-page Middle East reporting by my predecessors. They had been able to hitch their stories to the great locomotive of American journalism: an optimistic hope in a better world. The light of Middle East peace was burning bright at the end of the tunnel. But toward the end of the 1990s, this light dimmed again. American embassies in East Africa were bombed by al-Qaeda, the Arab-Israeli process stalled, and American editors lost interest. The Middle East was a place where one could expect nothing but failure.

"We could show exactly how wrecked the Middle East is, and who did it," I suggested.

I could almost physically feel the frustration and despair of the Arab Israelis around us in Jerusalem, for instance. I'd visited the building that might have housed the assembly and president of the Palestinian state foreseen by the moribund Oslo process. It was a half-built concrete carcass in a remote suburb of east Jerusalem. I climbed up through the building site to what was presumably meant to be the leader's suite. From the balcony, far away over a jumble of chaotic apartment block rooftops, I could just make out the Dome of the Rock. That symbol of everything dear to the Palestinians was becoming ever more inaccessible. In the backstreets in between the would-be assembly and the old city, bulldozers were already pushing up big piles of rubble to seal Jerusalem off from the West Bank. It was the precursor of the future wall. But Spindle had no illusions about the challenge ahead of us. The Palestinians were yesterday's news. They'd missed the train to the promised future.

"The front page isn't interested in explaining why the Middle East is a basket case. We expect it to be a basket case. To the extent that it might not be a basket case, they are possibly interested," he explained.

No wonder Palestinian poet Mahmoud Darwish felt his cause so marginalized that he was reduced to writing that "I defend my right to defend my right."

"How about the economy? The *Journal* likes that stuff. What about the slumping tourism business?"

"Given the intifada, it's just not surprising that nobody's visiting," Spindle reckoned. "They're not interested in what's happening to the Israeli economy."

It wasn't Spindle's fault. The Palestinians were parochial. For a story to fly to the front page from anywhere in the world, it had to be unusual, big, panregional, even universal. Before leaving, Stephen Glain had proved the near impossibility of Arab-Israel stories satisfying these criteria at that time. The other former Middle East correspondent, the late Danny Pearl, had felt the tide of front-page interest running out a year before and had left for new horizons in India.

There was another issue on the Arab-Israeli front that we stepped gingerly around. The powerful editorial pages of our newspaper were filled with a deep disdain for the non-Israeli Middle East. Their commentaries, so incisive and iconoclastic when applied to subjects they saw with a clear, well-informed, and familiar eye, became perverse. What they published was quite divorced from the unfortunate reality of what it was like to be actually born and live in the Middle East. No concession was made to how hobbled societies could be by never-ending wars, refugee camps, and dictatorships co-opted by the U.S. government in order to make "peace" agreements, open up oil fields, and accommodate Israel.

The Israeli dimension of the opinion pages surely shaped, even led, the neoconservative thinking of the presidency of George W. Bush as he headed toward his disastrous invasion of Iraq. When it was all too late, another of the *Journal*'s former Middle East correspondents, Peter Waldman, was belatedly allowed to analyze the neoconservative view of the Middle East for the front page. He concluded that it boiled down to the ideas of British-American historian Bernard Lewis, the "boldest shift in U.S. foreign policy in 50 years." The Lewis doctrine, according to Waldman, held that the Middle East perceived America as weak, and that the United States should therefore use force to instill respect or, failing that, fear. Somehow, democracy was supposed to follow. Iraq was the test run. By accident or design, this was exactly the worldview of Israeli hard-liners. Indeed, Israel was the only country in the world that really supported the U.S.-led invasion of Iraq. And while the news pages might have no real Israel correspondent, barely a month went by without our opinion pages printing long commentaries on what to do by a stable of uncompromising Israelis like Ariel Sharon, Benjamin Netanyahu, Ehud Barak, Ehud Olmert, Dore Gold, and Natan Sharansky. Usually the argument boiled down to Lewis's "get tough or get out," or in other words, hit the Arabs hard and they'll soon obey. It didn't work in Iraq, and I doubted it would ever bring peace to Israel.

Supposedly, we were separated from the editorial pages of the newspaper by what was referred to as a Chinese wall, as if we were a bank handling cold financial secrets. Certainly, the op-ed folks were on a different floor and there was little personal traffic between us. But some one-way news traffic was allowed through. Although the opinion pages piously ignored anything we reported from the ground that didn't fit their doctrines, they glowingly cited a reporter by name who turned up evidence they liked.

A week after the intifada broke out in 2000, Glain told me that an opinion page editor had asked him for ideas for fresh voices.

"How about an Arab?" Glain had said.

The editor gasped.

"We want to keep an open mind on this," he prevaricated.

Glain suggested it was worth contacting an Israeli Arab. This Palestinian minority was once seen as passively loyal by Israelis, but Israeli Arab towns and villages had staged protests in sympathy with the intifada, resenting the fact that they were not fully included in the Israeli economy and politics. The editor said he'd look at some possible commentators' names, which Glain forwarded to him in the vain hope that change was on the way. After all, one reason for the non-Israeli Middle East's lack of profile in the United States is that it produces almost nobody who can write a biting editorial commentary in English. The well-educated, internationalized Israeli and Jewish worlds excel at it. There was one fine Arab writer who appeared regularly on the opinion pages, Fouad Ajami, but he lived in America and his critique of the Arab world's failings only encouraged those Americans who wanted to get tough. A few weeks later, Glain told me, he asked the editor whether he'd contacted any of the names Glain had sent along to help give a new perspective.

"Steve," the editor said, lowering his voice, as if he might be overheard, "there's no way I'm going to get an Arab on the page around here."

In Jerusalem, however, people know that ignoring something doesn't make it go away and that legitimacy is meaningful. Jewish taxi drivers are reluctant to cross an invisible line on an apparently open four-lane highway, explaining that they don't want to stray over to the Palestinian side of the 1948 cease-fire lines, open since 1967. For my part, I instinctively felt more comfortable spending my nights among the old stone colonnades of the American Colony Hotel on the Palestinian side. Our upright Israeli-American assistant in Israel also felt a moral imperative, insisting on buying a more expensive house because it was on the pre-1967 Israeli side of her home suburb.

As I tried to turn these moral complications into readable story ideas, I discovered, as Glain had done before me, that the well-staffed New York Times bureau had left few stones unturned. The Journal would run nothing on its front page that wasn't completely original. And as Spindle had warned, any hint that the grim standoff we lived with was likely to go on for decades would kill a story.

"Peace" was a magic word that could open up space, at least on the foreign pages of the newspaper. But using it was like kissing a beautiful princess who then turns into a wicked witch. Glain and I had once worked up a story on the likelihood of Ariel Sharon taking over as prime minister of Israel. We managed to list all the stains on the veteran politician-general's record, despite severe time pressure and appalling cell phone lines between Glain in Jerusalem and me in Beirut that ended up costing the Journal $6,000. But guided by editors too far away and too confident of goodwill in the world, the story ended up suggesting that as a "strongman," only Sharon could make "peace." It was just plausible, of course. But it was as utterly wrong as the headline was horrible: TOUGH DOVE.

Realizing afterward what had happened, I couldn't believe how I'd betrayed everything I thought I stood for. For me, Sharon was first and foremost the architect of the 1982 invasion of Lebanon. With complete clarity I remember how I stood motionless in my shower one morning in Damascus, weeping in impotent despair as news reports began to come in over the radio of the 1982 massacre in the Beirut

Palestinian refugee slums of Sabra and Shatila. An Israeli commission later found that Sharon bore "personal responsibility," both morally and professionally, for the eight hundred rape and torture killings by Israel's Lebanese Christian allies whom he had sent in. The commission effectively forced him to resign his post as defense minister, but he suffered no further penalty. Sharon was sometimes ready to say he regretted what happened, but when asked if he'd apologize, he asked, "Apologize for what?" Infected in those days by a truly Middle Eastern desire for vengeance, I had fantasized about shooting Sharon personally at a press conference if I ever got the chance. Offered a tribune in print from which I could at least commit a character assassination, I had become part of the mendacious "it can all get better" machine.

The virtual story of exaggerated peace hopes that had taken root in Americans' minds took over again after I visited Hebron, crisscrossing the front lines of the ancient and contested West Bank city. One moment I was with wild-eyed Palestinian boys in the bazaar who were throwing stones toward Israeli machine-gun nests. The next I was visiting the bunkered home of a legendarily uncompromising Jewish settler in the heart of the Palestinian town, New Jersey native David Wilder. No peace in sight here. The text of my story spelled out the intractability of the conflict, the usefulness of international observers of Israeli actions, and the inevitability that Israel would reject UN suggestions that more of them would be a good idea. But the headline OBSERVERS KEEP PEACE IN ISRAEL—SOMETIMES/ SCANDINAVIAN PATROL COULD SERVE AS WORLD MODEL left the reader with the impression that Israelis and Palestinians were agreeing on something.

Gaza, I thought, would be a compelling story to put Americans straight about how hard it was to expect Palestinians to accept their current situation in a peace settlement. Already as I made my way through the fortifications of the crossing point from Israel into northern Gaza, it was clear I was entering an open-air prison. Years of small steps and decisions had allowed a ghetto of inhumanity to fester and grow. One and a half million people lived cooped up behind barbed wire, guard towers, and walls, with Israeli patrol boats off the beaches and Israeli F-16s in the air above. At that time the thin strip of land was cut in seven by Israeli settlements, which looked like supercharged gated communities guarded by slit-windowed Israeli forts and surrounded by slums. A withdrawal ordered by Sharon in 2005 was to make little difference to Israel's strategic control of Gaza; indeed, his adviser later told an Israeli newspaper he had ordered it, with Western approval, to supply "the amount of formaldehyde that is necessary so there will not be a political process with the Palestinians," unless, of course, they submitted. No wonder that the Gazans were to prove the most hard-bitten adversaries of Israel, and elected a radical Islamist government.

"It must be alarming, worrying that you could be assassinated out of the blue,

Graffito in Gaza depicting the suicide bombing of an Israeli bus. The painting is signed by the Islamic Resistance Movement (Hamas), and its title spells out the main Palestinian motive: not someplace in an Islamic paradise, but "Revenge." 2000. *(Hugh Pope)*

just sitting in your house," I commented as I sat with one of the bosses of Islamic Jihad in Gaza. In fact, I was the one looking nervously out of the window. An Israeli warplane could wipe us out any time it wanted.

"Don't worry!" the Islamist cheerfully replied. "As long as you're with me, I feel completely safe."

Fate intervened before I had time to find the right narrative to show the injustices of Gaza. On September 11, 2001, I was vainly working on interesting the front page in what I hoped was an irresistible, original story: Some Israeli companies, perhaps nervous about long-term prospects in Israel, were hedging their bets and moving back into the Eastern European towns from where they or their parents had been forced out in the 1930s and 1940s. I had gone to Tel Aviv to interview one entrepreneur, who, in a subtle act of coming to terms, was building a shopping center overlooking the Polish town square where his parents and family had been rounded up for the Nazi gas chambers sixty years before. When I arrived in his office overlooking the Israeli Ministry of Defense, however, the television beside his desk was showing the flames leaping out from the first tower of the World Trade Center.

I didn't know it then, but my editor Bill Spindle was at that minute sitting at his desk in the next-door World Financial Center wondering what do with another of my ideas to change American attitudes, a story about a conflicted Palestinian refugee soccer team in Jordan. As bits of burning building and jumping people from the World Trade Center flashed past Bill's window, and were relayed to the desk TV beside me in Tel Aviv, I tried to restart my hard-to-arrange interview about Israeli investors heading back into Eastern Europe. Then a plane hit the second tower, and even I realized that today was not the day to talk about shopping centers in Poland. Bill never mentioned my Palestinian soccer team again, either. This was not the time to explore Arab agonies: America was in pain and shock, and Arab terrorism was now the issue. Before I left the entrepreneur, however, I asked him what he thought the attacks meant for U.S.-Israeli relations. He smiled serenely and his hand described a sharp, upward takeoff.

Still, ten days earlier, I had managed to land a big story about Israel on the front page. It told how it felt to be Jewish and living in an Israeli settlement on the West Bank, under attack from Palestinian snipers, and what it was like for the poor, hamstrung Palestinian village next door, where people felt that the Jewish settlers from twenty mostly richer countries had stolen their old land. I was delighted that the feature aired much that I wanted to say about rising tensions, the lingering illegitimacy of Israel's claims to Palestinian land, the patronizing Israeli assumption of superiority, the Palestinian inability to catch up, and the resulting Palestinian radicalization.

In passing, I made a point about the real capacity of Jews and Arabs to live together in times of calm. It was only later that I noticed that it had come to be the major dramatic springboard of the article. The headline, which I had agreed to, and which was technically correct, was once again firmly anchored in the virtual world of the Middle East "peace process": BROKEN IDYLL/ON THE WEST BANK, A RARE PEACE FALLS TO SNIPERS' BULLETS/TWO TOWNS, JEWISH AND ARAB, LIVED AS "ONE COUNTRY"; NOW, FEAR AND LOATHING/YARMULKES SEWN BY MUSLIMS. I had thus added another layer of gilt to the false idol, making Americans think that the normality of Israel/Palestine was peace and that Jews and Arabs had lived together as "one country" before snipers had spoiled it all—Palestinian gunmen, of course, as readers would discover in the second paragraph.

References to what the settlers were doing there in the first place were edited down to make way for the journalistic narrative. There was no place for existential conversations, like the one I had with Shlomo Kaniel, the settlement's security coordinator and a survivor of Bergen-Belsen. He readily acknowledged that the majority of Israelis didn't share his ideology, which took its authority from God and viewed Palestinians as second-class citizens with no political rights. But as we sat chatting in his imported Scandinavian wooden house filled with modern art, he insisted the settlement represented the real Israel.

"What is happening is not a war over settlements, but a war over Israel. All Israel is a settlement and as such is an obstacle to peace. My assumption is that it will be a long, violent war. My hope is that our government will throw out those

[Arabs] who do not want to be our guests. Who will be the refugees, if it's not them? Us!" he said, handing me another succulent black fig from his garden. "We are in the forefront of what our society needs, not watching the train but leading the train of religious Zionism. We don't give ourselves the right to kill, like the Nazis. What I want is that my great-great-grandchildren will say, 'We made some mistakes, and Grandpa Shlomo was a bit naughty. But look what we've got now!'"

6. THE DRUNKEN LOVER

Revolutionary Iran's Struggle with Its Poetic Soul

I veil my words in curtains, friends
Let balladeers tease out their ends
—HAFEZ, FOURTEENTH-CENTURY PERSIAN POET

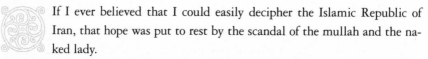 If I ever believed that I could easily decipher the Islamic Republic of Iran, that hope was put to rest by the scandal of the mullah and the naked lady.

It was back in 1986, and times were bleak. Glorious reports from the war front with Iraq barely concealed the reality of a bloody stalemate. Food was rationed and foreign travel was hard. The nation was tiring of the young, awkward Islamic Revolution that had overthrown the oppressive shah, or king, seven years before. Then the naked lady came, and she offered us all a sweet moment of escape. Tehran's rumor mill flashed the news of her arrival around the city. Within hours delighted whispers had spread to a giggling conclave in my office in north Tehran. I'd understood that this female apparition could be found nestling in the beard of the mullah in question.

"I've heard it's a fox," countered my assistant, Mohammad, a precise mathematician who now wore the quiet smile he reserved for the most satisfying of paradoxes.

I turned to Rahmati, the office manager, whom I'd sent out to obtain the evidence. Back then I was one of the only Western correspondents resident in Iran and was eager to impress my bosses at Reuters with such an extraordinary scoop.

"Where is she? Is there a fox? Can you see anything?" I asked.

"No!" said Rahmati, bending gleefully yet uneasily with the rest of us over the evidence. My willful twenty-six-year-old's inability to understand the niceties of submitting to revolutionary regimes, combined with the demands put upon Rahmati's life by government agencies of all sorts, were turning him into an ever-greater bundle of nerves. "She'll be very hard to find!"

We were looking at Iran's smart new purple one-hundred-rial banknote, printed in Britain and just issued by the government. One side featured the doleful countenance of Ayatollah Seyyed Hassan Modarres, a religious grandee and politician who died in one of the shah's jails in 1937. But, as all Tehran now knew, an ingenious engraver had woven a luscious nude into the curls of the thick growth on his chin! Everyone wanted to admire this cheeky revelation of what everyone had long suspected to be on a mullah's mind. Within a day the banknote soared to a premium against other notes, 20, 30, 50 percent above the face value. We pored over the newly minted bill, fingers pointing here and there. There the naked lady was, we eventually all agreed, in a sensuous recline. Amazing! Or was she? Could it be a fox? A national psychosis swept aside all such questioning. Soon people were describing snakes in the mullah's turban and a calligraphic swirl in the note's geometric surrounds that spelled out "Death to Khomeini," the revered leader of the Islamic Republic.

This proof of all the wildest conspiracies that any Iranian could ever dream up made the nation positively tipsy. The regime reeled under the onslaught, so much more dangerous for being completely outside the tightly controlled public media. To regain control, it withdrew the banknotes. Several days later, after a public holiday, *Islamic Republic* newspaper splashed the counterstrike across the front page. A plot by the little Satan, Britain, had been crushed! A certain attempt to meddle with the currency of the Islamic Republic had been foiled! The victorious government would now reissue the cleaned-up banknotes!

To me, the bills seemed unchanged. The same long-faced ayatollah looked ponderously out at the world. But now Iranians acted surprised when I suggested that a naked lady had ever nestled in his bushy beard. We all went back to our routines.

Yet, as I traveled to Iran over the years, the problem posed by the naked lady kept surfacing: What you see in Iran is not what you get. I felt it most deeply when I arrived in Tehran in January 2001. My editors at the *Wall Street Journal* were interested in a typical bill of fare: Iran's nuclear ambitions, its rabble-rousing rhetoric against Israel, its oil, and the latest round of brutal suppression of "reformers" by "conservatives." I slogged up and down the traffic-clogged expressways of the sprawling metropolis to report these matters in the fashion of the day. Thanks to the ascendancy of roughshod revolutionary thugs as the dominant class, my stories once again reinforced the idea that Iran was a mortal enemy of civilization.

But I knew this was far from the truth, and my role in perpetuating this myth began to upset me. Being a bit crazy sometimes didn't make nations wholly mad and bad. The sophistication of Persian culture had made my heart soar when I studied at university. Many Iranians I admired were clever and amusing. Their literary talents and fine taste made me count them among the most civilized people in the Middle East. I became determined to write something to show that everything in Iran was not as it appeared in the sterile rhetorical cockfight between U.S. spokesmen and Iranian hard-liners. At a deeper level, too, I wanted to explain that no Iranian ever took anything at face value, so we should be wary of doing that ourselves when dealing with them. Indeed, the naked lady had proved how the extraordinary vitality of the Iranian imagination meant that the country might actually be lost in a mental maze of its own devising.

But how to explain this uniquely mercurial country to the fact-loving readers of the *Journal*? I searched for inspiration by flicking through the Iranian channels of the television in my rented apartment. Postrevolutionary TV was predictable. A mullah preaching in a monotone. A poet. An Iranian film director discussing a heartbreaking cinematic triumph. A lugubrious Persian poetry reading. A mullah preaching. A soulful film, another mullah. A new poet who began to declaim about roses, nightingales, the beloved . . . Aha, I realized, that was it! I would travel to Shiraz, city of poetry and roses. There I would write about the one person I knew who gave voice to Iran's full complexity of inner truths and multiple meanings.

I telephoned Bill Spindle in New York to give him the good news. He needed me, as usual, to find a strong newsy front-page story.

"We have to explain everything at once, right?" I said. "What better subject than a poet!"

Spindle's sigh turned to rebukeful protest when I added that the poet I had in mind had been dead since 1389. But my arguments were ready for turning our media spotlight on Mohammad Shams al-Din Hafez, a poet of love, mystical paths to union with God, and lampooner of hypocrisy. Even in his own lifetime, this scourge of religious bigotry was well on his way to fame. The earlier Persian poet Omar Khayyam is more famous in the English-speaking world thanks to a felicitous translation, but it is Hafez who is Iran's most admired source of literary wisdom.

Iran's poetic tradition, I maintained, could help explain Iranian political rhetoric to the world. Understanding Iran was like deconstructing a magician's tricks: The secret lay in the trick, and there was no underlying sorcery. One reason none of us understood what Iran really wanted was that there was no consensus on policy even within the Iranian regime. I gave Spindle the example of restoring relations with the United States, broken since revolutionary students seized the U.S. embassy in

1979 and held sixty-six Americans hostage, some of them for 444 days. Contrary to appearances, mainstream Iranian politicians and the public quietly supported reopening the embassy. But neither of Iran's big factions could allow the other side to get the credit for it. The United States, of course, didn't help. It was vengeful about its humiliation and allied with Israel in viewing Iran's regime as uniquely diabolical. So the old American embassy became a high school for Iranian Islamic Revolutionary Guards, its brick walls painted with fading slogans and a Statue of Liberty with a spooky skull.

You shouldn't forget, I told Spindle, that Iranians consider straight talk vulgar, almost rude. When I asked an Iranian the way somewhere, he would often first try to assess in which direction I already wanted to go. Iranian clergymen reserved special debate for the *mantuq* and the *mafhum,* or what is said and what should be understood. In one of my two expulsion orders from Iran, only one of which was fully implemented, the ministry responsible formally charged me with seeing "the glass half empty when in fact it is half full." Some Iranians would scold me about how literally the West took slogans like "Wipe out Israel," and insisted they did not mean a new holocaust, just a change in Israeli policies. One friend who worked for the Iranian news agency IRNA said he and his bored colleagues deliberately sought out anti-West hell-raising by provincial mullahs, translated it, and published it to the world. Their purpose was not global Islamic revolution, as everyone thought. It was the opposite: to embarrass or trip up the Islamist regime.

The way to dissect this grand complication, I insisted to Spindle, was to dive deep into a poetic tradition that derived its power from a kaleidoscopic range of meanings. Every Iranian agrees, more or less, that Hafez is the paragon of this ancient and gorgeous art. His ghazals, a kind of sonnet usually of seven couplets, have a deep, resonant beauty and a sweep of Shakespearean majesty. Their apparently simple settings—usually rose gardens or wine taverns, perfumed by sweet breezes, nightingales, lovers, and wine bearers—disguise a vast complexity. Persian scholars can attribute several meanings to every word, weighing overtones of the mundane, the metaphoric, the mystical, and even the cosmic. Thus the phrase "That Turk of Shiraz" from one of his most famous poems can mean a Turkic tribesman from the Shiraz area; a pale-skinned male or female beauty; a face with a mole, in which the darkness of the mole indicates the mystical unknowable; the planet Mars; and so on. Hafez even mixes spiritual imagery with the wild-edged erotic:

With disheveled hair and gleaming skin and laughing mouth and drunk
With shirt ripped open, singing sonnets and a wine jar in his hand
With a trouble-loving eye and a finger on his lips
At midnight he came and sat here by my pillowside . . .

Every generation of foreign Persian scholars tries its hands at translating Hafez, while disparaging the efforts of the last. In studies of Hafez, debate rages about which ghazals he wrote, when he wrote them, and whether certain lines in them are really his. Nobody can quite tell if the love of which he speaks is for boys, women, or God. Hafez at times clearly revels in earthly pleasures of wine and song, flying in the face of orthodox Muslim disapproval. And yet it could all be metaphorical and refer simply to his path to union with the divine essence. One thing is for sure: He hated religious authoritarianism, and a widely accepted tradition has it that the blinkered clergy of his day tried to prevent him receiving a Muslim burial. Biting verses like the following show why he is more popular than ever among dissidents in today's Islamic Republic:

Preachers who boast of probity from pulpits and in the mosque
Behave quite differently when none other is on hand to watch.

I became so intoxicated with his idiom that when asked in my final exam at Oxford to critique the construction of a ghazal, I wrote out one that I had composed in honor of a lovely Persian woman in my college and duly discussed it with myself. I thought it wiser not to tell Spindle that last part. Still, to me the evidence that this was a story was overwhelming. But through the silence on the phone line, I could feel him leaning back skeptically in his swivel chair.

"People should understand that 'Death to America!' sometimes means, 'Please, America, show me more love!'" I insisted. "I'm also fed up with writing about Islamic this, Islamic that. We treat the whole region as if nobody goes out-of-doors without consulting the Koran. Well, the fact is that in Iran today, the poems of Hafez may well outsell the Koran. It's a secret counterculture—for me, actually, it's the main culture of Iran. This Islamic revolutionary nonsense is the counterculture. And six hundred years old or not, a new Iranian pop group is now using his lyrics as a form of protest!"

Spindle heard me out patiently. He allowed that this all might be the case but predicted that it would be hard to get onto the front page, the holy grail of all our efforts. This was a process with as many stages as the mystic's path to union with the godhead. First, a reporter had to write a formal proposal, an art form in itself that could take weeks to agree with an editor. Then it would be submitted to the front-page editors, who might dismiss the idea with a throwaway one-liner or wait silently for days. Then, perhaps, the story would be approved, plot, content, and all. After weeks more reporting, editing, coming and going, it might still be rejected. More often it would be published, to a satisfying e-mail cascade of self-congratulation that embraced all concerned. If a reporter didn't manage that half a dozen times by year's end, his last nightingale had sung.

This was a burden to bear for the *Journal*'s "fixer" in Iran, Afshin Abtahi. He despaired at the way his frustrated visitors ran from interview to interview, trying to wring quotes out of people that would flesh out and validate their presold story ideas before their short visas ran out. The front page often lost interest when research showed reality was different from the story advertised. Nobody liked trying to switch horses midway through the reporting. Bill knew that a six hundred-years-dead foreign poet was unlikely to jump the first fence. Still, he gamely allowed me to pack my saddlebags and try.

The airplane carrying Afshin and me landed in the plain between the barren mountains around Shiraz just as the sun began to clear a soft morning haze. The air was fragrant compared to the brown smog that constantly dulls Tehran. A billboard-sized line of Hafez's poetry in flowery calligraphy welcomed us at an intersection on the Shiraz ring road, the modern-day gates of the city:

> *You're late, O drunken-headed lover!*
> *I won't let your skirt slip easily from my embrace.*

I felt as if I was entering a liberated zone. The Islamic Republic was slipping into the background. As we continued, we saw a small crowd at a beaten-up brick building by a roundabout.

"*Aash!*" whispered Afshin, reverently. Soup.

Making out the curves of a cauldron the size of a small car in the shadows of the shop, I begged our driver to stop. Here was a scene that could hardly have changed since the time of Hafez. Each person carried a pot or pan to receive dollops of steaming green goo from a man with a capacious ladle. Then they headed back to their homes with their family's breakfast. We each took a portion of what turned out to be a broth so thick with lentils that our spoons stood up straight in it. I associated the taste with English pease pottage, a favorite dish, and felt at home.

I had fallen under the spell of the city sixteen years before, when the naked lady scandal was the only light relief and the national slogan was "War, War, to Victory." Shiraz had shown its rose-tinted spectacles back then with little asides, like the local graffiti artist who awkwardly translated the war slogan into the poetic language of mysticism: "War, War, Until We Reach the Alley of the Friend [God] and Meet Him." To get published in the local paper, young Shirazi poets struggled with the domineering spirit of the age. "My flower takes its scent from the Koran," one had written. Another: "Come, take wing like a dove, let's take up position in a front-line trench."

Peace of a kind had come now, and off-duty soldiers, Iraqi refugees, and penniless Afghan exiles no longer thronged the public spaces. It was Friday, Iran's official day of rest, but, as ever, still the regime's day for show-and-tell at the weekly prayer ceremony. I set out for the Friday mosque, a building a thousand years old in parts. Hafez must have stepped through these arches too. During times that he was in political favor, Hafez was chief of Koranic instruction at the main religious college here, and his pen name, which means "he who has memorized," honors his memorization of the whole holy book. At other times censorious rulers forced him to leave Shiraz, just as many of the most talented Iranians today are in France or America. I thought that if Hafez were alive now, he would probably be in exile too. The shabby crowd in the courtyard of the mosque was led by the kind of Islamic revolutionary bigots who enraged the conscience of Hafez as he penned the lines:

Drink wine, Hafez, be glad, be wild!
Don't copy those who make the Koran a hypocritical trap.

I was witnessing what Hafez hated. His old mosque was now an eyesore. Where were the subjects of his songs, the rose gardens, the nightingales, the wine shops, and the beauties? Maybe Spindle was right, and my thesis that Hafez represented Iran's truer culture was too far-flung. I headed to the bazaar, where I hoped the covered warrens of shop-lined alleyways would restore my morale and determination to make the story work.

At least I was correct in one matter. I stopped in a bookshop where the bookseller, Abbas, confirmed that sales of the poet Hafez easily rivaled that of the Koran. Nothing else came close. Every family wanted Hafez on hand to be able to consult it for the occasional *fal,* the oracle that might point them in the right direction when a difficult decision or situation loomed. After all, Hafez reputedly composed the best of his poems in a state of divine inspiration, just as Muhammad had been in when he received the Koran from God. I opened up an ornate divan, or poetry collection, and let it fall open to find an oracle for me. The method is to choose the couplet on which one's eyes first fall. I spied one of my favorites, close to the beginning, and it was certainly appropriate.

Tell tales of wine and song, and seek less the secret of the world.
This deep riddle will ne'er be solved by science and research.

I asked Abbas what he thought it meant.

"Hafez is right. Don't bother digging too deep. People live with lots of meanings, because everything is hidden from us," he said.

"That's why I like Hafez," I told him. "His poems seem to be able to bring all those meanings into an artistic whole. Why do you think people still like him so much?"

"We need him more than ever these days."

Hafez would have quickly spotted the hypocrisy in one huge slogan painted on a wall in today's Shiraz: THE REGENCY OF THE JURISPRUDENT IS THE SAME AS THE RULE OF THE PROPHET OF GOD. At the time, Iran's jurisprudent and supreme leader was Ayatollah Ali Khamenei. The word "jurisprudent" implies great wisdom, or at least authorship of many volumes of religious rulings on matters ranging from love and war to, say, dieting. Khamenei was, however, a hard-bitten revolutionary plotter whose religious claim to even the high title ayatollah was privately dismissed by some in the priesthood. After several loftier grand ayatollahs objected, he was forced to withdraw his claim to being the imam, or supreme religious authority of Shia Islam. Even the paintwork propounding the claim to divine sanction for his temporal role was bleached and chipped.

The slogan appeared on the compound wall of Khamenei's representative in Shiraz, Ayatollah Mohieddin Haeri Shirazi, who kept his offices in a jumble of box-like concrete constructions softened by palms and eucalyptus trees. He also carried the traditional title of the senior mullah of the city, the Friday prayer leader. The joy of an outlying city like Shiraz is that a foreign reporter can sometimes ask for and win an audience with a local dignitary without much delay, and can use him as a proxy for the great and unreachable folk in the capital. I was soon ushered into a guest room with simple white walls and flat cushions around the edge. The ayatollah joined me in a swoosh of elegant robes and sat down behind a small writing table designed to be used while cross-legged. The axis of political conflict in Iran those days was represented by hard-line conservatives loyal to supreme leader Ayatollah Khamenei and reformists around President Khatami, also a high cleric.

I asked him to define these two men's roles, but his account of Iran's tangled lines of authority made things no easier for me.

"The leader protects independence and Islam; the president defends freedom and the republic," he said.

The ayatollah was mocking my reporter's need for neat categorizations, and he tossed his chaff into the air with a trouble-loving twinkle in his eyes. He clearly did not often have the chance to address "the West." He moved to a subject close to his heart: Why, why, did America not realize that Iran was its friend?

Surprised at this turn in the conversation, I mumbled something about Americans finding it hard to think well of a country that kept saying "Death to America."

"Oh, Americans take all that stuff far too literally!" said the ayatollah, happily hitting his stride. "It's just propaganda. We are at war, after all. The difference between Americans and us, though, is that we are only waging a war of words. How many Americans did we kill? None. But in our war with Iraq the Americans were helping the Iraqis use chemical weapons, you were selling the Iraqis Phantoms and Mirages."

I could only nod. During my visits to the front lines of the 1980–88 war I had seen how Iraq enjoyed far more Western supplies than Iran, which could barely find spare parts. Washington also helped Iraq with satellite photographs of Iranian troop formations, knowing full well that Iraq was using chemical weapons to break Iranian advances. Toward the end there were U.S. military officers giving advice to Saddam Hussein's men in Baghdad. One night after a major Iraqi offensive that the Americans helped plan in 1988, the United States, which was by then waging an undeclared naval war with Iran in the Persian Gulf, furthered Iraq's cause by destroying half the entire Iranian navy.

"All the Americans want is for us to say, 'Yes, sir!' just like the shah used to," the ayatollah continued, two false lower front teeth leaping out of their places as he became excited. "We don't want to be good, obedient kids. We want to be independent with honor. But we are not your enemy. We are your friend. Your trouble is that you cannot distinguish between the two."

"Well, what about the taking hostage of all those American diplomats?"

"We kept them hostage for four hundred and forty-four days. But the Americans kept our country hostage for forty years."

The ayatollah's rhetoric was exaggerated, but he had a point. The United States had kept a tight grip after it imposed the shah's monarchy on the country in 1953.

"Why do you want to be friends with America now?"

He argued that the United States should join forces with Iran against the Taliban. In hindsight it made sense. This was eight months before September 11, but Osama bin Laden's terrorists, protected by the Taliban in Afghanistan, had already attacked U.S. embassies in Africa and other American targets. Iran would have been a natural U.S. ally in this struggle, opposing the Taliban because of all kinds of religious, ethnic, and geopolitical differences. I couldn't beat his logic on this point and gave up on the politics. I moved our battle of wits onto the mystery of Hafez. Soon his hands and teeth were flying in a dramatic recitation of one of the poet's best-known ghazals in praise of Shiraz's old natural beauty.

Bedeh, sāqi, mey bāqi ke dar jennat nakhāhi yāft
Kenār-e āb-e roknābād o golgasht-e mosālārā . . .

Pass the wine, cupbearer, because in paradise you'll never find
The flowing banks of Roknabad or the rose gardens of Mosala . . .

I saw my chance. Surely, I pointed out to the ayatollah, this "wine" was not just a metaphor for the love of God but Hafez clearly praising real alcohol that his government had so puritanically banned. After all, an earthenware pot has been found in Shiraz showing that wine production began seven thousand years ago, one of the earliest such finds in the world. Shiraz's name is most famous as a wine-grape variety first brought to France's Rhône Valley by a crusader knight returning from the Middle East. Grapes are still a leading Shirazi crop.

It seemed clear to me that Hafez liked both meanings. How else could we explain this couplet?

Whatever God poured into our cup, we drank it to the dregs
Whether it was intoxicating liquor or the wine of paradise.

The ayatollah laughed off my question without answering it, but this wine thing clearly bothered the Islamic Republican orthodoxy. When I later paid a call on the mayor of Shiraz, he presented me with a picture book introduced with a couplet from Hafez:

Just because I saw one drunken eye in this town
I'm now drunk, even though I don't drink wine.

Or perhaps the ayatollah was pouring me a draft of the perplexing Shia doctrine of *taqiyyeh,* which allows dissimulation of one's true beliefs to protect oneself from danger. The abuse of *taqiyyeh* is yet another reason why nobody can ever be quite sure who truly believes what in Iran. We tacitly agreed that there was no single answer. As I was taking my leave, the ayatollah produced a little porcelain ewer that looked exactly

like the wine pitchers used by lovers in Persian miniatures painted in more tolerant times.

"Oh, no," he said with a laugh, amused at the surprised look in my eye, "it's just rosewater to pour over your hands."

My fixer, Afshin, politely refused the ayatollah's perfume. Later

Iranian mullahs chat in north Tehran as they wait for the late supreme leader Ayatollah Ruhollah Khomeini to make a speech. 1985. *(Hugh Pope)*

he explained that he loathed the smell because everyone used it during his years as a religious high school student. Although an accredited descendant of the Prophet, Afshin had stopped halfway on the path to becoming a mullah. Clerical life was too thickly stuffed with hypocrisy and too thinly supplied with naked ladies.

Journalism wasn't much better in giving an Iranian a clean-cut life, mind you. To be allowed to work, some of our fixers said they had to give the Iranian secret service a plausible report about whatever their clients did. They also had to give a cut of their earnings to a man who headed a private "companionship office," a supplier of translators and fixers for foreign journalists. This man had been nepotistically appointed by his brother-in-law, the head of the office in the Ministry of Culture and Islamic Guidance that supervised the foreign media.

Still, Afshin was determined to find me the best advice on why Iranians seek refuge from corrupt hypocrisy in mysterious metaphysical poetry. For that, he proudly introduced me to a professor of literature at Shiraz University who specialized in Hafez. We met in the city center and drove to a characterless crush of cream-painted concrete buildings in a new development on the edge of town. The professor broke his silence.

"French built," he intoned, as if, when it came to designing apartment buildings, nothing else would do.

When we reached the door of his home, a transformation began to take place. The professor shed his shoes among the neat pile in front of the door. Then he stripped off his trousers to reveal voluminous white long johns. Looking with pity at my tighter-fitting trousers, he offered me a change of clothing too. I demurred. He pulled on a black Arabian robe: a complete metamorphosis from a citizen of a drab Western-style apartment block into something far more exotic and Eastern. When I asked if I could cite him by name, he refused. Instead, he insisted that I refer to him as a *rend,* a term in Persian poetry that is officially translated as "wild, drunk, divinely inspired, reasonless yet deeply wise lover." This was the soubriquet with which he signed his poems, he said.

The *rend* led us in his billowing gown into what seemed to be the playroom of his grandchildren and we cleared a space among the toys to sit on the Persian-carpeted floor. Above us was a poster of the Brazilian footballer Ronaldo and next to me was a cheap electric organ. The *rend* lit up a Kent Light cigarette and began by reminding me that Hafez was a universal genius, embracing the full history of Perso-Iranian culture. His poetry included references not just to Islam but to pre-Islamic Zoroastrianism, Christian culture, and even Jewish synagogues. For the *rend,* Iran's current-day practice of Islam had atrophied, and people just went on without much belief because it was what they were used to.

"Marriage can be like that too; people can't enjoy it because the issues around it have hardened like stone," he said. "Hafez, however, is after the heart of happiness in the core of the universe."

He paused, as if allowing a student time to write down his words. I scribbled away.

"People have drawn closer to Hafez in the past twenty years as they have become more aware of their own culture, and because he speaks of a common pain," he went on, using a euphemism for his opposition to Islamic fundamentalism. "Still, Hafez is above politics, and nobody can say why he said this or that. He never gives advice on what to do or not to do. The reformists might think themselves closer to Hafez in their rebellion against bigotry, but the conservatives are the people who know his poetry better."

I wanted more clarity.

"You've studied Hafez for decades. Did he drink real wine or not?"

The *rend* folded up his thin limbs underneath his cloak.

"I believe he drank. It's not incompatible with his way of thinking. Hafez had trouble in his own days, remember. Before Hafez became a complete person, he was an ordinary person."

"Do you say that outright in your lectures?"

"I'm reluctant to teach at all, because the audience is not on the same wavelength as me. Sometimes, my pupils leave my class crying. Other times, when I feel that the audience doesn't understand, it's me who leaves. For instance, the idea that 'dawn' in Hafez also means 'before creation,' they just can't get it. Actually, I feel like I'm a character in a Samuel Beckett play. Nobody understands me."

Perhaps I was hoping for too much. After all, legend says that Hafez spent forty years on his quest for the truth, and even then achieved enlightenment only after sitting for forty days and nights inside a circle drawn around himself on the ground.

"I find everything in Iran hard to understand," I said, hoping the *rend* could help me with a few words to define Iran's approach to real meaning. "If I learned the whole mystic vocabulary, would that be the way?"

"Mysticism is at its core a mystery, and that is a secret," he said.

"Can't you explain a little more? What is the secret?"

The *rend* looked at me in mock horror.

"If I told you the secret," he said, eyes bright with amusement, "then it wouldn't be a secret anymore."

To further my quest for tangible keys to Iran's mysteries, Afshin ended our investigations in Shiraz by convening for me a small debating group of poets, critics, and writers. We met in the offices of the small newspaper *Asr,* the *Age,* in a room so cluttered with desks that we all had to sit behind one, incongruously facing this way and that. The shoulder-length hair of some of the men—they were all men—and the slightly flared cut on some trousers gave me a sense that I was back in that part of Iran that lived in a prerevolutionary 1970s time capsule. My Tehran apartment had been the same, a disorienting place whose big white blocks of furniture showed a design sense trapped in the past. After the Islamic Republic closed normal channels to progress and the outside world, the intellectuals who stayed on burrowed deep into history. It gave them hope. The spasms of strict Islamist rule that punctuate Iran's long history have always passed, eventually.

The group's leading light was Parviz Khaefi, sixty years old and the head of a study complex attached to the Hafeziyeh, the burial place of Hafez with a small park laid out in the poet's honor. He took the part of the professor and chief spokesman, resplendent with flowing curls, a gray beard, and thick-lensed glasses. The discussion began with a comfortable ramble over well-known territory: how pleasant the climate of Shiraz was compared to hot and polluted Tehran, how minorities of Sunnis and Zoroastrians still lived harmoniously with the Shia majority, and how easygoing its population was.

I steered the conversation to the equally congenial subject of poetry. A chorus of voices echoed how it was an integral part of Iranian cultural life, how an elegantly turned couplet carried more weight than a book of boring prose, and how the verses of the great Iranian poets were engraved into children's minds from their early schooldays. I then asked why of all Iranian poets it was Hafez who towered highest.

Khaefi cleared his throat.

"Hafez still speaks to us today because we are now under religious rule, just as in his times. We cannot solve all the problems of our own time on our own, so we need to rely on someone from the past. Hafez knew what to say about it, ahead of everyone else," he said.

It was a brave start. Jamil Saadi, a contemporary Shirazi poet, continued the theme from a nearby desk.

"Hafez was against money, power, and hypocrisy. But we love him because there are so many meanings in his words," he said. "He's not a perfect human, but he is perfectly human."

The group let out an approving sigh to honor this perfectly poetic phrasing.

"That doesn't mean anything!" I protested.

"I don't think it's a question of meanings. There's no fixed meaning. It's dimensions, lots of dimensions," Khaefi said. Everyone's eyes were on him now. "People see the words of Hafez as a mystery and then try to decipher them. So any group can use it to further its own ends."

"Like people do with the Koran, you mean?" I asked.

"Every couplet of Hafez is different and distinct, indeed, just like the verses of the Koran," chimed in a newspaper editor from the back.

"He reached absolute art, but you see only the surface of it in translation," said Khaefi. "This is the secret of Hafez. He uses the same words as other poets, but Hafez has woven these words in a special way that can express the happiness and grief of a human being at the same time. He's a symbol of a human being on earth, in all his pain."

A satisfied silence settled on the room. Someone lit another cigarette.

I pushed harder. "You really think he didn't choose sides between fundamentalism and hedonism?"

"I can't say my own interpretation in this circle of censorship," Khaefi said.

I looked around the room. Everyone seemed to be his friend. Perhaps this was yet another layer of meaning that I had missed. Or perhaps I had been typically Anglo-Saxon, seeking a vulgar black-and-white interpretation of the supremely uninterpretable. Even "hedonism" suddenly seemed a superficial word. Wasn't Hafez, I wondered to myself, just a believer in unreason?

Khaefi recognized the confused and fascinated look of the seeker of the truth about Hafez. He politely helped me out.

"The God of Hafez is not just the God that Muslims see," he said.

The editor underlined the point, noting that when Iran accepted Islam, it kept its original culture. He pointed to Nowruz, the pre-Islamic celebration of March 21 as New Year's Day that several Middle Eastern Muslim peoples still celebrate with varying spring-welcoming ceremonies and a cleansing act of jumping over fires. Indeed, this was something that was always hard to get across to my editors and readers in America: Although Islam claims to be "one," in practice it is no universal key to understanding the different cultures of the Middle East. Islam is different everywhere and is redefined by nationalism, ethnicity, tribes, rulers, and political parties.

"We are Muslims, but we are Iranians," said another graybeard from behind his desk, one with a linoleum top. "And our poets are the ones who preserved our real culture. Every article I write starts with a couplet from Hafez and ends with another."

The poet Jamil Saadi picked up the argument.

"When the Arabs conquered Iran, the violence they used to bring Islam is the reason why people wanted to stay Persian," he said. "The Arabs didn't understand the real Islam. They killed a grandchild of the Prophet."

More people arrived, and the conversation drifted. Perhaps the circle of censorship had grown too wide. I accepted a whispered invitation to visit Khaefi at his office at the Hafeziyeh, the poet's memorial, the next morning.

•   •   •

Me at the tomb of Hafez, fourteenth-century poet of the Persians and scourge of Islamic bigotry, in Shiraz, Iran. December 1985. *(Nicole Pope)*

Walking into the mausoleum of Shiraz's most famous son felt like entering another world. Unlike the crowded, shabby boisterousness of most public spaces in Iran, here were sharply defined lawns, neatly kept beds of roses, and a reverent, modest flow of visitors. The tall cypresses looked as though they belonged in one of Hafez's poems, where they stand for the slender stature of the beloved. I stopped to chat with a mother and daughter who had just performed a *fal*, or the consulting of Hafez as an oracle.

I joined the mother in puzzling over the ambiguous couplet they had chosen. When I looked up, I saw that Afshin's ever-wandering eye had alighted upon the pretty daughter. The "sweet breeze" had brought a "message." Sure enough, the nightingale and the rose began to chatter. I asked the mother what she thought the *fal* meant.

"It depends. The couplet is like a mirror to your heart."

"What about the rest of the poem?"

"It's like subsidiary advice."

"What did you consult Hafez about?"

The mother and daughter looked at each other and didn't want to say. What I understood of the couplet would have allowed them to decide anything. Subtly, I tried to test the line of thinking that the poetry of Hafez was an alternative to the Koran.

"If I respect Hafez, it's because he memorized the whole of the Koran!" the mother protested, looking quizzically at me. She had told me that she was a teacher, and she clearly did not suffer fools. I soldiered on.

"Do you think the Koran set cast-iron laws that must be literally obeyed?"

"We have certain rules. But we are not under pressure, like people say," she rebuked me.

My time was up. Unknown journalists with notepads were not worthy of the truth, even in this lovely garden in southern Iran. In fact, much better to make something up.

"We love the Islamic Republic. And especially the mullahs. Write that down!"

She spat the words out shrilly. We were standing right by Hafez's tomb, and I turned away, sadly feeling that we had all betrayed his legacy. We said good-bye and, with a small bow, Afshin presented the daughter with his card. We took a seat in the teahouse. I wished it was a wineshop. We had to make do with a hubble-bubble pipe decorated with a hand-painted early nineteenth-century prince in colorful robes. At least he had a little wine jar in his hand. Parviz Khaefi soon joined us.

"She's just unloading her complexes on you," he said when I told him of my last encounter. "This is not the Iran that Iranians want. Our society is waiting. The government feels under pressure because people are watching satellite TV from abroad. People are stressed because the young have no recreation, no hobby. Many of our youth are using opium and even heroin. Widespread depression has overcome everyone. People are migrating. If they had wings, they'd fly out."

This plain speaking was something rare to savor. I sipped my tea.

"Why does the government not change, then?"

"They're at a dead end. The clerics know they have to change, but every time they feel threatened, they cling together and nothing happens. The people can't accept that such a government is durable," he said. "The trouble is, if the regime goes, everything will go, because, unfortunately, there's no other organization to replace them. So the world goes one way and we go the other, stuck with all this petty and meaningless time wasting."

Khaefi took his leave. Afshin's cell phone rang. It was the mullah-loving teacher's daughter. As Afshin billed and cooed, I studied the tabletop furniture. Surely I could persuade the *Wall Street Journal* to publish a story that presented Iran as a game of puzzles that no Iranian wanted to end. Ultimately I did. But Spindle was also right. It didn't make the front page. Already, I felt a twinge of disappointment. My exploration of Hafez had produced no moment of mystical ecstasy. I might be in the Hafeziyeh, finding signs of Iran's alter ego of ease and poetic blooms, but the rose in the little tabletop vase was artificial. And the dewdrop on its petal, that essence of heaven in Hafez's poetry, was a blob of blurry plastic.

7. SUBVERSION IN THE HAREM

Women on the Rise, from Cairo to Istanbul

Though men can't see through window blinds,
still they try to ogle the women.
—CAIRENE ADAGE

The West has long enjoyed a virtual affair with the Middle Eastern woman. I too once donned a velvet medieval costume and bribed an African eunuch to gain access to one through the great wooden main gate of Istanbul's Topkapı Palace. Unfortunately, it was only a whispered walk-on role in a Dutch documentary about the fantastical dimensions of the Western view of the harem, the secluded and protected women's quarters of the palace, house, or hovel of the traditional Muslim world. Indeed, a whole branch of art criticism is now devoted to this so-called orientialist imagery. Particularly in its nineteenth-century French version with catamites and naked female slaves, some orientalist paintings' exaggerated overtones of sexual indulgence have more to do with male fantasy than the real world. In its more reserved British incarnation, this kitsch school of art had domestic purposes still to be observed in Westerners' interactions with the Middle East. One was a chance of visual escape from suffocating contemporary social constraints back home. Another was to act as a new form of touristic souvenir, the next new thing for aristocrats bored by paintings from the grand tour to Italy. Last, the genre served to demonstrate triumphantly on canvas Europe's growing imperial sway since the eighteenth century over the Middle East and its holy places. In any event, the models for demurely pining harem ladies were, surprisingly, often the artist's wife or other Europeans, holding props gathered during Eastern expeditions and actually painted in the home counties of England.

By no means did all harem visitors spread sensation and fables, of course. Lady Mary Wortley Montagu, the wife of an eighteenth-century British ambassador to the Ottoman Empire, wrote back home that the veil could sometimes be a liberating shield from intrusion, that Ottoman Muslim women lived lives comparable in freedom to those of the women in the European cultures she knew, and that, as any woman who has lived in the Middle East can still attest, the first question in female company is always about babies, not sex. Interestingly, one of the few paintings that shows a nineteenth-century Ottoman harem interior done by a woman who'd actually been in one shows a mundane scene: high, bare walls like a prison, elaborate visiting rituals and costumes, and one woman leaning against a wall smoking a cigarette with a look of utter boredom.

Some segregation of the sexes is still common all over the Middle East, even in Turkey, but it's a negotiable thing. Spending a night in a two-room village house early in her reporting career in Turkey's Kurdish southeast, my wife, Jessica, was offered the choice between the harem, the poky kitchen where the village headman's wives slept with their children in bedding laid out on a rough concrete floor around the refrigerator, or the men's equivalent, the spacious *selamlık,* where he and his sons slept on a raised floor and carpet. She chose to be an honorary man for the night, and the headman properly offered her a private corner and a freshly laundered set of his own pajamas.

On the whole, however, the peep-show approach to Middle Eastern women lives on in Western media today, often with blithe disregard for reality and deep differences in the traditions of Muslim countries. A novel published in 2007 by the Turkish writer Zülfü Livaneli about a Kurdish couple and an Istanbul professor reaches its climax on a yacht cruising in some comfort on the Aegean Sea; his New York publishers chose a jacket picture of a woman tripping through a desert in a tentlike blue Afghan burka—plus titillating high-heeled shoes. Similarly, *Time* magazine, supposedly illustrating a story about modernizing Turkey, once unthinkingly chose as its illustration a picture of obviously Iranian women in black wraparound chadors, a kind of dress rare in Turkey. Time and again when I was taking press photographs to accompany a Middle Eastern story, a sure route to publication was a pretty girl's head in a head scarf. The Iran-Iraq War? Young women in chadors with Kalashnikov rifles! That one earned me a half page in the *Economist.*

It is true that, in theory, the Koran allows Muslims to have up to four official wives, if they can support them equally. In practice, most states in Muslim countries are secular-minded; they discourage polygamy and sometimes ban it by law. As a result, keeping multiple wives for Muslims is uncommon, especially in towns, perhaps as unusual as keeping a full-time mistress in the Christian world. Still, old-fashioned traditions dominate the Middle East. As such, male-female encounters are more restricted, and more intense, than their modern Western equivalent. That's why Middle Eastern singers pitch their emotional register at the wit's end of the scale. Indeed, my first romance with a Middle Eastern woman, an Egyptian who hired me to teach her English, was a journey into both a forbidden land of sensuality and the past.

Leila's handshake was as soft as a brush with a feather. She lived in the still elegant Garden City quarter in the city center behind the government's great *mugamma,* a gloomy bureaucratic anthill of concrete where, after appropriately grinding weeks of waiting, the yellowing paperwork for my residence permits would detach itself from rooms piled high with forgotten files and powdery filth. Three times a week, I felt a heady sense of escape as I stepped off the dusty streets of Cairo's outer reality and made my way up a gleaming white marble staircase to her family's old and expensive apartment. Servants would usher me in. Leila would then stage a fine entrance, her hair immaculately blond and a bright, funny smile on her face.

I had been planned, I think, as a filler for an otherwise boring gap in the morning. I was recruited by her mother's second cousin-in-law, who lived in the flat above me. Leila had just returned from California, where she had held a secretarial job in the Los Angeles Tax Department. In fact, she spoke quite good English already. In our conversational practice, she talked of her recent divorce, and of the house and baby that for reasons she kept obscure she had left behind to return to her family in Cairo. Laughing infectiously, she joked about her attempts to stay thin for long enough to catch another husband before she blew up to the size of her enormous mother.

In turn, I teased her about letters to her Californian friends whose grammar she made me check, in which she described her new English teacher with hyperbolic enthusiasm: "He is the most good to me of all the persons here, please pray for him Mary . . ."

These references to a larger public made me uneasy. An intimacy had arisen between us that was not innocent. In fact, it was intoxicating. At last I was inside a Cairo home, not barred as a foreigner on the outside. It was perhaps the most exquisite of harems, a private place where I felt briefly cocooned in Leila's unconditional attention.

We moved quickly on from exercises in pronunciation that I would invent, like "The philosopher cuffed the soft cougher roughly." When I was still trying to retain a properly correct atmosphere for our hours together, I had chosen to read Jane Austen with her. Leila had a charmingly immediate grasp of early nineteenth-century

British provincial morality. Our subject was *Northanger Abbey,* Austen's simple first novel. For Leila, it contained few surprises. She thought the bullying of the overbearing patriarch, General Tilney, was perfectly natural, and that young women were wise to avoid confronting him.

She had picked up ideas of female emancipation in America, but in other ways she remained a Cairene Muslim through and through. In addition to her private lessons, she attended the same language school as I did, studying Executive Secretaryship and English for Ladies while I came to grips with colloquial Egyptian Arabic. She instructed me to ignore her completely in public, as she would do me. I didn't object. Wearing a defensive armor of makeup and starched, stylish clothing, Leila didn't look as attractive in the hot dusty world outside as she did in the cool oasis of her flat.

Nevertheless, a crescendo began building in the relationship. I was later to learn that an early showdown was the norm in most Middle Eastern relationships between men and women. For even the most daring girls in these conservative and traditional societies, the stakes of discovery were just too high to enjoy carefree courtships. The few affairs that I was to experience tended to be secretive, modest, and quick to culminate in a bluntly put question of whether I was ready to marry. Leila never asked.

"In Cairo, everybody thinks that the women are kept inside all days. No, we do what we want," Leila bravely said one day, her hand crossing over to mine as she suggested that we set off on a rare joint expedition to lunch at her elite club, the Gezira, an expanse of grass and trees on Zemalek island in the middle of the Nile.

She borrowed her father's car for the trip, and, even though we embraced in her father's dining room, Leila ordered me to lie on the floor in the rear in case someone in the city of six million people should chance to see her traveling with a strange man. On arrival, I had to walk up the long drive to the club, pay my own entrance, and eat alone.

From my table, I watched the muscle-rippled bodies of the red-bronze young Egyptian men strut about the pool, not yet stout like their fathers. Simpering girls in skin-tight trousers, including Leila, sat in groups at other tables, pretending not to be looking. However, I was now learning that all was not necessarily what it seemed on the surface in this Middle Eastern separation of the sexes. And, watching the poolside ballet at the Gezira Club, I saw that I belonged to a different world. I decided to put things straight at our next lesson.

As I passed through the colonnaded entrance hall of Leila's apartment building, three local *bawwabs,* or doormen, nodded to me cheerfully from their bench. All were gorgeously chocolate skinned, long-robed Nubians from Upper Egypt, displaced from their ancestral homes, they had told me, by the flooding of the Nile

Valley behind the Aswan Dam. I must have been odd and exotic to them too, the pink English teacher, like a big puppy with his unruly mop of hair, always in such a rush. I made myself perform in my best Egyptian dialect, which was a perpetual-motion machine of pumping iambic pentameters and rhyming, jocular absurdities.

"*Sabah al-kheir!*" I said. Good morning! How are you all?

"A Morning of Light!" replied the first.

"A Morning of Apricots!" intoned the second.

"A Morning of Beans!" said the third, completing the well-worn routine. "Praise be to God, we're well."

I was already halfway up the marble staircase to the first floor, where a broken window gave onto the light well, piled high with years of repulsive-looking rubbish. In the West, the hallway might well not have been squeaky clean, but such filth nearby would have been considered as bad as leaving rubbish inside one's own house, a shameful stain on the building's "inner" reputation. Here, since it was in the open air, it was considered to be quite "outside" and beyond the pale of the *baw-wabs*' cleaning duties. I climbed to Leila's floor. The landing was spacious and bless-edly quiet after the harsh collisions of Cairo's streets. I rang the bell.

Loud barking erupted. Most unusually, this Muslim family kept a dog, perhaps to underline their status in the Westernized elite. The Alsatian's nose and paws pressed and jabbed against the loose glass panel in the door, filling the stairwell with clattering echoes. The dog was pulled away, the door opened a crack.

"Good morning!"

The maid peered suspiciously at me, ushered me wordlessly into the cool, shuttered reception room, and dragged the Alsatian off out of sight. I sat down on a dust-covered reproduction French Empire chair, its gilt feet just poking out from under the skirt. In the half-light I got out my compilation of spelling test sentences and crossed out an effort that now seemed too close to home to be funny: "succulent sensual sexuality sucks in such unsuspicious charlatans."

Leila shimmied in, radiating luxuriance and flouncy peroxide blond hair. She put her hand on my shoulder.

"We will go through to the dining room?" she asked.

"Shall." I swallowed. "Shall we go through to the dining room?"

"Yes," she said and opened the door.

The dog who had been shut up there tore out and bounded at me. I froze. He faltered, paws on my chest, sniffing at me, before another servant dragged him off. When we sat down at our normal chairs at the corner of the glass-topped table, I mumbled that I was traveling in the coming weeks and I would have to stop our English lessons. Leila looked down. I opened our copy of *Northanger Abbey* and began to read.

" '*The housemaid's folding back her window-shutters at eight o'clock the next day, was the sound which first roused Catherine.'* Didn't we get past this? Where were we? The general has already chucked her out, hasn't he?"

I glanced across at Leila. She was leaning forward, gazing at the page in rapt attention, pressing her ample bosom against the edge of the table. She was either in another world or hadn't realized that I wasn't reading anymore. I pulled myself together. I flicked through the pages. We were quite near the end, ah, here in the coach, chapter twenty-nine.

"If you remember, Leila, General Tilney has just sent Catherine back home without telling her why, she has been treated very—"

"Yes, it is discovered that she is not such good family, I know."

"Well . . . okay, let's carry on then: *'Catherine was too wretched to be fearful. The journey . . .'*"

Under the table, Leila's hand slipped into mine.

"*'The journey in itself had no terrors for her; and she began it without either dreading its length, or feeling its solitariness.'*"

I took a deep breath. I prayed for strength to say something to end our affair. I suspected that the family servants knew exactly what was up, since they took great delight in timing their entrance with coffee or 7Up at the most embarrassing moments possible. Leila's father seemed suspicious too. When he was around, he would pace up and down the passage outside the dining room, his beloved Alsatian at his heel, and let us see their double shadow project onto the frosted glass doors. A more traditional man would have supervised us; perhaps he was hoping that our lessons would lead to something for his divorcée daughter. Leila would joke that I would have to marry her if her father found out about our kissing, and tease me about the intricacies of Egyptian law court powers of detention, not to mention her family's construction business sidekicks. I half believed her. The family was proud to be descended from an ominous-sounding Ottoman Turkish pasha. Luckily her father was not around today.

Leila, sensing a lack of ardor on my part, excused herself and left the room. She stood pointedly behind the frosted glass door, obviously removing her bra. Like many Egyptian women whom I watched in their white wedding dresses, parading on the arms of their new husbands before a noisy band through the open-plan stairs and corridors of the Nile Hilton, she was roundly plump but without an ounce of flab. Things were not going well for my good intentions.

I needed divine intervention—and got some. When she sat primly back down again, the room exploded with noise. It was Friday, the Muslim holy day of the week, and the local mosque loudspeaker beamed a stern call to the noon prayer straight through an empty air-conditioner hole in the dining room wall. Leila's religious sensibility was of a general kind, and when I had first pressed my lips against hers, she had simply gasped *"Allahu Akbar,"* God is most great. Now, as the dining room filled with the amplified rustling of prostrations and muttered invocations by the faithful in the prayer hall, by unspoken agreement we tried to turn back to the trial of Catherine 150 years before.

" 'Leaning back in one corner of the carriage, in a violent burst of tears, she was conveyed some miles beyond the walls of the Abbey before she raised her head; and the highest point of ground within the park was almost closed to her view before she was capable of turning her eyes towards it.' "

I turned to explain to Leila, but she simply looked expectantly at me. It was pointless to talk: The imam was building up momentum with an earnest, killjoy sermon laced with warnings of hellfire burning hot for those who strayed from the straight path of Islam. We sank into each other's arms. Later, I recalled that I had once heard the same tone from one of the guest preachers at school. Pure self-righteousness. Now I hypocritically tried to put my own life back into a supposedly righteous orbit. Our last lesson was over, I said.

"I hope you enjoy the rest of the book. I'm sorry we didn't finish it. You needn't worry, because Catherine's honor is saved in the end. Henry goes to find her."

"Does he?"

She looked up at me quickly and then back down. Jane Austen would perhaps have found a better outcome or, knowing her, appropriate punishment for my chickening out of our relationship. Later I was to see that friends who married Middle Easterners, men or women, often had to work much harder than other couples to overcome differences of education, outlook, and expectation. It didn't have much to do with religion, since Middle Eastern Christians and Jews can be just as traditional as Muslims, and similar issues challenged friends who married spouses from any significantly different culture. Perhaps it was just proof that, for everybody, tribalism can matter much more than we expect.

Changes to the traditional moral and household duties of women are recent in the Middle East, following the lead of the West. Family honor and submissiveness are still usually considered to be essential and symbolized by the appearance of women, yet women also use their appearance to make political points. The Turks consciously unveiled in their 1920s secular revolution to show how they were turning toward the West. Iranian women covered up during the 1979 Islamic revolution to turn their backs on the West and its support for the shah's dictatorship. In the 2000s, these two countries swapped places, with Iranian women pushing back their head scarves to register opposition to the regime and Turkish women wrapping themselves up. Each nation had its own struggle with modernity rushing in, and paradoxes abounded. In Saudi Arabia, for instance, a woman could control a great corporate empire but not drive a car in public.

The debate in Western media is often framed as being about "Islam." But Islam is different everywhere and the Koranic word on veiling up is an interpretation, not a clear order. Just as important for a religion are national jurisdictions and, especially in the case of women, cultural traditions. In *The Girl from the Golden Horn,* his delightful pre–Second World War novel about what makes the Middle East tick, Kurban Said portrays an exiled Ottoman princess who finds that she cannot return her Austrian doctor husband's love because he is simply unable to display jealousy or any desire to kill to protect her honor. In my own time, a friend from Austria told me how he rued the possessiveness of his Kurdish girlfriend from the far eastern borderlands of Turkey, and who, just like Kurban Said's Princess Asiadeh, hated being asked to dance with strange men at a ball.

The Middle Eastern culture of paternalistic control is taken to a brutal extreme by killings of women by husbands or by a group of relatives to "cleanse" the family name if a female is suspected of having had an unauthorized male relationship, even if she was raped. This control system is not just a way for males to perpetuate their dominance; it is rooted in village clans obsessed with solidarity in the face of lawlessness and hardship. This has little to do with religion. The bishop of Mosul, in northern Iraq, told me his Christian community had the same problem with honor crimes as their Muslim neighbors. The Middle East seems especially prone to such family group crimes against women, although hardly exceptional in violence against women. In Spain, for instance, macho motivations of possession, jealousy, and even envy pushed individual, poorly educated men to kill seventy-four wives or girlfriends in 2008. Half of the women murdered in Ireland and between two thousand and four thousand women in the United States are killed by their partners every year.

Women's roles and rights reflect many national differences, both between the Middle East and Western countries and within the Middle East itself. They often have a rough deal: 40 percent of women in Turkey are beaten and 20 percent sexually abused; 50 percent of women in Iraq make arranged marriages to second cousins or closer relatives; and 90 percent of Egyptian women are forced to undergo female circumcision, even though it has been legally forbidden since 1997. All this is open to change, however, as evidenced by those Middle Eastern places where middle-class values, rights, and security have begun to flourish along with rising wealth, education, travel, and urbanization.

In the Syrian village where I once lived, if I returned home unexpectedly during the day, I would be surprised at how empty it seemed. It took me a while to realize that the women of the house all went out to sit on the pavement while I was inside until their menfolk got home. But in the more advanced city, daring Muslim girls would visit my house in Damascus, slipping off their head scarves after they entered the door. One became a kind of girlfriend, although we didn't go far together.

She reminded me most of the girls from the Roman Catholic convent near my boarding school in conservative, western England and shared the same defensive propriety about the many parts of her body that were quite off-limits.

I learned that just as a disciplinarian father was likely to have a wild daughter, authoritarian regimes spawned promiscuous rebellion. I could get boldly propositioned by women covered in black in Saudi shopping malls. Two decades after Iran's Islamic Revolution had stifled all forms of public entertainment, bored Iranian girls in north Tehran went much farther for kicks—"hitting on cars," as they put it, stopping a male-driven vehicle at random to escape from the jealous stupidity of the regime in anonymous, recreational sex. My wife's Istanbul gynecologist assured her that women in head scarves tended to have the raciest underwear. Indeed, some of the most daring thongs and g-strings—some can be eaten or have electronic songbirds attached—can be found in the conservative Arab city of Damascus. They inspired a playful recent picture book called *The Secret Life of Syrian Lingerie.*

On the other hand, women are becoming more publicly prominent in many Muslim societies, notably in the country that has advanced the farthest, Turkey. Professions like law, medicine, and education are staffed by more women than in some Western nations, even though few rise to high executive positions and those

Wearing colored cloaks instead of the white for men, Turkish women now also whirl in the ceremonies of the main Istanbul lodge of the Mevlevi sect, often known in the West as the whirling dervishes. 2000. *(Hugh Pope)*

who lead big companies are often members of the founder's family. Turkey's first woman prime minister, Tansu Çiller, was parachuted into her position by the old guard, although she knew well how to manipulate the men around her. Everyone thought they were special to her. Generals, ministers, female visitors, even me—all were taken to her back office. There she would press her hand softly on the inside of my forearm as I tried to remember the questions I was supposed to ask in my interview.

Turkey is almost schizophrenic in its attitude to women. Despite much progress, it lingers stubbornly at the bottom of world rankings that measure the freedom, education, and status of its female citizens. At the same time, the country's republican secularists and its religious conservatives use women as their favorite political battleground. Paradoxically, both sides use the language of freedom and rights to back their arguments about whether the state should or should not allow adult women to wear head scarves in university. The protagonists in this debate, mostly older men with mustaches, rarely even consult women or women's groups about this. Women might answer the call to demonstrate for their side of the argument, but on the streets of Turkish cities, it remains a common sight to see best female friends chatting arm in arm, one with and one without a head scarf.

The men claim, and may even believe, that this conflict is all about the place of Islam in society. But head scarves are also a new front in a long-running conflict about communities and social class. The religious-minded two-thirds of the population that is rooted in the villages of Anatolia, or have recently arrived in Turkish cities, tend to be conservative, pragmatic, and open-minded about head scarves. The more secular third is urban and often descended from refugees who built the Turkish Republic up from the wreckage of the Ottoman Empire after the 1920s, and view head scarves as the nemesis of their ideological goal to create a modern state.

The actual wearing of a head scarf in private is, it seems to me, a matter that outsiders have no right to judge. If religious scholars persuade adult women that this is God's law, so be it, even if other jurists have strong reasons to disagree. Nobody complains about Sikhs wearing turbans or ultra-Orthodox Jewish women wearing wigs. The problem for me lies more in the Islamists' other main justification for head scarves; that they are part of women's duty to stop men lusting after them. Innocently enough, many young women therefore wear an often chic head scarf to signal not that they are fundamentalists but that they are morally upright and marriageable, or are dutiful wives. But for exactly the same reason, the secularists are quite right, as in France, to insist that no head scarves be allowed in schools. A schoolgirl wearing a head scarf implies that I, as a man, might be lusting after her. I find the insinuation repugnant—if people really think there is such a general problem, they should first start reeducating the men.

· · ·

In Saudi Arabia, men were the first people who alerted me to the fact that I should reassess my Western ideas about the veil. Around the edges of interviews they revealed deep frustrations with restrictions on women. This is particularly the case in the coastal city of Jeddah, where the cosmopolitan bourgeoisie chafes under the ultrastrict Islamic mores of the Saudi monarchy and desert bedouin of central Arabia who conquered them in the 1920s.

I hadn't realized how problematic it is for husbands, fathers, and brothers. They have to rush home to drive women about, and to do themselves all the things women are prohibited from doing. Women can't drive, travel without their husband's permission, make bank transfers alone, stay in hotels alone. Arguments based on Islamic precedent—the Prophet Muhammad's first wife and sponsor, Khadijah, had been a major trader of Mecca—made little impact on the official ideology. On the other hand, unlike in Iran, where foreign women are required to veil as strictly as Iranians, in Saudi Arabia they are theoretically allowed not to wear a head scarf. The hard-charging American consul in Jeddah, a woman who purposefully went about her meetings without even the light shawl draped over her head that most foreign women used as a sign of politeness, said that sometimes she entered offices where there was no women's toilet in the whole high-rise block. The Prophet had certainly not ordered that. Even Iran's Islamic Republic gives far more civic, educational, and social rights to women.

"Those reactionaries are holding up the country, like this," said Omar, a businessman friend from the supposedly reactionary capital, Riyadh, holding up his hand like a policeman. "I don't want my wife to be Western or Eastern. She's a teacher. I want her to be something in the middle, to be productive, to be able to think. I'm worried about tomorrow for my daughter. If they let us have a tomorrow."

Walking through an old town in the mountains of the Asir near the Yemeni border, another Saudi friend, Mohammed, thought the way his countrymen could see women as a source only of shame, never of pride, was not an Islamic problem but an Arab one. By that, he meant a problem with tradition. As evidence, he pointed out how non-Arab Pakistan, Bangladesh, and Turkey had all elected women prime ministers, something he felt inconceivable in the paternalistic Arab world. And he had another explanation why Saudi Arabia kept its women figuratively locked up: to sustain its image as the holy land of Islamic pilgrimage.

"Our visitors think we're very holy and want us to keep it that way, especially those from farthest away. Those who are closer know how corrupt we are," he said, illustrating this point by suddenly seizing an old wooden boss on a door in an alleyway and fondling it in frustration as if it were a woman's breast. Mohammed was forty-five years old.

The elite had tried to rebel. In 1991, forty-seven women went out demurely for a drive beside their chauffeur husbands, then swapped around to take the wheel in a long, slow drive for liberation. The religious police jailed them for a day and harassed their families for years. In 1993, news got out of a bowling club party that included eighty women. The religious police came around to the man who organized it and accused him of being an infidel.

But what cannot come into Saudi Arabia through the front door is coming in through the window. The country delayed, but it could no longer stop the arrival of satellite dishes, travel, education, cell phones with cameras, and a need for women in the labor force. In the late 1990s, low oil prices had forced more families to seek incomes from their women. Companies working in Saudi Arabia needed women marketers to sell to women and to understand who was doing the buying. Women were pushing too. By 2001, more than half of the Saudi student body was female— about two hundred thousand girls compared to just seventy female students twenty-five years before. By the turn of the century, 7 percent of members of the country's chambers of commerce were women and, in Jeddah, one-quarter of the businesses were owned by women. For sure, many of these are stand-ins for husbands who can't own shares because they are civil servants. But the country is changing. With one contact passing on the names of others, I soon connected with the parallel world of real Saudi businesswomen.

The women I met acknowledged that Saudi society had a long way to go but hated the patronizing Western sense of superiority. Mayan al-Kurdi, the daughter of a Saudi diplomat, who ran a website design company in Jeddah, said it was just a different way of doing things, using discretion and having to work around restrictions. It brought her some frustration but a sense of progress nevertheless.

"I don't like to dwell on this man-woman thing. The West has this bizarre fascination with us. It's fueled by stereotypes, like a fairy tale. People there don't want to hear that we have a normal life," she told me, claiming that Western women suffered more depression, suicide, and oppression. "Western women judge by their own standards. We're no different. The girls here have boyfriends and dates, arranging their own lives as they want. In some households their voices are stronger. Women tend to be very pampered here."

Mayan, of course, was speaking for the middle class. The backstreets of Jeddah look impoverished. I had no confidence that every Saudi woman enjoyed such freedoms. And as one Saudi woman told me, reminding me of the daily carnage of car accidents on the streets of Saudi Arabia, "We need to get everyone to start wearing seat belts before getting women to drive. Right now, if women start driving, reactionary men are just going to beat them up."

·　　·　　·

Nevertheless, plenty is moving beneath the surface of Saudi society. I headed out one night in one of the Intercontinental Hotel's luxurious BMW limousines to meet with another businesswoman, Seham Abu Rashed, or Sam, as she liked to be called. The Pakistani chauffeur followed my directions deep into the suburbs until we bumped along a half-paved side street and drew up before the wrought-iron gates of an American-style villa. I rang a bell and after a while a maid ushered me into an interior that seemed transplanted from a luxury African safari camp. After a few minutes a beautiful young woman appeared. She greeted me in excellent English. Far from being veiled, a mane of black hair tumbled over her shoulders.

It was exciting, but it also made me nervous, a kind of Saudi syndrome. A meeting like this was clearly against the social rules, and I'd be in trouble if the authorities found out. This sense of self-control was felt in another way by an American woman who told me that after a few months in Saudi Arabia she began to feel exposed if she didn't cover her head. The problem wasn't just the religious police. One Saudi matron told me that men could be so sexually hungry that even when she was eight months pregnant and completely wrapped in black, they verbally harassed her, touched her, and followed her home from the weekly vegetable bazaar. I was no young bull, but Abu Rashed's femininity was magnetic. I gripped the arms of my unusual safari chair and complimented her on its curving lines.

"I designed it. I specialize in the wild and exotic. That reflects my personality," she said, looking at me steadily until I blushed and looked down. "I get upset when I see all those films about us on television. It's like we're all bedouins."

Paradoxically, in the real bedouin areas, where the paved roads end and the desert begins, Saudi women have actually been driving the family pickups all along. Politics and visibility make city life much stricter. Still, Abu Rashed, when I met her thirty years old and a divorced mother of four, had become self-supporting in business through a series of informal arrangements. For four years she'd run a clothes boutique in the women's part of a mall. It had failed, partly because men didn't want their women going in there alone. Staying with her mother while her father lived with "another wife" in the Spanish resort town of Marbella, she'd started designing interiors for friends. Her business had slowly grown. She had enrolled in correspondence courses from Florida, took a (male) English tutor, and found business partners like a Lebanese furniture maker who quietly cut her a percentage. She dealt with men and women together in their houses, in businesses, and in restaurants. One day, she was shocked on turning up for a meeting to discover that her client's husband was a member of the *mutawwa*, the religious police.

"I thought, Mama! I was a bit afraid," she said. In the end, "They didn't give me the commission—maybe they didn't like the price—but he was cool about me doing the work."

"It still sounds like you have to do everything secretly," I said.

"I keep telling my friends, I'm going to do something to liberate us all. There are so many little things holding us back. You need a man to do anything—anything official, that is."

She remembered angrily how she'd been told to give a thumbprint for her cell phone contract by a male voice behind a wooden barrier drilled with holes. But in the years after our first meeting, she was able to get an ID instead of going around with her passport, and the idea of allowing women to drive came back onto the agenda.

One day, Abu Rashed picked me up from my hotel to show me how she conducted her business. I sat in the front seat with the Sudanese driver, who, as a servant, somehow didn't count as a nonfamily male. Whenever we slowed anywhere she might be recognized, she demurely pulled a fold of her abaya over everything but her eyes. We proceeded smoothly through a morning round: a meeting with a client and the client's husband, a supplier meeting, a trip to the furniture maker. But she would not accept my invitation to lunch. Abu Rashed was impatient for change, yet she was intensely loyal to the conservative extended family system that prevented anything changing.

"How can you resist grape juice champagne?!" I asked.

Back at the hotel, I told her, the restaurant had a handcart piled up with ice buckets of winelike bottles and simulated beer cans that looked exactly like the real thing. The menu even offered "cocktails" that, for instance, transfigured a Bloody Mary into a pious, spirit-free Sister Mary.

"Yes. We have things like that to try and pretend we're not here in Saudi Arabia." Abu Rashed laughed, still bubbling with rebellious impatience. "Don't get me wrong: The way things are going is fine with me. But if God wills, in the future we will get the chance to drive and travel without permission. I want my country to open up more, I want our religion to open up more, so that people will be attracted to it and see its good sides."

In 2004, men and women sat together for the first time at the Jeddah Economic Forum. Lubna Olayan, a woman heading one of Saudi Arabia's biggest corporations, talked of women's careers and demanded that the Arab world move on from its old belief that it could adopt Western techniques without Western ideas. A light screen partially separated the white thobes of the men and black abayas of the women, causing one American woman to observe tartly that a real reformer would stand up on stage and say, "Tear down this wall." Actually, the women's representatives told me that the removal of the screen had been permitted by the authorities, but the majority of women still felt uncomfortable at a complete absence of separation. Naturally, the boundary line became blurred as the conference went on. The excited chatter from the young Saudi women showed how giddy the new freedom was making them. The religious establishment condemned the proceedings and the forum was more conservative the following year.

As long as society feels secure, however, progress cannot be stopped. Amid all its dull religious programming, Saudi TV can pull huge audiences with a homegrown series that pokes fun at the Saudi condition, including all those male-female hang-ups. I joined an all-male family room in which every cushion was taken to watch a hilarious episode portraying Saudis as they tried to let their hair down while abroad on holiday, but then, when seeing another Saudi family in the restaurant, had to quickly make it look like they were still obeying all the rules.

Saudi women have begun to be asked to make the rules too. At the Jeddah forum, Amira Kashgari, a professor of linguistics at King Abdul Aziz University, told me she had just taken part—via closed-circuit television—in a newly launched national dialogue through which the Saudi royal family was seeking to develop new policies. On the third day, a conservative male attacked the fact that women and men had started debating face-to-face in the lobbies of the meeting. To the astonishment of participants, one of the women argued back that using Islam to justify sidelining women was a mere cover for backward social and cultural traditions.

"It was ugly for a while. But after the meetings ended, he was so polite, so understanding, so moderate," Kashgari told me. "We're actually all a bit schizophrenic, both men and women. But we are showing that we are pluralistic, we can coexist. I'm proud of what we have achieved."

8. WAR, WAR TO VICTORY

Iran's School of Martyrdom and Love

You lit the flame and then cried fire.
—MIDDLE EASTERN SAYING

A week after the September 11, 2001, attacks on the United States, I flew to Tehran. Iran was not a prime suspect in the catastrophe, and young Iranians had won the hearts of Americans by staging candlelight vigils for the victims. Yet there was nervousness that the United States might lash out, given the two decades of unequal feuding between the two countries. In the back of everyone's mind in Tehran was the fear of a link between the U.S. declaration of a "war on terror" and it's long-standing position that Iran was a "terrorist state." One evening at dinner with Iranian friends, an explosion boomed out near our part of the city. Everyone dived for cover, believing that an American air attack had begun. It turned out to be a firework.

As I cast about for story ideas, I wondered what I could do to explore the concept of Iran as a "terrorist state" and what connection that had, if any, with the September 11 plotters. Paging through a newspaper, I spotted an event that looked like a promising window on the question. An announcement trumpeted the opening of the First Universal Exhibition of Sacred Culture and Defense. The next morning I drove up to have a look. The exhibition turned out to be strung out among the buildings of the Musalla of Imam Khomeini, which I thought of as his "prayer-drome," a half-built hybrid of the world's biggest mosque and Moscow's Red Square on the way to the northern suburbs of the city. Its foundations had already been laid when I was a correspondent in Tehran sixteen years before and, like so much about the Islamic Republic, was still under sporadic construction.

According to the special news sheet handed out with the entrance ticket, the long-planned exhibition was to celebrate the anniversary of the Iran-Iraq War of 1980–88. The Islamic Revolutionary Guards Corps, which had organized much of the event, wanted to remember the heady spirit of those days, honor the war dead, and consolidate its core constituency, the men who had fought in the war. But its propaganda purpose was more ambitious. It was seeking to inculcate the old values of self-sacrificing martyrdom in today's different and more cynical youth, show the difficulties overcome, remember the foreign states that opposed the Islamic Republic, and renew loyalty to the regime. Radical Islamists like Hamas from Palestine and Hezbollah from Lebanon were also listed as having stands, proving that Iran was not alone in the world—or, to Americans, that all the terrorists had got together for a big party. I now knew I'd have a story.

First, though, I wanted to see the exhibition. The entrance section stirred disturbing memories. The waxworks were primitive, but they portrayed a war that I had shared in. A section titled "The Memory of Heroic Deeds" featured reconstructions of familiar scenes from recruiting offices, emotional family leave-takings as young men headed off to the front, loudspeakers blaring out songs about "Our Jihad," mystical invocations of paradise waiting for the martyrs played to the troops before battle, and the dramatic martial music once broadcast all over the country during big offensives. There were also three-dimensional recreations of the dikes and bunkers of the front lines, scattered with battered Toyota Land Cruisers, antiaircraft guns, barbed wire, and depictions of Iran's two hundred thousand war dead.

A walk-through diorama portrayed the reed beds in the Iraqi border marshes, where I had also been during the war. Back in 1985, the great marshes had not yet been drained by Iraqi President Saddam Hussein. The Tehran exhibit got the otherworldly atmosphere exactly right. I'd passed down the same canals cut through the reed beds, and remembered the flat-bottomed Iranian metal boats plying along them, one weighed down with fuel, another jerry-rigged with a 50-mm cannon, a third with wide ammunition boxes for rockets. Half hidden in the reed beds were a small frontline clinic helpfully signposted in Persian EMERGENCY, barges mounted with Katyusha rocket batteries, and outposts where soldiers waved and brandished their Kalashnikov rifles. Once we zoomed past a timeless dugout canoe being poled through the reeds by a native white-robed Marsh Arab doing his daily rounds despite the war.

The next diorama was an artillery emplacement. I introduced myself to a bearded veteran inspecting a howitzer. Abdulreza was explaining a memory from those times to his wife, who was shrouded in a black chador.

Under attack from an unseen Iraqi mortar battery in the reed beds of the great Iraqi marshes during the Iran-Iraq war, Iranian-backed Iraqi rebels seek a route to safety. October 1985. *(Hugh Pope)*

"Do you think it was all worth it?" I asked.

"Those were the good days." He sighed. "What I remember was the spiritual atmosphere, the togetherness. We've lost so much since then, the value system is changing, the way money is so important, the way women no longer dress properly."

Seventeen years old when he enlisted, Abdulreza became a frontline medic. He now worked in an automobile paint shop.

"I longed to be a martyr. I didn't deserve it, apparently," he said. "People think of war as bloody, and it was very ugly. But if a casualty was brought to us, we saw his spirit. He would smile, and it was transcendent. It was beautiful to see people ready to give their lives for God."

I saw emotional remembering on the faces of many of the veterans touring the exhibits. For them the culture of the front had been the most meaningful time of their lives. This holy state of mind inspired slogans around the trenches that Western soldiers would find peculiar, like "Smile, Warrior!" firebases named after prominent martyrs, and obscure Shia Muslim invocations like "Remember to Avenge the Slap Given to Zehra."

I stopped to chat with a stall holder manning a "Sacred Defense" exhibition booth sponsored by his employer, Bank Melli Iran. Nariman was handing out key chains, cards with website addresses, and Korans to promote his bank. He'd been just thirteen years old when he rushed to the front at the outbreak of the war.

"Shouldn't you have been at school?" I asked.

"The war front was my school. A school of love . . . a lost paradise!" Nariman said with a faraway smile.

The next hall was filled entirely with poster-sized pictures of carnage: the mutilated stump of a leg, the blistered face of one of the sixty thousand Iranians poisoned by Iraqi gas, the face of a thickly bearded soldier in the trenches as he picks up his bandaged but now dead comrade, whose eyelids are not yet closed over the whites of his eyes. The soldier looks up, perhaps to a commanding officer, perhaps to God, and the expression reflects everything that the Islamic Revolution wanted from its supporters, and that they wanted to give: obedience, simplicity, resilience, pain, love, sorrow, piety. In a band wound around his helmet was printed a prayer to the "Lord of the Martyrs."

The underlying message to the visitors shuffling past was always the same: Look at the heroism of the revolutionaries who defended us in this war imposed on us by the outside world. The exhibition quiz sheet underlined the depth of the American plot. The question to be answered was *What were America's interests and objectives in the Iraqi attack on Iran?* The possible answers were

A. The liberation of the American spies.
B. To make Iran retreat from its revolutionary and fundamental positions in the international arena.
C. So that Iran would block Iraq from attacking America.
D. All of the above.

It's true that Iraq started the war in September 1980 by invading the oil-rich, Arabic-speaking south of Iran, and true too that Baghdad was quietly supported by the United States, France, and pro-American Persian Gulf oil states. But Iran was not innocent, either. It had threatened Iraq by talk of Islamic revolution for the country's restive Shia majority. It had ensured enmity with the United States by seizing the U.S. embassy in Tehran and taking American diplomats hostage.

The Iranians had chosen the spirit of martyrdom as their national ethos, and they also wanted to show that the Islamic Republic had international appeal. Many other groups shared a common real or rhetorical conflict with Israel. Iran's most prominent friend at the exhibition was Hezbollah of Lebanon, where Islamists first deployed the suicide car bomb in the early 1980s as part of a successful campaign to drive the U.S., Israeli, French, and other armies out of their country. There was the Supreme Assembly of the Islamic Revolution of Iraq. Other Islamists from Albania, Bosnia, and Africa were briefly represented. Most fashionable of all were the Palestinians, whose smartly decked-out booths were lined with gory pictures of young men who had blown themselves up, or had been liquidated by Israelis, as recently as the month before.

Like Iran in its war with Iraq, these anti-Israel groups were ready to sacrifice martyrs to gain an asymmetrical advantage. To this end, religion was pressed into service to justify martyrdom. It was a political business, however: Seeking to win domestic and regional popularity for their dictatorial regimes, Iran at times competed with Iraq to help groups involved in suicide bombings. Saddam sent money to the families of Palestinian martyrs; Iran was behind Lebanon's Hezbollah, whose yellow flag bears the symbol of Iran's Islamic Revolutionary Guards Corps, made up of the Arabic word for "no" turning into a hand clenching a rifle and the Koranic motto: "Oppose them until the last of your strength." When added to the ruthlessness of Israel itself, the conflict had warped everyone's values. At the stand of the Palestinian Islamist movement Hamas, their Tehran representative pointed to the photograph of a smiling young man.

"Look at this boy, this beautiful boy," he said.

Then, with a mix of well-practiced wistfulness and outrage, he pointed to the next picture, in which the same man burned to death in a car struck by an Israeli missile.

"Look, he's a martyr now."

At the Hezbollah display, pictures of shell-blasted babies and twisted corpses from Israeli attacks on Lebanon hung alongside a delightfully elaborate piece of Arabic calligraphy that spelled out "Death to America, Death to Israel." On a television screen, the movement's satellite station was broadcasting a speech by its black-turbaned leader Sheikh Hassan Nasrallah, baring his teeth and shaking his fist in militaristic diatribe. Across the convention-style walkway, where visitors crossed a Star of David being stamped on by an oversize, bloodred footprint, was a memorial for the death toll of Hezbollah martyrs over twenty-five years: 1,281 dead, registered in six-foot-high numerals dripping with red-paint blood.

"Why so much blood?" I asked the young man supervising the Hezbollah stand. "Doesn't it make you uncomfortable?"

Fadi turned out to be a Lebanese student of Persian language and literature—my own subjects at university. But he had no time for talk of poetry.

"Blood is sacred for us," Fadi said. "It's not terrorism. It's our resistance against Israel. We didn't have guns, so we gave our lives. That's what liberated our country."

I'd reported in south Lebanon in the 1980s as the Shia resistance movement that became Hezbollah pushed the Israelis out, and what he said was partly true. But I also knew how much Iran's domestic propaganda needs had come to dominate Hezbollah rhetoric. The Israeli "Zionist racist entity" and American "global arrogance" were now being blamed for all the ills of Iran and the Middle East, if not the world.

In the next hall was a stand run by the Iranian Foreign Ministry. Thinking of all my fair-minded American editors, whose blameless lives had been blown apart along with the World Trade Center the week before, I challenged the diplomat on duty.

"Aren't you making things worse?" I asked. "Don't you think this kind of show, this whole cult of martyrdom, encourages suicide bombers? How can you say some of this is not terrorism?"

"People have different views of what terrorism is," he replied. "We condemn it, whether it is in New York, in Palestinian refugee camps like Sabra and Shatila, or in Afghanistan. You've got to look at the context of each case. We want a dialogue of civilizations, not a clash of civilizations."

The diplomat's fair words suited the delicate patterns on a fine pair of Persian carpets in his booth. But the ethic was in stark contrast to the exhibit right opposite. Here, looking through one of the holes artistically blasted through a mock street wall with a sign reading MARTYR ROAD, visitors could spy the corner of an anonymous battlefield where a green military radio lay abandoned by the ruins of a house that glistened with fresh fake blood and gore.

Around the next corner, an Iranian elementary school group stood in mesmerized horror before a video monitor showing Iran-Iraq War scenes from a medical tent. In the recording, a man displayed the contents of a sack of amputated body parts: a foot, an arm, lumps of flesh. When some children flinched and looked away as doctors hacked at an open wound that filled the screen, their teacher ordered them to keep watching. I could barely look, and asked the man next to me whether he thought the scene appropriate for young people.

"Certainly!" he said.

He was the prayer leader of a Tehran mosque, and he told me he'd seen much the same on his trips to the front with food and morale-raising sermons during the war.

"We want to inculcate the new generation with the spirit of sacrifice we had then, in an unequal situation," he explained.

The Revolutionary Guards were trying to inculcate a willingness to die, and they started young. In one diorama, an Iraqi tank smashed through the wall of a schoolroom. On the blackboard, the first writing lesson of Iranian primary school, *bābā āb dād,* "Dad gave water," had been given an incomplete second line, "Dad . . ." which trailed melodramatically off to ". . . blood." Visiting children were encouraged to gambol on the tank itself, as the exhibition newspaper said, "to get acquainted with the engines of war."

Some mothers in long black chador cloaks dropped their children at the exhibition's day-care center, a camouflage-netted tent. Here the recreational painting was eye-opening. Supervising the children was Shabnam Yahyazadeh, a twenty-two-year-old art student, who asked them to create a child's-eye view of what they had

Regional elites, from the Saudi puritans of the Saudi/Wahhabi school to the modernizing secularists of Turkey, often perceive a threat to their authoritarian ideologies not just in permissive tendencies from the West but also in superstitious practices, as seen here in the Lebanese Shia town of Nabatiyeh during an annual march to lament the murders thirteen hundred years ago of members of the prophet's family. 1985. (*Hugh Pope*)

learned from the exhibition. Most of the work hung up to dry around the tent was of tanks, battles in palm groves, and soldiers dying bloody deaths.

"This is the air force," said a five-year-old at his worktable, pointing to a rendering of a warplane. Then, pointing to red streaks over most of the page, he added, "These ones are dead. They're gone."

When I sat down with the supervisor, she said the regime was manipulating feelings of being oppressed to shore up its legitimacy.

"I've been ordered to make them paint these things. But this is just the surface. It's politics, a minority view," she said. "The real Islam has no killing. If some people have flipped it upside down for their own benefit, I don't agree, the majority doesn't agree."

In her opinion the hard-liners were successfully exploiting Iran's Shia Muslim tradition of keeping a sense of victimhood alive for hundreds of years. This includes the retelling in graphic detail of the thirteen-hundred-year-old story of the murder of members of the Prophet Muhammad's family, part of the early Islamic civil war that divided the Muslim world into Shia (the "faction" loyal to the Prophet's family, mainly in Iran, Iraq, parts of the Persian Gulf, and Lebanon) and Sunni (those of the "tradition," mainly in the Arabian heartland, Egypt, Turkey, North Africa, and Asia). The murdered men have become the greatest martyrs of the Shia, and their deaths are remembered each year during the ten days known as ashura. Blood is always part of it, whether the occasional excesses of young men lacerating their backs with chains during the mourning processions in Tehran, or the extravagant scenes I'd watched in the Lebanese town of Nabatiyeh, where Shia celebrants perform a circuit of a town square beating their heads with the flats of swords—often having cut the forehead with a razor to ensure that the white sheet over their shoulders, symbolizing a funeral shroud, was suitably drenched in bright red blood. Similarly, a two-layer fountain in the heart of Tehran's cemetery for the dead in the war with Iraq overflowed with fluid dyed bloodred.

"Iranians like mythology. It's in our blood," the teacher said. "Unfortunately, here some people want to possess others by showing bloody pictures, by showing whose blood was sacrificed for Iran, and by showing why those Islamic revolutionary values must be kept up."

I knew that the *Journal*'s editors would love this story. But I felt hesitant. Neither the Iranians nor their exhibition had anything directly to do with Osama bin Laden's attack on the United States. The Revolutionary Guards who organized it could have had no warning of the plot. The Iranian government had long been at odds with bin Laden and his protectors in Afghanistan's Taliban regime; it was inconceivable that either al-Qaeda or the Taliban would have been offered a stand at the exhibition. There were no Chechen jihadists, presumably because Iran had warm relations with Russia. Politics trumped Islamist ideology most of the time. The point of the show was not really to be a rally of international Islamism, let alone terrorism. Iranian visitors were focused mainly on the nightmare of the Iran-Iraq War. And there, ordinary Iranians had a claim to my sympathy.

My most vivid of several days on the front lines was during the eighth phase of an offensive called "I Swear by the Dawn." I'd first become aware of it on a rare day off in the mountains high above Tehran, when the loudspeakers on the primitive ski lift suddenly started blaring triumphant martial music. After three years of stalemate, the news for Iran appeared to be good. A surprise attack had allowed them to occupy the southern tip of Iraq, the Faw peninsula. Iranian troops were threatening Iraq's access to the sea. Soon enough came the late-night call from the Ministry of Islamic Guidance.

"Be at the airport tomorrow morning at six. The military terminal!"

It was always a curious feeling when the Iranian propaganda machine, a permanent obstruction in our work, suddenly became obsequiously supportive. We became part of the war effort, in which, paradoxically for such an anti-American regime, much of the military machinery inherited from the time of the monarchy was still American. A Hercules transport plane flew us to the airport at Ahvaz, at the southern end of the front. Bell helicopters were waiting on the tarmac, surrounded by bearded young men in scruffy uniforms. We were invited to step into chemical warfare suits, thin plastic affairs for skinny Iranian village boys little suited to our thicker Western build and our need to reach into odd pockets for pens and cameras. A middle-aged German correspondent from *Der Spiegel* magazine could hardly squeeze his on, and it stretched taut over his large frame. We were handed gas masks and invited to board the helicopters. Then followed the hangers-on—soldiers, local journalists, and Revolutionary Guards in a sweaty, wrestling scrum.

"How many people are these helicopters built to carry?" I asked the American-trained crewman.

"Fifteen, including the crew."

As the crewman stepped out to begin his preflight checks with the pilot, I counted the passengers. At least twenty-three people. I could sense the Iranians around me gleefully relaxing, beginning to decouple everyday common sense in favor of a glorious ever after. I rebelled. I pushed my way back out, pulling the man from the ministry with me.

"Either you get eight people off the helicopter or I won't go!"

I am not brave for the sake of it and really didn't want to be part of the trip. Clearly it made my threat appear real. The freeloaders were removed. I had little moral choice but to get back in. Then came a long wheeze from the engine, a poorly oiled screech, and a slow build of thudding from the rotors. The crewman hopped back in, slid the door shut, and heavily we lifted up into the air. Two or three other helicopters rose up behind us, all tipped their noses forward, and soon we were beating high and fast across the Khuzestan deserts.

I sat on a side bench looking through the scratched plastic window at the gray flatness racing past. It was too noisy to think. Past the shoulders of the pilots I could see the desert road running ahead of us, straight as a ruled line. The helicopters gradually dropped height to skim along at what seemed almost ground level. We sped past a long convoy of Iranian heavy trucks, close enough to see the drivers, trundling forward to the war front with containers of supplies. From time to time the helicopters swooped up and down over the remains of power lines stretched across the plain, sucking my stomach down to the metal floor and then dragging it up to my throat. I kept an eye out for the great border marshes where on our last expedition an Iraqi Shia rebel group had taken us to the front line in speedboats and ran us into a Iraqi mortar barrage. We narrowly escaped, only to get lost in the reed beds. At the end of the day we had felt lucky to survive and return to dry land.

Suddenly, in the distance ahead, I saw a jagged explosion strike the road and a cloud of smoke shoot into the sky. Then another, and several more. The heavy-topped clouds merged into a billowing bank of dark density. The Iraqi air force high above us was bombing the highway! A missile streaked up from an Iranian battery near the road. I had no idea at the time that I had just seen real news: a first sighting of ground-to-air missiles supplied by America in return for Iran's role in securing the release of Western hostages in Lebanon. In fact, I couldn't think at all, astonished that the pilot was taking no evasive action whatsoever. In front of us, a bomb dug under one of the long flatbed trucks, sending it arching high into the air, somersaulting lazily onto its back, and then crashing back to earth. I started counting. We were heading straight into the maelstrom.

"One, two, three, four . . ."

After five seconds we hit the first of the black smoke. The pilot showed no fear. Burning trucks flashed by underneath us. Then we were out of it, back into the expressionless plain. Nobody was joking in the helicopter anymore. We lurched up and over more power lines. I pulled out my notebook to write a farewell note to my wife. Just a few hours before, I had left her in north Tehran, asleep in a warm bed in our small palace surrounded by a garden with fine rosebushes and a swimming pool.

I didn't know what to write. Expressions of sentiment seemed pointless and insincere amid the trapped, meaningless terror of our situation. I tried a few lines and gave up. I wondered at friends who loved this warfront adrenaline rush, a time of total focus on the present, the ultimate carpe diem. Perhaps such people are the ones who make great soldiers too. They would not pen silly notes to their wives.

We were skimming over the tips of date palms now, clearly closing on Mesopotamia, Iraq's rich lands watered by the Tigris and Euphrates. I spotted what must be the channel that was the Iran-Iraq border, the Shatt al-Arab, a surprisingly modest waterway whose *thalweg,* or central shipping line, we kept writing about as a principal pretext for the war that had triggered this mad adventure. It was here, we learned later, that the Iranians had taken the Iraqis by surprise one recent day at dawn with submerged pontoons that allowed the attackers literally to walk on water to cross the border. The helicopters banked over the wide, palm-fringed canal and slam-dunk landed in a wasteland on the outskirts of a war-ruined small town on the Iraqi side. We had reached Faw.

The helicopter pilots barely throttled back as we struggled out of our seat belts. We realized why only after we had stumbled out onto the chewed earth. The whole area was under attack, apparently from the air. It was surreal to watch the bombs explode around the helicopters as we ran for cover, our reporting paraphernalia flying from straps around our necks. I turned to take a photograph of the last of us, the German, struggling to keep on his feet. Then another bomb exploded nearby, the helicopters roared off, and I took cover in a broken-down concrete villa. Just as I used to in Beirut, I cowered under the stairwell.

When it seemed several minutes since the last of the bombs had fallen, I realized I was on my own and had no idea where anyone else was. I ventured out. Colleagues emerged from behind earthen banks and other buildings. Our Iranian guides were gesturing that we should gather on the back of some heavy trucks that had appeared. We clambered in, our nerves raw and jangling, feeling exposed to unseen dangers and overheated from the chemical suits. The Iranians were trying to check we'd all got on board.

"Where's the *Spiegel* correspondent?" somebody asked.

We looked about. There were a dozen of us crowded onto the open back of our truck, but clearly he wasn't among us or those on the other truck. But there weren't that many other places for him to be hiding in the blasted landscape around us. Losing my balance as we jostled each other again, I stepped on something soft. I looked down.

"Hey! Here he is! I think something's wrong!"

We made space and looked hard. He was motionless and pale. There was no sign of blood, or of life. This was in the years before correspondents went on courses for war reporters, and nobody had a clue what medical action to take. The Iranians were seized with an alarming panic. Soon his bulky frame was dragged off the metal floor and manhandled into the back of a jeep, which bumped off at speed, we presumed to a frontline clinic. Neither I nor any of the other correspondents offered to accompany him. Reporting can be a lonely profession. I later learned that he had died of a heart attack, leaving a wife and daughter.

We were consumed with worry about surviving ourselves. Our small convoy of trucks soon lumbered out of the town center. A rumbling boom of artillery rolled over from the middle distance. We were heading due west and soon came to the other side of the Faw peninsula. Here a Revolutionary Guard stopped the trucks to point over the sea to what might or might not have been Kuwait's flat-sand island of Bubiyan. He underlined the point of bringing us here: Iran could now threaten this oil sheikhdom, one of the several Arab states which, alarmed by Iran and its Shia revolution, supported Iraq's war effort with oil, loans, or manpower.

As we set off north toward where we were told the front lines lay, I became less convinced of the other point Iran was trying to make that January of 1986, that it was victoriously in control of a new salient that would force the outcome of the war.

"Gas! Gas!" shouted one of the Iranians. The trucks juddered to a halt. I couldn't see what exactly had triggered this reaction. Iraqi planes might be overhead. Perhaps he was referring to the big white cloud that had billowed up a few miles ahead, apparently from an explosion. I didn't wait to discuss it. Nine parts of fear is ignorance, and I had no idea what to do as I pulled on the gas mask. It didn't fit properly and seemed to be a design from the First World War. I gave up. Then I saw a trench next to the road and jumped into it. There was a kind of hole next to it, and I burrowed in.

To my astonishment, I found myself surrounded by Iranian soldiers. There were half a dozen of them, sitting around the edge of their dugout cave. They were amazed at the appearance of a flustered foreigner in a chemical warfare suit.

"Where are you from?"

"England. Where are you from?"

It sounded forced, but conventions are conventions.

"Mazandaran," they said in nostalgic unison. I pictured the lush rain forests of Iran's Caspian Sea coast, where I'd recently driven on a happy long weekend escaping from Tehran. We looked at each other. They were part of a battalion from the auxiliary volunteers known as the Baseej, the paramilitary used by the Revolutionary Guards. They had been brought in to hold the territory after the initial assault, dropped on the side of the road. With nothing but flat desert for miles around, they had wisely dug a hole and were hiding in it. It wasn't the death-defying bravado that was usually put on show. In fact, they were as terrified as I was.

"Bop! BOP! We are going now!"

I realized it was my mangled name being called. One of our guides had found me. Back onto the trucks. The Iraqis were clearly piling on pressure, and we retreated to Faw. We arrived in time for another air raid, with bombs falling thick and fast.

"The helicopters can't come now. We have to wait," the guides told us.

So we waited. This time the only place I could find to hide was an open trench. In the bottom were two dead Iraqi soldiers, slightly decomposed. But my fear of the bombs was far greater than of these corpses. I sat in the bottom and looked up in mesmerized amazement at the formations of Iraqi bombers. Some flew high overhead, long, thin, and silver. Fighter-bombers roared in lower, looking for targets, of which our helicopter field was a prime one. There was even one that looked like a passenger plane, which dropped bombs on parachutes. It seemed sinister. When I saw those, I readied my gas mask.

As the bombs came closer during the second raid, one of the toughest-looking Revolutionary Guards, a bulky, bearded fellow, jumped into my trench shaking with fear. Some of the Iranians appeared very brave, however. The man I admired most was one of the truck drivers, who sat casually out in the open throughout, leafing through one of the newspapers someone had brought from Tehran.

Iraq's air superiority was total. A third wave of planes circled overhead, bombs exploded all around, and the Revolutionary Guard and I made ourselves as small as possible in our dead men's ditch. The afternoon shadows began to lengthen. Our Iranian minders emerged to debate what to do about their two dozen foreign charges. I had no confidence in them. My penultimate predecessor as Reuters correspondent in Tehran, Najmul Hassan, had been killed when his guide from the Ministry of Islamic Guidance guided him deep into a minefield. The guide died too.

In a break in the air attacks on us we could hear the *whump* of Iraqi long-range artillery, feeling for the supply roads on the other side of the Shatt al-Arab waterway. Several seconds later we'd hear a louder thump when the shells landed. Then we got our marching orders.

"Quick! To the boats!"

We ran over to the Shatt and jumped into metal boats with outboard motors. On the other side trucks had arrived for us, and we clambered up and into them. Then came the supply road. The thump of outgoing artillery took on a new meaning, but luckily their shells didn't find us. After an hour, we had left the front behind. We began to relax. When out of danger, we stopped for water. We took photographs of ourselves. The one of me shows me to be absolutely green: I was still tinged with the same color when I returned home the next day.

My story from the war front, even if it failed to reflect much of the chaos and fear of our expedition, won wide play and a slot in the *Washington Post,* a rare honor for an agency dispatch. But the photos I developed and printed were not a success. The Islamic Republic News Agency refused to transmit a photograph that showed a turbaned Iranian mullah with his boot kicking the hand of a dead Iraqi pilot spilling out of his crashed warplane. And when it came to my backup image, I was too shell-shocked to realize that without the sights and sounds of the Iraqi air force blasting Faw to pieces, editors around the world would be puzzled by a hastily snapped photograph of a man reading a newspaper.

In short, the Iranian side of the war was an intense experience. The hard-line

An Iranian Baseej volunteer kisses his children farewell on his way to the front lines of the Iran-Iraq war. Morale was high inside the bus. Several of the soldiers said they'd done many tours of duty, even though some had been gassed several times. 1986. *(Hugh Pope)*

leadership that really controls Iran, men like President Mahmoud Ahmadinejad, are a group that bonded on those front lines. Much later, amid the plush sofas of London's Dorchester hotel conference rooms, a former frontline auxiliary who had become an Iranian oil executive explained why.

"I was with the defenders of Khorramshahr, early in the war. The only way we could keep the Iraqi tanks at bay was by digging a trench with a bulldozer," he said. "Sitting in the cab meant the Iraqi snipers could shoot you. One by one, the men who volunteered for the job got killed. There was a queue in the trenches to take their place, I tell you, a long queue! In that queue we all felt so calm, it was the most beautiful feeling in the world. Never again have I experienced such love!"

I felt more than one conflict of conscience, in fact, as I contemplated the story I'd write about the First Universal Exhibition of Sacred Culture and Defense. There was my disgust for the blood and gore versus my respect for the love-bonded spirituality of the Iran-Iraq War front; my scorn for the Iranian regime versus my admiration for Persian culture; my own wariness of Israel versus my suspicion that a big part of the Islamic Republic's anti-Israel stand was rabble-rousing and racism. When I rang up Bill Spindle to tell him what I had seen, he immediately wanted to push the story to the front page. Spindle had lived abroad and let me try to explain my Middle Eastern perspectives, at least the more rational ones. But as the story moved through the editing process, I realized that I was not on the same wavelength as some other editors.

As I had feared, for my faraway American audience, Iran's obsession with blood, suicide bombings, and anti-Israel, anti-American rhetoric epitomized the idea that they were grappling with the same Islamist terrorist nihilist crazies who'd just brought down the World Trade Center. I was shocked by what al-Qaeda had done and had no sympathy for that group. But I understood the sense of desperate impotence against overwhelming odds that had spawned Iranian human-wave attacks, Hamas, and Hezbollah. I'd been on one set of front lines; my colleagues had suddenly found themselves on the other.

The *Journal* is an honest newspaper and always lets the reporter have the last say. But editors control priorities and are in charge of attracting readers to the story and making them read it to the end. Even setting the scene was hard to get straight. I had led with the way the exhibition was a bit like a Western trade show, what with the key chains and commercial stands. So an editor inserted the idea that the whole thing was on a convention floor, as if it were taking place in some mall-like center in America. In fact, the prayerdrome venue was a vast, incoherent jumble, whose missilelike minarets and grandiose arches were covered in scaffolding. Five times the story came back with changes and questions, five times I tried to square the result with reality on the ground. There was much e-mailing about details. My front-page stories for the *Journal* typically took six weeks to appear, or, in one unusual case, six years. From start to finish we did this one in a record twenty-four hours.

This speed came at a price. In the spirit of the times, I'd mistakenly dragged Islam into it, saying that the fact the great prayer courtyard was filled with enough military hardware for an armaments fair "symbolized militant Islam." They cut out a rejection of the terrorist label by the Lebanese student manning the Hezbollah stand, who made a key point often ignored by Americans that Hezbollah was originally a resistance movement fighting an Israeli occupation. At least I managed to weed out one editor's view that the whole show was a celebration of "international terror." Exhausted in the early hours of the morning, I sometimes had to compromise. The front page insisted on having the word "terrorism" in the headline. I tried to soften the blow by making it indirect. It ended up as THE FRUITS OF TERRORISM ARE THE STOCK IN TRADE AT A TEHRAN EXHIBITION.

My heart sank when I woke up the next morning and realized what I'd let happen. Part of my reaction was fear. Getting a single word wrong can be disastrous in relations with Middle Eastern governments. I had been officially expelled from Iran in 1985 over the misuse of just one word in an article about an ayatollah in line to succeed Khomeini. I had called him *"owlish,"* thinking that his bookish eyeglasses made him look wise, but forgetting that in Iran, the owl is the bird of ill omen. I traveled to the holy Shia seminary city of Qom to deliver a letter of abject apology. A few days later the official in charge of foreign media grudgingly told me that I could stay. Middle Eastern institutions may be deficient, but personal intervention can often set things straight.

Luckily, the ministry minders didn't react to my cult of martyrdom story. Still, I felt that once again I'd failed to bridge fully the gap between Middle Eastern reality and American perceptions. Using "terrorism" as a blanket word looked as though I'd taken sides and insulted Iran. The same thing happened when reporting on the Palestinians' struggle against Israel, or that of the Turkish Kurds against the Turkish government. Militant groups' actions could deliberately or inevitably kill civilians—my understanding of a terrorist act—but then so could the actions of the state they were fighting, which people called terrorist only if they disapproved of its politics. I was ready to use the word "terrorist" as an adjective in relation to individual outrages. But I always tried to avoid using it as a noun or to describe groups that had real popular support, and among whom I lived and reported. There was, however, no perfect answer if I wanted to appear neutral. Whether I used or did not use the word "terrorist," it made one side or the other think I'd taken sides against it.

Even so, I did feel that I'd got some of our mad, sometimes perverted reality through to American readers. This was the case in a number of stories we wrote in those early weeks after September 11. Our editors and America as a whole were listening at last to us in the Middle East, searching for a reason for the attacks that had shocked them so much. But our distant voices were soon drowned out by others closer to home. As time went by, the explanations of the traditionally more influential American pro-Israel interest groups won the upper hand, followed by the rise of those who believed that the United States had to impose a new order on the Middle East by military force.

After September 11, the U.S.-led intervention against the Taliban and al-Qaeda in Afghanistan was presumably inevitable. But Iran, Syria, and Iraq were publicly mentioned as possible next targets, all states that were hostile to Israel but had nothing to do with the attacks on America. It was exactly such hard-line Western misrepresentations, and the eventual invasion and takeover of Iraq, that justified the politics of the radicals at the Tehran exhibition. Iran's Islamic Republic gleefully welcomed the legitimacy provided by the perception that it was the target of a campaign to be crushed and martyred by America. A strengthened us-against-the-world ideology, along with steady oil income, helped Iran's ruling group put off the day when it would actually have to face up to its failure to make Iran into a prosperous, pluralistic modern state.

The day my story came out, I switched on the Iranian television in my luxurious Tehran apartment. Iran's supreme leader, Ayatollah Ali Khamenei, was making a speech to veterans and relatives of the Iran-Iraq War dead.

"Martyrdom," Khamenei was telling them, "is a pleasant-smelling and scented flower that can be reached and smelled only by those chosen people and those chosen by God."

I wondered how any of these aggrieved people could accept such easy talk. But as I listened on, I realized that Khamenei had a convincing story for them. He lauded the achievement of Iran, which had defended itself against an Iraqi invasion quietly supported by the West. He rhetorically rebelled against what he called America's post–September 11 attitude, which he described as, "We are angry, so don't say anything that contradicts us." He rejected being labeled a "terrorist" by a country that so unflinchingly supported a country like Israel.

He went through the list of Israel's sins: its prime minister and White House intimate was Ariel Sharon, the same warrior-politician who had terrorized Palestinians into leaving Israel in its early wars and had been found "indirectly" responsible for the 1982 Sabra and Shatila Palestinian refugee camp massacre in Lebanon; Israel's "targeted assassinations" of Palestinians unilaterally judged by Israel to be militant leaders; and the 1996 massacre when Israel shelled a UN outpost that killed more than one hundred civilians.

I couldn't stop myself from nodding. A Dutch investigating general, Amnesty

International, Human Rights Watch, and the UN all found Israeli artillery guilty of some level of intent to attack the Qana outpost crowded with civilians, beyond the need to respond to Hezbollah mortars fired from more than 220 yards away. Violence breeds violence. Mohammed Atta, the Egypt-born pilot and lead planner of the September 11 suicide attacks, had written out his pledge to martyrdom as a vow to avenge the victims of the Israeli onslaught on Lebanon of which the Qana massacre was a part.

Khamenei now turned his attention to America's plea for help against terrorism.

"Have you ever respected the interests of others, that you now expect everyone to respect yours?" he continued. "If American interests in the Persian Gulf are threatened, everyone has to cooperate. But if the interests of the Persian Gulf countries [like Iran] are threatened, it doesn't matter."

Okay, fair point, I thought.

Khamenei lost me with a condemnation of Israeli kidnappings in Lebanon—Iran's close allies had done exactly the same—and some gratuitous criticism of American attitudes to Muslims. Then he went on to remember twenty-two years of U.S. efforts to cut the Islamic Republic down to size, its not-so-secret alliance with Iraq in the war against Iran, and one of the indirect results of that alliance, the 1988 shooting down by the USS *Vincennes* of an Iranian airliner in the Persian Gulf, killing 290 people.

The Americans, Khamenei said, "divide terrorism into good and bad . . . they blow up the airplane, tear the people into pieces, and drown them in the sea—a clear case of terrorism. But then they give the commander of the warship a prize."

"Yes," I involuntarily said to the television, out loud this time.

The commander of the sophisticated *Vincennes* may not have known that he was targeting a civilian airliner, but he should have. American claims that the airliner was giving the signals of an Iranian warplane flying outside the commercial air corridor and on a descending course of attack were later all proved to be false. Stress and tension clouded the captain's judgment because he'd sailed inside Iranian territorial waters to shoot up a flotilla of Iranian gunboats in a sting operation, part of an undeclared naval war with Iran. The U.S. commander in chief of the Pacific Fleet later publicly told ABC News's *Nightline* that within this conflict with the Iranians, the United States was prepared to "drill them back to the fourth century." Richard Armitage, the assistant secretary of defense, kindly said on the same show that eventually "the decision was made not to completely obliterate Iran." That was because intense U.S. military support for the Iraqis did the job more discreetly. And on return to port the U.S. president did give the *Vincennes*'s captain a Legion of Merit award for "exceptionally meritorious conduct."

For sure, double standards were not just for Iran. It was of course prestigious

American media like *Nightline* and *Newsweek* that exposed U.S. official lies about the incident, something that would not have happened in Tehran. But I despaired of my own side for giving so many winning arguments to someone as sanctimonious and hypocritical as Khamenei, and became more convinced than ever that the word "terrorism" was just too loaded for everyday use.

9. MAMMON IN MECCA

Crushing Religious Diversity in the Name of Islam

You kiss your lover, but tear out her teeth.
—ARABIC SAYING

The signs at the desert intersection outside the city are clear: No non-Muslims allowed into Mecca. I could get no closer to the holy focal point for all the billion-plus Muslims of the world. The Koran, the direct word of God for Muslims, says that all Muslims should try once in their lifetime to cleanse their sins by making the hajj, or pilgrimage to the holy city. Five times a day, the Muslims of the world prostrate themselves in the direction of the kaaba, the house-sized cube in the heart of Mecca's great mosque. Many Muslims thrill to the variety of Islamic nations and peoples who converge for the annual event in the city where the Prophet Muhammad had his first revelation. Shrouded in black silk, the kaaba's image is woven into carpets, printed onto calendars, and hung on posters in Muslim sitting rooms all over the globe.

Once a Saudi invited me to come with him to Mecca and break the Muslims-only edict, following in the steps of non-Muslim European adventurers who had secretly visited the city. Usually tempted to break rules, for once I declined. Few people who look as north European as I do are Muslim, and, if I were stopped, my visa specified my religion as Christian. I didn't feel the need to convert to see what was one of the most photographed places on the planet. Going secretly would mean I couldn't do much that was special, and writing about what I had seen and how I had seen it would compromise me forever in the eyes of most Muslims. I also resented the idea that my mere presence could be thought polluting, and what such a ban said about the insecure, absolutist side of Islam.

I felt an edge of it one day on a flight from Riyadh to Jeddah, sitting next to a chubby twelve-year-old boy in his pilgrim whites. After a while he looked up from his electronic toy.

"Are you a Christian?" he asked.

I weighed up my response. Posed in most places in the Middle East, the question does not mean the same as in the West. The boy's manner epitomized how much this was not about religious belief but a them-and-us affair. Becoming a Muslim is theoretically as easy as saying the creed of "God is One and Muhammad is His Prophet," but it is a one-way street: Try and turn back, and in theory the Koranic punishment for apostasy is death, even if rarely applied. As I hesitated, the boy on the Saudi Airlines flight came to his own conclusion that the inches that separated us were an unbridgeable civilizational divide. He had all the certainty of his young age, reinforced by the illiberal education that makes Saudi Arabia an archetype of Middle Eastern intolerance.

An English Saudi Arabian Airlines hostess reached our row and offered us a stale sandwich and tea, adjusting her head scarf, craftily designed by the airline to look like glamorous medieval headwear.

"You're an infidel, aren't you?" the boy going to Mecca said. "You'll be going to hell."

"Thanks. Same to you."

Rebuffs and skepticism couldn't rein in my curiosity, however. Most Muslims are not extremists, and Mecca is the most important Islamic city in the world. It had been a place of pilgrimage to a pantheon of gods long before the Prophet Muhammad received his call to choose one of them, Allah, to become God in the new Muslim monotheism. The thick old stonework of the kaaba, with a black stone, perhaps an old meteorite, set in one of its corners, has been damaged and reconstructed in sectarian wars but still stands where it has been since ancient times. Muslims believe the original builder was Abraham. A Lebanese academic, Kamal Salibi, even put a cat among the pigeons by arguing that the occurrence of similar place-names shows that much of the Old Testament may in fact have taken place around Mecca too.

Was there more to Mecca, I wondered, than I was giving it credit for? I looked closer at the pictures and studied the immaculate models of Mecca in the deserted halls of the National Museum in Riyadh. I tried to work out what it felt like, where the great mosque and the town fitted in with the craggy mountains around it, or how it was possible to feed, lodge, and water millions of pilgrims each year in a desert city. It seemed scary to be in the same place as so many people trying to do the same thing, including, at the emotional peak of the pilgrimage, hurling stones at a pillar representing Satan. Every year seemed to bring news of some deadly bridge collapse or stampede during the hajj. Perhaps the promise of paradise for a death on the pilgrimage assuaged pilgrims' fears. Dangers were even greater in the past, when pilgrims had to form great caravans for the last desert stages of their journey for fear of plundering raids by bedouin Arabs.

The pilgrimage also symbolizes the monotheistic clarity of Islam and simple insistence on the finality of Muhammad as God's last prophet. Muslim thinkers claim that this means there is an "Islamic world." Muslim leaders speak out for "1.3 billion Muslims," as if this were one homogenous block. This false idea of unity is open to abuse, not just by insufferable twelve-year-olds but also by militants like Osama bin Laden, claiming to act in the name of one big constituency. There were also misunderstandings, as in Britain's debate about possible sharia courts for Muslims, as if there is an objective thing called "Islamic law" that exists independently of a political jurisdiction. Friends told me of the brilliant chief of a Washington think tank, pacing the corridors and speed-reading the Koran in the misguided belief it held the key to the syndromes of September 11 and the aftermath. And, of course, the fallacy gives rise to the impossible question so often posed by faraway editors to Middle East correspondents: What does the Islamic world think about this?

At the same time, the illusion that there is, or should be, Islamic unity has great consequences for the rulers of Mecca, both as a responsibility and an opportunity. For more than fourteen centuries prior to the impact of oil money in the 1970s, the main source of income on the Arabian Peninsula was the flow of pilgrims to the holy city. Even today, the frankincense-laden bazaars and great shopping malls of the nearby port city of Jeddah continue the Muslim tradition of combining trade with sacred purpose.

As I began to learn more about Mecca, I began to notice reports about how the Saudi government was pulling down the built heritage of Mecca to make way for yet more glitzy malls and high-rises. These expressed both the oil wealth of the Saudi elite and its desire to cash in on the faith tourism of the hajj. Saudi Airlines magazine advertised apartments with kaaba views and crazy prices. Though not a Muslim, I have always admired the egalitarian spirit of Islam that dictates plain unsewn robes for everyone who makes the pilgrimage. I felt it must be offensive to some Muslims that people could now buy better access than others, and that one's acts of devotion would be observed by hotel guests behind smoked-glass windows. The newer-is-better attitude of the Saudi elite seemed to be perverting the one rite of passage that, for a few days at least, did symbolize what unity there was between the poor and the rich and the legendary "seventy-two nations" of Islam.

I searched for signs of Muslim dissent, but they were hard to find. Saudi Arabia is rich enough to buy a good press at home and in the Middle East to nurture its king's image as the "servant of the two holy shrines." One note of opposition was sounded by

Turkey, independent enough to dare publicly to protest the razing of an Ottoman fort that occupied the last open space in the ring of high-rises around Mecca's great mosque. Inside Saudi Arabia, there were also murmurs, a stirring of debate, a standing up for the right to think differently, and a respect for history. On one trip to Saudi Arabia, Judith Kipper, one of America's doyennes of Middle Eastern studies, swept me up in her tireless progress to palaces and princes. Hearing of my interest in Mecca, she passed me the telephone number of a man who seemed to her especially brave in his defense of the holy city and, as a result, in his challenge to the blinkered political and spiritual authoritarianism of the Saudi establishment: Sami Angawi.

Behind the high, blank walls that keep the hot and dusty streets of Saudi cities at bay, I had become familiar with a surprising variety of architecture and company. Inside I could join a banquet, for instance, with a dozen men in immaculately pressed white robes and equipped with Western doctorates. I once had lunch in the palace of a sheikhly grandmother, the table laid out before a saltwater aquarium the size of a bus and featuring the Red Sea coast coral reef and its schools of dazzling fish. I also took tea with an industrialist's family in their beachside mansion where, at the call to prayer, servants would roll out prayer mats and the men and women would together perform their devotions next to the swimming pool.

Sami Angawi's palace, however, wore its individuality on the outside: a cross between an old Arabian castle, a ducal residence in Italy, and the Alhambra in Spain. I knocked on a front door of age-blackened wood. No response. Five minutes later a servant appeared from the side of the house to open the door and lead me inside. It was cool and dark, and it took a while to absorb the scene around a covered atrium. Here were Jeddah's latticed balconies, overlooking an indoor swimming pool decked out with mosaic and green columns. I could make out stone capitals from the ancient world, pointed arches as in Lebanon, double arches as in India, glass lamps as in Egyptian mosques, striped stonework as in Syria, floral Turkish tilework, and intricate marble inlays that reminded me of Iran.

At the top of a spiral staircase, cramped compared to the vast scale of the house, I nearly bumped into a half-naked, bearded figure hurrying along a passageway with a towel wrapped around his waist. We politely pretended that we hadn't seen each other. The servant showed me to a library where I was offered a green-and-red cushioned divan on which to wait, drinking in the scent of incense curling up from a brass brazier.

Left to my own devices, I studied the books that filled floor-to-ceiling shelves. Soon I happened on a leather-bound volume bearing the name of my host on the spine. Taking it out, I found it to be his doctoral thesis, presented to London's

School of Oriental and African Studies, on the subject of the diversity of Meccan architecture. I was poring over the remarkable variety of carvings and stonework when the freshly showered Angawi appeared in the doorway.

A tall man in his early fifties, he wore a white robe topped by the thin woolen gown of a Sufi mystic, an extravagantly woven turban, and, despite the half-light of this inner recess, tinted glasses. As he talked, he passed a cane that showed his sheikhly status from hand to hand.

"Peace be upon you," he said.

"And on you be peace," I replied.

We settled down on separate divans and pulled up round bolsters to lean against. "Your house is wonderful, like an encyclopedia of Middle Eastern architecture."

"Everything is a reflection of the idea of the unity and the diversity. We shouldn't forget our traditions."

An architect, married to an interior decorator, he explained that adding windows visible from the street symbolized an openness to add to the my-home-is-my-castle privacy of Middle Eastern compounds. He pointed out the references to Meccan architecture around me, many of them original, like the ancient front door. The house was a shrine to the memory of the old holy city.

"Our reference point is Mecca. It is the link that brings Muslims together, the heart of the Islamic world. But the changes have been heartbreaking. In the past fifty years, we've done more damage than in the last fifteen hundred years," Angawi said. "Mecca is becoming Manhattan. It's not just buildings. Whole mountains have been blown away."

He meant a hillock or two rather than a mountain, but the reason for his outrage became clear as he explained the extent of the destruction and wholesale alteration of the city where Islam began in the seventh century. The same was happening in Medina, a city half a day's drive through the desert to the north where, fleeing initial hostility in Mecca, the Prophet Muhammad had nurtured his new faith. The buildings destroyed are usually graves of, or places associated with, saints, relatives of the Prophet, or the Prophet himself. The Saudi authorities do not do this just for the commercial benefits of redevelopment. A key justification is Wahhabism, the official doctrine of modern Saudi Arabia. Wahhabism started with an eighteenth-century preacher, Mohammed ibn Abd al-Wahhab. He was a puritan who wanted to reverse what he saw as the degeneration of high Islam into the veneration of dubious holy men, tombs, and even trees. From almost the beginning, he joined forces with the leader of the powerful Saud clan of central Arabia. The two men's families have kept up this alliance of church and state to the present day, intermarrying and supporting each other to mutual advantage. Wahhabis still believe it is wrong to worship buildings, because anything other than worship of

Urban sculpture on the seafront road in Jeddah can take unusual forms, like this one known as the Auto Cube. Other public art on display includes installations of old naval boats, a cut-up desalination plant, and a giant Arab beaked coffeepot. *(OTE Riyadh)*

God alone panders at best to popular superstitions, and at worst constitutes *shirk,* or worshipping more than one God, one of Islam's gravest sins.

For me, it seemed ironic that the Saudis were breaking down monuments linked to the history of Islam on the basis of an antibuilding doctrine only to erect new buildings that worshipped another deity, the god of profit. Islam doesn't see commercial gain as irreligious, and in other ways Saudi Wahhabis were consistent in their doctrines. I told Angawi how I stumbled by accident on the mud-brick house where the founder of the sect supposedly lived. I was wandering in the ruins of the old town of Diriya, the capital of the first Saudi state in the desert outside modern Riyadh, when the great barrel of an early nineteenth-century cannon, lying abandoned in a modest doorway, had beckoned me inside. The courtyard of the house was a junkyard of upended metal-frame beds and British-style wiring from the 1940s, against which, on its side, an old metal sign announced that this was the site of the house of Abd al-Wahhab himself. The house must have been extensively rebuilt since the preacher's death in 1792, but a tourist map of Diriya confirmed that it was indeed right here.

"Diriya was shut off in the middle of the desert for seven hundred years. Of course the people there separated from mainstream Islam. Abd al-Wahhab brought them back into the 'right Islam.' Then they went out and saw the whole Muslim world in this light," said Angawi.

Pouring out of the desert in the early 1800s, Wahhabi-Saudi forces headed west to take over Mecca and Medina, then nominally ruled by the Ottoman Empire. While they held the holy cities, they destroyed many shrines, including some over the graves of companions of Muhammad. Outrage over these acts in the wider Muslim world contributed to their military defeat in 1818 by rival Egyptian and Ottoman forces. Pious and wealthy families rebuilt the tombs in the holy cities. Many Muslims, particularly the Shia, who believe in a sacred role for the family of the Prophet, believe that worshipping at favorite shrines is entirely appropriate.

A century later, in the 1920s, when the Wahhabi-Saudi alliance once again conquered the west of the Arabian Peninsula as it founded the modern state of Saudi Arabia, there was a similar culture clash between the coastal cities and the Saudis' fervent shock troops, the *ikhwan,* or brothers, from the tribes of the Arabian Peninsula heartland.

"The *ikhwan* called the people of Mecca and Medina 'infidels,'" Angawi said with a sigh, pointing out that he comes from one of the leading clans of Mecca, one of those on the jealously guarded list of thirty-two hundred Meccan families authorized by ancient tradition to guide and care for pilgrims.

The shrines again started coming down. Early casualties included the hillock where legend put Muhammad's first school. Then a building came down where Muhammad had lived with his first wife, the rich merchant Khadijah. At first, nothing else was built in its place, and the site was fenced off to keep out the goats. Than the historic buildings within the old courtyard at the great mosque that were the symbolic seats of the four main schools of orthodox Sunni Islam were demolished. While unimportant for most everyday purposes—in practice, they differ on only minor details of interpretation and ablution—the schools did represent the whole concept of a pluralistic approach to religion. Angawi remembered how in his youth it was legendary that pilgrims could sample the wisdom of three dozen study circles that would form around Muslim sages in and around the shaded colonnades of the main Meccan sanctuary. In the early 1980s, the Wahhabi hierarchy banned the famed ancestral sheikh of the Maliki school from teaching his traditionalist and mystical approach inside the mosque precincts. Put under a kind of house arrest and banned from the media, he could never reenter the mosque and died in 2004.

"He was the last of our real teachers," Angawi said.

The arrival of oil money in the 1970s gave the Saudi state even more power to remodel Mecca and impose a new Wahhabi orthodoxy on the country's diverse population, including significant minorities of Shia and Ismailis. Then, of course, there was the matter of personal enrichment for those who could redevelop prime sites of value because of the pilgrimage. As in many Saudi cities, some older quarters of Mecca are surprisingly impoverished and run-down. But the main motive for development was that Mecca had to be modernized to cater to the growing numbers of pilgrims, now three million a year in the ten-day main hajj season, one-third of them Saudis.

There was a price to pay. Standing up to pull out his university thesis, Angawi pointed to illustrations of the precious history woven into the fabric of the city's architecture: shapes of birds and dragons fashioned under balconies by immigrants from Asia, different floral patterns from Morocco and Turkey, and windowframe patterns from near and far.

Angawi's resistance began early. As a twenty-seven-year-old in 1975, he set up an institute to study the architecture of Mecca and the best way to adapt the city to the needs of the pilgrimage season. He borrowed money to pay salaries, burning up a big chunk of his inheritance. But his idealism made him powerful enemies. He was ousted from the institute in what he calls a coup in 1988, while he was out of the country for the final presentation of his thesis. Despite sympathy among some high princes and an audience with the king, he was from then onward kept off planning committees in Mecca and Medina.

"Every time I see a building going down, it's like watching a relative being slaughtered in front of me," he said.

Angawi wasn't exaggerating. In 1990, a caller tipped him off that the site of Muhammad and Khadijah's house was about to be paved over. He rushed to intervene, even threatening to put his young son in the bulldozer's path. His contacts won him permission for a last-minute archaeological dig. It lasted forty days, and his team uncovered stone foundations that appeared to be those of the Prophet's abode. But in the end, the site was buried in concrete and unmarked marble. A public toilet now stands nearby.

The commercial complex that began to take the place of the Ottoman Turkish fortress next to the Great Mosque after 2002 now rises thirty-one floors over the kaaba. In Medina, fundamentalist clergy and developers destroyed the famed old mosque of Abu Bakr, Muhammad's successor and caliph of all the Muslims, and the tombs of the close relatives of Muhammad in Medina. They turned the sites of Muhammad's great early military victories at Uhud and Badr into a parking lot and an area of empty tarmac. Then came overpowering towers of hotels, apartments, and shopping malls. Of three hundred sacred places in these two holiest cities of Islam, Angawi reckoned fewer than ten remained when I talked to him. In 2008, the last pre-1920 mosque in Mecca was removed.

"Only they are right and all others are wrong. It's authoritarianism. They don't recognize history, and they are trapped between being extremely modern and extremely conservative," he said.

"How can that happen? Why does nobody else speak up?" I asked.

"They really think they are doing something that is a great service to Islam. However, the Muslim world isn't asked if it wants that service." He shrugged.

Angawi complained that today's Wahhabi power over the Saudi state was increased in 1979 after the seizure of the Great Mosque in Mecca by a group of tribal *ikhwan*. Alienated and left behind by the modernization of the country, they believed they had found a messiah foretold for the turn of the Muslim lunar-calendar century, the year 1400. The Saudi monarchy flushed them out two weeks later, but only after nearly four hundred people were killed and the weakness of the security forces was amply demonstrated when foreign and non-Muslim special forces had to be called in to help. Angawi at one point flew over the precincts with the prince who was minister of interior, and was for the first time truly appreciated for his unique knowledge of what lay underneath and around the mosque. But the monarchy was so rattled by this threat to its authority from its core constituency that it essentially adopted the fundamentalist ideology of the attackers. The relative freedoms of the 1970s ended, throwing into reverse the development of areas of life like hotel restaurants and swimming pools where men and women had increasingly been allowed to mingle. The long illness of the king, and resulting brittle weakness in the royal family, pushed the royals farther behind their Wahhabi protective shield.

A quarter century later, Angawi believed it would still take much longer to "build institutions that will take us from being a tribe to being a country." He wanted to bring different opinions into the open, to give young people a wider choice, since he believed they now faced an impossible choice between Wahhabi fundamentalism or an utterly Westernized lifestyle. This lack of pluralism meant Saudi society was polarized, intolerant, and dangerous.

The Wahhabis say, " 'al-Qaeda is not us,' and it's believable. But for me it's the difference between Marlboro and Marlboro Light," Angawi said.

"How can you get past the whole culture of denial?" I asked, meaning the way many of his countrymen, shocked by the participation of fifteen Saudis in the September 11 attacks, refused to believe that Muslims could have been responsible, or that it could have anything to do with the xenophobic intolerance of Wahhabi Islam.

"The government has opened the door to change. Some are pushing to get in. Others are pushing to keep the door closed," he said. "Some people concentrate on women or the constitution. I'm focused on Mecca and Medina. I'm the heart specialist. It is the heart of the Muslim world. I don't mind what body it's in."

Angawi led me to a desk inlaid with mother-of-pearl on which he kept his laptop computer. We sat side by side as he clicked through to a PowerPoint presentation. He started with a striking set of images that moved from Saudi zealots raising their arms to cheer as they dynamited the minaret of a shrine near Medina. The second showed the giant monumental stone Buddhas of Bamiyan in Afghanistan just before they were blown to bits by the Taliban, with whom the Saudis had many links. A third pictured the World Trade Center engulfed in flames.

"My point is, shouldn't we be learning to think before blowing everything up? Intolerance of diversity is due to a monopoly of religious opinion, and that has to end," Angawi said. "We can't beat terrorism, because its roots go back so far. I keep telling them [the princes], if you don't allow other points of view to be discussed, our huge numbers of unemployed youth will face only two choices: to become fanatics or to reject religion completely."

"How many people have you shown this to?"

"It's probably in the thousands now. They are students, teachers. It keeps evolving. I keep going. Sometimes, in private, people from a very high level come. But they don't want other people to know that they've seen it," he said. "People always cry when they see it. I do too."

Angawi's iconic struggle for a pluralistic Saudi religious culture made a great *Journal* story, but I puzzled over the underlying question: Did it represent hope for the future or mourning for a lost past? Saudi Arabia's liberal class seemed small and diffuse. A reappraisal of how the country should be run that started during the oil price slump of the late 1990s slackened when a new tidal wave of oil money arrived in the 2000s, giving the authoritarianism of the ruling Saudi dynasty a new lease on life.

Even among educated Saudis, there was no consensus that someone like Angawi was right in his battle to preserve the past. As in many places in the Middle East, what is old has for a long time reminded people only of backwardness and poverty.

"This policy of razing the past makes me think of all those old pre-Islamic poems we used to have to read about leaving nothing behind but the ash of the campfire!" I said as we finally said good-bye.

"A desert mentality dictates that everything you have should fit either into your mind or onto your camel," Angawi said. "They want to preserve the letter of the past but remove all physical trace of our heritage."

Before I left, Angawi led me on a tour of his palace. One by one he pointed to a three-hundred-year-old door, knobs, carved stone flourishes, and wooden windows that had been salvaged by him or his friends from Meccan houses bulldozed for redevelopment. In one graceful niche, I noticed that he had given pride of place to an ancient-looking block of stone. Instinctively, I knelt down and put the palms of my hands onto its rough-hewn surface. I wondered if, after Angawi's excavations, the whole of the house where Muhammad had once lived was really left to be buried under the marble. I looked at Angawi with the question in my eyes. He smiled. As I pressed my hands down I felt the energy of my own Meccan moment.

●　　　●　　　●

In the weeks that followed, I asked every Saudi I met about Mecca. In the capital, Riyadh, a leading lawyer told me it was hard to feel loyal to the ancient sites because so many of them had been destroyed and rebuilt over the years. A politics professor felt alienated by the loss of the old Meccan quarters and the arrival of American franchises—despite Saudi prickliness over U.S. backing of Israel, the cultural warmth of the American-Saudi relationship means that pilgrims coming out of the gates of the Great Mosque can be greeted by Kentucky Fried Chicken and Pizza Hut—but he could see no alternative to the modernization of the city. The chief of the chamber of commerce preferred the new marble being laid everywhere to the narrow old streets. He didn't want unnecessary ties to history to hold back the chance for his members to make money.

Suleyman al-Hatlan, a writer so literate in English he could get commentaries into American papers, thought modern Mecca was an unhappy "holy Manhattan." But when we met in the lobby of an ultramodern Saudi hotel, reclining on the cushions of a carpeted faux Oriental corner that such establishments always seemed to have, he didn't think his views counted for much at home.

"In my family I have no credibility. I'm the Western-educated infidel," he joked as we bit into the succulent dates on offer for guests. "My cousin didn't finish school but goes to the mosque five times a day. Whenever he speaks, it's him they listen to."

Later that day I sat talking to one of the liberals who'd been invited by the royals to have a grand discussion to broaden the common ground among Sunnis, Shia, and Sufi-leaning clerics in the kingdom. Such meetings at first generated excitement and hope for change, but this gave way to cynicism. All the talk failed to bring progress on the road to reform or real Islamic unity in diversity.

"It makes sense for the regime to choose the conservatives as partners. The conservatives ask for control only of education and mosques. They don't get in the way of foreign policy, money, anything else," the liberal said bitterly. "In fact, since September 11, the monarchy has actually increased the budgetary payment to religious schooling. I found the royal decree on the Internet. They think liberals are nothing, have no power. And they are right."

One warm Riyadh evening I went to discuss the way ahead with Khalil Kordi, not a prince but high in the outer courtyards of royal life. He took me down to the den in his mansion in a suburb and fired up the electrical coil on his hubble-bubble pipe, a vast contraption that was taller than I was. A television screen filled most of one wall. He caught my eyes wandering.

"I like rich people," he told me calmly in highly educated English. "I'm making an exception for you."

Kordi shared an attractive trait in Saudi Arabia that in private, and sometimes even in public, many people retain the frank openness of their bedouin Arab forefathers. He was pushing for the Wahhabi ideologues to loosen their grip on Saudi life, but, unlike Angawi, only to have easier access to a Western lifestyle.

"You can never neutralize religion, but you can liberalize the way we think of it. We are not a society of saints. I'd like to see religion only in the mosque," he said, taking another puff. "But this isn't possible in the short run."

Diplomats weren't much more optimistic, despite the Saudis' constant talk of reform. Sipping fruit juice at a party thrown by a reformist prince, the German ambassador told me he'd seen it all before during his postings to the Soviet Union.

"It seems so daring when you read about it in the papers, but reality is different," he said. "They compare the 'best of Islam' with the 'best of the West.' But they don't compare the Saudi reality with the Western reality."

I told him of my latest trip to the desert, where I'd stayed in a Saudi town where the real world was alive and well. I met the police chief when he popped around to the local Internet whiz to get a new bootleg card to decode the satellite sex channels. My friends drove me past a gypsy brothel on the outskirts of town. The local population was pragmatic and viewed working life as what happened between long religious holidays and the never-ending obligations to one's family.

An American envoy joined us and pointed out that nobody could expect liberalism to flourish when two-thirds of the subjects at Saudi universities were Islam-oriented, and that one-third of the students were at all-religious universities. I had toured the most famous of them on the outskirts of the capital, feeling desolate at the stark, blank-faced architecture favored by the Wahhabis. Such education kept young people nominally busy but seemed no way to construct a modern state.

I tried and failed to compare it to my own "Christian" education. More than half of my father's generation studied Latin and ancient Greek at university, which, on the surface, seemed as otherworldly as looking at life through the prism of Islamic theology. I myself took eight years of Latin and five of ancient Greek, and we marched in military-style platoons into chapel twice a day at my primary school. My secondary school had been founded along religious lines, too, as the choir school attached to a great abbey, and, five hundred years later, chapel attendance was still obligatory. But it was not like Saudi Arabia, with its lack of debate and narrow, rote-learning approach. Very few of my contemporaries saw the religious side as more than cultural background noise. Classical Greek and Latin embraced a huge spectrum of philosophy. We knew and appreciated the diverse real subjects that we studied. Saudi schoolchildren, however, took an extravagant revenge on their far more blinkered education. To celebrate the end of each school year, they poured into the streets and dumped their schoolbooks into garbage containers or made sacrificial piles on the roadway and set fire to them.

"In the Arab world, books are written in Egypt, published in Beirut, read in

Iraq, and burned in Saudi Arabia," quipped a Saudi friend over coffee one day, adding a new last line to an old cliché about Arabic written culture. "They teach us to hate knowledge. At the same time, there is big confusion about the outside world, how to deal with new things. You see a woman wearing a bikini on TV but never in real life. We're supposed to be rushing into business, but commerce is a bureaucratic nightmare. So we live in a sea of helplessness and cynicism."

In the coastal, cosmopolitan city of Jeddah, a powerless resentment seethes against domination by the dour Wahhabi Islam of the desert highlands. Women wear looser veils and can be found smoking hubble-bubble pipes at seafront open-air cafés. Young men can leap out of their cars in traffic jams to dance madly to music on car loudspeaker systems turned up to the max. A bank clerk whispered how he had smuggled works of mystical poetry into the kingdom. In the office of one publishing magnate, Hussein Shobokshi, I was astonished to find the walls filled from floor to ceiling with drawings and calligraphy in honor of Sufi mysticism and whirling dervishes. At least he appreciated Angawi's efforts.

"He's seen as an eccentric, but he's got respect. He's breaking a taboo," Shobokshi said. "A singular approach to religion has cost us a lot, led to extremism and suffocated our people."

I went back to Angawi to discuss people's reactions. He thought that the older elite, people like himself and Shobokshi, were preserving liberal traditions at home and passing them on within the family. This tendency, however, was weakened by being individual, not communal. He was doing his best to spread his own approach and invited me to one of his weekly discussion groups for young Saudis, dealing with such subjects as the mercy of God, individual freedom, and the national heritage.

We met in his house, in one of those rooms that set the Middle East apart—the meeting room, or majlis, where all gather with their backs to the walls, whether in a simple mud-brick dwelling in the mountains of Kurdistan, a reed-bundle cathedral in the marshes of southern Iraq, or the gold-curled chairs in the palace of a Persian Gulf prince. Angawi preferred modest wooden benches with intricate woodwork. He was joined by one or two older university teachers. Most of the younger people who came were professionals. Two-thirds wore the national dress of Saudi Arabia, the white robe, meticulously starched, with a white cloth over the head. The other third wore versions of Western casual clothing, although in distinctively Saudi style, big and loose, and once again, pressed and starched by their Asian servants. One wore a suit. Another concession was made to the traditions of Saudi Arabia: All those who came were men.

One of the older men present called the majlis to order with some words of introduction and a reading of one key house rule—respect for the rulers, even when criticizing. The agenda included freedom, education, the Islamic heritage, interpretations of Islam, and the search for a new balance between stability and change. The floor was opened for debate. The first intervention came from a bearded youth.

"The link between all this is mercy. Our slogan should be that we Muslims are merciful, with everyone. Our view of mercy is sick. Finding this link again would link us to God!"

It was true, I thought. Despite the Western view of an aggressive Islam, "mercy" is the most repeated word in the Koran and gives Muslim life as a whole its most common phrase, the invocation traditionally rendered in English as "In the name of God, the merciful, the loving-kind." In 2008, exiled Iranian writer Kader Abdolah, fed up with being confronted with the Koran's most warlike lines by his new compatriots in the Netherlands, went so far as to retranslate the Muslim holy book. His gentler take on the invocation: "In the name of God, who is loving, who gives, who forgives."

An unhappy-looking older member of the majlis, Osama, didn't buy it. He said he was still waiting for a more moderate Islam to appear. Angawi stirred in his corner, telling the gathering that mercy was a beacon to the traditions of the Prophet.

"First we have to have mercy on ourselves, though," commented Esam, a marketing executive with the multinational Unilever.

"The last meeting we agreed that freedom was Islam, Islam is freedom. Is this freedom a dream or is it chaos?" broke in a student called Tariq. "People look at us as unfree and bound by rules. But even airing these questions is half of the solution."

Juma, a bearded youth, murmured through an obscure philosophical point based on the orthography of the Arabic word for "freedom." "Do angels have freedom of will?" he asked. "Or mountains?"

The pragmatic part of my brain was losing its grip on the meeting. Angawi too sensed a need to anchor the conversation to his favorite theme.

"Remember, the first universities in Islam were in Mecca. There was freedom of thought and expression. People would go and ask something from everybody. One of my goals is to get back the variety of Mecca, its original balance. In the past twenty-five years it's become just one view. It's not that the view is wrong, but the fact is that there is just one view is wrong."

The older Osama reckoned that Saudi Arabia was now far more open, influenced by the more permissive sheikhdoms of the Persian Gulf. People were now freer in the choice of a spouse, divorce, and access to five hundred channels of international satellite television. He remembered that when he left Saudi Arabia in the 1970s—when there were just four to five hours a day of television—he was overwhelmed by the women and freedoms of Egypt.

Change was indeed in the air. In a sharp reversal of the old days when Saudis tended to look down on foreigners as the hired help, I'd just met my first Saudi bellhop, overweight and unhappily squeezed into his hotel uniform, but nevertheless determined to ask me if he could be of service. Farther afield, I'd even gone down to the bottom of a Saudi gold mine and met Saudi Arabians who worked like anyone else.

At that point, the call for prayer sounded out. All shed their slippers and formed an impromptu line. Even the servant who kept us fueled with tea joined in. Angawi led them through the prayer in a firm, fine voice. Here was a version of the egalitarian Islam that had seemed noble to me as a student. But, as an agnostic of no fixed address, such public displays always left me feeling uncomfortable, particularly since I was the only one of the group sitting to one side, not taking part in this act of devotion.

Afterward, participants took up the thread of the conversation as if there had been no interruption, but it didn't lead anywhere. Conservative and liberal lines emerged: The conservatives thought moral standards were degenerating, people were not following the tradition of Muhammad, people were copying the West. The modernists hoped for more rationality and innovation. But if this debate represented the front line of intellectual change in Saudi Arabia, reform was going to take a long time.

The *Journal* enthusiastically ran my story about Angawi, rightly profiling him as a plucky and admirable intellectual taking on the Saudi establishment. The front page even took the highly unusual step of printing a photo instead of a line drawing, the one showing Wahhabis cheering as they blew up a minaret of a shrine. I suspected that I had changed Americans' existing impression that Saudi Arabia was full of Islamist crazies only insofar as they would now think it was full of Islamist crazies mad enough to blow up their own religious buildings. My job was to dig out stories that were strange, unique, and true, but since Americans had no idea of the everyday reality of a country like Saudi Arabia, I feared they would take my narrative of the extraordinary as the normal state of affairs.

10. DINING WITH AL-QAEDA

A Saudi Missionary and the "Wonderful Boys" of September 11

If a serpent appears to love you, wear him as a necklace.
—ARABIC PROVERB

I liked many things about visiting Riyadh, and near the top of my list of favorite places there was the Khozama Hotel. It had been built for an earlier oil boom, when tastes were simpler and being a few stories high was grand enough in the Saudi Arabian capital. It always felt interesting, familiar, and safe, with beds and furniture fitted at an eccentric angle to the walls, a staff from all over Asia, a lobby full of idle Saudi coffee sippers, and a swimming pool nobody else seemed to use but me. Indeed, after twenty-five years of shuttling around the Middle East, my social base became so fragmented that its manager ended up being one of the only people who, for a while, sent me an old-fashioned birthday card every year. By now, of course, the hotel was dwarfed by the smoked glass luxury towers of the new millennium. But the Khozama still had a well-tended lawn where guests could eat outside. To cool the heat on summer evenings, discreet black pipes slung around the outer edge of the dining area sent a delicate mist of water floating over the tables.

Two months after the September 11 attacks on America, I returned to the Khozama on a mission for the *Journal* to try to explain Saudi Arabia and its link to al-Qaeda. The kingdom had become a heart of darkness as the home to fifteen of the nineteen suicide hijackers, whose catastrophic mission had suddenly propelled the Middle East to the front and center of the American consciousness. It was

Ramadan, the Muslim month of dawn-to-dusk fasting, and the daily life I shared with Saudis revolved around the evening feasts. At the Khozama, sideboards groaned with tropical fruit, spit-roasted lamb, and urns of sweet rice pudding known as *Umm Ali,* or Ali's Mum. The gap between perception and reality would be tough to bridge this time, I could tell.

In Saudi Arabia, like much of the Middle East, people had mixed feelings about the September 11 attacks. Almost all regretted the shocking loss of life. But there was also a widespread satisfaction that America had at last tasted some of the mayhem so common in the region. Some hoped that the moment of "why did they attack us?" introspection would turn into a rethink of U.S. policy. There was something else as well. When I left my hotel window open to listen to the Friday preacher's amplified voice, I was surprised at the raw anger that burst out of the loudspeakers. After all, it came from the mosque of the Faisaliyeh, think tank and cultural center of the most liberal and intellectual wing of the royal family. The prayer leader went on and on about the many Koranic injunctions against non-Muslims, pointing out that even the Muslim lord's prayer, the *fatiha,* explicitly underlines the gulf between Muslims and Jews ("those against whom one is angry") and between Muslims and Christians ("those who have been led astray"). I could clearly hear the congregation's reaction, their voices picked up by the mosque microphones, murmuring in fervent unison, "God, please smash America. Please smash Britain."

This was not the Islam that I had tuned into as a twenty-year-old student of Arabic in Cairo. I had skimmed over the long, tiresome chapters at the beginning of the Koran that deal with community administration, theology, and urging the faithful to fight against the Jews and polytheist Arabs, who opposed the Prophet Muhammad in seventh-century Mecca and Medina. I preferred the short inspirational chapters at the end. I committed them to memory, along with the *fatiha* and the call to prayer. Some have always stayed with me, like the chapter known as "Power":

> *The Koran we sent down on the night of power*
> *Do you know what it is, understand that great force?*
> *It's a fateful night better than one thousand months*
> *On that night descend angels and Spirit as one*
> *With the future in hand and empowered by their Lord*
> *Spreading peace as all wait for the break of dawn.*

Even though I found some words hard to understand, or perhaps because I could bend what I did understand to my own taste, the verses of these parts of the Koran swirled like mystical poetry for me. Indeed, trying to set down a pragmatic English "meaning" detracted from the impact of its gorgeous Arabic cadences. It never occurred to me to take its strictures any more seriously than one or two favorite Christian hymns. Only later did it sink in how Muslims took seriously the constant self-references of the Koran that state that this is the word of God. Indeed, many Muslims also believe that because the Koran is in Arabic, God speaks only Arabic. For all these reasons, there can never really be a translation of the Koran, only renderings of it.

There remains, however, the problem of the provenance of the actual Arabic text. In the Prophet Muhammad's day people had well-trained memories, but of course different versions soon began to multiply. So nearly twenty years after the Prophet's death, the third caliph recalled all extant versions of the Koran, written haphazardly on skins, parchment, and even bones. He created an authorized version of the Koran, which has stayed almost unchanged to today.

To me, the idea that humans could record and transmit something with 100 percent accuracy was dubious—journalism offers daily proof that whenever anything is said, everyone hears something slightly different. It seemed crazy that anyone could be sure enough of the text of the Koran to base a rigid and total manual for life on it. And that was before trying to tease out all those shifting meanings within the text. Non-Muslim skeptics and Muslims debate at least one hundred significant areas of apparent contradiction within the Koran, about the prohibition of wine, the punishment for adultery, the Koranic creation story, or Islam's perception of its overlap with Christianity or Judaism. Indeed, the Koran shares so many stories of Jewish and Christian prophets that Islam was viewed by some medieval scholars in Europe as a heretical Christian sect. Yet today's anti-Islamic movements seize on warlike Koranic phrases to prove it cannot be a peaceful world religion, as in the film *Fitna* by Dutch right-wing politician Geert Wilders. But the Koran's violent side is shared with parts of the Old Testament, and Christians too use their religion for warlike purposes, as pointed out by a Saudi who posted a YouTube film response to *Fitna* showing, for instance, German Nazis at Christian prayer.

Still, Muslim fundamentalist like the Faisaliyeh's Friday preacher do believe that Islam and Islamic law can exist as a unified religious ideology without the need to compromise with the real world. Indeed, any cleric, state official, or militant can take the Koranic text and claim both universality and infallibility for his interpretation of it. This fits with the Middle East's tendency to absolutism. It thus opens Islam up to abuse by authoritarian regimes, their opponents, and rogue elements like al-Qaeda. Real-life Islam is tailored to political and national jurisdictions. For all the claims of countries like Iran, Pakistan, and Saudi Arabia to have based their systems on the same Islamic law, they are manifestly very different in doctrine and practice.

The problem I faced as I pondered how to unpick the complex relationship between al-Qaeda, the Saudis' Wahhabi ideology, and Islam was that the Islamists and their enemies had convinced many Americans that Islam was this monolithic faith. Furthermore, many Americans thought that Islam was the main reason that Middle Easterners in general, and Saudi Arabia in particular, hated the United States. I, on the other hand, was sure that anti-Americanism was based far more on the extraordinary, decades-long bias in U.S. foreign policy in support of Israel and all its doings. There was also the matter of U.S. support for oppressive Middle Eastern autocrats. Saudi princes, for instance, backed by America to rule a country with 25 percent of the world's oil reserves, could be greedy, corrupt, and unjust. The Saudi king was clearly a loyal U.S. friend, customer, and oil supplier in the region, like the rulers of Egypt, Kuwait, Jordan, and elsewhere. America called these regimes "moderate," apparently because they allied themselves with Washington. Osama bin Laden and his September 11 attacks had, however, exposed once again the fact that the populations of Saudi Arabia and other Middle Eastern "moderate" states strongly opposed many American policies.

Reasons for popular frustration were not hard to find. Saudi life could mix the glitter of Dubai and the clutter of Egypt. Poorer Saudis' hopes were fixed on the lottery of charity, which meant waiting in long lines outside the lavish reception halls of top princes, as now in the holy feast days of Ramadan. Cities suffered from neglect

Boys dressed up as soldiers at a 1985 demonstration in Tehran. Families often bring children up strictly in the Middle East, making some more susceptible to authoritarianism, fundamentalism—and occasional wild acts of rebellion. (*Hugh Pope*)

and mismanagement. In Jeddah, the Red Sea coastal highway had crushed the porous substructure of the plain, so when it rained hard in winter, whole suburbs could flood. And because a prince had pocketed the money for a wastewater system, sewage then floated up to the surface. What was normally done with effluent was hardly more attractive. One day I drove up into the mountains behind Jeddah in a crawling convoy of cesspit pump trucks, which then lined up to spew their contents into a river of stink that ran down a dry desert wadi toward the heart of Arabia.

Perhaps, I decided, I could show the *Journal*'s readers where September 11 came from through a story on the Saudi opposition, of which al-Qaeda was a radical offshoot. Paradoxically, the most potent criticism of this most fundamentalist of Middle Eastern regimes has always come from the ultra-Orthodox Islamists. Such opposition had surged in 1990–91 after "Christian" U.S. troops arrived to protect the Saudi status quo and to help drive the Iraqis out of neighboring Kuwait. Some Saudis perceived it as an occupation of the holy Muslim territory of the Arabian Peninsula. Religious sheikhs took the lead in criticizing the monarchy as little better than a gang of infidels. In response, by the mid-1990s the monarchy had jailed nearly four hundred opposition clerics. Long skilled in handling such matters, it gradually won most of them back into the establishment with flattery, mosque sinecures, and money. None of those whom I telephoned from my hotel room were ready to talk to me. Indeed, public silence was a condition of their freedom.

There was one notable holdout, however, whom a Saudi dissident in London suggested I try to contact: Sheikh Said bin Zuair. His son Saad answered the phone. After a week of conversations that lowered his suspicions of me, Saad agreed to receive me. I delayed my flight home for a day. Soon the Khozama's limousine was nosing through a middle-class suburb of Riyadh, following Saad's directions to the Zuair home. He'd invited me after the family had broken their Ramadan fast. It was nearly dark.

The house lay across the street from one of Wahhabism's rectangular mosques, whose straight lines are so different from, say, the domed baroque of Turkish places of worship. Bin Zuair was previously the imam of this mosque, as well as a professor at the equally austere university of Imam Saud on the outskirts of Riyadh. Saad ushered me into one of the main guest rooms and invited me to sit on one of the cushioned benches that lined the edge of the room. The concrete-built home felt large and bare.

I may not have agreed with the fundamentalist ideology of the Zuair family, but anyone who dares defy a Middle Eastern state deserves respect. About twenty-five years old, Saad kept flicking his red-checked headdress over the shoulder of his white gown.

He told me that his father, like many of the other Saudi preachers, had not gone into opposition over the question of U.S. troops in particular. The real reason was linked to Israel. It happened after the chief Muslim dignitary of the kingdom, Sheikh Abdulaziz bin Baz endorsed U.S. moves to make peace between Israel and Arabs.

"My father was one of those who remonstrated and got Baz to say that the peace should be only 'temporary,'" Saad said. "The security forces came to take him away after the dawn prayer in March 1995."

"Were you there too? Did you try to stop them?"

"I was very sad, but my father was very confident, laughing. He didn't show anything. He was as cool as an Englishman. The next day, they came at about 2 A.M., with a female officer to be with the women of the house. They inspected the library and the other rooms, they confiscated some books. Then we didn't hear anything for a month. When he called at last, we gathered around the phone. We wanted to visit, but he refused it, to start with. We called him every week, then every fortnight, then every month."

A knock on the door announced the arrival of a servant bearing a beaked brass pot of aromatic green Arabic coffee, which Saad poured for me in sips until I wiggled the little porcelain cup to indicate I'd reached my limit. I relished the bitter elegance of the taste, such a surprise compared to its murky texture. The caffeine made my head sing.

"Was your father ever charged with any crime?" I asked.

"The government never gave a reason why they took him in. I think the problem was that he was meeting together with other imams. They were popular. The government may have feared a revolution. The imams began objecting to the politics of the government, things like usury, advertising."

"Did he oppose the rule of the Sauds?"

"He didn't criticize the royal family directly. In fact, he had a good relationship with the crown prince, would meet with him for two or three hours at a time. He would criticize the monarchy's performance; the prince would listen, and accept the criticism, or say my father had misunderstood what happened."

Bin Zuair had been locked up with other Islamist dissidents in Hayir prison outside Riyadh. As the years went by, pressure mounted on the group to recant. The government asked them to write out their demands, and they listed things like freedom of expression and political reform. Some won their release by signing promises not to oppose the regime. Soon only the toughest four were left. Then the three others won their freedom with a verbal promise not to talk without government permission. Only bin Zuair remained in prison, refusing, as then Saudi chief of intelligence, Prince Turki al-Faisal, put it to me later, "all clemency."

"My father didn't enter into debate with the government. He'd say, 'I don't want anything from you. I haven't attacked you. I haven't committed any crime. You can't ask me for anything.' It's like a psychological war," Saad said.

Sometimes the regime left bin Zuair free to use the phone, to talk to his family for an hour at a time if he wanted. He was allowed to move freely around the prison. At other times they'd put him under pressure. Punishments included the forced retirement of bin Zuair from state employment. As a pension, he was offered a half salary for his twenty years' service.

"He said he would take nothing from them. He wanted to challenge them," Saad said proudly. "My two elder brothers are both teachers and they pay for everything we need."

"Can you still talk to him?"

"The government told the other three sheikhs on a Tuesday that they would be released on the next Saturday but ordered them not to tell anyone. But my father told us anyway. The government got angry. They said, 'Now you can only use the phone for five minutes at a time.' So my father called us up and said, 'I'm well. I won't talk to you again.' That was two years ago."

Bin Zuair was building moral stature. In detention, he had started reading the autobiography of South Africa's Nelson Mandela, and busily annotating it. The war of nerves made the state uncomfortable.

"They're an Islamic state, but they're imprisoning a sheikh. Our government won't stand down. The prison governor called in my father, saying, 'You have to get in touch with your family, it's not right.' The governor suggested allowing us to visit again. My father said, 'I don't want my family to see me in jail, they'll be searched, and I don't want to be watched over. Hire me a place outside the prison, and I'll think about it.'"

In the end, the governor agreed to offer a building inside the outer prison wall, and that anyone who asked could come and see the sheikh without being searched.

"Visits went on freely for seventy days. At eleven P.M. one night they called him and said, 'Write what you think of the prison, are you happy, do you need anything. But if you don't write, we'll stop the visits.' 'I didn't ask for these visits,' he said. They said, 'We have orders, we have to implement them.' They came to us that same night and sent us out. Since then we haven't heard from him. Of course we do hear from secret sources that he is well and his morale is high," Saad said.

The Saudi authorities continued to target the bin Zuair family. Saad was arrested a few months later in Riyadh airport, in July 2002, on his way to put his father's case on the al-Jazeera satellite television station. He was held incommunicado for three years. His brother Mubarek was arrested in 2004 and held for ten months. Their father was released in March 2003, rearrested in 2004 for speaking to al-Jazeera, released in 2005 in the traditional general amnesty for the enthronement of a new Saudi king, then rearrested in 2007. Amnesty International and Human Rights Watch kept media attention on the injustice of his case.

When Saad came back from taking a break for evening prayers in the mosque, he remarked in passing that the preacher was still calling for the congregation to raise money for al-Qaeda. Osama bin Laden also called for the release of bin Zuair in an audiotape made public in February 2003.

Was there a connection between the bin Zuairs and bin Laden? Were the bin Zuairs a front for al-Qaeda terrorism? Or was bin Laden publicly citing the case of bin Zuair, a widely respected Islamist, in an attempt to put a polish of legitimacy on his grisly record?

I wanted to find out more. At the end of my conversation with Saad, I had asked if he could introduce me to anyone from al-Qaeda. He said he might know someone. After a couple of calls, he invited me round again to meet a special guest the next evening, my last in Riyadh. He'd pick me up with my luggage and drop me at the airport afterward.

Saad took me back to the hotel in the family's battered Toyota pickup. Navigating the wide freeways of Riyadh, he played a cassette recording of his father's old sermons. In a passionate, fine tenor voice, his father railed against sin, women singers, Western-style advertising, and popular television programs. It wasn't anything illegal, and my own high-minded English father, who forbade his family to watch commercial television, would have agreed with many of the targets of his disapproval. But anger filled the sheikh's voice as he said nothing has validity that isn't strictly based on the Koran, or the *hadith*, the traditional accounts of the behavior and sayings of the Prophet Muhammad and his companions. He warned against Satan and his soldiers and the enemies of Islam.

Back then, even though it was just a couple of months after September 11, it didn't occur to me to worry much about risks to my life from al-Qaeda in Saudi Arabia. I was far more scared of the wildly erratic Saudi driving. I still believed in the cloak of innocence, the idea that my reporting represented an honest, universal right to know. Every voice, color, and smell helped build up the story of a situation. No one person could ever tell me the whole truth. The trick was to keep moving, to explore as much as possible of the terrain of a subject, to win confidences. Sometimes it felt like making a meal of crumbs instead of baking a cake.

On some reporting trips I liked it when a colleague or a fixer helped me find my bearings or kept me company, but in places where I felt confident and spoke the language, like Saudi Arabia, I usually worked alone. It was easier to strike the necessary intense rapport with an interlocutor that way. I tried to cast my net wide, from princes in their palaces to random conversations in bazaars, from bedouin with their pickups and corrugated iron shack camps to ambassadors in their grand reception rooms.

I felt safe enough in 2001 in Saudi Arabia, a functioning state. Despite the multiple Saudi connections to the attacks, I didn't fear al-Qaeda personally. Bin Laden's strategy seemed aimed at the United States in general, and, sometimes indirectly, at the government of Saudi Arabia. He used the media in an established manner, and at that point there had been no attacks on Western individuals in the name of the organization. Nevertheless, a later period between 2003 and 2007 would produce a rash of murders of foreigners by al-Qaeda in the Arabian Peninsula.

I trust my instincts, and Saad Zuair seemed to be a moral person who wouldn't have anything to do with terrorism himself. His gown was full-length, not the shortened version favored by the Islamists to imitate the companions of the Prophet and to make easier the ritual washing of the feet before prayer. As he arranged the meeting, he described the person whom he had contacted as a *da'i,* a caller-to-the-faith, in other words, a missionary. When Saad arrived in the hotel parking lot in his pickup the next evening, I thought nothing of loading my bags in the back and setting off with him. Only later did I realize that I had told nobody where I was going.

This time we entered a different reception room. Suddenly, the missionary made a dramatic entrance: no handshake, no real introduction, and no name. He wore a youthful and untrimmed beard—I learned that he was just twenty-four years old—and a robe that was not only short in the fundamentalist Wahhabi fashion, but gray, a signal of dissent against the starched white thobe, the flowing, floor-length shirt that is the Saudi national dress.

The first flurry of greetings over, we sat side by side on a cushioned bench. Saad sat down opposite. A mild, fleshy fellow came with the missionary and sat to one side. In my most correct Arabic, I told the missionary of my interest in telling readers in America about al-Qaeda's motives and goals.

"I know that Western media seems distant and hostile, but that's because your voice is not heard. People are not familiar with your perspective. If you can speak to me, I can make your viewpoint known."

He hadn't really engaged in the conversation yet, and I had no real idea of exactly who he was. Then he stated something that had clearly been on his mind for the past few minutes.

"Shouldn't I kill you?"

"That's quite unnecessary, I assure you!" I replied without thinking, giving a calm and pleasant laugh. I kept looking into his eyes. With a twinge in my belly, I realized that he was serious.

I still found it hard to believe that I was in dangerous territory. Word games and political joshing are common currency in the Arab world. This certainly wasn't the scenario that I had imagined for myself since friends began being kidnapped in 1980s Lebanon: burly toughs, a journey in a car trunk, and an unpleasant concrete cell. This missionary was slight and thoughtful. I looked across at his heavy friend. He appeared somehow too soft and young to be an executioner. I sipped at my glass of ice-cold water.

"You are an infidel, one of those-whom-it-is-obligatory-to-smite!" the missionary continued, as if he was debating with himself. I responded in kind. He was twenty years younger than me, and I felt he was out of order.

"Not at all. The Prophet Muhammad, peace be upon him, quite clearly stated that those who have permission to be among the believers must have safe passage. Besides, I am a guest in this house."

The missionary waved away such an appeal to tradition. He focused on the Islamic argument.

"What permission?" he snapped.

I looked askance at Saad. He looked blankly back at me. This wasn't going quite as planned. I had a visa, of course, but to get into the country more quickly I had arranged it privately through a Saudi businessman. Did I really have permission? I wondered. Or was I just assuming my right as a Westerner to go where I pleased in the world? Or was I counting on the fact that I had called the Saudi Ministry of Information once in a gesture of politeness? There could be no help from them now, anyway. It was evening and all Saudi bureaucrats fade away by midafternoon.

"The Koran states, quite clearly, that it is the duty of the believer to kill intruders and spies."

My disbelief left my instincts intact. If this was bargaining, why then, I would bargain. The first rule of that was to stay in control, not to lose face or cool, as if it was about a matter not directly related to me.

"Why take the Koran literally? How can you be sure of every word?"

"I've memorized the Koran. All my friends have too. It's the word of God. I think that maybe even talking to you is to leave the sunna, the tradition of the Prophet. Then I'll become a *mubdi* [one who innovates]."

He drew a long face at this dreadful prospect. I hid my happiness at having innovated a more congenial subject to pursue. I leaned forward with the urgent interest of an eager student.

"That's right! Exactly. The traditions of the Prophet. Do they have the same weight? How many have you memorized? How many should one know?"

"Oh, two thousand is fine, but forty thousand commands real respect."

"Extraordinary. People in the West have lost their ability to memorize," I said.

"Yes, you should never use your head, never use your own reason."

"What about *ijtihad*? Doesn't that give one the right to draw one's own conclusions?"

Ijtihad, or rational deduction, was one of the few things I remembered from the mind-numbing lessons on the history of Islam at Oxford. For a brief period eight hundred years ago, one group advocated the use of reason to explain the Islamic revelations. They hadn't lasted long, but it seemed to me like a glimmer of intellectual life in a long tradition of dull repetition and authoritarian crushing of dissent.

"*Ijtihad?* We don't need that. Everything we require comes from God and the traditions."

I tried to keep the conversation on such well-established areas of neutral discussion. But he kept coming back to the question of killing me. It made me uncomfortable.

"So, I'm a Christian, fine. But the Koran says that Muslims must respect people of the book."

The missionary paused. His light build gave him a look of a man of the hills. He'd already proudly let slip that his family originally came from Yemen, like Osama bin Laden's, and he lived in the province of Asir, on the Saudi border with Yemen, like four of the September 11 hijackers.

"Well, Islamic law takes a position on whether it's permitted or not, that is, can you go to the infidel and kill him?" the missionary continued.

Saad was studying his hands in his lap. I realized that however decent he might be, if push came to shove, he was not going to stand up for me.

"The priesthood divides the infidels into two groups, those who pay taxes, and those with whom Muslims have a treaty," the missionary went on. "But actually the infidels are all one. They will become Muslims, through God's mercy."

I twisted the water glass in my hand and looked seriously into his soft black eyes. It was vital to coax him out of whatever he was thinking, before anything irreversible took place. I was searching my memory for arguments and suddenly had an idea.

"Look, I have this written treaty of which you speak. I have permission from the sultan of this land to be here. He is the guardian of the two holy shrines. So I can be here and not be killed," I said. I was searching my memory for something about foreign ambassadors to Muhammad who got safe passage but couldn't remember where it was written down, so I winged it. "The Koran and the traditions say I should not be harmed."

"What proof do you have?"

"Here," I said, pulling my passport carefully out of my pocket and paging through it as if it, too, was holy scripture. "Here. The king's firman, his royal permission."

Getting a visa to the Kingdom of Saudi Arabia is not easy, so my aplomb was not entirely out of place. It was a long and elaborate sticker, with a picture of me and details like the fact that I was a Christian. The missionary read every word of it.

"Indeed, this permit is from the king of Saudi Arabia. But there are some clerics who say the king is illegitimate."

"But the Friday prayers are read in his name."

"That's true," said the missionary. Then, with a proper display of magnanimity: "All right. I can accept that you do have permission to be here."

The drama of our conversation evaporated as if it had never been. His one-man tribunal had passed a not-guilty verdict. All of us felt relieved, including Saad and the missionary's friend. Up until my passing of this mysterious test, they had stayed ominously silent.

"Thanks for your confidence," I said.

"Well, I suppose if we killed Americans like you it would be hard on the religious leaders here," the missionary said generously. "The principle of success is to balance knowledge and jihad [holy war or struggle]. The official religious leaders go too far toward knowledge. But if you go too far toward jihad, you end up like Algeria."

As I led the missionary through his life story, the conversation became almost conspiratorial, the closest I would ever get to the world of the September 11 hijackers. He had studied Islamic theology and was the only one of his brothers who had become religious. He considered that only 20 percent of Saudis were true Wahhabis who imitated the lifestyle of the companions of the Prophet with their short thobes and brushing their teeth with *miswak*, the fibrous ends of a desert bush. Other people were *fussaq*, corrupted. They wanted things like women driving cars.

"Sure, there's nothing wrong in Islam with women driving a car. But it would open the door wider to sin. The rope breaks and anything can happen. It's like petrol and fire."

Such youthful absolutism drew him into the worldwide Wahhabi missionary movement that Saudi Arabians of all kinds supported before 2001. His mother sold her gold bangles so he could go to Chechnya, but he gave her the money back. A seventeen-year-old girl gave him a special Koran, and he arranged for it to go into the pocket of a boy fighter on jihad.

"Young boys came to kiss my hand and beg to go on the jihad," he said. He extracted from the depths of his thobe pocket a photocopied magazine from the mosque, with a picture of Osama bin Laden on the front. "Most of the editorial board is under fifteen," he noted admiringly. "For us the warriors doing jihad are like the aristocracy, the knights. Your aristocracy too are the descendants of people who were brave and who fought."

The missionary's first assignment had been in Baku, in the former Soviet Republic of Azerbaijan. I knew it well and could sympathize with the uphill task he faced in that relatively modern country. He told of his shock at seeing people kissing in a car, the ever-present vodka consumption, and the continual religious complication of sharing a stairwell with four unveiled women neighbors. He'd made only one convert, he admitted, who'd stopped drinking and begun to pray.

Then he discovered Afghanistan, and his life changed. He did three tours of duty there, lasting between one to three months each time, paying his own way and reveling in the way his Saudi Arabian identity and Koranic learning gave him a holy aura with the Afghans. The high point of one tour was giving a Friday sermon in a mosque in Kandahar, in which he told the faithful about the need to stick close to religion and about the great war in progress between Islam and the infidel West.

"The hotel in Afghanistan was very cheap, and they didn't even ask for my passport," he said, his face lighting up. "They said, you're a Muslim, and this is the land of Islam."

"I know. Talking to some Afghans is like drinking water from the purest mountain stream."

"There's two kinds of simplicity, though. One is pure. The other is stupidity, like trying to cut with the wrong end of the knife," he said, demonstrating for my benefit. "They are very poor."

The missionary's frankness and our shared experience of foreign travel made me feel closer to him. But he was pretty naïve.

"I took two hundred *miswak* sticks for cleaning teeth with me. I wanted to teach them the tradition of how Muhammad let his beard grow with just some clipping of the mustache, how one should wash one's elbow joint, the armpits, and the pubic hair," he said. "This is what sets us apart from the animals."

"Did you meet other Arabs there?"

"Yes, I gave lessons to al-Qaeda, in their al-Farouq training camp. There were Saudis, but also Germans, Turks, Australians, an American, a Russian, all sorts."

"And the group that carried out the attacks on America?"

"Yes, them too. I knew several of them. Wonderful boys."

I took a deep breath. Two months after September 11, nobody had found out much about the fifteen hijackers from Saudi Arabia. They didn't seem to be the leaders or pilots, rather cannon fodder chosen because their mere nationality sent a clear political message from Osama bin Laden to the United States and the Saudi king.

I told the missionary that four days after the attacks, I'd been one of the first reporters to reach the house of one of the pilots, Marwan al-Shehhi, in a little-known Persian Gulf emirate called Ras al-Khaimah. It was an unpretentious walled villa amid haphazardly planned, sandy, unpaved streets. The son of the ruler had told me the emirate had sent al-Shehhi on a training program in Germany related to a purchase of naval frigates. It turned out that he failed his German-language exams. He fell in with a radical group that tried to go to fight the Russians in Chechnya but diverted to Afghanistan. Then, still as part of the same group, the relatively privileged, religiously observant young man had turned into the pilot of the United Airlines plane that sliced into the second World Trade Center tower.

We didn't know this then, but if the September 11 group was motivated by an observant Islamist culture, it didn't stop Marwan al-Shehhi drinking rum and Cokes in America. For sure, their motivation was more complicated than "Islam" or "nihilism," as American conservatives would have it, although it was certainly aimed to terrorize the United States. In Germany, it turned out later, al-Shehhi once told people he didn't smile because "people are being killed in Palestine." Indeed, the day I visited his local social club in Ras al-Khaimah, clansmen there—tribal enough to still be carrying light ceremonial hand axes, and bewildered because it was unimaginable that one of their own could be part of such a world-shaking event—were sure that Palestine featured among his motives. It wasn't hard to see why when I sat watching the television news together with the sheikhs. The reporting moved seamlessly from American suffering on the streets of New York to scenes of mayhem from the Palestinian territories. Film showed the Palestinian city of Gaza reeling from rocket attacks by U.S.-made Israeli Apache helicopters, of doctors displaying the blown-off stump of a young boy's arm, of Palestinians fleeing in terror. "Where is the Arab world to help us?" screamed a Palestinian woman to the reporter from the emirates' television station, displaying part of a munitions casing that showed that it too had been made in America.

The missionary in Riyadh also believed that the motivation of the hijackers he had known was vengeance.

"Why did al-Qaeda want to kill Americans? Because America acts as a shield for Israel. Because it protects corrupt Arab governments. Because America occupies the Arabian Peninsula. And because America is the strongest. Al-Qaeda thinks that a really good attack will break this powerful government, that Islam will be able to expand. We believe that Islam will come to embrace the whole world one day."

"What about all the innocents in the World Trade Center?"

"It's asymmetric warfare! That's something that was predicted in the Koran. They were the 'towers of usury'! Hitting them was fulfilling a prediction in the hadith traditions about the 'collapse of a mountain of gold.'"

"But Muslims were killed too."

"It was okay. You can't help it, and they'll go to heaven anyway."

"Are you actually with al-Qaeda?"

"I might be, I might not. We might agree on the goals, we might share interests. I have a cause, that is, to gain knowledge. Al-Qaeda are the military side, the sword."

We discussed several of the hijackers he'd met as a missionary in Afghanistan. One was Majed Moqed on American Airlines Flight 77, the plane that plunged into the Pentagon with its throttles thrust full open, a "laughing, social, religious person." Waleed al-Shehri, one of two brothers on AA Flight 11 that Mohammed Atta flew into the World Trade Center, was a painting teacher in air force school. According to the missionary, he had reformed from being "corrupt" and self-indulgent into an activist "when he saw the massacres in Chechnya" and wept. Aboard United Airlines Flight 175, heading for the World Trade Center with the emirati clansman Marwan al-Shehhi at the controls, Ahmed al-Ghamdi knew the Koran, was very sweet, and wrote "modern poetry about the massacres of Muslims." Hamza al-Ghamdi was "aristocratic, very polite." Mohammed al-Shehri loved books and had a stamp made for books in his collection with the motto "Let your death be in the way of God." The missionary remembered best Ahmed al-Naimi, on United Flight 93, in which passengers overwhelmed the hijackers before the plane crashed, as someone who had been sinful but who believed that his sins could be cleared with jihad. He was "studious and quiet. When he was chosen for the September 11 teams, he said it was an ecstatic feeling, like a marriage."

A wildly adventurous dynamic seemed to knit together this group of ill-adjusted, angry young men, easily manipulated by Osama bin Laden. But a desire to get even with Israel was cited as a main motive in the testimony of Khalid Sheikh Mohammed, the ringleader of the attacks and three months later to become the confessed murderer of my colleague Danny Pearl. The chief of Saudi intelligence, Prince Turki al-Faisal, later told me that bin Laden became popular mainly on the back of anger over Israeli actions in the West Bank and Gaza after the Second Intifada began in October 2000. Realizing the danger, Saudi Arabia had sent a letter to the United States in the summer of 2001 warning that such perceptions could lead to "many terrorist activities."

Later I was to meet high British officials who had studied the secret files on the Pakistani youths who bombed the London underground on July 7, 2005. They said the only common thread they could discern in the suicide bombers' life stories was teenage rebellion gone ballistic. Other studies of suicide actions talk of the importance of group loyalty, rather than ideology or family background. But the missionary, now in his stride, and fully in tune with bin Laden's rhetoric, was spinning it the way Americans would soon spin it too, as an attack purely motivated by winning glory for "Islam," by which he meant the peoples of the Islamic world. He was seeking a clash of civilizations.

"If you are a Muslim, you must be independent, different, beyond the UN, beyond the IMF! And America is helping al-Qaeda in this," he gloated. "Al-Qaeda is beyond an organization; it's a global phenomenon. Nobody in particular chose the hijackers. It wasn't just Osama bin Laden or [his deputy] Zawahiri. They have no ranks. They work for God."

My working time was up. It was the middle of the night already and I had to catch a plane. I wanted to hear more of the story, which felt, at close quarters, like a miraculous scoop. As so often in Middle East, my hosts generously suggested that I stay. For once I gave in. I called my understanding wife, delayed my flight again, and we talked on for hours more.

"If you want the thing the [hijackers] had in common, it was the fact that they would cry when they read the Koran," the missionary insisted. "They read a lot. If someone cries when reading the Koran, then he's really good."

Another thing at least nine of them had in common was al-Qaeda's training camp near Kandahar in Afghanistan. Many of them had told their parents that they were going on jihad in Chechnya, but many got stuck in neighboring countries like Georgia or Azerbaijan. It cost much money to be smuggled in and the Chechens preferred experienced fighters. So they took the money they'd collected back home and went to Camp al-Farouq, meaning "he who distinguishes truth from false-hood." This was the epithet for the second caliph of Islam, Omar, the Muslim leader who conquered Jerusalem. As always, a reference to the Israeli-Arab conflict was a central point in al-Qaeda's efforts to win ideological legitimacy.

"The food was always bad. People got sick. People were always tired. There was no food, no women, no music, no alcohol. Sometimes there would be meat twice a week, sometimes once a month. We'd have special training weeks during which all that everyone got was a little bit of bread and a bit of salt. Many of us came from rich families, and had left homes, cars, even wives. Osama's house in Kandahar had no air-conditioning!" said the missionary.

"Did you never take time off?" I asked.

"Some of the Arab Afghans were so excited to be there they would play football, mess around in a way," he said, frowning. He'd already told me that in his view, playing football once a week after Thursday prayers was the limit for someone as-piring to imitate the early Muslims. One was killed for indulging in heroin. Two others were caught in a homosexual relationship and executed.

"Oh, they repented, they pleaded for mercy. But they were judged by the Af-ghan judge. And they were killed."

"It sounds pretty tough," I told him.

I found it hard to believe that someone so clearly ill at ease with the real world could have dealt with all this hardship.

"Everyone felt an internal peace. There would be a special hour of prayer before the dawn prayer. Afterward we'd read the Koran at length."

Then they'd have training. Occasional videos recovered from the camp after the U.S.-led invasion of Afghanistan showed the elementary military obstacle course training involved. Before we broke up at dawn, the missionary told of training with poison—"they had a recipe so that when an infidel comes to a car and opens the door handle, he dies"—sniping, urban guerrilla tactics, lock breaking, explosives, map reading, how to deal with security agencies, and how to kill "while swimming, walking, or riding a bike."

When we reconvened the next day, the missionary arrived with Saad at my hotel looking like a medieval monk or caricature from a film. The cloth on his head was starched but loose like a cowl, and he glowered at the evidence of luxury.

"I hate hotels!" he harrumphed.

We inspected the Khozama's restaurants, which sought to transport guests as far as possible from the Saudi reality. One was done up in a kind of French boudoir taste, the other looked like something from a South Pacific island. The missionary growled, made for the reception desk as if to complain, then thought better of it. All the more worldly Saudis sipping coffee and gossiping in the reception area were looking with curiosity and some scorn at our little group. His type was highly recognizable, but marginal too.

So we repaired to a mall with a Chinese restaurant with Saad and the missionary's heavy friend, Abu Faisal. The missionary tried and failed to keep up his tradecraft. He would take the battery out of his phone, knowing that cell phones send signals even when turned off. But then he'd put the battery back in and make a call. A spring roll arrived, which he poked but didn't touch. When a European woman's voice trilled over the background noise, his head reared up like a startled forest deer.

"What was that?" he asked.

Once he spotted me drinking water with my left hand and, ever the missionary, told me off about how impure that was.

Life in the Afghan camp had clearly been a strain. He'd got so sick from the water that his friends had had to carry him around. Weak and delirious one night, he woke and saw one of the trainees for the jihad sitting up to watch over him. For the missionary, that was the kind of moment of love, exhilaration, and common purpose that made it all worth it.

"In Afghanistan, everything changes. Your mind opens up. You begin to think globally. When you meet Osama, you realize he's not just doing something regional; he's got a global plan. Osama's a belief, not a person. Even if he's killed, someone else will carry on. One of my friends once saw Osama looking at a map. He had the misty look in his eyes that he got when he talked about the future. My friend asked him, 'Oh, sheikh, what are you doing?' He responded, 'I'm thinking of changing the map of the world. There will be the Abode of Islam, and the Abode of Infidels.'"

Abu Faisal chimed in with some of his ideas as he picked over his noodles. For him, the black flag of al-Qaeda symbolized a historic revolt that arose from Afghanistan. He thought a "pillar of light" in the Scriptures might be a nuclear bomb. It got flakier. The King of Terror was abroad in the land, about to liberate Palestine and intending to march on Rome.

"It's possible that nuclear war is coming. The Jews are not going to give up easily. This is the cycle of history," said Abu Faisal, his eyes alight with the fantasies of the impotent. The man had lived in America, tried to study communications for a semester, dropped out, and believed he couldn't get credit because he was an Arab and a Saudi. "Constantinople has not been conquered yet. It will be a fight like never before!"

Satisfied with his noodles, he lit a cigarette.

"You should stop smoking, Abu Faisal," the missionary admonished him.

"Are you sure you're on the right path? Can you really win?" I asked them both.

"In Afghanistan, Osama used to say that when a lion puts its head into a beehive, the bees only have to sting in seven or eight places and the lion will die," the missionary said.

"The hadith says the Christians will bounce back quickly," Abu Faisal cautioned.

"The world has changed. We've changed too," the missionary insisted. "We used to think there's a long way to go. Now there may be just five or six years to the universal Islamic caliphate. We have broken the neck band of weakness, with justice and jihad."

"Did you actually do much guerrilla training?" I asked the missionary.

"Me? No. Some people do the fighting. I do ideology."

One piece of tradecraft, though, I did admire the missionary for. As the Asian waitress cleared away our Chinese tea, the missionary pulled out a five-hundred-riyal banknote to pay for the meal, far too much for the transaction. It was crumpled and had clearly performed this role before. I waved it away and the *Wall Street Journal* picked up the tab.

I returned to Istanbul exhausted and exhilarated at my hours of reeling in a new perspective on al-Qaeda. After all, in those early days there was a real hunger for insights into the group. To my astonishment, the *Journal* wasn't interested in publishing the account. The main reason was that the missionary was unidentified. He'd naturally been reluctant to give me his name and full life story, since he had been picked up four times by the Saudi police since September 11. Then of course there was the fact that he hadn't really been close enough to the action. He wasn't a would-be hijacker, he was flaky, he was vulnerable, and as a walk-on al-Qaeda actor he didn't add much to the mechanical, blow-by-blow accounts of the buildup to September 11 that were the newspaper's priority.

It was pointless to complain that September 11 wasn't just a matter that could have been stopped by better airport security, or that the U.S. problem with the Middle East went beyond the Islamic religion. Once again, I was left with notebooks full of marginal Middle Easterners complaining about U.S. policies, blaming Israel, dreaming of a universal caliphate, people who, from the perspective of the *Journal*'s headquarters in the wrecked Manhattan financial district, just weren't hard news.

I had a generic problem with the missionary story too: the Middle East's disdain for transparency and reliable information. Age twenty-two in Syria, it had taken me three weeks of struggle to write my first published story, and that was only a purple word portrait of the village I lived in. Even as a professional, it could still take me days to understand what was going on before writing a news report from one of the Middle East's more dictatorial states. In Turkey, with its free but distorted burlesque of conflicting viewpoints, I could frame an issue by midafternoon. But when I first left the Middle East, to report for three months in South Africa for the London *Independent,* I was surprised to find that I could see the story clearly before lunch, just from reading the newspapers. The penny finally dropped in New York, where, a couple of weeks into my life as a recruit to the *Journal,* marketing page editor Mike Miller sailed by my desk.

"Ah, Hugh! Can you do the marketing column? Digital yellow pages looks like a good story!" Miller said.

"How long have I got?" I replied gamely, thinking a week would do the trick.

"Two hours or so should be fine," he said cheerfully and disappeared.

So off I went. Within half an hour I'd read excellent background surveys in specialist magazines available on a database. Soon the chief executives of the major companies involved began returning my calls. The terrain was clear, the challenges obvious. Writing it up seemed like child's play. Miller had his column in time. That day I understood why the United States was often one step ahead of the part of the world I lived in.

For the same reason, when I needed information or a new insight about the Middle East, I often found myself calling Middle Easterners at the dozens of specialist American think tanks and universities. It wasn't just that they could speak to the culture of the *Journal*'s readers. Very few such think tanks existed inside the region itself, and their denizens could be as mired in the sewer of local disinformation as I was.

Even in the United States, of course, investigative reporting requires much more work. But it also has supporting rituals that a reporter rarely sees in the Middle

East: the whistle-blower who will not be executed, an assumption of shared moral values, freedom of information legislation, accessible and trustworthy public domain material and, of course, the fact that the reporter, the sources, and the officials all live, work, and belong in the same country. This means that American stories arriving for New York editors are usually crystal-clear.

I was expected to match this standard. The shadowy world of the missionary story, by contrast, was the kind that exposed my weakness to the *Journal*. It wasn't just a lack of names, court papers, or second sources. This was as close to an investigation as I was prepared to go in Saudi Arabia. I was even less daring in states where government authority was weak, or if the British or American governments were direct parties to the conflict. I had long headed off to report around wars, but the risk/benefit ratio seemed to be worsening. I knew my growing caution meant that my range of informants was shrinking and could strip my stories of originality and impact. Sensing the change in climate, I declined to go and cover the brewing war in 2001 in Afghanistan or subsequent Islamist-related events in Pakistan.

My *Journal* colleague Danny Pearl also declined to go to the war—in fact, he led efforts to make the newspaper more conscious of the risks we ran—but he did volunteer to go to Pakistan. He was ambitious, original, generous, and always funny, which shone through in his talent for the *Journal*'s idiosyncratic front-page feature stories known to us as A-heds. On handing over his part of the Middle Eastern beat, he had dispatched his files to me with captions scribbled on them like "Sand Skiing? There HAS to be an A-hed in that." We'd worked together on a number of stories. We weren't always right. Impressed by the way the more conciliatory administration of President Clinton had reduced tensions in the Middle East, we jointly produced a series in the late 1990s about the declining sway in the region of violent political Islam.

I knew that Pearl had been frustrated at the *Journal*'s disinterest in India, where he'd gone to work, and I understood why he'd risk going to Pakistan. It was one way to bump up the critical average of front-page stories that we needed to achieve. Two months after my encounter with the Saudi missionary, Pearl was still in Pakistan, tracking down connections between al-Qaeda, militant Pakistani sheikhs, and Richard Reid, a British convert to Islam who, with a bomb in his shoe, had attempted to blow up an American Airlines flight from Paris in December 2001.

Pearl was not as lucky as I was in his brush with al-Qaeda. As often seems to happen, he dropped his guard on the last evening of his reporting tour, seeking that breakthrough interview to make the story sing. Instead he was kidnapped and handed into the control of Osama bin Laden's group. Pearl probably never had a chance. They soon understood that he was Jewish, American, and had Israeli connections. He was probing a terrorist case that could have dire repercussions for Pakistanis and worked for a newspaper that backed the U.S. establishment. Our editors had proudly and publicly announced that they had handed over to the CIA an al-Qaeda computer that other colleagues had managed to buy in the Kabul bazaar. A week later, probably on February 1, 2002, Pearl's head was hacked off and brandished to the world in an early Internet hate video. I have never dared watch it. But I admired to the roots of my soul his courage in standing up for his Jewish identity.

The *Journal,* traumatized by the collapse of the nearby World Trade Center, was completely unprepared for a hostage situation, let alone a brutal, public murder of one of its best-loved writers. Perhaps there was some miracle we could have engineered, but I feared the die was cast as soon as he was kidnapped. When the final blow fell, they did everything they could to deal with the disaster that befell Pearl's family. I went alone to see the film based on his wife Mariane's book *A Mighty Heart* in a London West End cinema. The actors got amazingly close to reproducing the real characters, especially Mariane. But I felt hollow. Either life in the Middle East had burned out my emotional responses, or something was missing.

It was at a memorial ceremony in New York that I felt most awkward. Speaker after speaker lauded qualities I hadn't known about my late colleague. That he played violin in a bluegrass band. That he was so remarkably popular throughout the newspaper. That he once filed an article as a long poem. That he kept a beach chair in his London cubicle. But I had never heard him say that he was motivated by a desire for the brotherhood of man or dialogue between East and West. I'm sure he wouldn't have been against that, of course. We never talked much about our motivation for what we both did, but I'd say that our principal goals must have been similar: adventurously to travel the world; seek out unnoticed success, hypocrisy, injustice, or paradox and turn them into stories that would shine on the front page of the newspaper. In her book, Mariane remembers challenging him about his mission in life and getting back a considered response that he was searching for ethics and the truth.

If anything, what I remember him talking about was exposing hypocrisy of all kinds, whether in the Middle East or in U.S. policy. He had been furious, Mariane later told me, when the *Journal,* fearful of offending its readers, had refused to use a story he had written about how Muslims had become so prejudiced and angry at the West that many truly believed a baseless rumor that Israel was behind the September 11 attacks. It wasn't just thoroughness, as the memorial speakers said, that caused him to stay for a month in Khartoum to pin down a story proving that the United States bombed an innocent medicine factory in Sudan in 1998. He had no choice, in fact, if he wanted the detail needed to get his report to run on the front page. But what they did not say at his New York memorial service was that his decision to stick it out in Khartoum was, as I saw it, the result of his determination to expose a U.S. wrong. Nobody seemed to acknowledge that. And that led to something else that shocked me most about his killing, a lesson that helped stanch my tears: The ignorant bigots who cut off his head cared not a whit for Pearl's attempts to get more justice for Muslims.

Three years later, I was sitting in my hotel room in Jeddah, Saudi Arabia, as news began to come in that a BBC journalist had been shot in the capital, Riyadh. The next day the main Saudi newspaper pictured Frank Gardner on his knees in the street, begging for his life. He had been filming in a suburb known for its al-Qaeda sympathies. The photo showed passersby watching his agony. None went up to him to help, but someone had clearly felt poised enough to take a cell phone photo. Riddled with bullets, Gardner owed his life to the skill of a South African surgeon. An elegant Arabist who had left banking for a journalist's life, Gardner had selflessly helped me out in Riyadh on one of my first trips. I felt he was like me too, someone who accepted a measure of hardship on the road in exchange for adventure and the chance to publish stories that would narrow the gap between the Middle East and the West. Motivation made no difference. His role on the Mideast stage had made him a target. For sure, Western actions in the Middle East had resulted in many innocent Muslim deaths. But this was not the way to fix it.

A week later in Riyadh, the British ambassador, Sherard Cowper-Coles, invited me to stay on for an impromptu memorial service for Simon Cumbers, the Irish BBC cameraman who had been shot near Gardner and who had died on the spot. A dozen of us present held hands in the residency garden, standing on a flagstoned circle. I held the hand of Gardner's wife, Amanda. Opposite me was Louise, the dead cameraman's wife. Words were said by Cowper-Coles and by an Irish envoy. Silence fell over our group. Later I would read in Gardner's book about how he pleaded in Arabic with the wispy-bearded gunmen to spare his life, and, after being shot many times and left for dead, how people just watched him bleeding and weakening until the police turned up half an hour later. He also told about his long struggle to win back his dignity and employability. Standing in the circle in the embassy, I was already beginning to wonder about me, about whether what I was doing was worth the risk of leaving a grieving wife and children behind. Through my head went the nineteenth-century German folk song that I was then singing to put my one-year-old daughter to sleep at night. It told about the death on a battlefield of the singer's best friend:

Waiting on the Beirut beachfront for U.S. marines to land in Lebanon, *Newsweek* photographer John Hoagland points his long lens at the head of then UPI photographer Leighton Mark. Six months later, Hoagland was killed by an army bullet in crossfire in San Salvador. Mark was shot by a Lebanese gunman, narrowly surviving and losing the use of one arm. 1983. *(Hugh Pope)*

A musket ball came flying
Is the target me or thee?
Him that ball did rip away
He lies there at my feet today
But still seems part of me.

Of course, my daughter didn't understand the words. It was actually a lullaby for me, one of my few outward reactions to the steady toll of colleagues, friends, and acquaintances ripped away by the events around us. It wasn't just the dozen or more people I knew who had been killed in the wars I hovered on the edges of. There were all the near misses too and the memory of the hostage-taking years in Beirut. A geologist who was hosting me in Jeddah around the time that Gardner was shot asked how I dared to do the journalistic things I did. Flattering though it is to be considered courageous, only the war junkie actually seeks out frontline action. I survived partly because I was cautious and withdrew at the first sound of gunfire. So I shot the question back to him: Isn't it dangerous going down mines, climbing mountains, crossing deserts? And it turned out that he too had known a dozen people killed in his line of work, falling down crevasses or crashing in helicopters.

So was reporting worth the risk? A lot wiser than when my first two girls were born at the beginning of my career, I started contemplating this question seriously after covering the northern front of the U.S. invasion of Iraq during the months before the arrival of my youngest daughter. When she was born I took three months of leave. Then I tried to go back to work as usual in the Middle East. I now realized that my sense of winkling out truths protected by a cloak of innocence had been replaced by a new consciousness of threats and my own impotence. I tried to convince myself that I'd done my best, but I could now see that all the risks I had taken had made no perceptible difference to U.S. public opinion or government.

My growing suspicion that I should guard carefully those of my nine lives that remained was confirmed when I enjoyed a chance breakfast with the publisher of the *International Herald Tribune,* Michael Golden. What switched the light on for me was the genuine, admiring delight in his laugh as he told me how, when his newsroom gathered to find a volunteer for a dangerous assignment, there was always one person who'd raise his or her hand. I felt like a fool. Within six months I gave up my job as the *Journal*'s Middle East correspondent.

11. TEA WITH THE BRIGADIER

Failing the Famished of South Sudan

The riches of Egypt are for the foreigners.
—ARABIC PROVERB

It was 1986, I was still learning the business of Middle Eastern reporting, and I was given what looked like a straightforward mission. A special envoy from the UN had just announced that more than two million people were at risk of starvation in south Sudan. So Reuters sent me to Khartoum to write about the tragedy and how the West was mobilizing to save the country from itself. The world would be wiser and send help to where it was really needed.

But when I arrived in Khartoum, I felt bewildered and lost. I was an agency journalist raised on the Iran-Iraq War and Arab states confronting Israel. I had recently been expelled from Tehran, given twenty-four hours' notice to leave for an overdetailed report that the Iranians had judged "revealed military secrets" about an Iraqi bombing raid. Unlike such urgent bulletins required of me in the past, my masters at Reuters were vague about what they wanted to know about Sudan. An insurgency was then vaguely threatening this vast, dysfunctional country, worsening the split in its identity and geography between the Arab and Muslim north and the more African south, which at Reuters we always described quaintly as "Christian and animist." But the Sudanese I met were gentle and soft-spoken and did not shout out the kind of passionate crossfire of propaganda I was used to. The days I spent crisscrossing Khartoum from embassy to aid agency revealed little. Newspapers were unclear about any famine and the guerrilla war in the south. When I eventually tracked down the national news agency, it seemed that the entire staff was out for lunch and unlikely to return that day.

The Horn of Africa's great famine of the previous two years seemed remote from the Sudanese capital, and all I had to go on were comments by aid workers who had every interest in making the emergency seem dire. The intractability of the poverty, war, and poor governance was depressing and demotivating. I felt heavily that responsibility for the mess seemed to lie again with the British Empire, which, as elsewhere in the Middle East, had cobbled the country uneasily together with great pieces unable to coexist—the Christian and animist south, Muslim Darfur in the west, and the more Arab and Muslim north. The colonial past taunted the present. The broken-down streets I labored over in central Khartoum were still laid out on the pattern of Britain's Union flag.

The Sudanese head of state, perhaps, could supply the newsy copy Reuters needed. A laconic veteran from the *Financial Times,* John Murray Brown, helped me join the small crowd that was at the airport late one evening to greet the leader's return from a fund-raising trip to Libya. Sudan was so poor that he even had to come back in a Libyan plane. Politely respecting revolutionary Libya's favorite color, he came down the steps into the Sudanese night wearing a pale green robe. I found it stirring to be in the presence of someone called Mahdi, or the Messiah, after an ancestor who led a great rebellion against the British. We sat down on the false leather benches in what passed for a VIP lounge.

Then the power cut out.

"Allah!" said Mahdi, more in resignation than in anger.

I froze. My instincts clenched for the worst—muzzle flashes, explosions, an assassination attempt, a coup. Nothing came. A thick African silence settled on the blackened room. Five minutes later, the power came back on. Bored, Mahdi left before Murray Brown and I could ask him about anything of significance, let alone about the claim that millions of his countrymen were at death's door.

Back in town, I moved at Murray Brown's suggestion into the Acropole Hotel, an establishment run by Greeks, a group whose presence in towns all over Sudan was the legacy of an even older colonial heritage than the British. A collegial, family feel to the establishment tempered the first-days-at-school insecurity I always felt in a new country. Guests gathered informally at tables where we were served the menu of the day, washed down with cold water with half a fresh lemon squeezed into it. Most were people like me from far away, and I soon began to feel more at home.

The community of the Acropole soon offered me what seemed like a small breakthrough. One of my dinner companions suggested that I fly the following morning to a town called Wau, deep in south Sudan. This was, I had already learned, one center of the supposed famine; it was also remote, roughly at the spot in the heart of Africa where, if you cut out a map of the continent, it might balance on a needle. In recent days it had become clear that the great and generous West would step in to help through an action named Operation Rainbow. I hoped that I might also meet and write about the legendary animists. I telexed my editor, the imperturbable François Duriaud, who agreed that I could go, suggesting I stay a couple of days. I noted that if things didn't look good I could fly back on the same aircraft. I doubted that I would, though. The only other story I'd managed to interest my editors in was about locust swarms forming in the Sudanese deserts.

My fatigue from pacing the streets of Khartoum fell away as the small propeller plane lifted off from the airport. I felt I had sorted out a comprehensible mission, a way to fit my Sudanese confusion into the manageable frame of a news story. Added to my new sense of purpose, of course, was the familiar buoyancy of an adventure beckoning. I relished the name of the aviation company that ran the plane: Nile Safaris. Beneath us, the dry plains of north Sudan gave way to the savannah, trees, and then thicker jungle of the south. The Middle East was turning into Africa. Six hundred miles later, we bumped down along Wau's rough landing strip.

The tall, hugely fat Nile Safaris representative, Manolis, welcomed us. I came to know well this half Greek, half Arab trader, one of the leading businessmen in the town of 100,000 souls. I was later to learn that there was nothing worth having that he had not got stockpiled in his padlocked, guarded warehouses. He certainly seemed the man in control at the airfield.

"Can I ask you something?" I ventured. "If I don't go back with this plane, how likely is it that there will be another one back to Khartoum in a few days' time?"

"Take this plane back," Manolis warned me without hesitation. "The situation here is not good. People got killed last night. There is no guarantee there will be another flight out."

The pilot gave me an hour to get back to the plane. I walked along an earth track into town. It felt like I had been transported to the Stone Age. Herds of cattle with great wide curved horns worthy of holding a pharaonic sun disk jostled past me. Between thick green trees stood clusters of thatched rondavels. Single-file lines of emaciated, half-naked Dinka tribesmen walked to the market bearing thin staves, spears, or fighting clubs. Then I came to the buildings around the great redbrick Catholic cathedral that rose over the town and saw those who could no longer find food for themselves clustered on porches around the mission buildings.

Most people I'd seen in the town so far had seemed thin but active. This was the first time I had come face-to-face with true hunger. Children with bloated stomachs stared at me blankly. Women with breasts reduced to folds of skin sat motionless. Their powerlessness seemed to have robbed them of the will to live, let alone fight for food from the market.

In his house beside the cathedral, the bishop of Wau, Joseph Nyekindi, told me the last truck convoy reached the town the month before. The last train had made it through two years ago. There had been no electricity for three years. The town's population had been swollen by twenty thousand people as news spread of the possible new Operation Rainbow airlift. But the same news attracted the attention of the rebels in the south, the Sudan People's Liberation Army, or SPLA, which had pushed forward to lay siege to Wau. It was the first time they had reached the town in the three-year-old bush war.

"The Red Cross is now our only hope," Nyekindi said. "What food we already have at our disposal is nearly exhausted."

I rushed on to the small compound housing the International Committee of the Red Cross. In the wider population, I was told by Stéphane Jaquemet, the head of delegation, 18 percent of the children were severely undernourished and many could die.

It was already time to go back to the airport. Everything seemed normal. Airfield staff said one of Operation Rainbow's planes was due in the next morning. Scuttling back to Khartoum seemed silly now that I was here, especially since the ICRC appeared well established and pursuing a full aid program. I had seen battlefields that seemed far more dangerous. I would learn about where the starving people were and what the world should do. I let my seat on the flight go. The twin-engine Nile Safaris plane taxied off without me, rose up over the jungle canopy, and disappeared.

Back in town, Bishop Nyekindi offered me a bare room off a courtyard of his house. As the black night emptied the town before the eight P.M. curfew and I settled in, I discovered that I was surrounded by a remarkable library of first-edition books on Africa by British explorers. I wasn't just back in Africa, reconnecting with the continent where I had been born and spent the first eight years of my life. As I leafed through their old lithographs of magnificent tribesmen, I compared them to the similar scenes I had seen during the day and felt as though I too was embarked on a mission whose exciting possibilities far outweighed the uncertainties.

The next morning, a big Hercules cargo plane emblazoned with a big red cross landed at Wau airport as expected. Its sacks of corn were duly off-loaded on the backs of thin but willing workers. Trucks bore them off to a warehouse. All seemed to be going according to plan.

Busily filling my notebook with news and views, and overwhelmed by how many people said they were hungry, I found my way to the Jesuit mission, a one-story wooden building on a low hill at the edge of town. The two Jesuits at home were large, patrician, and welcoming. They invited me to join them for lunch on their wide porch. We ate a modest, sober meal, looking through a thin mesh of insect wire at the open African plain and the flame trees with their flat tops floating high over the tall green grasses.

After our meal, as one of the priests served tea, a sudden commotion broke out to our right. The noise resolved itself into a black shape flashing through the grass about fifty yards away. It was a man, leaping and dodging. Behind him an armored military vehicle careered across the landscape. On top of it were Sudanese soldiers, struggling for balance and firing at the fugitive. The big wheels of the armored personnel carrier gradually closed the gap with the running man. A shot hit home, then another. He stumbled, struggled up, and then fell out of sight. The vehicle stopped. The soldiers inspected their work and drove away.

My cup of tea was still halfway between the saucer and my lips.

"There was shooting last night too. The rebels have burned and looted huts just one hundred yards from here," one of the missionaries said softly. "In Rome, Wau is considered the most difficult mission in the world."

The missionaries said it was unwise to venture out to the body just yet (a few hours later, after I had gone, one of them went out with a spade to bury him). For the time being, they looked at their watches and suggested that we go to listen to the rebel SPLA radio station's daily three o'clock news. In a back room they tuned to the shortwave frequency, which soon crackled into chaotic life. Instead of a few bars of a musical signature tune, the battery-powered radio played a wild recording of machine-gun fire. Then an excited announcer came on the air. He declared that the SPLA had shot down a government airliner over another south Sudanese town.

"The airspace of south Sudan is closed to all air traffic until further notice," the rebel spokesman said. He went on to tell guerrillas that all their leave was canceled while they participated in the new SPLA offensive against a dozen army garrisons in the south. That included Wau.

I bade the missionaries good afternoon and headed back into town in a daze. That evening in my mission room I tuned in to the BBC to hear that sixty people on board the airliner had been killed. I realized I might be stuck.

The familiar sense of a deteriorating situation made me feel exposed in the lonely, overgrown bishopric. I decided to approach the Red Cross delegation and ask to stay with them. Back in the mid-1980s, the International Committee of the Red Cross was still a rigorously all-Swiss organization primarily dedicated to the welfare of prisoners of war. After a day or two of discussion with Geneva, the group of nine people let me in, partly because I was the only other foreigner in town who wasn't a long-term missionary, and partly because my then wife, Nicole, was a Swiss ex-ICRC employee. I felt privileged and greatly relieved. Aside from a well-honed instinct to find the safest place in town, I was keenly aware that the ICRC had the only dependable radio link to the outside world.

My instinct to take cover was sound. The night before my arrival a rebel SPLA attack on the edge of town killed ten people and burned thirty thatched huts and the wood-branch fences around them down to blackened ashes. A few nights later the rebels fired a clutch of mortars to sow confusion in the town center, setting the street dogs howling. Some mornings dead bodies lay on the bank of the White Nile, which ran through town. In continuing strikes on outlying huts, the rebels kidnapped women and children to work as porters and camp followers for their guerrilla army.

Since the guerrillas were largely a Dinka tribal group, and Wau was mainly populated by Dinka, the army garrison started taking revenge for their losses by killing suspected rebel sympathizers, as I had seen from the Jesuits' porch. Within days matters came to a head in a confused running battle through our quarter of town between the local Dinka police and army soldiers. We barricaded ourselves behind the high walls of our little compound as bullets whizzed and cracked overhead. Half jauntily and half desperately, we discussed what we would do if the rebels managed to take over the town. For a week, events seemed to hang in the balance. At last the Sudanese government's military governor of Wau, Brigadier Akol Akol—a tall, dignified, English-speaking officer whose first name was Albino, despite his pitch-black skin color—managed to arrange a truce that held for the rest

Disturbed onlookers on the bank of a tributary of the Nile inspect a body washed up overnight, another casualty of a rebel guerrilla siege of the Sudanese town of Wau. 1986. *(Hugh Pope)*

of our stay. Then the rebels stopped attacking, for reasons that SPLA radio never explained. The SPLA's air exclusion zone, however, remained in force.

Just three flights loaded with food made it to Wau before the SPLA flight ban took effect. A fourth flight passed by high overhead, but it did not dare land. From then on the huge sky was empty. We were so far from the rest of the world that there weren't even any vapor trails from high-flying passenger jets. All that were left were wheeling groups of hundreds of kites and vultures. With each flight costing $30,000, not to mention the expenses of the ICRC mission, the corn and milk powder on those three planes must rank among the most expensive food in the history of humanitarian relief.

As the days wore on and urgent radio-telexing revealed no change in the SPLA's decision to close Sudan's airspace, the delegates decided to distribute the food they had. I went to help. It all started well enough, but word soon spread that the warehouses had been opened, and our small group gradually lost control of the situation. The day ended with a free-for-all. Most impressive was the looting of the milk powder stocks, coating those involved with a layer of white. We just managed to get there in time to seize ten sacks of corn and flour for our own survival.

Gradually the twenty thousand or so displaced people who'd arrived in Wau hoping for foreign food slipped back into the bush. Good rains began to fall, making crops perk up and lowering fears of famine. Over the ensuing weeks I realized the hunger wasn't the result of some kind of natural disaster, although the recent drought had made things worse. Indeed, in Wau, except for traders like Manolis and his ilk, people often suffered from hunger before the rainy season. They subsisted on hoarded stocks, fish from the river, leaves, wild roots, and fruit from the trees in the fertile plain around town.

It was politics and war that turned hunger into famine. The SPLA said it opposed the airlift because it was a ruse by which Libyan war materiel could reach the isolated garrison towns of the south: Only we, who saw the plane's cargo bags, knew that to be a lie. Governor Akol said SPLA leader John Garang's recent attacks were just a show of force. As we sipped tea in his pleasant garrison gazebo, he correctly predicted they wouldn't do much more.

"The question is whether John Garang can starve the south into submission. No, he can't," Brigadier Akol said. "Garang hopes people will abandon the town to leave the military isolated. But the people know very well that it is Garang who is stopping the food supplies."

This would all have sounded quite reasonable if I didn't know that the Sudanese government and its forces were also capable of cruelty toward the people of the south that increased their hunger. The lesson slowly sank in that the two sides were just like militia leaders and governments that I knew elsewhere in the Middle East, for whom there is never any clear distinction between war and peace. When they feel strong and want to put pressure on the other side, they start a battle here or place a bomb there; when it suits them to have a period of calm, they go back to appealing for some new forum for peace talks. The welfare of the people in their charge is a completely secondary issue.

The Swiss delegation's mood grew gloomy. Their leading role in food distribution in Wau had been a new departure for the organization. I already knew the ICRC as consummate professionals, rigorous in their official neutrality and predictability, obsessed with maintaining high Swiss standards, and respected by all sides, whether Israelis running prison camps or furtive Palestinian guerrilla groups. Unfortunately, however, neutrality didn't sell. Governments and especially ordinary people in the West saw less and less reason to give money for the ICRC's work as the unique lifeline between, say, the tens of thousands of prisoners of war in Iran and Iraq. My wife Nicole had spent a year in Baghdad on such an ICRC mission and said money was so tight that she even had to keep count of the delegation's pencils. Westerners would, however, open their wallets and give huge sums if starving children appeared on television screens. The ICRC, the delegates privately confided to me, hoped that by involving itself in famine relief in the Sudan, it could somehow raise its profile and fund-raising capacity for all its activities.

It worked. I myself had unwittingly been part of the organization's new strategy just the day before I left Khartoum, sending a glowing story with the headline RED CROSS AIRLIFT RELIEVES HUNGRY SUDAN TOWN to newspapers all over the world. I quoted the station chief in Khartoum, Ruedi Kueng, talking of a town where 65–85 percent of the population was "malnourished or severely under-nourished." In other reports I noted the UN estimates that 1 million of south Sudan's 6 million people were short of food, and 2.5 million were "at risk." Who wouldn't give money for such work?

The delegates, however, felt multiple layers of guilt at the failure of the ICRC mission to bring food to Wau. It wasn't only the huge expense of bringing the forty tons of corn but also the fact that they had spent weeks measuring and sorting everyone out into various categories of aid recipients. Now there was no food to distribute to them, yet here we all still were. They tried not to show themselves about town too much.

There seemed to be nothing left for us to do. The days of isolation turned to weeks. I slowly worked my way through the books in the mission library, ever more amazed at the wealth, power, and self-confidence of my British predecessors. Sundays could include a visit to the Roman Catholic Mass, where a choir of women in immaculately clean dresses and their woman conductor sang their hearts out under friezes of African angels, to the accompaniment of a swinging band. Shopping expeditions to market stalls brought back supplies of everything from live chickens to succulent, whiskered fish from the White Nile. We played hilarious games of volleyball against a team of students from the local college. I learned to distinguish among Wau's many different tribal groups. I sat for hours watching blacksmiths heat charcoal and beat out elegant custom-made spearheads for fishing, for hunting lions, and even for killing men. With nothing much else to do, I started to collect them.

Sleeping three to a room in the small ICRC mission, we battled to keep cabin fever at bay. Red Cross ration tickets became playing cards. We cut a chess set from cardboard and played through long competitions. The odd-smelling water brought by the waterman in jerry cans suspended from a yoke had to be filtered, maggots had to be sieved from the bug-infested flour, and to bake our own bread we had to devise a system of loading red-hot charcoal into the ex-gas oven. After years of writing about nations' production of millions of barrels of oil, I learned the critical value of our last barrel of petrol and how many days of electricity a barrel of diesel represented. We took occasional solace in Manolis's Arizona Beer Garden, where a fizzy, lukewarm Zairean brew was served in jam jars, along with the tops to keep out the flies. The rainy season brought occasional wild chances to shower, which we would do communally, naked and fearfully under water gushing from a broken roof gutter behind the house as thunder rolled and lightning flashed overhead.

On birthdays, we scoured the idiosyncratic Wau market for gifts, concocted a new recipe for our diminishing stocks of maize flour, and taped together the megaphones that were to have been used for crowd control, put them in front of my little cassette recorder, and danced through the night to bubbling Congolese music. We walked along the Nile, climbing in the tall trees, but did not stray far. Two foreigners captured by the SPLA, I had read, became slaves carrying ammunition through the bush until ransomed out after a whole year.

"Why don't you just wait for the end of the rainy season, and then leave by road? You'll be fine," Manolis said one day over a whiskey in his sitting room.

"When does the rainy season end?" I asked.

"December or so," he said. That was still three months away.

Because I could still pass occasional messages home through the ICRC, I learned that others had begun to become concerned at our situation, not least my family. My father had called the British Foreign Office to ask if they had any suggestions about how I could escape. "Why doesn't he hire a car and drive out?" was the Sudan desk officer's suggestion. When my father protested that this was absurd, the officer brushed aside such objections and added a new, sharply logical, reason to do nothing: "If as you say he cannot communicate with you, how do you know your son wants to leave?"

Increasingly frustrated, I did want to do something to get out. An idea blossomed when our isolation was broken by the sudden appearance of an army convoy of supply trucks from the border with Zaire. Everyone in town turned up to watch them parade toward the market square, each one topped by a dozen soldiers obviously delighted to have survived the journey. A second convoy arrived soon afterward. For a town supposed to be starving, market forces had dictated an odd cargo: one thousand cases of beer. Better still, from my perspective, the trucks would head back.

"Will you give me permission to travel out with the convoy?" I asked Brigadier Akol over another afternoon tea.

"Of course, if you like!" he said, delighted to satisfy me so easily.

Soon I had a "Certificate: To Whom It May Concern" permission to travel to Tombora with the convoy and then on to Zaire, typed out in triplicate. I bore it back to the ICRC delegation in triumph. Indeed, I still have it.

"That doesn't seem safe to me," said Jaquemet, our sensible leader. "Do you know where Tombora is, actually?"

"No," I admitted. "But I've got enough money to get me across Zaire!"

My enthusiasm faded when I found a map in the back of one of the less ancient British travel books. Even if I got to Tombora, there was a great deal of Africa still left to cross. I gave up on the idea, bid the convoy a regretful farewell when it left, and slumped back into my uninspired routine.

Being cut off was a sobering exposure to a basic fact of life in the Middle East: utter powerlessness over one's own fate. It eroded my willpower to do anything long term. I could have done a real study of those extraordinary books in the mission library, for instance, or taught a class at one of the Wau schools, or written an account of my past year in revolutionary Iran, a traumatic period that was then still vivid in my mind. Instead, like all Middle Easterners, trapped as they are in endless insecurity, most of us expended our energy on discussing "the situation." Jaquemet was in talks every day on the radio with headquarters of various kinds, all of whom were seeking a "green light" from the SPLA for a flight to take us out. Every optimistic rumor spurred false hopes. We always thought we would leave in a few more days at most. I now understand a little better the groups of men immobile in coffeehouses, living out their lives in unpredictable societies in which planning and personal initiative are irrelevant or doomed.

Only one of the ten of us assumed from the start that we were stuck indefinitely and therefore developed an appropriate can-do spirit. Fred reverted to his civilian work as an engineer, going out every day to consult with doctors and local chiefs on a proper architectural plan that could one day turn into a new hospital for the town. The bishop wanted to build it for the poor. Others also tried to do good. Anne gave French lessons. Andreas fixed the water tanks. The ICRC radioman, Peter, dismantled and rebuilt the electricity generator once a week.

Our supplies began to run out. We bid ceremonial farewells to the last coffee, the last washing powder, the last thermal paper for the radio-fax, the last toilet paper, the last toothpaste, the last filters for the water brought by the waterman. As one month holed up in Wau stretched toward two months, time seemed to stand still. I caught myself feeling unmanly when I walked about town, since I didn't carry any spears. I sometimes despaired of leaving so deeply that I even wondered what it would be like to take a new wife and set up house and home in one of the round, grass-roofed huts.

Elegant officials from the Wau government were our frequent visitors, to hear news of our negotiations with the SPLA, to enjoy some educated company, and to escape from the population's incessant demands for food.

"A journalist, hmm?" commented one with grim satisfaction. "Well, at least you can now live out your story, not hear it from other people."

In fact, I felt useless, a journalist without an outlet, yet knowing nothing else but to go out each day to pursue my trade, interviewing people, seeing things, trying to find ways to get the story out.

The ICRC allowed me to send one article out by the radio-telex that told the world about Wau's hunger, life in our town under siege, and what had happened to the aborted aid effort. Thereafter their Swiss standards of neutrality kicked in and I was on my own. I scouted around town looking for alternatives. I discovered the Sudan News Agency, which occupied a few concrete huts in a corner of Governor Akol's government compound. Luckily, a couple of men were there, with a radio. And a Morse code key.

A message made it through to Khartoum, care of the Acropole Hotel. The radio man carefully wrote out the acknowledgment that it had arrived. I was amazed.

"Can I send a whole story?"

"Sure," the man agreed with a warm smile. "But we have no fuel for our generator."

The next day I gave Manolis $15 for a half barrel of diesel and even handed over my last half packet of biscuits to the emaciated operator. He began beep-beeping away. Soon he plugged in earphones, but little did he know how familiar the strained expression on his face was to me. I had messed about with ham radio as a Royal Air Force cadet, spending long afternoons trying to talk to other school cadets on a valve transmitter salvaged from a First World War British battleship. Like the Wau machine, it often looked as if it was working, but it hardly ever really did. Still, at a painfully slow and imprecise rate, he virtuously dot-dashed my whole piece into the ether. As far as I know, my story duly disappeared off the face of the earth.

I had more luck later. I had been holed up in Wau for five weeks when my employers sent Cairo bureau chief John Rogers to Khartoum. I suggested in an ICRC

A Dinka tribesman stands in the Sudanese town of Wau, undaunted by the hunger and the insecurity that persuaded him and his family to leave their village in search of promised Western food supplies that failed to arrive. 1986. *(Hugh Pope)*

message that he call me on the Nile Safaris radio. Manolis, however, insisted that anything we talked about should be cleared by the authorities. I went to see Governor Akol to seek his permission. When he read the first draft of my dispatch, he began with some old-fashioned editing.

"There is no starvation here," he ordered. "Write 'malnutrition-related diseases.'"

That was only the beginning. For a whole week I met him for tea and censorship. Brigadier Akol had the time to discuss not only content but also tone, style, grammar, and punctuation. Rogers just had to wait. Finally we had our rendezvous on Manolis's radio. I would say a phrase, Rogers would repeat it, sometimes four or five times. The story took an hour of struggle against the static and interruptions of Khartoum air traffic control to dictate. For two weeks I had a bruise on my thumb where I had gripped the transmit button on the handheld microphone with all my might, willing the report all the way into Rogers's consciousness.

It was to be the last time I could send a story. While the searchlight of news interest moved elsewhere, we became obsessed with the efforts to send in a plane to get us out. Sometimes the plane got as far as another town in the Sudan to talk to the SPLA, but for one reason or another, the green light all the way to Wau was withdrawn at the last minute. We suspected it was because the SPLA actually had no contact with the rebels around Wau and were thus reluctant to take responsibility in case something bad happened. My experience with the government radio operators appeared to confirm that theory. For our own sanity, after ten near misses, we simply stopped believing the news that arrived from ICRC negotiators. Still, we kept crowding around the radio-fax for our three contacts each day.

So when at last I heard the buzz of an engine of a light aircraft over Wau, I was sitting with a few ICRC companions in the Arizona Beer Garden. I didn't immediately understand what was happening until the ICRC jeep tore up to take us off to the airfield. A Dutch pilot with a broken arm in a cast had dared to fly in. And somehow he let all of us on—with our luggage. Fred and Andreas bravely stayed behind as a skeleton staff.

Manolis broke open two of his last barrels of Jet A-1 aviation kerosene. The engines started. With shining eyes we waved good-byes. None of us wanted to revive the discussion about whether or not the SPLA really could talk to its rebels around Wau. The plane lumbered down the runway. Faster and faster, it approached the edge of the jungle. Now we were hurtling toward the trees. At the very last second possible, it seemed, we unstuck from the ground and groaned a few feet over the treetops. The SPLA wouldn't have needed a missile to bring us down; a pistol would have done. Slowly we climbed into the sky. Ten minutes later, high over a glistening network of tributaries of the Nile, it seemed almost unbelievable that I could be talking on the plane radio directly with my editors at Reuters headquarters.

The pilot put down at Lokichokio in northern Kenya for the night. We all experienced a mix of exhilaration of having safely escaped, survivor's guilt about those we'd left behind, and depression that this ten-week period of intense friendships and community was breaking up. My main memory is sitting before the small hostel where we had our last and rather quiet meal together, contemplating the perfect smiling curve of the little wooden stools that people there used as pillows. My good fortune was underlined on our flight onward to Nairobi. We had to make space in our airplane for a British television cameraman who was also coming out of south Sudan, wounded by a land mine explosion and on a stretcher. His producer had been killed.

I was lucky too in my editor, François Duriaud. Not only did he let me take a week's safari with Nicole at Reuters' expense, but he also allowed me the unusual privilege of sitting down to write real, lengthy feature stories about what I had seen and done.

The first was perhaps not surprising: If people were hungry, the solution didn't lie in expensive Western-run aid efforts. The real problem was the war between the government and the rebels. Normally, we would sum up its causes with a bland, catchall agency paragraph like "the SPLA is waging a bush war in southern Sudan to press demands for a secular state and political reforms. The mostly Christian and animist southerners resent what they see as political dominance by the Arab, Muslim north." For once, I got the chance to explain the conflict as I now saw it, a struggle over the legacy of Western colonial borders, the new ideologies of religion and ethnicity that were trying to fill the postcolonial vacuum, and the authoritarian governments that outside powers found it convenient to deal with.

Publishing the second piece was a braver editorial decision for Duriaud to make. The UN had said that more than two million people were "at risk" of starvation. I knew that this was an exaggeration in Wau, supposedly one of the centers of the famine. I had also seen how promises of aid created as much of a problem as the aid itself, encouraging people to leave their subsistence living in the countryside and become entirely dependent on charity in the towns. Development and security were needed, not showy Western interventions. Of course, I could never have been so sure of myself without being stuck for ten weeks contemplating this reality, something that few reporters have the time or wish to do for one newspaper story.

Still, looking back, I search for evidence that living through and writing about the siege of Wau served some purpose. For sure, *Middle East* magazine highlighted as an "explosive story" my claim that the extent of the Sudan famine of 1986 was a "myth". But even that magazine's veteran reporter could come to no conclusion about exactly how many people were at risk, or what to do about a country that seemed impossible to help. For sure, the world still prefers cure over prevention. People give billions of dollars to relief agencies offering to help refugees and hungry victims of war. But in 2007, when I joined International Crisis Group, one of the few organizations actively working to stop these damaging conflicts breaking out in the first place, I learned that they made do with just $15 million a year.

I cringe now at what I wrote in our *Reuters* magazine, that when the white man's plane plucked me off the airstrip at Wau, I felt that the suffering I left behind me "became just another story." Perhaps all cultures are narcissistic when recounting their experiences, as I was when discussing the pros and cons of the Western aid effort for a Western audience. Perhaps my attitudes bore comparison to the accounts of memorable African elephant hunts in the Wau bishopric library, solely designed to glorify the writer in the eyes of imperial London's clubland, or the paintings of the orientalist school, which had less to do with the Middle East than with the upper-class British drawing rooms for which they were destined.

In Wau, indeed, over tea with the Sudanese governor in his military garrison, I had perhaps experienced a last gasp of old-fashioned colonialism, that of Arab north Sudan's rule over the more African south. The trouble for Sudan as a whole, of course, was that neither north nor south was strong enough to control its own fate, laying it wide open to wars, famines, and foreign manipulation, whether by oil-rich Libya then or resource-hungry China today. Arguably worse, however, was what happened to a country in which the state disappeared entirely, as I was to discover in Afghanistan.

12. THE CENTRAL BANK
GOVERNOR HAS NO SOCKS

Taliban Warlords, Pakistani Feudals, and the Nation-State

The tyranny of the cat is better than the justice of the mouse.
—ARABIC PROVERB

As a student of Oriental languages, pride of place in my rooms at the top of an Oxford college staircase was given to a map of the Middle East. Pinned up over the mid-twentieth-century electric bars that glowed inadequately in the old fireplace, my eyes would trace great virtual journeys on it, from Aswan to Zonguldak, and then from Zabol to Ashgabat. Each place-name conjured up romantic promise. As the years went by, I assiduously rubbed every Aladdin's lamp I stumbled across. Magic carpets did miraculously appear. I reached most points on that map, and I was rarely disappointed.

A critic would say I was inspired by a false idea, a postimperial urge aroused by the sometimes artificial images of Cairo and the Holy Land conjured up by colonial-era-orientalist painters. To be charitable to myself, I preferred the heady purples and stark watercolor landscapes done in the eastern Mediterranean by Edward Lear, better known for his nonsense rhymes. True, I really did think I would find orderly societies in pristine premodern condition, I already knew that I bonded with the more openhearted Middle Easterners, and I was sure that their societies were in the grip of great changes, more exciting than in a university city where the top priority—duly articulated by the vice-chancellor's only flash of emotion in our welcoming speech—was to preserve the treasured fabric of the past. I also felt a desire to be different, which is why I applied to be a rare student of Oriental languages, rather than one of the hundreds of students rehearsing the canon of English literature. Having then learned Arabic and Persian, I felt a curiosity to find out what really made the Middle East tick and a sense of mission to try to explain it. Much as I liked England—the countryside, my privileged class, high English culture—I was unsure that the daily grind of London would offer more than a predictable, gray struggle through life.

The romantic expectations that ignited my wanderlust proved hard to satisfy. Perhaps my love affair was with an imagined East. Instead of the fragrant rose gardens of medieval poetry, or the camel driver's solitary bell calling me to join a timeless caravan in the wide-open desert, I was trapped in a cacophony of traffic jams. Walking about on broken, much-parked-on pavements was even more stressful than being stuck in a car. Ancient cities and stone courtyards were crushed, bombed, or elbowed aside by brutally designed, badly built concrete apartment buildings. Instead of spending my time debating imagery in Persian poetry in coffeeshops with like-minded enthusiasts, I found Iran barred to me as an Englishman. It was hard to find common subjects of interest with those to whom I could speak Arabic in public places, mainly due to the great gap in education and interests. On the other hand, most educated Middle Easterners of my age spoke far better English than I spoke Arabic. They were keen to improve it in pursuit of their goal to leave the backward Middle East as soon as the opportunity presented itself.

Cairo in 1980, for instance, was not for the faint of heart. Rubbish drifted like desert dunes against the buildings, beggars advertised their festering stumps on old cardboard boxes, and ragged children kept running up to touch me. Each day as I set out along the unpaved road outside my apartment block, the cringing pack of dogs that inhabited the building site next door bid me farewell with desultory barks. Some of the conscript soldiers at the army truck motor reconditioning workshop would look up and yell me a cheery, "Hallo mizter, haw arr yu? I luvv yu!" Then I would pass a mustachioed barber, merrily plying his trade on the street side, whetting his razor on a strop beside his lathered-up customer's thrown-back chin and pale open neck. The next shop's business was the white necks of chickens. These would be seized by the proprietor when he completed a sale and snapped with a carefree twist. He then tossed the chicken onto a rubbish heap across my path, where it would cavort, jibbering, teetering between this world and the next.

I would set out to my destination of the day by bus. At rush hour it was often so full that a bulge of people hung from the door. I would have to spot a gap in the hands clutching the vertical handrail and hurl myself up at it. The crush would somehow divide, giving me a grip and a helping pull up. A couple of hops later I would be safely cocooned in the solid human body of the bus. If not Sufi union with the godhead, it was a complete loss of control of one's own fate. Once, suspended outside the bus as it picked up speed, I stared with impotent surprise as a hand appeared from the mass of bodies, clenched its fingers around my watch strap, and ripped the timepiece off my wrist. The conductors had it worst of all, forced to make their way down the bus by climbing along the backs of the seats, backs curled against the roof. They let nobody escape from the fare of three *qoroush*, even those hanging on to windowframes and bumpers outside. Yet somehow they managed a split second of good-humored, exaggerated respect for each customer: *"Ya doktor! Ya sheikh! Ya brofesor! Ya mu'allim! Ya bey! Ya basha!"* O doctor! O sheikh! O professor! O teacher! O sir! O my lord general!

The raw human spirit of people trying to survive all this impressed me, part of the cocktail that kept me addicted to the Middle East. Only as the years went by did I begin to understand how the rulers of the Middle East had mismanaged their countries into this state. The governments gave many dubious excuses: the colonial legacy, the wars with Israel, U.S. policies. Then came urbanization, population explosions, and the tranquilizing drug of oil income. More insidious were the corruption, bureaucratic pettiness, and misguided ideologies. I rarely met the dignified Arab sheikhs of my imagination. I did spend frustrating hours and days in decrepit bureaucratic warrens, updating my flimsy papers in offices where dusty old files sometimes spilled out of doorways onto the scuffed corridor floors. It took me a long time to realize that states, like many other areas of human activity that leave their mark, have a beginning, some kind of imperial or golden period, and then a decline. Even this simple paradigm seemed to have passed by much of the modern Middle East, so many of whose governments were barely legitimate, lacking in common purpose and dependent on outside powers. Change could be dramatic at times, however. The very real dynamism of better-run Istanbul and Dubai transformed those cities before my eyes. On the other hand, in Oxford, I have to look hard to see changes over the past three decades. Bus lanes have been painted and a few buildings rebuilt in the same style as before. Such contrasts engendered a fascination for all the very different ways countries and states were run.

For instance, what happened when there was virtually no state? Would this, at some level, constitute a natural purity in which society ran itself? There was one country to experience this, one that to me always seemed the most remote, the hardest to get to, and hence highly attractive: Afghanistan. Reuters had assigned me to cover the Soviet withdrawal in 1989, but to my great disappointment I failed to secure a visa. After that it seemed too dangerous, or not in my reporting territory. But as the *Wall Street Journal* realized that we had a mutual interest—theirs to find someone ready to go to the obscurest Middle Eastern places, mine to tick off those last destinations on the map—the chance arose again.

There were a number of catches. Afghanistan was in 1998 mostly run by the Taliban, with whom I had no relationship. I didn't know how visas were obtained, since the Taliban were represented only in Pakistan, Dubai, Saudi Arabia, and somewhere in Queens, New York. I had to be back for a promised holiday with my children two weeks later. Even if everything had been organized in advance, it would be a race against time. But, as I flew eastward through the night from Turkey over Iran to Pakistan, I felt my horizons expanding again. Trans-Afghan gas pipelines from Central Asia were in the news, the little-known Taliban were said to be seeking international respectability, and I still had no idea how I would get into the country or quite what I would find there.

It was always pleasant to visit Islamabad, the capital of Pakistan, a government town of modern villas, mountain backdrops, and subtropical greens. I was bright and early in the queue that Monday morning at the villa that housed the Embassy of the Islamic Emirate of Afghanistan, as the Taliban called their two-year-old regime. The previous government, run by the quarreling warlords who ousted the Soviets, had been called the Islamic State of Afghanistan. On some of the official documentation the word "state" had been crossed out, and the word "emirate" written above it with a blue ballpoint. The black-turbaned embassy staff were polite as I filled in the visa application forms. Of course, I knew this deference and my dutiful repetition of my mother's first name were the traditional opening shots in a long bureaucratic battle. Only an incurable curiosity can have kept me filling out such hopeless papers for so long, the naïve but lasting belief that because the government in question didn't want to be openly inspected, it might be hiding the romantic secret of the East I was searching for.

"How long will the visa take to be approved?" I asked, privately delighted that my rusty Farsi was still proving serviceable, being similar to Dari, once the main Afghan language of government. The Taliban are almost all from the ethnic Pushtun tribes that straddle the Pakistan-Afghanistan border, the biggest single group and making up about half of the twenty-five million people of Afghanistan.

"Sometimes it's quick. Sometimes it takes a long time," the clerk replied and gave me a winning smile. It was impossible not to feel optimistic.

I filled the subsequent days by going to all the big Western embassies to ask them about the latest news from over the Afghan border. What I already knew seemed straightforward to me. The Taliban had taken power in Kabul two years before. They had recently captured all the big cities. Declarations had been made that seemed to indicate they were backing down from their early idealism about creating a universal Islamic caliphate. Their organization and moral tone implied that they wanted to move from warlordism to become the government of Afghanistan. I assumed that Western diplomats would sit down to settle things soon and give them Afghanistan's seat in the UN. As the days went by, I grew uncertain. Not only was my visa not coming through, but the embassies seemed unsympathetic or guarded about the Afghan situation.

Much later, the story would become clearer. My *Journal* colleagues who found and bought two of al-Qaeda's computers in the Kabul bazaar in 2001 pieced together the narrative, with me translating some of the Arabic. Three months before my visit, it turned out that a first and last U.S. mission to Taliban-ruled Kabul had in fact tried to break the ice with the country's new overlords. The Americans sought cooperation against the al-Qaeda chief, Osama bin Laden. They wanted to talk about a possible U.S.-built oil pipeline from Central Asia through to the Indian subcontinent. They sought a partner against Iran. The Taliban were keen, even canceling the usual Friday display of "Islamic" punishments in the football stadium. The al-Qaeda computer showed the Taliban were angry with bin Laden's arrogance and lust for publicity, and the ex-Taliban intelligence chief told my colleagues that the Taliban leadership had been warning bin Laden that they wanted peace, not more wars. Just before my arrival in Islamabad, in fact, the Taliban had even agreed to expel bin Laden, although the Americans still believed that there was collusion between the two.

I learned more of this from the then Saudi chief of intelligence, Turki al-Faisal. In the incense-laden air of his grand apartment in Paris, he told how a deal with the Taliban made in June 1998, two months before my visit, would have delivered bin Laden to the Saudis for trial on charges of treason. All that was needed was for top Saudi clerics to endorse Taliban leader Mullah Omar's betrayal of his unruly guest, by means of a ruling on religious grounds.

"Mullah Omar was getting very upset with Osama bin Laden. He wanted to find a legal way of breaking his word," said Prince Turki. "I believe he was sincere because of his need for aid, political support, and diplomatic recognition. He stripped bin Laden of his personal bodyguard and put Taliban soldiers around him."

Focused on ways to secure my Afghan visa, however, I learned nothing of this. By Thursday morning, just before the Pakistani weekend, I was running out of time and my nerves were stretched taut. The embassy clerk was as polite as ever and highly optimistic about my visa chances at some point in the not too distant future, even if it was mysterious to me whether he'd even sent my application through to Kabul. I knew that a UN flight was leaving for Afghanistan that afternoon. At that moment, in the corridor behind the consul's desk, I saw the great black turban and beard of a man already pointed out to me as the Taliban ambassador. This was my last chance. I plunged in and threw myself at his mercy. It was not a pretty sight.

"Mr. Ambassador, peace be upon you. I am from the biggest and most serious newspaper distributed throughout the United States. We are very interested in developments in Afghanistan. I would like to visit your important country so that a proper up-to-date assessment of the Islamic Emirate can be laid before the American people . . ."

The ambassador looked at me quizzically, and at the clerk following me apologetically. I pushed my ragged Persian onward.

"Please, I request your sympathy with all my heart. I know my visa could take awhile but there is a flight this afternoon and I want to spend as long as I possibly can in the emirate . . ."

"Of course," he said, turning to the clerk. "Give this reporter a visa." He then turned back to me and added, "Please write the truth about what you see."

Little can dim the glamour of flying in small planes, especially the safe ones that the United Nations operates in difficult spots on the globe. Our group of travelers instantly felt a camaraderie, knowing that we'd spared ourselves a difficult and time-consuming road trip and were part of a privileged, rare expedition. We bumped into the air from Islamabad and headed up to the Afghan town of Jalalabad, making small talk and competitively comparing experiences.

I fell silent as we descended over the other side of the mountain range. The plane landed and trundled along the ragged Jalalabad runway. On both sides were the wrecks of planes and equipment left behind by the Soviet occupiers a decade before. I suddenly felt out of my depth and wanted to stay in my international bubble for a while longer. Luckily, the UN had a spare seat in a jeep running up to Kabul in a small convoy. I gratefully accepted the offer of a lift from Carmine Calo, an Italian army officer who was the military adviser of the UN Special Mission to Afghanistan. Back then, this was one of the few international efforts to reconcile the Afghan factions and to rebuild the Afghan state.

If I wanted to see a land bereft of government, I had found it. Twenty years of war had ravaged the countryside so badly it looked like a moonscape. Kabul was just ninety miles away, but traveling the road took us hours. The potholes were unrelenting, deep pits in the road through which the UN Land Rover pitched and rolled. All around us was parched desolation. Afghanistan was supposed to be an agricultural country, but I saw no trees, no fields, no villages. My neck began to hurt from all the slow-motion whiplash and would give me pain for several weeks to come. Calo tried to keep up my spirits.

"It's best this way. They used to lay land mines in places next to the road, for when you try to drive round the holes," he pointed out. "Things are better now, people can use the road, even at night. The Taliban have brought security to the country."

Indeed, as we emerged from the jagged narrow gorge that led up to the plain of Kabul, there was a new customs shed to tax commercial trucks. Its traffic cones were old artillery shell cases decorated with streamers of cassette tapes confiscated in the Taliban's puritan drive against music, television, and all forms of modern entertainment. The speed bump was an old tank track. As we drove through the city itself the shock of what had happened to the country began to sink in. Whole quarters had been flattened. The wrecked houses on main boulevards had been abandoned and shopkeepers had set up stalls in the streets in front of the ruins of the old shops. Mud-brick dwellings were melting back into the yellow-brown earth. Wreckage of Soviet-made armor from past battles still lay about on the roadsides. Later I searched the old industrial zone for signs of economic life amid corrugated iron roofs peeled back by explosions, walls raked with shrapnel, buildings stripped to their metal skeletons, and orphaned walls of concrete blocks. The only surviving factory I found was a German pharmaceuticals plant, its manager fighting against closure behind a sign riddled with bullets.

Some central suburbs, however, had survived, especially an elite district of villas, Wazir Akbar Khan. Here lived aid workers and, increasingly, high Taliban officials. I was headed here thanks to BBC correspondent Richard Galpin's generous offer of a place to stay. His assistant let me in, thickly bearded as the Taliban had ordered all Afghan men to be, and immediately made me feel at home. Still, at almost six thousand feet above sea level, the thin air was making my head spin.

On the UN plane in I had sat next to Bashir, the Afghan representative of a British aid agency. He had matter-of-factly brought me up to speed about Afghanistan

Taliban loyalist Afghans set up camp after preemptively taking flight to the southwestern corner of their country during the U.S.-led invasion in October 2001. (*Hugh Pope*)

and its place at the bottom of most global indexes of civilization, as measured by literacy, nutrition, infant mortality, and life expectancy. At the time I was visiting, one-quarter of the Afghan people were living in poverty as refugees in Iran and Pakistan. The Taliban's economic policy was the ultimate bare-bones approach: subsistence and fate. Two-thirds of the economy was based on growing opium poppies and the "transit" trade, that is, smuggling to the better organized states all around them. Two-thirds of the country's wheat was imported from Pakistan. One of the many successive central bank governors had told Bashir that if money came in, that was fine. If not, that was also fine. If international nongovernmental organizations wanted to continue running all Kabul's basic services, the Taliban let them alone if they didn't meddle politically; but if the foreigners left, that was all right too. The Taliban had no administrative capacity, felt no responsibility to feed the people, and were greatly skeptical of the grant-making, do-good outfits from the West. They cared only about their Taliban system and winning the war.

"They are themselves well coordinated. They tax goods heavily and quite efficiently," said Bashir. "They're not honest. They just punish severely."

"Why do you stay?"

"I refuse to be a refugee," he replied. "But I'm the only one of my family, or even from my school class, still in Kabul. It's lonely."

Once settled in, I began to tour the national ministries and government institutions, such as they were. After eighteen years of war, the Taliban appeared to be squatting in some of them, deprived of staff, budget, plans, or purpose. Mullah Omar kept everyone on their toes in Kabul under a six-man council. The city was on its sixth chief of water supply in two years. Ministers could suddenly be sent off to fight at the front. After all, there was still a war to win. They could not quite capture the last 10 percent of the country, an easily defended mountain corner mostly populated by ethnic Tajiks.

Two decades of involvement in the Middle East had convinced me that the predictability of some government was better than the chaos of no government. Initial impressions and interviews confirmed that, whatever their frustrations with the Taliban, Afghans were grateful that this militia had stopped the fighting that had turned their capital city into rubble. More and more refugees were returning. After years with no electricity, the power was back. Once omnipresent gunmen were banned from the streets, apart, of course, from the Taliban. Trucking costs to Kabul had halved, road-tax revenues were up fivefold in a year, and I later got stuck in a truck traffic jam on the Khyber Pass to Pakistan. In a shop in Chicken Street, a merchant told me he had already bought a new carpet loom, was thinking of setting up a match factory, and boasted that he'd recently driven all over the country feeling safe with the money in his pocket. In the bazaar, traders complained in low voices about having to wear their beards to the length of their fist. But they sat happily behind large piles of currency with only the most nominal of guards outside.

A gaunt older mullah with a red henna-dyed beard explained how he was negotiating with an American and an Argentine oil company to build a pipeline across the country. The twenty-nine-year-old deputy minister of finance wanted to negotiate a World Bank loan like other countries. At the Ministry of Mines and Industries I met the minister, an intelligent Talib with a white turban and a tartan waistcoat called Al Haj Mawlawi Ahmad Ahmadjan. He rightly boasted that the Taliban had ended a situation where everybody in Kabul had been imprisoned by rocket fire.

"We don't even have a subsistence economy. When we came here we started from zero," he said. "There were once fifteen big factories in Kabul, two hundred small ones. None were working. All the equipment had been broken or sold. Now two or three have started again, and we're rehabilitating more."

An onyx mine in Helmand had been reopened after twenty years of idleness. He wanted to open up berite and coal mines in Herat, chromite mines in Khust and Logar, marble quarries in Jalalabad, and deposits of mica, copper, and iron elsewhere. Cement and soap factories were about to start production. Then of course there were hopes for the exploitation of oil and gas. As for how this would happen, he was experimentally reinventing the financial system according to what he considered to be a good Islamic model, that is, without interest.

"We guarantee the money. Say someone invests $1 million, he operates the business, at the end of five years, we will return the $1 million," he said.

I had no idea how he thought this would work and was unable to interrupt the flow of the minister. I looked imploringly at the minister's elderly top bureaucrat for an explanation, but he remained inscrutable. The minister was, however, clearly trying to put modern economics to work in a way his countrymen could accept.

"In Islamic law there's more emphasis on private property, so we are privatizing, leasing the mines. We know that a person works on his own land better than any government organization!"

As I left, the old undersecretary pulled me aside. He was an educated civil servant who had survived and kept his dignity through everything so far, including one eleven-day period imprisoned in a small room in the ministry basement as a rocket battle raged in the city above.

"Don't be too hard on him. He's just thirty-one years old. He's trying, and you can't find anyone else like this in the whole administration!" he whispered.

Outside the ministry was a patrol of the bearded Taliban gunmen. They were clustered around a couple of 4×4 pickups with chrome roll bars, recently shipped up from a Persian Gulf emirate. They let me pause to joke with them.

"What makes the Taliban the Taliban?" I dared to ask.

"The way we look, I suppose!" the Talib joked back.

Around his eyes was a hint of kohl, black eyeliner. The Taliban were young, all-male seminarians, being a plural of Talib, meaning "student," usually, in Afghanistan, of religion. Their homogenous, deeply tanned, black-turbaned look didn't fit with Kabul's fair-skinned city folk, and the impression of a people from a different era was underlined by obsessive conversational references to following exactly the traditions of the Prophet Muhammad.

I dropped by Da Afghanistan Bank, the equivalent of the central bank. As a *Wall Street Journal* reporter, I hoped that here, at least, I would find people with their feet on solid ground. As I was led through the empty corridors and up a wide staircase, I was reminded of an obscure academic institute in a Soviet provincial city. On entering the central bank governor's suite, I found a substantial Talib warrior with a triangular beard, long shirt, and baggy trousers sitting behind the desk. Actually, Al Haj Mollah Haji Mahmad Ahmadi was sitting cross-legged on the former governor's wide chair. He didn't get up or shake hands, and, after serious mutual salutations, our conversation began. When he shifted about, I noticed his bare feet.

"Afghanistan doesn't have any problems, and we won't have any problems in the future," he ventured.

This was the most extravagant example of wishful denial I'd come across yet. It was hard to hide my impatience.

"If there is fighting, it will affect the country. We want to end the fighting," he insisted, but never looked me in the eyes. "We face some difficulties . . ."

Al Haj wanted a banking system, imports and exports. He brightened as he pointed out one advantage of the "zero government" the Taliban had inherited: zero foreign debt. He called for outside countries to help them extract and sell Afghanistan's mineral wealth. As we talked, he occasionally doodled, practicing his signature on a piece of paper. He'd been in the job for one month, having been minister of finance before.

"Is it hard to keep switching jobs?"

"This is the order of the commander of the faithful. Whatever he says, we do," said Al Haj.

A tough-faced, bearded Talib on a chair in the corner behind him, introduced as the chief of Kabul's other "bank," cracked open a broad smile and pointed to the telephone on the Soviet-style bank of telecommunications equipment. This, he said reverently, is the phone on which calls came from Mullah Omar, the one-eyed Taliban leader in the southern city of Kandahar.

"According to the basics of Islam, we will accept foreign investors," Al Haj continued, shifting his black turban on his head.

"Do many come?"

"You're the first one I've met."

It was hard to connect to him. I could only imagine the prejudices he must have had about me. A UN official had told me how he coached the Taliban in diplomatic protocol as part of their new strategy of meeting with outsiders. A day or two later they'd visit and ask, "How did we do?" and, with a flash of Afghan humor, "Were we conciliatory enough?" Unfortunately, the UN man said, every meeting started with the foreigners grandly telling off the Taliban for their restrictions on rights and culture, making the Taliban at first feel humiliated and then gradually prickly and defensive. Because of their policies on women, foreigners denied much-needed aid that would likely have benefitted women as well. When the Taliban blew up the great stone buddhas of Bamiyan three years later, supposedly in the name of the purity of Islam, one Afghan told me he reckoned it was pure defiant vengefulness, because they felt so insulted by the ungenerous, patronizing way the world had dealt with them.

The challenges Al Haj faced were daunting. He was forty but looked twenty years older. The previous central bank governor had been killed a few months earlier while on military campaign in the north. There were two national currencies, neither of which was under Kabul's control. There was the old afghani, which circulated in Taliban areas but had been issued by the former government. Then there was the new afghani, issued by the same people who had been in the former government but who were now the Taliban's enemies in the north. When the Taliban were winning battles, the old afghani would shoot up in value; and when they were beaten back, the new afghani surged.

"How about inflation? What's that running at?" I asked the bearded giant on the chair.

Al Haj shifted uncomfortably. He looked uncertainly over his shoulder at his fellow Talib bank chief behind him. They worked out what I meant but could find no answer. Soon we wrapped up our conversation. The deputy governor showed me out, a gentler, younger Talib in a white turban.

"We want to be part of the rest of the world. We need help. Tell the reality!" he pleaded with me. "You see this city, look at Herat and Kandahar! The real point is you can now put ten thousand dollars on your car and it'll still be there when you get back."

Aspects of Taliban-era Kabul verged on the otherworldly. One piece of Kabul graffiti in praise of the TALIBAN REVOLUTION announced DON'T TELL YOUR PRAYER IT'S TIME FOR WORK. TELL YOUR WORK IT'S TIME FOR PRAYER. Few really thought this way, of course. I met a former Afghan army colonel who hankered after the more rational state of affairs under the Soviet occupation.

"It's good that there's no more shooting and robbery," he said, conceding a common point of view. "But this business of beards and bans on music and these clothes is ridiculous. The kids are all losing their brains and their culture. What's the point in all of us becoming mullahs?!"

The Taliban's fundamentalist Islam didn't seem to me much different from that of the opposition warlords. From what I could see, most of the factions oppressed women and wanted to keep them covered up in burkas. And just as the identity of the Taliban was clearly ethnically Pushtun, so was their traditional *pushtunwali,* their powerful code of tribal law, clearly predominant in their interpretation of what Islamic law meant. The call of Islam was not meaningless, since it gave the Taliban an ideology and a mission. But it was money, Pakistani and Saudi support, good organization, and a focus on winning the war that had made their leader, Mullah Omar, the supreme Afghan warlord of the day.

While I was in Kabul, I felt I should go and see the main weekly morality play put on by the city's rulers, the so-called Islamic punishments in the soccer stadium. Again, the fact that they did this didn't seem to put the Taliban beyond the regional pale. The Saudis were friends of America and their executioners used swords to cut off miscreant heads after Friday prayers. In Iran, an awkward state but still part of the international system, I'd watched the judicial police use a purpose-built electric miniguillotine to chop the fingers off a thief. They chose a park by the main Tehran bus station to make sure they could round up a crowd, most of whom watched this display with a stony-faced mixture of curiosity and disgust.

"Why is this necessary?" I had asked the police chief of the city from which the thief came, Mashhad, a great center of Shia Muslim pilgrimage near Iran's border with Afghanistan.

"He was a multiple offender. It's the best way. Since we started doing this, you wouldn't believe how the number of burglaries has dropped!" he had replied.

In Kabul, the new Taliban chief of public morality similarly assured his interviewers that sex was as powerful as a loaded Kalashnikov and had to be as forcefully controlled, and that killing adulterers was a small price to pay for eradicating sin from a city. Now I waited for something to happen on a front row of the bare concrete bleachers, fitfully pestered for conversation by a few young boys with nothing better to do. The crowd of a few thousand were scattered around the stadium, the blue-clad women up on what might once have been the VIP stand. I wondered at the Olympic circles, still just visible on a wall.

"Why so few people?" I asked Malek, who'd accompanied me there to translate the Pushtun announcements.

"There's no beheading today," he replied.

At last the stadium loudspeaker system crackled into life with a prayer.

"People should come here not for fun but to learn a lesson!" the preacher admonished the crowd.

Some turbaned youths drove a four-door pickup with tinted windows onto the pitch and dumped a pile of little sacks at our end. The announcer said they contained opium and heroin. The youths poured petrol onto them and set them ablaze. Then an offender was frog-marched into the middle circle, hands bound but fully clothed. The announcer said he'd been drinking alcohol. A turbaned Talib gave him eighty strokes with a broad strap. The performance looked absurd, however, because the Talib kept his elbow close to his hip, awkwardly twisting his whole body to deliver the blows.

"That's their reading of the true practice of the Prophet Muhammad," Malek explained.

The next punishment—or "administration of heavenly order," as the Taliban's Radio Shariah put it—was delayed as the Taliban offered family members of an aggrieved party the chance to forgive a burglar, whose haul of forty-one items from their house was displayed on the pitch. No forgiveness was forthcoming. The burglar thus got his punishment, the climax of the "show." As in Tehran, the hand chopping was administered under the supervision of doctors in hospital cloaks. A Talib applied the anesthetic, a tourniquet was fastened, and the burglar fell over on his back. I could no longer see what exactly they were doing out in the midfield. I could not fail to notice, however, a certain bloodthirstiness among the stand of women, who jumped up in their seats and called down shrill imprecations and curses as the deed was done. Male spectators stormed onto the field for a better look.

A few weeks later, when a beheading drew record crowds, the Taliban pleaded publicly at great length for the families of two murder victims to spare the lives of their relatives' murderers. This included an offer to advance compensation, or blood money, to the victims' families if they would waive their right to an execution. Only after this had been exhaustively and comprehensively refused did they allow the relatives of the murdered men to slit the murderers' throats.

Throughout my week in the Islamic emirate, I was trying to find a dramatic illustration of the locked-up state of women and their lack of rights. The burka was obligatory and all travel had to be with a male relative. Females were banned from education and work. Supposedly, an on-the-spot beating could be the punishment for women who defied the bans, but among the dozens of people I asked, not one had seen this actually happen. The Taliban, after whipping and beating their way in to dominance in 1996, had not had to do much in recent months to sustain their social terror.

It was all but impossible for me to meet women. Proxy interviews didn't work either: "My sister sees veiling as security, not a restriction" was a typical comment from an Afghan male acquaintance. "Why have girls' schools, when we have none yet for the boys?" was another's. A first-year engineering student said he was "from the tribal areas, so it's okay by me. It's hard for these Kabulis, they're used to freedom. But they'll get used to the Taliban, too." Even in an international agency, the representative reckoned the plus side outweighed the minus: "Women have lost rights but gained security. There's less kidnapping, rape, and forced marriage to warlord commanders."

Women were criminally disadvantaged, no doubt. One Taliban order confined women to just one of Kabul's twenty-two hospitals. But that order was a year old, and I needed to find a new trend to prop up a journalistic story. International agencies seemed to have little real change to report on the matter. Indeed, the main problem seemed to be to keep remembering that it is not normal to oppress women. That's why there was a sign pinned up on a wall in the UN building urging officials: WE MUST NOT BEND UNDER THE WEIGHT OF SPURIOUS ARGUMENTS INVOLVING CULTURE OR TRADITIONAL VALUES . . . NO VALUE WORTH THE NAME SUPPORTS THE OPPRESSION AND ENSLAVEMENT OF WOMEN.

Frustratingly, I saw occasional women in their blue burkas in the streets going about their business, although I didn't dare address any. One day when there seemed to be no Taliban about I dodged into a burka shop. The salesman, Abdulghafor, seemed to be going as chattily and flatteringly about his business as any lingerie dealer might in the West. I didn't dare address the women, but Abdulghafor ordered me up some tea.

"I bet the Taliban have been good for business!" I ventured, watching the women checking cloth qualities between their fingers. Most of them were cheap synthetics.

"Sales are up a bit, but not much," he said.

We compared the benefits of the Iranian black chador, which leaves the face open, and the sky-blue Afghan burkas he was selling for between $4 and $20, which covers the face with a prisonlike grille. He was loyal to the Afghan national tradition. Faces should not be seen.

"The burkas are much better for sharia," he claimed.

"If you're so religious, why are you talking to these women who are not from your family?" I asked. The same social hypocrisy was evident in Iran, where the regime would separate male and female students with a curtain in class but did not stop them squashing into the same shared taxi to go home afterward.

"Oh, the Taliban come around and tell us not to talk to the women," Abdulghafor cheerily replied. "But we have to!"

"What do the women say about the burka?"

"In the old days, everyone wore it in the suburbs, not so much in the center. Some of the women are pretty angry, I admit."

I needed advice on what I should say. Mary MacMakin, a vivacious Boston native in her late sixties, had set up a nongovernmental organization to help war widows two years before. In and out of Afghanistan since the early 1960s, she was clear-eyed about the problem, and not just for women. In the past, four-fifths of schoolteachers had been women, so the social damage to the country of them not working was immense. Her upbeat appraisal shines through in my notes of our conversation, even though she had frequent arguments with the Taliban who raided her premises. Carpet weaving was "taking off like a jet plane," she said, "things have got a lot better in the last year," and even, "the atmosphere of oppression is much less, much less incidence of harassment of women." Quotation marks in my notepad showed that I had double-checked on my disbelief that I could cite a Western female activist saying such a thing about the Taliban, but MacMakin had insisted it was fine.

I gave up the idea of a Taliban-versus–Afghan women story. But after a few days, I did begin to understand why the Taliban were so obsessed with ankles and ordinances about shoes that "should not make a noise when stepping." The foot was the only part of a woman that anyone could ever see, or where a woman could express any individuality. Hence the sidewalks sported some of the wildest fishnet stockings I've ever seen. After a few days, I was compulsively checking out every ankle. That was the closest I got to any Afghan woman in Kabul.

After several days, my notebooks were replete with reportage on how, under the Taliban, Afghanistan seemed to be pulling itself together at last. There was one problem. On August 7, 1998, halfway through my trip, my shortwave radio had tuned in to broadcasts of grisly news. Two suicide truck bombs wrecked two U.S. embassies in East Africa, killing 250 people in Kenya and Tanzania and injuring 5,000. This was Osama bin Laden and al-Qaeda's breakthrough, their biggest attack to date.

In hindsight, it sealed the fate of Afghanistan. Even if the Taliban had wanted to have trans-Afghan pipelines, international relationships, and the rule of law, the embassy bombings blew up their bridge to normality. Two weeks later, on August 20, President Bill Clinton, beset with problems over his affair with intern Monica Lewinsky, unleashed a vengeful hail of missiles on Afghanistan and an innocent pharmaceutical plant in Sudan. In Khartoum, a political rally was held under the banner. CLINTON, SCREW MONICA, NOT SUDAN. No such gallows humor was on display in Kabul. Mullah Omar furiously refused to do any more business with the Americans. Bin Laden found that he had reinforced his Afghan safe haven, made himself into radical cult figure, and that goading America could help his cause.

The former Saudi intelligence chief, Turki al-Faisal, went back to see Mullah Omar in September. The meeting was brief.

"He started insulting the kingdom, words like 'the kingdom is a vassal to the U.S. Instead of putting your hands with the infidels you should put your hands with us and the righteous sheikh bin Laden to fight the infidels.' He was absolutely rude," Prince Turki said in his hypnotic monotone. "We suspended relations after that."

In Kabul, the Afghans I interviewed saw the East African bombings as happening on a different planet. To me it seemed that way too. I stuck to the story in my notebooks, published a month later under the headline TALIBAN REALITY CHECK. It suggested, broadly, that it would take a long time for a country that had lost all its educated classes and institutions to claw its way back to stability and normality, but that if there were any trains in Afghanistan, the Taliban would be trying to make them run on time. Indeed, nobody really challenged the story, making me luckier than a colleague from Reuters who wrote about far more progressive, peaceful scenes he saw in Soviet-run Kabul in the mid-1980s, and who was then hounded by accusations of being a stooge of Moscow.

In what my editors called the "to be sure" paragraph, I included the prediction of a wise American, Barnett Rubin, that the East African bombings had knocked the Taliban into the wilderness of a pariah state just as they were about to launch a big push for international recognition. Mullah Omar was snookered by his sense that his honor and the Afghan code required that he defend a guest from foreign attack. On top of that, his international isolation weakened him and made him and his circle vulnerable to bin Laden's flattery, presents, and advice. As always, a blanket Western refusal to deal with a Middle Eastern regime usually bolsters the hard-liners.

A day after the U.S. missiles struck, Carmine Calo, my companion from the UN on the road from Jalalabad, was shot and killed by a vengeful mob in a Kabul street while sitting in the same Land Rover in which we had driven together. That direst moment in Middle Eastern state implosion immediately followed. The UN and the International Committee of the Red Cross withdrew their international staff to keep them safe. Two years later, in July 2000, the Taliban arrested Mary MacMakin on charges of spying and proselytism and expelled her. Attacks on the Kabul bazaar left trade in disarray. Three gloomy years after my visit, bin Laden carried out his spectacular attacks on America, the United States invaded, and Afghanistan's civilizational stopwatch was set back to the beginning again.

Afghanistan's neighbor, Pakistan, was some way ahead in the spectrum of Middle Eastern governance, if not very far: Three-quarters of the population was illiterate and the average income was $420 a year. Shortly before one of my visits there,

Pakistan had exploded a nuclear device, raising all sorts of questions in my editors' minds about whose finger might one day be on the trigger. As far as I could tell, rich and poor, most Pakistanis were pretty exultant that they'd achieved this moment of international recognition, not to mention a kind of parity with their huge archrival, India. The outside world's mixture of ignorance and worried awe also allowed me a rare moment in journalism: a big blank sheet on which to describe the situation and ruling system of a country, without any need for finding sensational twists, dramatic predictions, or distracting prejudices.

As I began to explore, Pakistan seemed in some respects quite familiar to my home base in Turkey. It was a state founded from scratch on part of the ruins of an empire. Its charismatic and Westernized leader liked a glass of strong spirit but created a secular state based on the idea that it would be for Muslims. Also like Turkey, it had a powerful army that viewed itself as the guardian of the state. Another aspect of Pakistani governance was strange, familiar, and seductive at the same time: the country's ruling class of feudal lords. These were the heirs of a nineteenth-century landowning elite co-opted by the British Empire, and even today, the most tribal of them kept up their influence through an ability to command whole districts to vote in their favor. Indeed, tribal lords formally ruled the autonomous provinces along Pakistan's border with Afghanistan.

This version of democracy is by no means purely Pakistani: In all Middle Eastern countries where voting is part of the regime, from rural areas of Iran to Kurdish areas of southeastern Turkey, elections are partly managed in this way. In Pakistan, however, the system is at its most extensive, with some five hundred feudal lords. Quite a few of them descend directly from warlords who carved out territory in raids down from the mountains of Afghanistan, an age-old tradition in which Afghanistan is still largely stuck.

Feudal lords sounded like an irresistible subject. Many were educated at Atchison College in Lahore, just like my own boarding school. In speech, many cultivated an engaging Pakistani version of the English upper-class drawl. At times, one insider boasted, every single member of the cabinet had passed down Atchison's tree-lined avenues and worn the college blazer, even if "only the academic underachievers gravitated toward politics."

In business, in politics, in society, the ruling elite referred to itself, with British self-deprecation and a consistent certainty, as "the feudals." They sometimes seemed above the law, since they had long ago successfully merged with the state. But, increasingly, they were having to defend themselves from the democratic demands of Pakistan's growing middle class. Perhaps Pakistan had lessons for Afghanistan, showing how warlords could become responsible feudal lords and ultimately become irrelevant as a modern society emerged. In my own England, social hierarchies had developed from a similar starting point of liege lords. Some thought that events could go in the other direction, with Afghanistan's Taliban dragging Pakistan back into the past. Either way, many of the feudals I spoke to felt their privileged way of life was doomed. But they were resilient and believed they were doomed only one day, far in the future, a day of reckoning that might be delayed with sufficient guile.

A Lahore textile magnate cheerfully admitted how "thoroughly spoiled" the feudals were as a class and how they had no game plan to survive. Then he aristocratically waved in a servant with another tray of cucumber sandwiches and samosas. The ex-cricketer Imran Khan received me in his family mansion, where his living quarters, with bare lightbulbs, exercise machines, and a complete lack of any female touch, reminded me of what might be a prefect's room in my old school. He was trying to break the mold of Pakistani politics, he said, but there was as yet no democracy, "only alliances with mafias or feudals. Without a change in system, we're gone." The *Journal*'s legendary correspondent Ahmed Rashid split his time between lordly commentaries and running the family coal mines. Tehmina Durrani, a beautiful lady with smoldering eyes, told me as we sat together on a sofa at a party how she had written an indictment of the whole system in a book about her husband called *My Feudal Lord*. She still seemed to be doing pretty well.

One member of this engaging elite, Shehryar Mazari, impressed me with an unusual sense of moral duty. His father was a notably honest government minister who from the 1960s on opposed the dictatorial methods of Pakistan's successive rulers. He was also a lord of the Baluch, one of the country's principal ethnic groups. When I asked to see the system working at firsthand, Mazari invited me up to spend a few days in Rojhan, his tribal territory on the sun-scorched plain by the Indus River in the heart of Baluchistan.

As we flew up from Karachi together, Mazari told me how he had spent twenty-one years out of Pakistan, once as far away as New Zealand, before moving on to the quiet life of an international banker around the world. Then, as he took a sabbatical to reconnect with his homeland, his father ordered him back to rescue the family farm from clannish feuding. His first problem was one of scale. Islamic inheritance laws decree equal shares between children, so any landholding gets smaller with each generation. In Turkey, I once visited a plow factory whose success was entirely based on this phenomenon: Every new younger son would become a landowner and order his own equipment, and so the country was filled with a wasteful excess, not just of plows, but also of tractors and all kinds of duplicated and underused agricultural machinery. Mazari's father had inherited some eighty thousand acres but lost seventy-seven thousand to land reform legislation and sold two thousand to support his political career. He fell out with Pakistan's two

Pakistani feudal lord Shehryar Mazari *(right)* stands with his retainers before a family fort in his Baluch tribal fiefdom. *(Hugh Pope)*

main political factions, ending up in jail under both. By the time Mazari took it over in his name, there were just over a thousand acres left for his sons by his two wives.

We landed at a small airport named after the prince of a Gulf emirate who liked to come here with his falcons to hunt bustards in the deserts. After leaving the plane we had a choice: the "royal lounge," the "executive lounge," and "arrivals." Mazari modestly guided me through "arrivals" to a saloon car.

"This car shows I'm a failure as a feudal. I go for these cheap Jap jobs, not one of the expensive four-wheel drives," he said.

No longer, he added, did thirty horsemen stand ready to greet him outside the family fort as he remembered from his youth. Such forts were still built in the old style of "just one entrance—hope for the best, plan for the worst." He had struggled valiantly to make the fields of cotton and mango trees pay. He tried to be modern, inaugurating field-management methods to boost yields. He said he treated the three hundred people who depended on his decisions fairly and decently. He built and equipped a cotton-ginning factory. Other Mazaris had set up a Super Mazari Petrol Station and a fish farm, but this was the first industrial enterprise started by any member of the clan. He named it "Challenge."

"I ended the system of rents and put them all on salaries. I learned about fertilizer and crops. I was the first to bring international pruning methods to mangoes.

I wanted to progress," he said. "But when I tried to find out why the schools weren't getting better, the minister of education told me quietly that it was my own family that was blocking things."

He tried to bring in a doctor and improve the medical system but found a pharmacist in the bazaar selling the medicines he'd provided.

Mazari also kept up traditions, and I felt that I was for once glimpsing that untouched Middle East that my heart still sought. I was shown to my bedroom by a turbaned seventy-five-year-old servant who looked exactly like the water genie portrayed in the gorgeous Salman Rushdie tale of *Haroun and the Sea of Stories* that I often read to my eldest daughter.

"Malik Rahmin's family has been with us for two hundred years. His ancestor was originally a prisoner of war, who became a slave," Mazari whispered. This clan formerly went by the name of *ghulam,* meaning "slave," until half a century before, when they had sensibly shrugged this off in favor of the new surname of *malik,* or "king." "Feudalism is a state of mind, a mentality from the days of the moghuls when everyone was dependent on the emperor for a share of what was extracted from the empire. Now everyone wants to be a VIP."

The walls of Mazari's house were hung with crossed scimitars and a collection of jezails, antique rifles with inlaid stocks as curvaceous as harem pants. They dated from the eighteenth century, when Mazari's ancestors arrived as mercenaries from deeper in the interior.

"We used to live by piracy, preying on the ships going up and down the Indus. But nowadays our district is just a baking hot stretch of desert, and I wonder what we're doing here," Mazari complained as we sat in his front room, receiving principal tenants who had heard of his arrival. "I used to be a banking professional. Now all I talk about is fertilizers and crops."

A police chief arrived, then a tribesman on the run from manslaughter charges. Gradually a widening circle of smallholders clustered in his salon to watch the action. In each case the routine was the same. Mazari would give an account of his activities since the two men had last met. Then the visitor would give his full story. The monologue could last several minutes. It struck me as an excellent way of catching up. I now try to get a "Baluch report" whenever I meet a member of my family after a long parting.

Soon the electricity cut out, stopping the fans and raising the temperature in the room to the ambient heat. This elicited another round of reminiscences about the past.

"We were used to the heat then. Now we get hot whenever the fan stops," he said. "It was much better in the old days. There was simplicity, honesty, the food was simple. Everyone wore white, even twenty years ago, with no buttons or colors. Now everyone's in blues and pinks . . ."

"How many people are there in your tribe now?" I asked him.

"About eighty thousand. But there's not just me as the feudal lord, not just my father. We're very fragmented," Mazari replied.

"Still, at least you have these people's respect."

"It's like being a school prefect. I've learned to be firm but fair. If you're weak, they'll take advantage of you."

As the visitors came and went, and the stories multiplied, Mazari's mood became more somber.

"You need to be a lawyer to mediate this stuff. There's so much lying." He sighed. "It's about land, murder, honor killings, cattle theft, you name it. But basically it's about too many people and not enough land."

One of his ideas had caught on successfully, to sow winter wheat between the rows of cotton. But he often left the hot plain of Rojhan to travel. And every time he left, he said, new problems arose. Fertilizer disappeared. Agents cut corners. Farmers forgot or ignored his lectures on new methods. The uncertain business of running the cotton-ginning mill "was gambling against the forty families that own all the textile mills in Pakistan," so he passed it on to a risk-loving relative. One year he introduced a pest spotter to catch bug infestations early, then left on holiday; when boll weevils were seen, the farmers ignored the spotter's warnings. The crop was lost, angering family members who missed their rent money and were tired of the newfangled ways. Soon, against all the principles he'd learned while abroad, he was forced to go back to the old system of feudal rents. He focused on carving out a small tract of land to serve as a model farm and his plan to gather into his garden one example of each of Pakistan's flowering trees.

Mazari himself got into a feud with his half brother, who occupied their father's traditional Baluch fort in a move to take over more of the family land. A relative also took to roaming the countryside with armed men, intimidating farmers. A few nights before we arrived, one hundred machine-gun rounds had been fired outside Mazari's house.

"As we say, half a doctor is more dangerous than no doctor at all," Mazari groaned. "You have to be here the whole time, like a spider in the web, watching everything. For nine years, I've been trying to find an honest way to make money, but I've been hitting my head against the wall. The village is split by feuds and I hate lording it over the peasants."

The next day Mazari and I set out early to tour his Rojhan district estates, past and present. We picked up some cousins to go visit the family tombs, mosquelike buildings with intricately painted wooden ceilings in bold red, yellow, and indigo. They stood among acacia trees close to a sandy bank of the Indus and were losing a few more bricks with each season's flood. We sat down in the sweltering heat. One cousin brought out a bottle of *teeta,* a potent brandy distilled from local acacia bark. He tested it by dipping in his forefinger and setting it aflame with his cigarette lighter.

Lunch was in a pavilion in a big family fort, a rectangular enclosure of thick mud-brick walls, with a gatehouse and corners marked by fat, round, crenellated towers of pale brick. More and more tribesman gathered to watch our sophisticated picnic, all with the obligatory rifle hung from their shoulders. It was a modernized scene from a Persian miniature painting. To entertain everyone, Mazari suggested a shooting match. A tribesman was sent to set up some paving stones as targets about one hundred yards away, on a sandbank on the inside of the fort wall. I had been captain of shooting at school and felt confident I could hold my own. The family asked me to choose my weapon. I took a modern-looking Kalashnikov and loosed off round after round. Careful as I was, and able to support the barrel-grip arm on my knee, I still missed every shot. A cousin fired off a stream of shots from the shoulder and hit several. Perhaps I was too nervous about hitting the tribesman who was standing next to the stones to set them back up. Or I should have dared to use one of the tribesmen's old Lee-Enfield .303s, the same pre–First World War weapon I used in my days as a military cadet.

We drove to town to buy me two cases of mangoes to take home to Istanbul, and I dropped by the local bank to see which way the economy was moving. Feudals, the manager said, nowadays accounted for only 10 percent of his business. Hardworking owners of smallholdings were his new customers, as were the growing urban bourgeoisie. Then I sat with the local mullah, who opined that a recent trip to Afghanistan had convinced him that the direct Islamic rule of the Taliban was the best not just for Pakistan but for the whole world. He listed its benefits as the ban on alcohol, the cloistering of women, and an absence of the state. But his most devoted disciple that day was a ranking officer of the Pakistani army, sitting at the mullah's feet in full uniform and, of course, paid by the state. It reminded me of a French officer in Kabul who'd told me the incestuous relationship of Pakistani army intelligence and the Taliban was like someone who's pulled the pin of a hand grenade and then is doomed to keep holding the spring-loaded detonation lever to keep it from exploding.

Despite these conflicting images of a Pakistan that could either modernize or slip back into medieval backwardness, I couldn't believe that the fading away of the old masters was all bad. Instead of serving their feudal lords, one son of Mazari's ancient retainer Malik worked for Colgate-Palmolive in Karachi. Another had an electrical shop in Lahore. Television, money, travel were all carrying Pakistani society forward. Middle classes would have to arrive one day and begin to take responsibility for a new rule of law.

Mazari continued his struggle for a better country. Having learned the hard way, he gradually improved yields on his wheat and cotton crops, beating skeptics, fertilizer shortages, rapacious middlemen, and a summer when there was almost no electricity to power the irrigation pumps. In 2008, he ran for parliament in an attempt to defeat a "brigand political cousin" who was misgoverning a neighboring district for the ex-military national dictator of the day. By eight P.M. on election night, with 82 percent of the votes counted, Mazari was beating his cousin's proxy candidate by two votes to one. Then the cousin, the police, the paramilitaries, and even the officer in charge of the polls stuffed the ballot boxes with an extra thirty-five thousand ballot papers to "defeat" him. He told me that "dozens of my polling agents were kidnapped, hog-tied, and physically thrashed—some returning, bruised and battered, only three days later." When he challenged the outcome in court, the supposedly democratic party that he represented abandoned him. After the falsely elected incumbent died a few months later, the new president, from the same party, used the by-election to install unopposed a loyalist who was unknown among the Baluch.

In between times, Mazari published the story of his father's struggle against authoritarianism, and its title, *A Journey to Disillusionment*, spoke volumes. He was convinced that his family's old role was coming to an end and worried that nothing good seemed to be coming in its place.

"I can't stand it, Hugh. A decent person gets no respect in Pakistani society today. Decency is perceived as a weakness. Who are the dacoits [bandits]? The dacoits are us," Mazari said when we got back to Karachi after our trip, puffing on his small English pipe in the sumptuous library of his father's grand house. "There used to be tribal pressure to stay together. Now everyone's going his own way. People are better educated, but there are no jobs. They are free, but the freedom is false, because there is no safety, like in the old tribal system. My father was a strong, tough, just lord; now justice is arranged through touts, bribes, and bent police. The younger generation can't run everything, like in the old days. There is a change in fundamental values. In the end, I foresee anarchy. But it's much better to go down fighting the good fight."

The prevalence of warlords in Afghanistan and feudal lords in Pakistan was not just a developmental problem, although poverty and ignorance did play a role. The problem was that, like everywhere in the Middle East, the many wars and revolutions of the past century uprooted or destroyed existing societies, sometimes repeatedly. The sense of instability is now endemic. East of Europeanizing Turkey, almost no country has achieved a maturity that allows real political power to be transferred without the ruler's death, assassination, or execution—a situation analogous, say, to Britain under the Tudors.

Furthermore, democracy is tough to bring into a region where there is little political homogeneity. Almost all the states inherited borders artificially cutting through all manner of ethnic and religious groups to serve the needs of European empires. Lacking democratic legitimacy, most developed authoritarian tendencies, making them excessively dependent on armed forces and the security services, reliant on external support or vulnerable to foreign interference. Families close to the ruling group tend to become the economic version of feudal lords. This has all impeded the development of a stable bedrock of middle classes, a symptom and cause of further instability.

In the Eastern lands ruled by the Ottoman Empire until 1923, that is, much of what is now thought of as the Middle East, the bourgeoisie and even the majority communities of towns were often non-Muslim. In the part that became modern Turkey, the disappearance of these Greeks and Armenian Christian minorities in the first two decades of the twentieth century, through massacres, expulsions, and population transfers, dealt a developmental blow from which Turkish society is still trying to recover. Still, in 1923 Turkey became the first Middle Eastern country to found an independent republic and set out to construct a nation-state in Europe's image. For nearly three decades it was an oppressive, one-party regime and developed painfully slowly into a multiparty democracy thereafter. Eighty years later, Turkey has built up a broader middle class and the best-functioning democracy in the Muslim world, but the problem of representation and democracy within political parties themselves remains a big challenge. Each party still works as a miniature dictatorship, even if Turkish voters can and do vote their often authoritarian leaders in and out of office every few years.

The way Turkish society hit a civilizational air pocket with the end of the Ottoman Empire is obvious even in Istanbul's new Museum of Modern Art. As the cultured painters of the early twentieth century bourgeoisie died out, including the talented last caliph, whose work is represented by a radiant self-portrait and a cheerfully amateurish study of an elegant woman, their place was taken by the representatives of a far more limited, unimaginative national culture. Only now is the artistic scene in Istanbul—Europe's biggest city—really becoming world-class.

Turkey is not alone. The Palestinians saw their whole society atomized by the foundation of Israel in 1948 and subsequent wars, with millions forced into exile, the middle classes scattered, and the brightest minds usually finding it easiest to make better lives far from the region. The Egyptian revolution led by Jamal Abd al-Nasser ousted the monarchy in 1952 and destroyed the educated bourgeoisie. Within a decade or two, the great Egyptian film industry was a shadow of its former self, and the presidential system was a dictatorship at least as autocratic as that of dethroned King Farouk. In 1958 Iraq's monarchy fell to a bloody military coup d'état that led to the dictatorial regime of Saddam Hussein. It was eye-opening on visits to Iraqi Kurdistan in the 1990s to observe how sophisticated the culture of anybody over the age of fifty could be and how brutalized was the psychology of anyone under thirty. In 1961 it was Syria's turn to join the madness, with a revolution that soon stripped all initiative from its once great merchant cities of Damascus and Aleppo. Algeria's independence from France in 1962 was also effectively a revolution that drove out the principal pillars of middle-class culture. Urban centers were always more marginal in Libya, but the ascension to power of the eccentric Muammar Ghadafi in 1969 extinguished any hope of pluralism or economic and cultural depth. In 1975, Lebanon, once the most internationalized of Middle Eastern cultures, followed its neighbors into the morass, igniting a fifteen-year civil war that sucked in the ambitions and armies of Syria, Israel, and the United States, wrecked the country, and drove its middle classes into distant exiles. Then came the 1979 Islamic Revolution in Iran, shortly followed by the 1980–88 Iran-Iraq War. The best-educated three million people of Iran quickly fled to enrich the cultures of France and the United States. The exodus from Iraq sped up most during the U.S.-led sanctions of the 1990s and especially after the invasion of 2003. More than one-sixth of the population fled, often people with the most initiative. Iraqi doctors have become one of the mainstays of the British National Health Service.

In all cases, from the catastrophic collapse of the Ottoman Empire after the First World War onward, the destruction of the old elite usually put in power people with a rural background. This has put a suspicious, insecure, patriarchal, village-minded stamp on Middle Eastern governance. The new rulers often sprang from the best-organized group, the region's ex-colonial armies, adding an authoritarian streak to the mix. Introversion and clannishness are prevalent as well, partly because in villages, as well as states where you can't trust the government, families stick together.

With time, determination, and a measure of security, countries can bounce back. One June day in 2002 I flew into Kabul airport with a Turkish Airlines Airbus to celebrate a changing of the guard. A Turkish general was going to command the NATO force in Afghanistan. Alongside me in the specially chartered passenger jet, I soon realized, were members of the Symphonic Band of the Turkish Armed Forces. As we waited by a dusty parade ground for the ceremony to start, I braced for what would most likely be a humiliation in front of all these multinational force commanders and diplomats. A real band needs a breadth of tradition and culture that only a strong society can provide, and, having witnessed many a tinpot parade in Middle Eastern capitals, I feared that Turkey wouldn't make the grade. My premonitions were made worse by chatting with an old friend among the internationals in the audience, who, taking a different route from Oxford, had entered Her Majesty's secret service and here appeared in a thick Afghan-style beard as the latest incarnation of Western attempts to guide the future of Afghanistan. He joked how impossible it was to work with the Turks in Turkey because, even though they were NATO allies of the West, their prickly, suspicious Middle Eastern side refused to allow the British in on their real secrets. I sympathized with the Turks. It was the British who had carved up the Ottoman Empire.

Still, my friend's stories of how the poorly supplied British forces in Afghanistan struggled to make do were surprising. And watching the handover ceremony proceed from under the shade of a tree there in Kabul, it was the outgoing British contingent that made me wince. To say farewell to the Afghans, they produced a few fifes and marching drums, which pluckily tapped and whistled through the theme tune from the film *The Great Escape*. It was at the same time practical, ironic, and disappointing.

By contrast, the Turks, who had no inhibitions about demanding cash from the United States for subcontracting military work, had set up camp in such style that even the French were passing by to ask for bread from the Turkish bakery ovens. And soon a splendid sound rolled over the parade ground. Marching toward us in relaxed but excellent order, their crimson jackets immaculately pressed, brass instruments blazing in the sun, the Symphonic Band made a magnificent entry. As their maestro conducted them through rich versions of the Western canon, I felt my spirits lifting.

Then came their surprise gift: a new national anthem for Afghanistan. President Hamid Karzai was delighted, jumping up to his feet to clap. He later begged to be allowed to keep the music, and the maestro duly sent a minion to extract it from the band's selection of sheet music. I later learned that the colonel had, with just a few days' notice, taken a cassette sent with just a single melodic line and created this full-band musical arrangement. The two Afghan colonels who had taken refuge next to me in the shade of a tree had no idea that they even had an anthem. Under the Taliban, they joked, they had had to make do with "Praise be to God" in a plainsong chant.

13. REGAL REPUBLICS, DEMOCRATIC KINGS

Syria, Jordan, and the Dimensions of Dictatorship

He alone knows the heat of the bath who has entered it.
—ARABIC PROVERB

I walked toward the crudely welded double gate in the border fence. A crowd of travelers heading from Turkey into Syria stood to my left, their shapeless bundles of stuff wrapped in all kinds of cloth, their faces locked in expressionless submission to the God of Border Crossings. I unloaded my luggage to the right alongside a trader's stash of cheap water coolers and folded blankets in clear plastic carrying cases. I then adopted the national survival technique, a mental attitude of opportunistic indifference. I knew the score. A Syrian border point once detained me and my car for most of a day, filling two whole pages of my passport with stamps. At the last obstacle, I had to beg my way through by presenting my distressed small children at the office of the border station chief. Another time I was barred from crossing entirely and had to phone through my disappointment to my would-be hosts in Damascus at a 1930s wooden plug-and-line telephone exchange, from which mice popped in and out of the holes as if in a cartoon film.

A policeman in khaki uniform appeared from the Syrian side, his eyes covered by dark aviator glasses. He rasped the gate open and gestured toward me. I stepped through the fence and handed over my papers. With that, I exited Turkey, uptight but relatively efficient, and let myself be swept away by the swirling currents of

Syria, where decades of dull dictatorship have dimmed, but never conquered, the gallows humor, open spirit, and stubborn ungovernability of the Syrians.

Gesticulating with my passport, the policeman started shouting theatrically at the water cooler and blanket merchant. He seemed to be making clear that nobody would move any farther until his goods were through the gate. Then he gave up in midsentence, changed his mind, locked the merchant on the Turkish side, and began to deal with me. We walked to a new hut that he said was the passport control office. Halfway there, a second policeman took my passport. I was ushered into a glassed-off room with desks that had never been used.

"Just coming!" called the second Syrian, then left in another direction.

Five minutes later a third man came in behind the desks, carrying my passport. He tut-tutted, picked up some ledgers, and left again.

Another five minutes later, the first policeman with the aviator glasses came back and led me to a shopworn hut where people really were having their passports dealt with. He then got involved in a playful fight with a fellow border policeman, in which he used my passport as a kind of bat. They tussled, then he remembered me and put me in the chief's room and told me to sit down. Then he disappeared again. I sat down.

"No, no! Not there!" I heard him shout from around the corner. I jumped up again. "Please come here, mister!"

So round I went, through back corridors to another office, which a wooden desktop nameplate in elaborate jigsaw-cut calligraphy announced to be the preserve of a Captain Mardini. Papers and books and ledgers were piled up in front of a man with a dark-tanned skin and a round, jolly face. They all voiced great pleasure that I spoke Arabic, and, better still, that I had learned it in Damascus. Captain Mardini filled out my personal details yet again. I gave a faint, respectful groan.

"Ah, bureaucracy," he said, embracing me with a beaming smile. "That's what makes us Arabs great!"

I told Captain Mardini and his court how I remembered my trials at the main state bank in Damascus as a penniless student, passing by every working day to see if my latest English check had cleared. Once it took five weeks. The lady at the international counter would slowly peer at the ledger and then inform me blankly that the money wasn't there.

"The way she looked at me, it was as if someone from the rich West actually owed that money to her and her bank, not the other way around!" I said.

The passport officers roared with laughter. I did too—at the naïve student, at the thieving state, at the tyranny of bureaucrats like themselves. I was presented with another piece of paper that I had to fill out.

"What's this card for, anyway?" I asked.

"I've no idea!" Mardini retorted, delighted with a new paradox. "It's just part of the routine."

We puzzled together over my patchwork background—born in South Africa, British passport, speaks Arabic, lives in Turkey, works for Americans, Swiss children, Dutch wife, passport stamps from Albania to China. The questions kept coming. Father's name? Maurice. Mother's name? Johanna.

"Johanna? But that's a man's name."

More curious discussion. Strong sweet tea was summoned. Stamps were whacked into my paperwork. At last I dragged my bags out through the rough yard outside, past another registrar, to the last army post, and then surrendered myself to a corrupt gang of drivers. Ah, Syria. Infuriating or entrancing, terrorist or terrorized, one thing is for sure: Nothing happens very fast.

Luckily, when I rushed to Damascus to help report on the aftermath of the death of Syrian President Hafez al-Assad in 2000, I passed through the more user-friendly halls of the airport. Since my colleague Stephen Glain was already watching events in the capital, I headed straight up to the remote mountains of northwestern Syria, where the Assad family came from and where he would be buried. I hoped to catch a glimpse of his son and heir, Dr. Bashar al-Assad, a London-trained eye doctor and computer buff. I thought I could perhaps see some of the new dynamics of the country at the grand funeral for his father, who had ruled Syria with unflinching and brutal caution for three decades.

I staked out a spot in the Assads' mountain village and waited until the procession went by. Dr. Bashar was there, a tall, lanky figure in a black suit. I started to follow him. Dr. Bashar was frustrated. Security men were surrounding him, hemming him in. He made impatient hand gestures to get them to move away, to give him some space. They ignored him. This was a big day and they weren't going to let anybody risk spoiling it, not even the new president.

I had already learned at the 1989 funeral for Ayatollah Khomeini in Tehran how the death of a country's Big Man could be an awesome event in itself. I pushed and elbowed my way through the crowds to the heart of the funeral staged on the plain south of Tehran, to an inner stadium of rickety and hastily erected scaffolding. I knew that many people had been crushed to death at Stalin's funeral, and, far from being caught up in the black-clad Iranian crowd's passionate wailing, I became increasingly alarmed that the funeral might become my own. At the point where I could barely move my arms and was being bodily lifted up off my feet by the surging crowd, the imam's body appeared on the roof rack of a beige Toyota Land Cruiser. Seeking ways toward the grave, or perhaps just giving his most passionate supporters an intimate chance to bid farewell, the jeep lurched drunkenly forward and backward. Bearded Islamic Revolutionary Guards leaped onto the front bumpers, screaming with a desperate madness for people to make way. Everyone around me erupted in an ecstasy of grief, and for several minutes I felt that I was fighting to stay afloat in a stormy sea. Whenever the jeep passed by, hundreds of hands reached up to grab a piece of Khomeini's burial shroud, making it gradually unwind to reveal his naked body. The last time their imam came past me he was lying half naked on his side, the wounds and stitches of the surgeon's last stomach cancer operations running up his chest like rough wooden steps nailed to a telephone pole. Even in death, however, the great man's long gray beard and hooded eyes maintained a stern and thoughtful dignity.

Up in the Assads' mountain village, in the heartland of his minority Alawite sect, there was no mass hysteria. Still, an unshaven youth had taken one of the black-edged photographs of Hafez al-Assad distributed by the funeral organizers and had dug its safety pin directly into his own bare and bleeding arm, part of a self-mutilation that included scores of gashes over his arms and torso.

"When I heard the news of his death, I went crazy. I didn't know what I was doing. I don't know how many times I cut myself. For him, I had the love for a father or a brother, I loved him with my soul and blood. He was everything for me. He was life itself."

"Doesn't it hurt?" I asked.

"I feel no pain. The pain is bigger in my heart!" he replied.

A Big Man can indeed inspire such loyalty. It was hard to explain to individualistic, educated, and empowered Westerners that a significant number of people in Syria were bound into patronage networks that were a vital and perhaps only buffer between themselves and poverty. To them, dependent on the corruption and even the brutality of the one-party state, the death of the patron was an utterly devastating event.

Many Syrians, whatever they thought of President Assad's domestic record, could also voice grudging agreement with the international outlook of the Baath Party, an Arabic word that means "renaissance." The Baath originally represented

One Syrian felt such grief at the funeral of Hafez al-Assad that he pinned into the flesh of his arm a picture of the deceased leader and his two sons, the late Basil (left) and the new president Dr. Bashar (right). (Hugh Pope)

the 1950s Arab nationalist dream of rebirth and unity after the struggle for freedom from the Ottoman Empire and the European colonialist rule that took its place. The success of the Baath Party, which came to power in both Syria and Iraq, was also a reaction to the way Israel had trounced the previous, softer postcolonial Arab regimes. Even though the Baathist presidents of both countries wrote new chapters in the story of Arab failures, their rhetorical stand of confrontation against Israel did at least fit the popular mood.

But the Baath Party itself had grown stale. Many Syrians wanted change and more democracy, but feared, as the regime wanted them to, that political liberalization could lead to destructive revolution at home and weakness abroad. And they certainly did not trust any change delivered by the United States, which was visibly hostile to them and was an unquestioning supporter of their most obvious enemy, Israel.

At the top of Syrian government, the corrupt, bullying barons of Hafez al-Assad's court were loyal to Dr. Bashar, and also dependent on him for their wealth and power. They sought to control him like the security guards did at the burial. Dr. Bashar depended on them too, to defend himself against the likes of his uncle Rifaat, the brother of Hafez, in exile after mobilizing his tanks once too often in disputes over the succession. The barons had helped Dr. Bashar just before his father's death, staging the bloody military seizure of Uncle Rifaat's home compound on the coast, which also acted as a lucrative illegal port. Now Uncle Rifaat was working the phones to his old army friends, publicly claiming to be the legitimate heir. In some ways he was, since succession in Arab clan and kingly leadership usually goes to the oldest surviving brother. He also offered to "take up his responsibilities at any time" in interviews with the BBC—and to whoever was listening in Washington, D.C.

Despite these ominous signs, there was hope that Syria might be waking from its decadeslong sleep. There was much talk then about the youthful Dr. Bashar ushering in a new era of renewal in Syria. People began to talk about the onset of a "Damascus Spring," partly because it was that time of year. Perhaps, people dared to hope, the Americans might then even change their approach to Syria.

I drove back down from the Assads' ancestral hills to the city I reckoned would be gladdest of change if there was to be a springtime of new freedoms: Hama. If Syria was really changing, at last I'd have the chance to give the *Wall Street Journal* an uplifting narrative of the kind they loved and do something to broaden the image of Syria, to which I felt sympathetic, despite the regime's manifest shortcomings. I had lived among its people, had childhood memories of the country, had explored many of its obscurest corners, and had shared in its political turmoil.

The people of Hama had reason to hate the regime of Hafez al-Assad. I last saw their city in one piece in 1980, when my bus from Damascus to Aleppo stopped in the late evening by the Orontes River that runs through its heart. The air was thick with an agonized concert known in Arabic as *anina,* the juddering groans and wrenching wails of the giant wooden waterwheels, the norias, that have for centuries heaved water up to high aqueducts feeding irrigation systems around the city. I stood on the parapet by the slow-moving river, soaking in the atmosphere of this ancient urban fabric. In my hand was a plate of a favorite specialty of Hama, a chewy, almost liquid pastry that flows in slow-motion waterfalls off treelike trays in the cake shops and is served wrapped around clotted cream cheese and drowned in rose-scented syrup.

Two years after this visit, in 1982, armed militants from the Muslim Brothers staged a rebellion, seized the city center, and killed any officials, party members, and even teachers they found. Uncle Rifaat then parked the nation's tanks and artillery on the outskirts of town. Ineffectual against the might of Israel, for which they were purchased, Syria's big guns simply pounded the city center into submission. At least ten thousand innocents may have been killed, but nobody really knows. Then a whole district of the town center was flattened and expropriated. Many people abandoned it.

For years afterward, piles of rubble stood where the trucks dumped them on secondary roads leading out of town. In 1992, wandering in backstreets, I still found a car trapped in an overgrown stone-arched garage blown apart ten years before. In 2000, when Dr. Bashar took over, big swathes of the center still lay empty, scarred with rubble-strewn hillocks and the bombed-out ruins of once-graceful stone mansions. To add insult to injury, the only decent hotel in town had been erected on a bulldozed lot on a bend in the river, where once the vaulted terraces of a medieval palace stepped down to the bank of the Orontes. The concrete and marble hotel was designed with the town's trademark architecture of stripes of pale and dark stone, but too obviously done. Traces of rubble lay right next to it. The regime certainly wanted Hama to remember its lesson. Only a few waterwheels on the other side of the river survived to tell their tortured tale.

What surprised me, as I began to talk to the Hamawis, was how the population seemed to have left the past behind. Two young men whom I had coffee with were not frightened to talk of it but were far more interested in coining Arabic nicknames for different models of cell phones that had just become the rage. Mobile phones, the Internet, and commerce were small steps forward by which the regime manipulated and defused popular expectations for political change.

"People are not pushing Bashar to move too quickly. We feel we would not be better off if he did that," said Maen, up visiting relatives from his day job, which, coincidentally, was running one of the security details around the U.S. embassy. He excused his apathy as typical of the "destroyed generation" of the 1960s and 1970s when schools were so full there were fifty students per class, Syria was mauled in two wars with Israel, and political instability wrecked the economy. Things changed so slowly that there were still cars from the 1950s on the roads.

"For goodness' sake! How long can you go on making parts for your old cars by hand?" I remonstrated. "You've been to Lebanon, you've seen how far Syria has fallen behind!"

"Sure, we go to Lebanon, we enjoy it. But we still feel better off than Lebanon. I would not want to be them. I don't like that much democracy. I prefer a good dictator."

The two men started debating the maze of regulations holding back their business dreams, the scams of exporting rotten fruit to get "export dollars," and their hopes invested in Law No. 10, a regulation to encourage investment in the Syrian infrastructure, which had achieved little since it was part of the last Damascus Spring in 1991. Their concern was how to make the system work for them, not how to destroy it.

"We will continue to resist globalization for a while. It would destroy what little economy we have. I don't want to catch up. I don't have long enough legs!" said Maen.

All they expected from Dr. Bashar was a slow Chinese-style liberalization of the economy. Already here in Hama, the government was allowing people to found joint-stock companies. I tracked down a group of traditional Hama grandees who had set up a successful intercity bus company and were now building a vegetable oil factory, mostly with local shareholders' money.

This, indeed, was a story the readers of the *Wall Street Journal* could connect to. Editors' sudden interest in where a new leader would take Syria, and that indispensable and real element of hope, allowed me to write a straight story. Of course, onto the locomotive of optimism I hooked a trainload of Syrian problems: a brutal history, incorrigible bureaucrats, deadbeat banks, and the near impossibility of running an honest business. But the title in one of the *Journal*'s editions brimmed with enthusiasm: ONCE-DECIMATED SYRIAN CITY POINTS TOWARD ERA OF REFORM.

I was back in Syria a year later, in 2001, keen to update *Journal* readers on the fate of the Damascus Spring. Dr. Bashar had closed a notorious desert jail and released six hundred political prisoners. He had allowed a first private school to open. Parliament had passed new laws to introduce private banks and to protect banking secrecy. Steps were being taken to liberalize the currency and customs regulations that had choked Syrian business for so long. Satellite television dishes spread thickly across the Damascus skyline.

One symbol of this era was a caricature-filled weekly magazine called *al-Dumari,* the *Lamplighter*. When it appeared in 2001, it outsold the entire print run of the three turgid state-run daily newspapers in an hour. Syrians had seen nothing like it since thirty-eight years before, when private newspapers were banned.

"Aren't you scared to be stocking this?" I asked at a newsstand, looking over my shoulder.

"There's no fear anymore. We want to see criticism, something good at last," the newspaper seller said. "I ordered one hundred copies this week, but I've asked for five hundred for next week!"

Even though the colorful *Lamplighter*'s satire was light, and mainly directed against obvious corruption, the idea of a publication entirely outside state control seemed unbelievable. I tracked down the magazine's offices to a well-off middle-class neighborhood. The owner, publisher, and chief editor, Ali Farzat, had a full beard, neatly pressed jeans, and a taste for big Cuban cigars.

Farzat said he'd been encouraged to found the weekly by Dr. Bashar seven years before, but even though Dr. Bashar was then the president's son and had now been president for a year, the press laws had only just changed.

"I rang up Dr. Bashar after the first edition hit the streets. He was very happy," Farzat said. "He loves this kind of thing."

"But Syria is still ruled by fear!" I insisted.

Farzat hunkered down in his chair with his head under his arms as if protecting himself from being beaten, then laughed.

"There is a new period that has started. Bashar loves initiative, he respects it. He loves arts and sciences. He is young. He has a map in his head and he's implementing it step by step. Reform is something that imposes itself, like the need for oxygen."

Three months after Dr. Bashar took power in June 2000, ninety-nine opinion leaders wrote to him asking for more civil liberties. The following January, one thousand politicians and reformists went farther and demanded an end to four decades of martial law during which they said "society was desecrated, its wealth plundered, and its destiny commandeered by tyrants and corrupt people." It seemed like something was on the move in Syria. But the more I looked into what had really changed, the less I found.

The state nipped in the bud a movement of left-leaning intellectual home discussion groups. Dr. Bashar, who had given a green light for these National Dialogue Forums, now suddenly criticized them as "futile intellectual exercises," telling an Arab newspaper that Syrians should "avoid the possibility that the process of advancement is exploited by seekers of leadership. It is more important for development to be stable and effective than to be rapid." When a society lady was caught distributing by e-mail a caricature of the Syrian leader in unseemly union with the president of Lebanon, she was detained.

In the first issue of *Lamplighter,* Farzat suggested that there might be a cabinet reshuffle, which, in Syria, is discreet code for getting rid of corrupt old guard ministers. In private, Farzat told me these people were "profiting from the state of fear, like thieves after an earthquake." Still, his next issue's front page was more careful: an article on coeducation in a distant province on the Euphrates River.

"Does that count as self-censorship?" I asked.

On the cover of the latest issue in front of us was his drawing of a man walking down a darkened street, looking nervously over his shoulder and worriedly realizing that the armed secret service agent on his tail was his own shadow.

"None of our stories have been stopped. But there are conditions for the newspaper. There can be no opposition to the army, no personal attacks. Like everywhere, there are red lines, like state secrets," he said.

Just then, a Lebanese man in uniform with a thick black beard put his head around the door. I registered that he had a pistol tucked into his belt. He kissed Farzat on both cheeks and they chatted like old friends until it turned out he was looking for someone next door.

"Who was that?" I asked.

"No idea!" Farzat laughed. "But this is exactly the kind of thing the magazine is about. What we are representing is the street, the Syrian street. We criticize things about the traditions of our society. Like when you get a guest who stays for three days and you don't ask why, and you don't know why. You can't spend your time that way. The oppression we suffer is within our society itself, not the government."

Farzat was constantly being oppressed by the telephone—as in many Syrian offices, there was no secretary—as was his brother, who was on the line to the state printing house. Although everything had been paid up front, the printers had stopped the presses. He wheedled and negotiated. A big tip was promised. The presses started rolling again.

Another guest was one of his young contributors who had traveled for hours by bus just to pick up a pay packet of $15. The man would talk to me only while outside and on the move. So we strolled through a jasmine-scented district whose confident curved houses dated back to the first flush of Syria's 1944 independence from France.

"Syria is waking up culturally. But we are still frightened," the contributor said, looking around to see if his shadow was a policeman. "For intellectuals, the *Lamplighter* is as light as a soap bubble. It's a symbol of how the government is talking a lot but doing nothing."

For sure, the censors at the Ministry of Information didn't feel much of a threat. Their office was on a high floor of an aging office block known as the Palace of the

Baath. Work on a new façade had been proceeding for years, and renovations were in fitful progress inside. Wires dangled loose in the corridors and the false ceiling was missing slats. Metal filing cabinet doors hung open. Stacks of dusty files on top of cupboards were tied together with string.

"Some tea?" one censor asked me from behind one of half a dozen desks piled high with papers and magazines.

Everyone in the room had studied somewhere in the former Soviet bloc, and all welcomed a chance to chat and communicate their convictions about the Zionist-Israeli-American plot to hold Syria back. The families of two of them lost homes in the Six-Day War when Israel captured the Golan Heights, a significant chunk of Syria that Israel still occupies southwest of Damascus. One had taken part in the latest demonstration outside the U.S. embassy.

"The only problem was that we couldn't find any stones to throw!" he said, but confided, "I hope the *Lamplighter* strengthens into something special. But right now, it looks a bit weak."

The censors knew that the magazine, just like Syrian business franchises, was not exercising any right. Farzat had merely won an individual and temporary favor granted by their ruler. Everyone seemed to know his or her place. Syria's few legal political parties, locked in a "front" with the Baath Party for decades, had been allowed to start publishing their newspapers too. But they seemed to be fighting the same battles as before they were all closed down in 1963. An editorial in the new organ of the Communist Party was a didactic exposé of class war under the Rip Van Winkle–esqe motto "Workers of the World Unite." Even more amazing was the reappearance of the *Unionist*—a relic of Syria's short-lived political union with Egypt in the early 1960s—featuring a front-page news photograph of legendary Egyptian leader Jamal Abd al-Nasser. He died in 1970.

No wonder they gave censors little trouble. Real opponents fared much worse, men like Riad Seif, Syria's most outspoken opposition politician. That spring of 2001, we could still meet in his modern office. He was bright eyed then, a maverick who had just dared to challenge the Assad family's control of lucrative cell phone licenses.

"It's dangerous. They bankrupted me!" he said.

"Who's they?"

"The Baathists! There's no competition, no vitality, no ideology with which to defend themselves. The Baathists in the 1950s were all idealists. Now they are opportunists. Their brains have calcified. They believe their own lies."

"Like what?"

"There's been a drought for two years, farmers cannot pay back their loans, there are no jobs in the provinces, and unemployment is a huge problem. Against all that, the *Lamplighter* is just an aspirin," Seif told me. "There is still no basis for fighting the roots of corruption, there are no popular organizations, no real unions, no opposition parties, no separation of powers, no free press."

"What's happened to you for speaking like this?"

"They put the knife on the neck and leave it there. My supporters are very silent people. Nobody likes to take a risk. Some friends don't phone me anymore. I became isolated. It doesn't mean I'm not supported. The intellectuals are determined to go on. These months of breathing some freedoms, expressing ourselves by getting rid of some taboos—we enjoyed it. It's difficult to go back to being humble. It's not 1980. There's the Internet, satellite TV stations. The Syrians are just playing at being sheep."

But Seif was wrong that the Syrians would rise up in any significant way. Perhaps they were wise to act cautiously, given the country's forty-year absence of political experience. The subsequent example of Iraq showed the danger of knocking out a dictatorship when a population had no idea how to exercise freedom. In any event, it was clear that the Syrian regime had no intention of anything more than minimal change. Bill Spindle and I discussed my week's reporting and decided that there was too little change to justify publishing anything in the *Journal*.

Back in Syria in the spring of 2002, two years after Dr. Bashar's takeover, Damascus felt better. Shops seemed fuller of imported goods, restaurants were more brightly lit, people were better informed, and even the ancient columns and street of the main Souk al-Hamidiyeh were undergoing a sensitive restoration. Government officials insisted that if everyone would only be patient, change was now really on its way. In his State of the Union address in January 2002, President Bush had categorized Syria as part of an "axis of evil." I felt this was wrong. I went back to Ali Farzat's office to see whether his magazine's slow struggle might now epitomize a possible reawakening in Syria.

When I sat down with Farzat, however, he waved a piece of paper in front of me. It informed him that the government had decided that the *Lamplighter* could sell no more then 14,420 copies. And all had to go through the government distribution system.

"To cover our expenses I have to sell thirty-five thousand copies! There should be rules to allow us to work as a private press. They issued this with no warning, no discussion. They just say: We have to distribute it. And they want to take a forty percent cut. It's as if we, the private sector, are producing for the state. Then they have ordered all ads to go through the government's Arab Advertising Organization, which takes a twenty-seven percent cut. They do absolutely nothing, and the state gives me no advertising at all!"

"Can't you complain? What about Dr. Bashar?"

"Even the minister of information refuses to see me or to talk on the phone."

"I know how that feels."

"What can I tell you? Our research affects people, hits those responsible. People who fear their interests will be damaged find ways to fight innovation. We need to find a new way to push our civilization forward. The newspaper isn't a success just for us, but for the country itself. It is a symbol of development. It should have gone farther."

I continued on my rounds, reluctant to give up. I learned that six months before, Riad Seif, the brave opposition politician, had organized a meeting of a few hundred democracy activists. He was thrown into jail, where he would remain for more than four years. An American diplomat told me the regime was no longer about the Big Man, but the Big Lie: Outwardly the most stable place in the world, inwardly scrambling to save itself every day.

Of course, like all the oil-fueled dictatorships of the Middle East, one reason for the lack of change was that oil supplied 70 percent of Syria's export income. The situation was similar in Iran: As long as the regime had enough money to bankroll its support base, it could survive. Leaders tolerated corruption because, in the absence of popular legitimacy, corrupt ministers could be relied on to be loyal. As in the Soviet Union, which had a similar resource-based source of funds for the regime, dissidents could be tolerated as long as they mounted no direct challenge. On the other hand, a country like Turkey, with few natural resources, is forced to be more pluralistic, open, and democratic, since it has to borrow money every week from domestic and international markets.

I paid a call on Haitham Maleh, an elderly lawyer who still insisted on holding the regime to account from an old colonial-era apartment building in the heart of Damascus. It was a feature of Syria's dictatorship that few young people bothered fighting for human rights. In the absence of domestic publicity, Maleh pursued his cause meeting with diplomats and Arab and international correspondents. He sent Dr. Bashar letters pointing out the contradictions between Syria's constitution and its emergency laws. He waved a copy of a secret ordinance showing that civil servants could be brought to account only if their superiors permitted it. Sitting under a piece of elaborate embroidery he had done in jail, Maleh laughed at the idea that the United States would ever really help someone like him promote democracy in Syria or elsewhere in the Middle East.

"All our Arab dictators are made in the USA. It's because the U.S. just wants one person to talk to, to get their business done. Here they've made us a very strong, fascist dictator. What can we do about it?" he asked.

Indeed, in the months after September 11, the rhetoric from the United States toward Syria had grown threatening once again. I passed by a shop that sold elaborately woven Damascus fabrics, which I used to visit often as a student, and from which I bought the sparkling turquoise silk that my wife used to make her wedding gown. I remembered in 1980 how the bolts of cloth formed a rippling wall of golds, silvers, and scarlets. Now just a few rolls remained, and the Kurdish owner complained that his business was nearly dead. Tour agencies minimized their stays in difficult, corrupt Syria and the tourists no longer had time to shop.

By 2009, the opposition gadfly Riad Seif was still not being allowed out of the country to have his prostate cancer treated. Instead, he was sent back to jail. The 1963 state of emergency was still in force and hundreds of political prisoners remained confined, including many who came to prominence in the stillborn Damascus Spring. The three years of difficulties of the *Lamplighter*, which collapsed under all the pressure in 2003, might have made a story in another newspaper. But the *Journal* did not think that Americans wanted to dwell on failure as usual. The editors preferred upbeat narratives.

"Let's just drop the Syria story, Hugh. It's not happening. It's not your fault," Bill Spindle said after we'd talked through another wasted week of interviews. "Syria hasn't changed, so we just won't write a story about it."

In February 2003, three years after the great change that never was, I was once again passing through Syria. I was going to Iraq and had to report to the border base of the *mukhabarat,* Syrian Intelligence, that apparent oxymoron that wagging tongues savor all over the Middle East. My driver dropped me at the end of a long series of barricades leading to a compound sealed off by high concrete walls. I had no idea which of Syria's many secret services this actually housed. At the guard hut, I explained my mission to a Syrian plainclothes agent with a Kalashnikov rifle on his shoulder. When I was a student in Damascus, such guards stood outside the houses of the elite, and at night sometimes suspiciously trained the barrel of the gun on me as I walked by.

"Do you know the way?" he asked me, taking another sip on a brass straw of South American maté, beloved of Syrian minorities like Alawis and Druze. Their communities had picked up the taste after migrations there to escape from past poverty and persecution by the Sunni Muslim majority and now consumed it as a badge of empowerment.

"Of course not!" I said.

He gave some peremptory directions and sent me off alone into the intelligence compound. I wandered through overgrown streets of what in French colonial days must have been a delightful row of villas. The buildings were in various stages of collapse, and vegetation was running riot. The nondescript one-story house pointed out to me had the same tumbledown appearance. In front, water overflowed from the bowl of a fountain with dirty green tiles. The outside wings of the villa were falling down and had many missing windows, but toward the center of the building I saw signs of renovation.

Next to where I stood were three Russian military trucks alongside a white van that had collapsed with a broken axle. I felt that I was visiting the commander of a rebel unit that had just captured some far-flung third-world outpost, not the executive arm of a working government. The idea that such a tumbledown country should ever trouble the strategic vision of the United States seemed absurd.

Somebody was trying to attract my attention from the top of the steps. Inside, two rooms had been fixed up for the man I had to see, Colonel Suleyman. He sported a loud blue-checked jacket and a very soft handshake. Two teenage boys sat on a sofa to one side, one of them his son, playing annoyingly with a Samsung mobile phone that produced irregular, loud bursts of reverberant music. The colonel looked on indulgently. He called for coffee as we began to go through the paperwork. He happily volunteered that I was in a Military Intelligence base.

He also made clear that he was a Christian, a Syriac Orthodox. I knew the ancient center of this faith in nearby Turkey well, and I was struck by a paradox. Syria was Washington's enemy, mainly because of its below-the-belt kicks at Israel and the West, and partly because of its dictatorship. Turkey was America's friend, for all kinds of reasons including its democracy and its cooperation with Israel. But it struck me suddenly that no Christian, like this man in Syria, would ever be allowed into a position of authority in Turkey. In fact, there were hardly any Syriacs left in the country thanks to Ankara's centurylong drive for ethnoreligious purity. Taking the paradox one step farther, the Christian colonel believed he owed his luck to the secular Arab nationalist ideology of Syria's ruling Baath Party, the target of so much U.S. criticism. Syria and its surviving ethnic mosaic could seem the society that had remained truest to the old ways of the Middle East. Indeed, when I first lived in Aleppo, I used to pass by the shop of a middle-aged Armenian who still made that symbol of Ottoman times, the red and tasseled fez, a brimless hat pressed in heavy metal molds.

Since I was going to Iraq, which was ruled by another Baath Party and which the United States was about to invade, I asked Colonel Suleyman what the difference was between a Syrian and an Iraqi Baathist.

"Oh, very different!" he said, as if we were talking about Nigeria and Switzerland. "They're rightist. We're leftist. We're more open-minded. And our leader is Dr. Bashar!'

We filled in more papers. We savored the paradox of my mother's apparently male name. We worried about his son's education. He took time off for a phone call in which he only picked up the receiver, listened, and replaced it. I waited deferentially to be released from my penance. Time stood still.

My eyes drifted back to the television on the ornamental display case in front of a bookshelf with no books in it. Syrian state TV had gone live to parliament, where Dr. Bashar was addressing the deputies and the people. We all watched him launch into a series of off-the-cuff remarks, his trademark I'm-one-of-the-people style that seems to show him to be a radical patriot, or potential populist.

Normally, Syrian posters of the British-trained eye doctor showed him striking the Hamlet-like pose of a man deeply pained by the state of the world, angry at the injustice of it, and possibly, or just as possibly not, gearing up to take revenge. On his wall, Colonel Suleyman preferred an unusual picture of Dr. Bashar in a cruel tyrant pose: black suit, dark glasses, unflinching expression. Elsewhere, people who were unsatisfied by Bashar's to-be-or-not-to-be ambivalence added a picture of his father Hafez al-Assad, who looked undeniably tough and decisive, even if dead, or a militaristic pose struck by Hafez's first heir apparent, his son Basil, also dead, killed long before in a car accident while speeding to the airport to catch a plane. With this spooky triumvirate, Syria's father, son, and holy ghost, the regime wanted to maintain the illusion of being led by the toughest thugs on the block, a warning to any who might plot to take on their tribe or their country.

"Look at Dr. Bashar," said Colonel Suleyman, admiringly pointing at the TV. "He's speaking without a written speech. That shows he's really got brains."

I thought that Dr. Bashar was a prisoner, a bit like everyone in Syria, but politely said nothing. The Syrians, even Colonel Suleyman as he cheerily waved me off, still wanted to believe that the change from the old Assad to the new Assad meant that something better was on the way in their politically blighted lives. But it was surely going to take a terribly long time.

While Syria languishes on the U.S. list of "state sponsors of terrorism," mainly due to its tactical alliance with violent anti-Israel groups, some Middle Eastern countries seem charmed with an ability to keep America sweet: Saudi Arabia, Morocco, the Gulf emirates, Egypt, and Jordan. One reason was their willingness to make peace or accommodating gestures to Israel; other reasons, not unrelated, were their happier ideological relations with Washington and need for U.S. protection. With the exception of Egypt, a republican dictatorship that won huge U.S. subsidies and political support in return for signing a peace with Israel in 1978, most of these were also old-fashioned monarchies that had avoided the disruptive revolutions of the 1950s and 1960s and had not become mired in state-heavy Socialist populism. Indeed, these latter-day kings, sultans, and sheikhs began to seem more effective, and perhaps even democratic, than the republican regimes that had elbowed kings aside in other countries. In Iraq, older people still sigh with nostalgia for the calmer days of the pre-1958 monarchy. Dubai looks globally glamorous under Sheikh

Mohammed, patron of a glitzy building boom and a sleek-bearded practitioner of the endurance sport of marathon horse racing.

Commentators in Arabic newspapers began to discuss whether progressive monarchs weren't doing a better job at modernizing. They noted that the old Arab monarchies lost less of Palestine in 1948 than the republics did in 1967, that they enjoyed more legitimacy than those who had seized power more recently by force, that the new generation of royals were proving better at resolving petty disputes in the Gulf, that the Moroccan king was offering new rights to minorities, and that in Jordan the government was moving bravely forward into the Internet age. The power of all Arab regimes rests on managing tribal loyalties, security chiefs, foreign powers, and the barons of state-connected business. While doing this, kings conveniently didn't have to fake elections or referendums like all the main republican presidents did; they could claim a royal legitimacy, and some were not shy of claiming or hinting at a divine right to rule.

Meanwhile, the republican presidents are becoming regally dynastic, following the example of Dr. Bashar's takeover from his father Hafez al-Assad. The presidents of Egypt and Libya, Hosni Mubarak and Muammar al-Ghadafi, are readying their sons to take over the leadership when they die. This has already happened in Azerbaijan, a nearby ex-Soviet country happily emulating the Middle Eastern model of oil-fueled despotism. Saddam Hussein would have liked to arrange such a transfer of power in Iraq too, before the United States ousted him and troops of the 101st Airborne drilled his sons full of bullets in Mosul.

I asked a Syrian government official about my theory of democratic monarchs over a delicious dinner of dips from eggplant, yogurt, and chickpea paste and succulent barbecued lamb in the stone courtyard of one of the newly restored Arab houses in Damascus. It was the beguiling kind of place that kept making me want to write glowingly about Syria despite its sclerotic dictatorship.

"Maybe you're right, Hugh. I know what you mean. In Morocco, things are moving under the new king. But in republics like Algeria or Tunisia, nothing's happening. Look at us. We're taking small steps, but not enough. I can't explain it. You'd have to ask a specialist."

The specialist to whom I decided to put my questions about modernizing monarchs was King Abdullah II of Jordan. I'd first met him thirty years before. His mother was English, and she and his father King Hussein sent him to my preparatory school, St. Edmund's, deep in the rolling forested hills of Surrey south of London. His arrival, along with his brother, brought a buzz to the establishment. Forbidden expeditions for midnight feasts in the cricket pavilion became adventures full of fearful talk of armed secret agents patrolling the grounds. Indeed, as we shook hands in his palace in the hills above Amman, I was proud to present him with a copy of my first journalistic photograph: the two young princes in their English prep school uniforms.

"Oh, St. Edmund's! Were you there too? That dump!" The king groaned.

I felt defensive. The school had treated me well. But it was true that he'd stayed in our English backwater for only a few months before moving on to schools in the United States. He came back to the British military college at Sandhurst to be educated into a Cobra helicopter–piloting, skydiving action man. My Jordanian friends thought him unimpressive intellectually and laughed at the way Jordanian newspapers pandered to his car-racing skills with headlines like PRINCE ABDULLAH WINS THIRD PLACE IN JORDANIAN RALLY, without reporting the name of the winner. Now that he was king, however, elite businessmen in Amman referred to him as Jordan's new chief executive officer, the same expression used by Dubai for its sheikhly ruler. King Abdullah wasn't slim, but he looked pretty fit, not unlike his pictures in commando uniform that were popular downtown. It gave a different feel of possibility to all the old tribal knives on the table around which we sat.

The man I remembered as a shy and excitable ten-year-old had become confident and impressive just two years after assuming the title. I was surprised. King Abdullah hadn't been given the title of crown prince until a few weeks before the death in 1999 of his father, King Hussein, who thus broke with the Arab tradition of succession down the line of brothers before passing to the new generation. He was an open, fluent, and fast talker. The transcript of our conversation filled eleven pages. Sensibly keeping alive his late father's mythically astute powers of political survival, he still referred to him as "King Hussein" or "His Majesty."

Being king of Jordan entailed much stress and juggling. He was trying to pioneer modernization in a country steeped in tradition and religiosity, drawn arbitrarily on a map by British imperial officials in the 1920s. He was managing an economy in a region that kept throwing up crises, a volatility that kept upsetting the national industry of tourism. He had to bridge a population split not only between native Jordanians and Palestinian refugees, from Israel/Palestine next door, but also between native Jordanian minorities, as when a bedouin Arab politician had recently bitten off part of a Circassian rival's ear in parliament. That's before taking into account his international balancing act, between Israelis and Palestinians, between Israelis and other Arab states, and between the United States, a chief source of aid and trade, and the neighboring Iraq of Saddam Hussein, always a threat to Jordanian security but also a source of cheap oil and Jordan's cousin in a thousand and one social and cultural ways.

"Jordan's between Iraq and a hard place," King Abdullah joked. "We've learned to live in a very difficult neighborhood."

He'd symbolically bridged one of Jordan's divides by marrying the beautiful

The picture I took of the young Prince Abdullah, circa 1972, at the school we briefly shared in England *(left)*, and the king of Jordan that he became. *(Photos: Hugh Pope; Royal Poster, 2000)*

Rania, of Palestinian origin. But this had given rise to insulting shouts at soccer matches between Palestinian-Jordanian and native Jordanian teams.

"How do you feel about the, umm, recent unpleasantness in football stadiums?"

King Abdullah's smooth patter missed a stride or two before he muttered that football stadiums should not be taken to represent the whole country.

"It really is not worth giving it time and attention."

I turned to the role of monarchies, and the king quickly moved up a gear.

"I think that it was Bismarck who said that the best form of government is monarchy," King Abdullah joked. "But the flip side of that is that you have to have a good king."

He said he felt like he was part of a regionwide movement of royal reform, and that young princes from more old-fashioned, oil-rich states in the Gulf were watching the television broadcasts of his participation in meetings on economic or civil service reform.

"I have some princes saying, for God's sake, please don't fail in what you're doing, because you're giving us ammunition to go to our elders and say: look at what's happening in Jordan," he said, adding that he was "surprised at how much they're watching, so it's having a very subtle but very positive impact."

"But how can there be real change in times of such turbulence?"

"We don't have the burdens, or the difficulties, that maybe our fathers had, the anxieties," he said, referring to the newness and legitimacy problems of the early postcolonial monarchs. "That allows us to move beyond what trapped the older generation. The important story in the Middle East is that there is a whole picture emerging. Look what we're doing for education, with computers and English in classrooms. You'd be surprised how many other Arab countries are asking how we do it."

I wondered whether educating the population would lead to demands for an end to the existing regime, a dilemma faced by all the Middle East's authoritarian elites, royal or republican, who want educated populations to bring greater prosperity but who want to keep control of everything too.

"Seventy percent of the country is younger than me. That's pretty frightening. And that's not unusual for this part of the Middle East."

"What's frightening about that?"

"I mean, kids watch Pokémon in China as they do in Jordan and as they do in America. You have a new generation that is going to have international perceptions because of the media, because the world is becoming a smaller place. We've set up Internet centers all over Jordan, they've have had a tremendous effect on villages. Kids are sponges. If you give them the ability to have the door of information open to them, they're going to see the world in a different way."

"Is that dangerous for you?"

"I don't think it's going to be a problem," he said. His survival strategy was "trying to keep our traditional values, which I think we can do in Jordan, but modernizing with the rest of the world. Just take the good points of Eastern and Western culture and use that. We are all going to have to change the way we do business. I fully understand that. It's the only way to go. Just do it smart."

King Abdullah of Jordan didn't mention the key requirement of Middle East kingship: To remember to keep renewing the monarchical insurance policy taken out in Washington, D.C. But he wasn't alone in trying to represent a change for the better. Saudi Arabia's royal family was also moving away from absolutism. It had always maintained its alliance with the main clerical family descended from the founder of its Wahhabi ideology more than three hundred years ago—if unhappy, clerics would even remind the Saudi royal family of the obligations of this partnership on public television. Still, since 1993 the monarchy had slowly given a consultative role to a council drawn from a cross section of the elite representing tribes and regions, businessmen, clerics, and academics. The council's members may have been relatively powerless, but half had doctorates from Western universities and included some of the more interesting and amusing conversationalists in the Middle East.

"The alternatives have not succeeded. The monarchical system has survived well in various countries. The republics have become monarchies and even hereditary. If the Middle East would go back to monarchies I would applaud it!" Prince Turki al-Faisal told me contentedly. The dividing line between monarchy and republic could be fluid. In Turkey, which ousted its sultan in 1923 as it turned its back on the former Middle Eastern empire of the Ottoman dynasty, I once received a fax from the Turkish armed forces, comparing their role in founding and leading the new republic to that of a modern European monarchy, which does not govern day-to-day but exists to guard the constitution.

The Saudis had steadily broadened their base from the state founded in the 1920s by King Abdulaziz, who died leaving more than fifty sons in 1953. This is a key difference with the doomed one-man-show monarchy of the shah of Iran. Princes seemed omnipresent—as political commissars in ministries, as governors of provinces, as intellectuals, and as leading public servants exuding intelligent bonhomie. A junior Saudi prince, one of dozens of grandsons of King Abdulaziz, told me in his office in the family foundation in Riyadh that I should think of their system as aiming at a broader integration of power rather than a separation of powers. After all, the country is unique in the world in bearing one family's name.

"The royal family is like society itself," the prince said. "It's in defense, education, poetry, painting, business. It's an integral part of the society."

I did hear plenty of whispered resentment about the royals' separate terminal at the airport, their pensions worth several thousand dollars per month, the rumors that black sheep princes controlled the distribution of work permits, and the illicit smuggling in of containers of strong spirits. One well-placed great-grandson of King Abdulaziz had built what was reputed to be a $2 billion palace in Jeddah with Spanish towers and internal roadways paved with Italian marble. I'd been a guest at his sumptuous, ranchlike compound outside the capital. It had included a cleaned-up rebuild of an old Saudi town, including a full cast of hired actors pretending to be blacksmiths, basket weavers, and camel drivers. Before the banquet we were even treated to a mock cavalry battle. The reception room had a wall where one could watch a dozen large flat-screen television screens at once. And the prince—whose reputation for generosity meant he wasn't necessarily unpopular with ordinary Saudis—hadn't even been there for his party.

It was unclear how much the royal family cost. Saudi bureaucrats and bankers reckoned it was anywhere between 15 and 35 percent of the oil income. Then there were the commissions that had to be paid to princely intermediaries for state contracts, sometimes extortionate. The culture of toadyism could be disturbing, as when a TV anchor purred "what an achievement" upon the news that the king had managed to publish yet another imprint of the Koran. Watching the mixture of stress and arrogance on the faces of a top prince's entourage at the Riyadh race-course reminded me entirely of officials' faces on the reviewing stands of Saddam Hussein's Iraq. I asked one gentlemanly prince, another grandson of King Abdulaziz, about the royal privileges that people criticized.

"Sure, I get one free phone line, free water, and a pension. But you have to remember that ten to fifteen princes get eighty percent of the money!" the prince said. I believed him. His daily job was in a modest professor's cubicle office in a university.

Again and again, leading Saudis told me that the royal family was the glue that held Saudi Arabia together, and, apart from any excesses, people actually liked it that way. The chief of the chamber of commerce wanted the royal family out of the state, but he admitted he didn't like criticizing the royal family's executive role since he felt it had a deeper legitimacy than any group that could win an election.

"Every five years someone tells them that their world is about to collapse. But these people have seen it all. You can't scare them. They're smart. They just have to keep their nerve," said a Saudi newspaper editor in Riyadh.

The lack of institutions was a problem. Someone with a complaint could do little more than send a telegram to the palace and hope for the best. Gulf sheikh-doms could seem unreal. They relied on the United States to defend them, depended for services on majorities of their resident populations who were temporary laborers with no political rights, and their native citizens numbered so few that the ruler could be in personal touch with most of the people who counted.

"All a regime is required to do to survive is listen to the community," I was told by a diminutive Gulf princess from the Emirates, chief of an Internet company, leaning passionately across the table on a hotel café balcony overlooking the beach in Dubai. "If I have a majlis [audience with the sheikh] and solve my problem, that's democracy!"

I once aired this topic in the pages of the *Wall Street Journal* in the context of what government might take over from Saddam Hussein in Iraq. I trekked through the Iraqi opposition haunts of West London to find the pretender to the old throne of Iraq, Sherif Ali, who held a modest court in his grand Notting Hill apartment full of heavy baroque gilt furniture. I reckoned Sherif Ali faced an uphill battle to win power in Iraq's political dogfights when I saw how decently and democratically he fussed over his school-age daughters. His quest to establish an Iraqi constitutional monarchy fizzled out after the United States invaded, as did the significant pre-2003 popularity in Iran of the America-based son of the deposed shah of Iran. Descendants of ousted monarchies linked to colonial regimes or Western intervention had few roots to graft themselves back on to.

Up in King Abdullah's palace in Amman, I felt how a sliver of a personal story with the king made me feel connected to him, which he was able to seal with the simple device of a regal New Year's greetings card. Such consumer politics are the duty of any leader who wants long-term success, even if he has oil revenue. This is different from offering power to the people. Breakthroughs to a more representative government are rare, and flowerings of liberal hope like the Damascus Spring are usually sacrificed to the security needs of regimes that feel brittle, both from lack of real legitimacy and the insecurities of a violent region. Bedrock loyalty is usually bought pragmatically through a hierarchy of patronage, and if the ruler can tie in the loyalty of at least one-third of the population, the regime is probably safe indefinitely.

14. SADDAMIZED

Inside Iraq's Psychotic Stress Machine

Dance for the monkey when he's on the throne.
—EGYPTIAN PROVERB

For the first two decades of my work as a reporter in the Middle East, I avoided Baghdad. I never forgot the first Iraqis I ever met. Overhearing a group of young men talking in a London street, I had greeted them in my student Arabic. What struck me wasn't that they assumed I was a spy or an agent provocateur; it was the hunted, fearful looks they cast over their shoulders back at me as they hurried away. The next Iraqi I met was the truck driver who tried to force himself upon me in a Syrian hotel room. Other Middle Easterners embellished tales of a brutalized country which, by the turn of the millennium, had been gripped by war, punitive sanctions, and revolution for nearly three decades. Since the bloody overthrow of the monarchy in 1958, dictatorship of one form or another had been the norm. This had honed a psychotic edge onto the already forceful Iraqi national character. The country was the ultimate example of how a tyrannous Middle Eastern dictatorship is run. I understood that and kept my distance.

But that didn't mean I could avoid Iraq altogether. The country seemed constantly to be at war, notably against Iran in 1980–88, against the Gulf sheikhdom of Kuwait and an international coalition in 1990–91, and against a U.S.-led invasion in 2003. As a result, I violated its borders dozens of times. I entered in Iranian military helicopters; with Iraqi rebel mujahideen in a speedboat through the great marshes; with the armies of France, Britain, and the United States in the 1991 war; in dinghies across the Tigris from Syria; on punitive raids with Turkish commandos; and on foot through mountain passes with columns of Iraqi Kurdish refugees. Only once was I given an Iraqi visa, and that was delivered by a petrified Iraqi official being watched over by a U.S. officer brandishing an M-16 rifle. No wonder that I felt apprehensive when, in the spring of 2002, I applied for a real visa from the Iraqi embassy in Jordan.

It was Saddam Hussein's birthday, and the Iraqis were calling for guests to flock to their country for the occasion. A tip to get quickly into the queue in Amman came from my predecessor as the *Journal*'s Middle East correspondent, Stephen Glain. A dedicated professional, the free-fall disconnect of trying to explain the Middle East to Americans via the *Journal* had caused him to leave our newspaper and nearly to abandon journalism altogether. Little did I know then that involvement with Iraq would ultimately teach me exactly why.

Saddam Hussein was turning sixty-five, and his regime decided this was a good excuse for a "glorious birthday celebration"—and for Iraq to open its door to outsiders for the first time since the September 11 attacks on America. Baghdad was increasingly rattled by unrelenting accusations from the highest levels in Washington that it was somehow responsible for the atrocities. So they promised to restart talks on welcoming back UN weapons inspectors and cranked up the regime's creaky PR machine, inviting sympathetic dignitaries and hungry reporters from around the world to witness that Saddam was not weak and alone. I couldn't see any reason to believe that Saddam would have had anything to do with September 11. Saddam's Baathist ideology was relentlessly secular, Iraqi Islamists were ruthlessly persecuted, and al-Qaeda's spokesman had personally attacked the Iraqi leader. Perhaps U.S. officials imputed such plotting to Iraq because they knew only too well how deeply implicated the United States was in forcing the UN to keep Iraq cut off from the world by sanctions after 1991.

Thanks to Glain's introductions, I was put on the birthday party invitation list. Looking at the visa, I assumed that this meant my past sins, amply proved by published datelines inside Iraq, had been forgiven. The Iraqis, surely, would not spoil the party by starting a spat with the *Wall Street Journal*. But I could not be sure. Iraq did hang a British-Iranian reporter as a spy in 1990. After stepping around the DOWN USA signs on the jetway pontoons at Baghdad Airport, I sweated past passport control. Iraqi law decreed the death penalty for much less than my long history of border violations.

The border control official displayed only a passing interest in my passport, however. More disconcerting was the immediate, in-your-face bribery culture that hit us as customs agents dragged us off one by one to an office behind baggage claim. If I wanted to take my equipment into Iraq, I had to pay. Further demands for cash were made by teams of grasping porters. The moral fabric of the country was clearly in tatters. The homemade banners strung across storefronts on the way in from the airport rang hollow: SADDAM HUSSEIN IS ETERNAL SPRING and THE GREATEST LEADER FOR THE MOST NOBLE PEOPLE.

My first mission was to find stories that would illustrate what the Iraqis really thought of their leader. All U.S. reporters in Baghdad were required to fuss over this quandary, since the war party in America claimed to speak in the name of a real Iraq that supposedly hated the man. Reporting on popular sentiment was a circumspect business, however. Iraqis would chuckle knowingly, look quickly over their shoulders before answering, or give heartfelt sighs of weariness. My tactic of standing in a busy place and waiting for someone curious to approach me didn't work well in Baghdad. When I started chatting with a man buying a small cassette player in a shop flush with goods newly smuggled in from Southeast Asia, he turned out to be a geography teacher, thirty years old, and well trained by Iraq's culture of fear.

"Just like some countries celebrate their king's birthday, this day is special for us," he said with a smile that could have been interpreted on 1,001 levels. "Please quote me. Saddam is a symbol of pure happiness."

Watching the one dreary channel of television in my hotel room, I teased the chambermaid about Mr. Hussein's constant television presence. She could have said nothing. But she looked genuinely shocked and replied that she loved her leader. Later she caught up with me again to explain.

"If he's not on television every evening," she said, "we'd be worried sick about what had happened to him."

Thus did the regime keep the machinery of dictatorship running. Newspapers printed laudatory poems like one written by General Ghazai Dara al-Tani, official poet of the armed forces. He compared the Iraqi leader to a palm tree that had survived a thousand storms, the protector of "an Iraq that is your paradise, where nobody is afraid." I remembered how a retired aide of President Hafez Assad in neighboring Syria once caught me figuring out an adulatory birthday poem framed on his wall. "You may laugh," he said. "But when you're out of office and the poems stop coming, you really feel bad."

I could only imagine the anguish of the high officials who competed to come up with ideas for sixty-fifth-birthday presents to keep Saddam feeling good, or at least satisfied with their level of loyalty. One by one, the gifts were displayed on Iraqi television. They included yet more statues of him striking heroic poses at various crossroads in Baghdad and house-high paintings of him wielding the fine German carbine from which he liked to squeeze off shots in salute during military parades.

One enterprising official put up a monument called the Meeting of the Leader and the People, two white rectangles curving 150 feet into the air to fuse in a concrete embrace. I watched its architect on Iraqi TV telling viewers that "seen from the side, it also forms the word 'no,' symbolizing our leader's 'no' to our enemies!"

On the great day, the government packed us off to Saddam's hometown of Tikrit to watch a parade in the president's honor. We took up our places below a well-defended stone reviewing balcony where the berets of a few senior Baathists could be seen mingled with the peaked caps of military attachés from embassies ready to sell weapons to Iraq. The procession was weirdly folkloric after the Saddamite Iraqi fashion: cheerful bedouin Arab dancers, resentful Kurdish girls in flower print dresses, long-haired dervishes from a Sufi mystical lodge, uncertain townspeople and young men apparently representing a legion of suicide bombers, with their heads in black hoods and white funeral shrouds over their shoulders. I plunged into the parade and began to march with them. The perspective from inside the procession was startlingly different, boiling with frustrations and tensions. I understood what the regime was trying to do but wanted to get to the bottom of what the participants felt about it all. Soon I found myself surrounded by schoolboys, but they were quicker to get to the bottom of me.

It was impossible to conduct a conversation, and not just because the boys were so utterly wound up. People kept bumping into me. I'd ask a question, and they'd yell one back. The routine of name identification ended as usual with cries of "Mr. Q!" then, less usually, "Mr. Q. You are beautiful!" Suddenly I was sure of it—my backside was being pinched. Not just once or twice. Serially pinched, grabbed, and fondled. "Mr. Q! I love you!" The boys yelled with laughter and intoxication at their power and my sudden fear, their completion of the circle of viciousness that was Saddamite Iraq. I fled back to the stand. Here, aside from a chuckling Stephen Glain, the older order was calmer. "Chemical" Ali al-Majid, gasser of the Kurds in 1988, cut one piece from the birthday cake, a monstrosity in the shape of a ten-foot-long pale pink rose. TV cameras peered silently and flunkies clapped. Nobody was offered or ate any of the confection.

Safely back at the hotel that evening, state TV showed Saddam receiving a two-foot-high golden statue of a horseman, a tribute from a grateful province. For five minutes, his vice president, Izzat Ibrahim al-Douri, pointed out in a soft voice how its solidity and sweep symbolized the glories of Saddam's rule. Saddam spoke gruff words of gratitude. Something didn't quite add up. The ubiquitous olive-green uniform adopted by officers of the Iraqi regime was the fashion of an outmoded generation. Vice President al-Douri, supposedly a seller of ice on the streets of Baghdad before the revolution changed his life, was barely articulate. And Saddam was careless, stepping away from his golden gift and then absentmindedly turning back to dedicate it, with a growling flourish, "to Palestine."

Only after a couple of days in Baghdad did I realize what being wrapped up in this totalitarian envelope reminded me of, and why my defenses were going down. It was like being back at boarding school: turning up to be bused to events, eating overcooked communal meals, and being propositioned by other boys. Freed of stressful choices that had made me into something of an insomniac at home, in Baghdad I began to sleep deeply and happily. As at school, I began to play harmlessly truant in town. I did move out of the Rashid Hotel, where dark wooden panels made every room look sinister and bugged, installing myself in the lighter-hearted Palestine Hotel, whose spiderweb-shaped balcony screens seemed merely peculiar, quite appropriate to the B-movie scene that was Saddam Hussein's Baghdad.

The idea of finding out and retelling to Americans what the Iraqis felt about the world was noble, but soon I came to believe that it was futile. And therein lay a fundamental problem in my Western journalistic approach: the assumption that if Iraqis knew what was going on in their country and what was best for them, they would believe they had a chance to do something about it. Americans, and to some extent Europeans, have a fundamental belief in the transformative power of the individual will, and believe that the rest of the world shares their rich, spacious country's feast of opportunity. By contrast, life in Iraq gave me daily proof that, in the public space at least, an individual had to be on maximum guard at all times, and that a mistake could condemn you forever.

That's probably why Dr. Ahlam Al-Hadi of the Baghdad Radiology Hospital refused to have anything to do with me.

"Please leave me alone," she said, looking at me and my government minder. "We get you foreign delegations all the time. But it never changes a thing. Go and see one of the other doctors."

She took me briskly down the crowded corridors, knocking on the door of one overworked doctor after another. They all refused to help. Dr. Hadi and I looked at each other. I gently explained to her once again the bureaucratic mountain that I had climbed just to get there to see her. My minder, weary of my constant questions and runs at the battlements of disinformation in Iraq, slumped into a chair that had come free in a waiting room. Dr. Hadi relented. The minder waved me on. He'd seen the Great Iraqi Cancer Show before.

So the white-coated deputy chief of radiology led me off through a crowd of patients, past signs warning of radioactive hazard, and into a thick-walled room. There, lurking in the dim light, stood a cancer-treatment machine the size of a pickup truck, dusty and flanked by battered lockers. The styling was dated, but it looked brand-new.

"When we installed this machine in 1990, it was the first of its kind in the Middle East," Dr. Hadi said, moving into the control room, where switches and never-twisted dials waited under plastic sheeting.

That was three years after she had started working the cancer wards. It was also the year that Iraq invaded Kuwait, triggering the Gulf War and international sanctions that prevented the hospital from obtaining the pellet of radioactive cobalt 60 the machine needed to work. Twelve years later, the machine had never even been turned on.

"We made this area into a storeroom," Dr. Hadi said. "Actually, this is also now our changing room."

We went on to the registry, where she opened bound medical books of hospital admissions for me to see. There was no doubt that there was substance to the Iraqi claim of a huge rise in cancer patients in the past ten years. Dr. Hadi leafed back through numbered, handwritten ledgers to show me that admissions were just under four thousand a year in the mid-1980s. In 2002, the rate had doubled to nearly four thousand in just the first six months. Deep in the corridors of the Ministry of Health, another official had also convinced me that half of Iraq's cancer patients were now dying, compared with one-third before.

"We don't even open a file until we have a medically confirmed tumor or lesion," the ministry woman had said. "Maybe outside they think it is all lies and exaggeration. But here it is real."

I was just the latest reporter to come to take the measure of an issue that nobody seemed able to resolve. Was Saddam, as America suggested, pocketing the money for medicines and cruelly exploiting the cancer-stricken victims of his neglect? Or were Iraq and most of the world's U.S.-skeptic press correct in saying that Washington, revealing a sadistic and evil streak, was wantonly preventing the treatment of cancer in Iraq's population, a cancer that was actually caused by America's own use of radioactive munitions? If I wanted to reach the front page of the *Journal,* I would have to prove the case one way or the other.

Iraqi officials blamed the cancer epidemic on a U.S. trade embargo, UN sanctions, Gulf War damage to Iraqi infrastructure, and the American use of shells tipped with depleted uranium, a dense and slightly radioactive metal that pierces armor. But I'd also found out from neutral international experts that the Iraqi government refused full medical surveys that could pin down the cancer's cause.

Dr. Hadi was off again, now fully committed to showing me her domain. Less than half her radiology machines remained in service. The only apparatus that had arrived since the Gulf War—a French machine installed in 1998, donated by the International Atomic Energy Agency—was working three shifts, twenty-four hours a day. A twenty-year-old German machine for treating skin cancer limped along at half power. Two Shimadzu machines from Japan were soldiering on with cobalt 60 "sources" left over from the mid-1980s. They were so weak that patients had to spend half an hour underneath them to kill their cancer cells, instead of the standard minute or so. One operator sat behind it, catching up on her knitting. The air was ice-cold, thanks to one brand-new foreign machine next to the scratched control room door.

"We keep asking for new cobalt sources for our patients, even though this treatment is now out of date in developed countries," Dr. Hadi said. "They never come, I don't know why. But they do send us air conditioners."

Iraqi officials could not explain this ban on cobalt. In theory, such radioactive sources were not subject to the UN embargo. When I later got back to Istanbul, I started calling whomever I could. Major international suppliers told me they had never received Iraqi requests for these sources. UN statistics showed that the Iraqi state bought only 5 percent of what they could have obtained of some of those very cancer medicines that harassed Iraqi doctors said they needed. I had met Middle Eastern wholesalers in neighboring Jordan who told me that five times as much money went into heart treatments as into cancer treatments. The implication seemed clear: Saddam was prioritizing the death of cancer patients, because people like me would come and write about them.

It was, after all, a central Iraqi propaganda platform. The cancer situation meant Arab attention focused entirely on Western responsibility for deaths of innocent Iraqis. While President Bush called Saddam a "cold-blooded killer," the Arab side remembered former U.S. secretary of state Madeleine Albright's response to a *60 Minutes* question in 1996. Lesley Stahl asked her about the relationship between sanctions and the hundreds of thousands of extra Iraqi children who started dying of malnutrition and disease in the 1990s. "I think that is a very hard choice, but the price, we think, the price is worth it," Albright replied. In her memoir *Madam Secretary,* she bitterly regretted this terrible mistake, wishing she had said that it was Saddam Hussein's fault and that for her nothing mattered more than the lives of innocents. But for Middle Easterners, this slip of the tongue came to epitomize the unfeeling cruelty of U.S. policy toward Iraq. Caught in the middle were increasing numbers of Iraqi cancer patients, including those who turned to Dr. Hadi and other overcrowded clinics for help. I met a group of them sitting forlornly on a bench outside a cancer clinic in southern Basra, next to a hospital so worn-out that raw sewage leaked into one of the operating rooms. Inside the clinic, graphs colored in by pencil on the wall showed how cancer deaths had risen from 34 in 1988 to 464 in 1996 to 603 in 2001. One of the waiting people, Kazem Youssef, a retired police sergeant, sat there with his wife, who was losing her battle with cancer. They invited me home. It was surprisingly spacious but empty of hope.

"It's just a slow death. There are never enough drugs. I've sold my two shops, my gold, my car, and my second house to save my wife," said Kazem Youssef. He used the money to get up to Dr. Hadi's machines in Baghdad.

Even so, his wife's breast cancer had returned. In his sitting room he sat on a line of flat cushions along an empty wall turning a package of a generic medication around and around in his fingers. He was happy that for once the pills he needed for his wife's chemotherapy were available. But still it wasn't enough.

"This pill is made in Jordan. It's too weak," he whispered. "Do you know any way that we can get the one from America? That's the really strong stuff that we need."

The Youssef family blamed their ills on some evil substance in an American missile that had exploded nearby in January 1991. To me, the filthy garbage-strewn streets outside seemed just as dangerous. The whole of Iraq was an unhealthy place, its cities' backstreets full of rubble and rubbish, its drinking water barely purified, and its once-famed expanses of date palms ragged and sick. Its doctors had migrated away to other countries. As a new piece of UN jargon put it, the country had been "de-developed."

The Iraqi leader preferred to spend his money elsewhere. A new, onion-domed Arabian Nights palace for Saddam was going up in his sprawling compound of palaces by the bank of the Tigris in Baghdad. On the outskirts of town rose the huge pylons of what never succeeded in becoming the biggest mosque in the world. And the vast headquarters of the ruling Baath Party was rising from the ruins for a third time, rebuilt defiantly bigger after each destruction by U.S. high explosive.

It wasn't only Saddam who was responsible. Western diplomats in Baghdad, uncomfortable with their moral dilemma, told me that great powers deliberately delayed fulfilling Iraqi requests in the UN. Tracking a case down was easy enough. Austrian cancer doctor Eva-Maria Hobiger came to Iraq to address a medical conference in 2001. Horrified at the sight of children dying of leukemia, she vowed to do something about it. Working with the Society for Austro-Arab Relations, she marshaled money from the Austrian church and Red Cross to fit out a lab in Basra with the blood-clotting equipment vital in the treatment of leukemia.

In January 2002, she submitted a list of fifty-five items to the UN sanctions committee. "Donation!!! No Payment Required!" she typed on the bottom, making sure a frequent problem was bypassed. Two weeks later, the committee approved the list—minus seven of its key components. She later faxed me a copy of the blocking hold order, requested, as was almost always the case, by the United States alone. The justification was that some of the equipment could be used to make weapons, and that "more information" was needed on others.

Dr. Hobiger and her NGO supplied the information and reapplied. On the question of the refrigerator, item number six, she pointed out: "This is a normal refrigerator as it is used for household purposes, produced by Bosch. We got it as a gift from the Teaching Hospital in Vienna." In May, the U.S. representative upheld the hold on a slightly changed seven items. Key blood centrifuges were by then both blocked. None of the shipment ever reached Iraq.

Then there was the natural inefficiency of the UN bureaucracy, coupled with corruption that was later shown to have spread from Iraq to the highest reaches of the UN program itself. There were also practical considerations. Whereas U.S. hospitals might order medications a week ahead, Iraqi ones had to look eighteen months into the future.

By this time, the United Nations Children's Fund said half of formerly wealthy Iraqi schools were unfit for use and more than one-fifth of children had dropped out entirely, often to work. Female adult literacy had dropped from a peak of 87 percent in 1985 to 45 percent in 1995. The physical growth of more than one-fifth of Iraqi children was stunted by malnutrition. One-fifth were anemic. When I visited the academic year opening at one school full of mold and chipped paint, one of the teachers said some children simply no longer had the capacity to concentrate. I found my focus terrifyingly at the flag-raising ceremony, when the music teacher suddenly loosed off three rounds from a Kalashnikov rifle.

In the Baghdad hospital, Dr. Hadi wound up her tour by taking me to a dusty room where rested three U.S.-made X-ray machines for treating deep cancers. The machines were in pieces, abandoned in the mid-1990s. When I called the maker, Varian Medical Systems of Palo Alto, California, their spokesman plausibly explained that the company would indeed have liked to meet repeated Iraqi requests for help, but the web of U.S. and UN sanctions made servicing them impossible. One result was that Dr. Hadi's doctors no longer even had the device to check whether, when servicing the machine, they had received an accidental dose of radiation.

When we got back to Dr. Hadi's office, her absence had turned the line of patients into a small mob. The ten doctors in the department were seeing forty people a day each, and patients had to wait as long as three months for radiation treatment. Dr. Hadi elbowed her way to the door and sat behind her desk. I stayed on to watch and listen. Nobody paid me much heed.

Finally only two people were left, a young couple from Nasiriya, a town in southern Iraq. He was an upright, bearded man, trying hard to do the best for his wife, Karima, a pretty thirty-five-year-old with a black chador over her head. As Dr. Hadi opened her file, I watched fear mix with hope in Karima's eyes. But she probably never had a chance. The file showed that Dr. Hadi had to compromise at the last session, because she didn't have a drug called Cytosar. Another time she didn't have two of the three drugs indicated. Overall, only fifteen of the fifty-one drugs needed for chemotherapy were regularly available. And only once did the file show that Karima got all the drugs she needed.

"We never say 'cancer' in front of them," Dr. Hadi said softly to me in English. "We just say tumor. But cancer is spreading all over this woman's body. We get a lot of cases from Nasiriya. And there was a lot of American shelling there."

Dr. Hadi asked Karima some questions about how she felt, then noticed she'd missed her appointment the month before. She upbraided the husband for not bringing his wife. He said he couldn't get leave from his army unit.

"Ultimately, the problem is always the war or the sanctions. And I'm left here facing the sick person, and I just can't solve it for them," Dr. Hadi said. "I used to be a euphoric kind of person. But now when I get home I'm just depressed."

As I tried to assess where the problem lay, I found that the U.S. attitude was a critical element. In Jordan, the transshipment point for much trade with Baghdad, I had stopped by wholesalers to ask about the unavailability of American drugs. They told me that in practice most of their U.S. suppliers simply forbade them from selling their products to Iraq. This was both out of fear of trouble back home or because sanctions made shipping even generic antibiotics cumbersome. There was no beating the system. For their part, the Japanese manufacturers of the aging radiology machines that were treating the wife of Youssef from Basra told me that the reason they wouldn't send in spare parts was fear of U.S. countermeasures elsewhere in the world.

I tried to dig deeper into the debate on the role in the cancer epidemic played by the U.S. military's use of shells covered with depleted uranium. More than three hundred tons of this substance jacketed one million U.S. shells fired in and around southern Iraq during the Gulf War, and the Pentagon claimed this was all relatively safe. But since 1991, thirty of one hundred Americans involved in the main depleted uranium cleanup unit had died, including several from various cancers, according to the man who led them, Doug Rokke. Like almost all of the others, Dr. Rokke was now also ill. But when I caught up with the head of the World Health Organization's cancer department on a visit to Baghdad, he said that, in the circumstances, there was no scientific way to prove anything.

After months of pushing and probing, I sat down to write what little seemed clear about Dr. Hadi's battles. But without a lawsuit or clear malefactor to blame, it faded into a fair but modest item on the *Journal*'s foreign pages. American readers were left with the feeling that Iraqis were the unlucky victims of an inexplicable, inevitable fate. I could not adequately illustrate my conviction that everyone—from Iraqi pen pushers to reporters recycling propaganda to vindictive U.S. policy makers to French bankers delaying payments—shared a truly cancerous responsibility.

My experience of Saddam Hussein's last year in power ended with his last hubristic set piece, the national referendum asking if he should be granted a new seven-year term in office. The United States was ratcheting up pressure on him through sanctions, verbal harassment, and physical attacks. The Iraqis were as confused as I was about what to think. For instance, if an Iraqi I talked to felt that the United States would subject Iraq to American occupation or some extension of its pro-Israel policies, he or she would react with anti-American defiance. But the majority reckoned U.S. pressure was solely directed at weakening Saddam's regime, not ousting him, and they were taking courage. The population could sense that the regime was on its back foot.

Taxi drivers had begun to openly favor the seductive, apolitical music and talk shows of an American-run broadcaster, Radio Sawa, now washing over the plains of Mesopotamia. One of my drivers slyly took me aside to let me know that he, for one, longed to see the United States smash the Baathist regime into pulp. Freedom of individual enterprise was widening, private sector business was flourishing, more people were ready to whisper their hatred of Saddam, and there was even a slight rise in prices at the Baghdad Stock Exchange. Forbidden dollars began to be freely taken. Internet use began to spread—even though each message was checked by censors—and I was allowed to wander about without the men from the ministry. My minders began to be nervous of going with me into crowds, where boisterousness could turn to mocking sarcasm about the regime. One minder admitted that his life of half-truths had driven him to drink and a dream of escaping Iraq. When

Democracy as depicted in a propaganda mural in Baghdad before the 2002 referendum. The slogan reads, YES, YES TO THE LEADER SADDAM HUSSEIN! (*Hugh Pope*)

I asked another if he would fight the Americans, he half mockingly shook his fist above his head and said "to the end, oh, to the bitter end."

When the regime tried to make a gesture to the population, it was like trying to twist off the lid of a hot pressure cooker. The result could be explosive. After Saddam Hussein magnanimously freed some prisoners, crowds broke into the main jail and several prisoners were killed in the crush. Anger began to overwhelm fear. Unprecedented protests began outside Iraqi secret police headquarters, staged by relatives seeking information about the many, many thousands who had disappeared in the regime's custody. I caught myself thinking that the United States was doing the right thing. I persuaded myself that just making noises about an invasion could topple the regime while keeping the state and country in one piece.

On the day of the referendum, I flew up to the northern city of Mosul. This was months before the invasion, and U.S. warplanes had bombed a target on the outskirts of the city that morning. Indeed, U.S. and British aircraft were overhead most days as part of an undeclared war in progress since 1991. Sensing that the cables binding the population to decades of totalitarianism were stretched to the breaking point, the referendum showed the regime in a mind-set of maximum mania. Media, street banners, and polling station officers all shrilly instructed the population to vote "Yes! Yes! Yes!" The government had a list of everybody. They all turned up. They all voted yes. There was no other candidate, but stressed election officials often filled out people's ballot papers just to make sure. Without exception—there were few curtains on polling booths and anyway the polling officers proudly showed me the lists—everyone did as he or she was told.

When our group of reporters and observers appeared at polling stations in Mosul, the hysteria magnified. Men and women began piercing their thumbs with toothpicks, needles, or knives to press a bloody thumbprint on the box for "yes." Bashar Youssef, a bearded thirty-six-year-old sweet seller from the Mosul bazaar, wanted to send an unmistakable message. Was it to us because he believed it, or to the secret police watching over us because he didn't? He drew a full syringe of blood from his arm.

Then he used his own blood to write "Yes, Yes, for my leader!" on his left arm with his right index finger.

"I am ready to sacrifice everything for my motherland, for Saddam Hussein, to die in order to liberate Jerusalem," Bashar informed us.

At a school decked out with colored holiday lights, plastic-bag bunting strung across the street, and slogans in poorly spelled English, a fifty-two-year-old headmaster went one self-abasing step lower.

"It is we who are unworthy!" he said. "We shouldn't be voting for Saddam but rather trying to make him accept us."

But his wild attempts to rouse anti-American slogan shouting from his female teachers acting as election officers drew only a lukewarm response. In another school voting station, a man stood alone in the mob of slogan shouters and signaled to me with his eyes that he hated what was going on. I followed him outside.

"I say no. I don't accept him," he hissed in a desperate whisper. He sliced the air with an angry karate chop and disappeared into the crowd. But he had almost certainly had to vote yes, and on his lips was the powdered sugar from the heaps of Turkish delight being handed out on trays at the entrance.

When I got back and looked at my photographs of these events, I realized that there was in fact no answer to the questions the *Journal* often asked me to address: What do the Iraqis really want? or Do Iraqis support Saddam Hussein? or Will the Iraqis support or resist a U.S. invasion? In the pictures, I could no longer hear the insults against President Bush or the adulation of Saddam Hussein. I couldn't see joy or excitement, anger or hatred. It was all exhaustion, ignorance and, above all, fear—of both oppression and the possibility of another war. The resulting stress was so acute that it froze people's faces; the corners of their mouths dragged right down, like the masks used in ancient Greek tragedies.

Back in Baghdad, we watched television in the Ministry of Information as someone announced that Saddam Hussein had won a cool 100 percent of the vote in the referendum. Going from office to office, I happened to bring the news to one of the senior Iraqi bureaucrats of the department. He simply started laughing. Out loud, deep from the bottom of his belly.

The West's mistake, however, was to think that killing off Saddam would kill off Saddamism and the Arab nationalist causes with which he sought to distract Iraqi attention from his evil excesses.

I was reminded of this in the same ministry, which had rare official access to the pan-Arab satellite newscaster al-Jazeera. The news was from Israel, and one of the popular Palestinian leaders, Marwan Barghouti, was in the dock of an Israeli court. It wasn't what he was saying that fascinated me. It was the fact that all our hypocritical minders were gathered around the television set. For once they were concentrating, spellbound with admiration as they drank in the defiant words being said by a real hero, a free spokesman for the one issue that all in the Middle East think they understand: the Palestinian cause. The news item over, the minders wearily dispersed. I wandered back to my hotel, taking a route through what had once been a pleasant colonial-era district of two-story shops and houses. It was now battered and filthy, and looked as though it was inhabited by squatters.

I stopped to chat with a group of men working out of a corner shop, busy reconditioning electric hand drills and sanding machines. The twenty-nine-year-old owner, Ahmed Hassan, turned out to have a university education. He had even done a doctoral thesis on the despair and alienation that suffused Iraqi short stories

Two stressed schoolgirls shout slogans for a group of visiting foreigners in a Baghdad schoolyard. 2002. *(Hugh Pope)*

of the current sanctions era. He had lost hope of ever being able to buy a house, own a car, or marry. He longed to join the millions of Iraqis in exile or working abroad.

"There is nothing here. I'll go anywhere. Even Yemen," he said. "Nothing changes, and nothing will change."

"Mr. Hassan . . ."

"Dr. Hassan."

"But Dr. Hassan, you've got a busy shop here."

"Yes, these three men earn sixty dollars a month for twelve-hour days and seven-day weeks. I come often to work with them too. I'm supposed to be a university lecturer, but I get just fifteen dollars a month for teaching," he said, resting his blackened hand on the chipped frame of his shop door. "In the evening I write poems, poems of unattainable love. You see, we always have to keep busy with something here. But it never adds up to anything."

15. JOUSTING WITH THE JUGGERNAUT

How Not to Stop a U.S. Invasion

Do not trust the prince if his minister cheats you.
—ARABIC PROVERB

When I slipped over the Tigris River on a small metal speedboat to visit Iraqi Kurdistan in early 2002, neither I nor my editors thought it likely that President George W. Bush's administration would invade Iraq. The juggernaut, that great holy cart of Indian mythology, had not yet started on its destructive and irresistible path. As the year progressed, contacts in Washington told me that the decision to go to war had been taken, but there remained little public consciousness that American ground troops would occupy the country. To publish the lengthy analysis that I longed to write on the premise "when the United States occupies Iraq, this and that will happen," therefore, would have looked incredible. Since the world's most powerful country must know how crazy it would be to take responsibility for the Arab world's most difficult state, I tried to persuade myself that any U.S. posturing about an invasion must be a brilliant bluff.

Still, I thought it wise to make a theme of occasionally challenging an American assumption that there would be a delirious welcome awaiting U.S. troops as liberators in Iraq. I was given my first lesson about this in April 2002. A tribal chieftain dressed in a long cloak and a white headdress had invited a group of official foreign visitors including myself into his ceremonial tent for a lunch of steaming piles of mutton on rice. He presided over his guests with traditional Arab dignity as we stood around the wide brass trays. Later, he noticed that I was watching him intently from the wall of the tent. He made a point of coming up to me and making sure we would have a short conversation alone.

"I know what you're thinking," he told me. He didn't have to say that he had marked me out as the obvious spy of our group—I could see it in the veil of hostility that had fallen over his piercing blue-eyed gaze. "Just let me tell you one thing. Whatever happens next, we will fight you."

I tried to encapsulate and communicate this defiance to the *Journal*'s readers. My first story was inspired by the face of President George H. W. Bush, cut from the finest Italian marble for visitors to trample underfoot at the entrance of Baghdad's Rashid Hotel. I always sidestepped it, just as I refused to step on American flags laid out everywhere in such countries, a gesture of respect for the America and Americans that I, unlike most people in the region, had had the good fortune to live among and get to know. What intrigued me was that any Iraqi I asked believed that, ten years before, the United States had deliberately targeted and killed one of the country's leading painters for designing the scowling image. In fact, the painter had nothing to do with it, and the U.S. missile, like much of U.S. policy toward Iraq, had missed its real target, a next-door secret police facility. The story of this Iraqi psychosis turned into one of those long, offbeat features that the *Journal* used to run from the left column on the front page, a richly textured mural about the artists of Iraq.

As it turned out, however, it could not be a story about "anti-Americanism," since my editors felt that Americans had read enough of that. It had to go farther, talking about how Iraqis' dislike of the West had made them almost irrationally suspicious in "a country isolated from independent sources of information by a dictatorial president and by a web of international sanctions." Somehow we never panned out to the big picture to explain how rationally this psychosis was connected to decades of wars pitting Iraq and Arab states against the West, whose countries had imposed these sanctions. Instead, the main lesson we underlined was "how easily legend overpowers reality in today's Iraq." Thinking about it in hindsight, most readers must have concluded that the subtext remained the same: A delirious welcome would await whoever revealed the reality, and that an invasion would therefore work.

In the fall, the beat of war drums was discernible and I tried again. I warned how exposed the Iraqi Christian minority felt at the prospect of regime change—indeed, vicious bombings and persecution after the invasion were to force most Iraqi Christians to flee the country. Then, under the headline DEFIANCE GROWS AMONG IRAQIS, I tried to point out that even if the main body of the Iraqi army might not fight a U.S. invasion, nobody could predict the reaction of ordinary people: "While diplomats and some Iraqis believe citizens are likely to stay on the sidelines of any fighting, many Iraqis say a decade of sanctions has turned many against the U.S." If that sounds bland, that last sentence in particular was deliberately so.

In the first draft, I had quoted my driver, fixer, and minder, Samir.

"You say you're coming to bring us freedom. Well, let me to tell you something. Here in Iraq, freedom means the freedom to kill whoever you want," he said. "Now you listen to me. Two of my relatives have died because of the lack of medicines because of sanctions. I blame the Americans for that. So when they get out of their tanks here in Baghdad, I'm going to kill two of them myself."

Bill Spindle had sighed and told me that no reader in America would be able to stomach that kind of talk, would not believe it, and would stop reading. He was probably right. Similarly, I originally ended the story with the words of one of the Baathist blowhards, a former ambassador: "Let the U.S. put their finger in the snake's mouth, and find out for themselves if it is poisonous or not." Spindle objected to that on the grounds that it undermined the strength of the story.

"Since it's so clearly propaganda," he said, "it makes one wonder whether what the other folks in the story have said isn't also."

I accepted that too. I was up to my eyeballs in Iraqi propaganda, and I didn't want to scare the readers into thinking that I couldn't be trusted. Then the battle would be completely lost. Reality was a broad spectrum, and the common zone between the diametrically different Iraqi and U.S. worldviews overlapped only a short hand span in the middle. Spindle was my adviser and protector in making sure that I stayed on this reservation. We didn't do too badly, ending the story by quoting a progovernment sheikh complaining that "the Americans say they are only after Saddam, but actually they are destroying our people." But why should an American believe a progovernment sheikh? We often put in such layers of distance so as not to upset people's comfort zones. The cause seemed hopeless.

The former chief UN arms inspector in Iraq, Scott Ritter, an ex–U.S. marine, dared to stray off the reservation. I went with no particular expectations to listen to Ritter give a speech to the Iraqi parliament, the first by any American. For once in Baghdad, however, I was filled with admiration. First, he stated clearly his belief that Iraq could not be hiding weapons of mass destruction and that the weapons inspection regime had been abused by the United States. He said the United States had planted agents in the inspection teams, cooked up the crisis that led to the Desert Fox bombardments of Iraq in 1998, and selected targets mainly to damage the Iraqi government, not weapons making. This was already like a breath of fresh air. He added, "There is more than enough blame to spread around regarding this situation, including among you, the leaders of Iraq." The bit about the leaders was not fully translated into Arabic. But to say that in Saddam Hussein's Baghdad took courage, and for me counteracted the fact that he was being hosted by Iraqi officials.

Above all, in that low-ceilinged room, he tried to get Americans to focus on what as a journalist I was trying and failing to say.

"My country seems on the verge of making a historical mistake . . . a policy of unilateral intervention . . . The consequences of such action are not only dire in terms of their near-term consequences as measured by death, destruction and lost opportunities, but also the long-term global destabilization that will result from the rejection of international law by the world's most powerful nation," he said. "My government is making a case for war against Iraq that is built upon the rhetoric of fear and ignorance as opposed to the reality of truth and fact."

When he got home, Ritter was interviewed by *Time* magazine and lots of other outlets about "waging peace," but even his effort couldn't stop the slide to war. Three weeks later, the opinion pages of my own newspaper hit back at "Baghdad Jane" and "Ritter of Arabia." Highlighting the switch in Ritter's stance from insistence on the dangers of Iraq's residual weaponry in 1998, and linking it to substantial financing from a pro-Saddam Iraqi-American businessmen, a commentary by the *Weekly Standard*'s Stephen Hayes said Ritter's arguments had shifted from "discrepant to disturbing." He was a foe of the war, a stooge of Baghdad, and, worst of all, damaged goods. He had left the reservation. His words would not be believed.

What to do? Ritter didn't need me to write about him. Journalists are not supposed to be advocates for any state, group, or person, but our "objective" reports often do have policy implications. I often wrote a story because I believed my reporting revealed a message. My idea of objectivity was to be fair while doing so, even if the message had to be dressed up with entertaining frills. But in Iraq, I felt that what I was writing was not getting close. I was certainly no match for the opinion pages of the *Journal,* which were dragging the American consensus their way with fallacies from the pens of Israeli and American hard-liners who'd rarely set foot in an Arab country. Saddam Hussein is bad, therefore removing him is good, they said. The use of force is necessary to win respect for America. Questioning this was immoral, since something called a "war on terror" could be "won" only if everyone supported it.

I couldn't discard what I thought of as my objectivity and become a peace activist. But I could report about the peace-waging individuals whom I kept bumping into in the lobby of the Palestine Hotel. They came from all over the world, and some weren't all that peaceful, like a Serb parliamentarian still bitter about the bombing of her own country by the United States. Still, others seemed noble to me, like Bert Sacks. The retired sixty-year-old software engineer from Seattle was taking more than the usual risks of travel to Iraq, since he was Jewish. I'd tagged along as he endured a tough day bringing a taped message of peace and love from American schoolchildren. His tape hadn't worked on Iraqi video players. Iraqi officials had kept him guessing about which school he could go to. His interpreter hadn't shown up. Then when we got to a school at last, politics broke out all over the yard full of children.

"Down, down, Bush!" the children screamed in English, waving schoolbooks with color pictures of Saddam Hussein. The kids were urged on by a gesticulating Baathist battle-ax of a headmistress. "Long live Saddam!"

Bert smiled pleasantly through this display.

"I come with a message from far away . . . where the children are just like you," he began.

"The professor says that he comes from a great distance and he greets you, children," one of the junior teachers translated, struggling with shyness and a lack of English.

Three volunteers from the Anglo-American group that helped Sacks organize the trip handed around thread bracelets and pencils in the background. They had to organize for a television monitor to be brought over from the offices of one of the TV news crews so Sacks could show a video of American children singing of peace. By the end of the event, artificial, amateur, and politicized at all levels, I wondered at how Sacks could maintain his kindly, grandfatherly demeanor throughout.

Afterward, I went up to his hotel room to share some of my whisky and to ask

American peace activist Bert Sacks discusses with a Baghdad headmistress how to broadcast a message of friendship that he had brought from an American school to Iraqi children. 2002. *(Hugh Pope)*

for his help to win back my lost sense of purpose. I was deeply grateful for the occasional encouragement by e-mail—"Thanks for humanism in reporting" or, even better, "I started to look forward to your byline. Your stories are a welcome tonic to the screeds on your editorial pages"—but sometimes not a single one of the supposed millions of readers that we told advertisers about responded at all. I was beginning to understand why most Middle Eastern journalists I knew were so cynical about their work. If the power is blowing against you, you feel you've been blown as flat as a blade of grass. Of course, Middle Eastern writers are then trampled on, facing real censorship, beatings, and murder if they stray far from their labyrinth of coded symbolism. The biggest danger I faced was solicitous editors. Even so, I was depressed at my failure to make any noticeably greater impact on the situation than Sacks himself.

"It's like swimming against a tide that's sweeping me away," I complained.

"You can't approach things like that, Hugh," he advised. "All people like us can do is hang on and keep chipping away."

With Bert Sacks's words ever present in my mind, I kept on chipping. In December, it was clear that war was probable, and that its likely shape and outcome were now legitimate subjects to address. With a colleague from Washington, David Cloud, I pulled together a survey of all the problems ahead. The first sentence declared that "the victors would inherit a traumatized society full of festering conflicts." The piece clearly laid out that only outside powers or dictatorships had ever held the country together. It warned of separatist Kurdish troubles, of tribalism and vengeance, of the vast expense of fixing up Iraqi infrastructure. We foretold the likely rise to power of the Shia Muslim majority and the advantage that would give Shia Iran. We warned of the need to keep a working relationship with the minority, yet traditionally dominant, Sunni Muslim Arabs in the army and Baath Party. The article sank without trace. Questioning the war's outcome was for wimps.

With a U.S. president apparently intent on sending in the troops, the fashion was for frothy articles about new techniques for victory and aspects of the might of the United States. Raising the question of Iraqi resistance seemed beside the point. So I decided to chip away on a more ambitious scale. I began to talk up a story that would frame any U.S. invasion of Iraq alongside the centuries-long history of failures of such ventures in the Middle East. Bill Spindle pushed me forward. With his help I got the assignment, and also kept my hand on the rudder when similar ideas for a global story were expressed by a former Middle East correspondent. Peter Waldman had covered the region in the optimistic 1990s, scoring one front-page article after another that articulated the hopes of many in the region that the Arab-Israeli conflict was burning out, and enumerating positive changes that could follow from that. His initial take on what we should say reflected Americans' confidence in their capacity to do good in the world.

"Without sounding like a Wolfowitz acolyte—which I'm surely not—I think it might be somewhat original and worthwhile to explore the question, What if the U.S. succeeds?" Peter wrote to me. "What if Iraq is transformed into a stable, open, pluralistic society with a semblance of democratic government? What does that mean for the region, but more interestingly, what does that mean for Iraq? Much of the story, I'd think, could focus on Iraq's unbelievably enormous potential—the only country with all three indispensable elements of success: lots of (educated) people, lots of water, and lots and lots of oil."

Indeed, six months before in Istanbul, I had been invited to listen to Deputy Secretary of Defense Paul Wolfowitz tell a group of opinion makers exactly the same thing. "Iraq's educated, industrious population—with the aid of its large endowment of natural resources—could rapidly build a modern and wealthy society that would be a source of prosperity, rather than insecurity, not only for the people of Iraq but also for its neighbors," he said. "That is why the United States continues to look for new leadership in Iraq."

Wolfowitz went on to say that he "valued Turkey's views highly," but he was clearly not listening to the Turks at all. Most Turkish leaders rightly viewed a U.S. invasion of Iraq as likely to shatter the country, Lebanon style. This would then ruin the already rough neighborhood to Turkey's east and, by speeding up the development of Iraqi Kurdish autonomy, possibly also threaten Turkey's territorial integrity. Turkey wasn't impressed with Wolfowitz's visit, or the fact that he was the only senior U.S. official to bother to come at all. As a result, a year later the Turkish parliament would refuse the Pentagon's plan to open a northern front through Turkey. This plunged the U.S.-Turkish relationship, once a cornerstone of U.S. regional policy, into a crisis that took five years to heal. It sent the U.S. approval rating among Turks down to 9 percent, the lowest in the world.

I was able to persuade Waldman to go with me down the gloomier path I saw. He was a strong partner to have, reminding me of the success of a previous joint article in which he had led the way. Published ten days after September 11, our article focused on President Bush's slip in announcing a Western "crusade." We warned that it "had already reinforced the anxiety of some Muslims that the war on terrorism is really a war on them. It also pointed up the vast gulf between two world views. In Washington, the violent attack spawned ringing vows to defend American values. In much of the Muslim world, it was viewed as a desperate call to America to rethink its support of Israel and, more subliminally, of authoritarian Mideast rulers who deny democracy to ordinary Muslims." It went on to warn of trouble being compounded if the United States did not reconsider this wayward Middle Eastern policy. The unusually frank tone of this piece—a front-page news article, not a commentary—reflected America's brief moment of freethinking and self-questioning about its policy after September 11. We both wanted to seize the chance once more.

Working together again had advantages. Pushing from the American side, Waldman helped the story rise to the top spot. It pulled no punches. "For two centuries, foreign powers have been conquering Mideast lands for their own purposes, promising to uplift Arab societies along the way. Sometimes they have modernized cities, taught new ideas and brought technologies. But in nearly every incursion, both sides have endured a raft of unintended consequences . . . Middle East nations have tempted conquerors only to send them reeling."

The two-thousand-word story led the front page of a newspaper whose editorial pages had arguably done much to whip up support for the war. For once I got dozens of e-mails thanking us for doing our best. The state of Oregon reprinted the article for use in its school system. David Byrne of Talking Heads bought the rights to distribute it as a flyer for all who attended a concert. But starting a project about the folly of the Iraq War in early February had almost no prospect of actually stopping the war juggernaut. Our warning was published only six weeks later, the day before the tanks began to roll into Iraq.

Wars pose dilemmas for correspondents. Their consequences are clearly terrible, but covering them is exciting and every editor is hungry for news about violence, disaster, or victory. The bipolarity of conflict easily supplies the drama needed to make a narrative readable, but at the same time it obscures commonalities, and the entrenching of divisions by our media chorus line makes wars more difficult to end. Many writers, including myself, established themselves professionally by doing frontline service in remote conflicts, but some correspondents become addicted to the adrenaline high of cheating death and basking in the maximum spotlight of attention. I gradually started betting on the safer side of the risk/benefit ratio. I realized this when I read a memoir by Thomas Goltz from one of our tours of the front lines in Nagorno-Karabakh. I had brought my photographer brother Patrick along for the trip. When I saw the bullet-riddled, overcrowded helicopter that would fly us over an enemy-held mountain to a besieged town, I decided to save the family gene pool. Goltz quoted me as bowing out with the words, "I've got a wife and kids." I don't remember saying that, but it's what I meant.

My caution was compounded when the Iraq War came over the horizon. Although fairly treated by my editors, I was demoralized by the way it counted for so little to be the only *Journal* correspondent actually to have been to Iraq, and many times, in the year before the invasion. Nobody asked me back to headquarters to talk about it and there were no invitations from Washington think tanks to give a taste of the bunkered, blinkered, brutalized life of the average Iraqis. Still, as the conflict approached, I felt a need to be a good sport. I signed up for lessons in reporters' battlefield safety.

One course, in an English country house, was far scarier than anything real I had seen in years. We would come around corners to find people apparently bleeding to death with bones sticking out of their skin. I'd only seen dead people on battlefields—anyone wounded was being dealt with elsewhere. It was salutary to have to act myself, given that I can faint while giving blood. Afterward I felt empowered in daily life, probably because my fear of blood was actually ignorance of first aid. I learned always to make sure an accident scene is safe before trying to intervene, that someone should take charge, and that moving a casualty can be more dangerous than making the person comfortable. I wondered why schools wasted so much time making me memorize the kings and queens of England. I realized that I might now actually be useful if I happened upon a car crash. I doubted, however, that a few days' theoretical class work and some bandage practice could help much in the conflict arenas I had known.

A course on chemical warfare at another English manor house felt completely unreal. Like Scott Ritter, I doubted that there were many chemical weapons left in Iraq, or that Saddam Hussein would use any if he had a few. After an hour listening to an ex-military instructor list all the horrors of chemical warfare, I put up my hand. I had the impression that he was bored and unconvinced that amateurs like us needed to learn these things.

"Basically, if there is a chemical attack, is what you're trying to say that there's no point in us even trying to do anything about it?"

There was a short silence. A couple of dozen war reporters were sitting behind wooden desks, just like schoolchildren.

"No, there probably isn't anything you can do," he said, looking relieved at being able to admit the truth. "Even in trained military units, with all the warning devices, the expected casualty rate is thirty percent."

Still, I felt queasy as we went for an experimental walk through the manor house grounds wearing chemical warfare suits, looking like a scene from a science fiction film. I had worn such suits on the Iran-Iraq War front, been terrified at what the Iranians said were chemical bombs exploding in the distance, and I'd spent days with the Iranian victims in hospitals, with their bubbly skins and suppurating eyes. The others were only imagining it, but it was enough to draw us all into the rhetoric of fear designed to make us subtly choose sides in the "war on terror."

One of my *Journal* colleagues ended up ordering all kinds of stuff—chemical warfare booties made in China, a drinking belt one was supposed to fill before a chemical attack, biological antiagent, and, if one had remembered all that, litmus papers to stick on your chemical warfare suit and watch them change color if you were in danger. He gave me some and they still sit on my desk, a curiosity like my great-uncle's binoculars from the First World War trenches. I declined the *Journal*'s offer of a massive flak jacket with thirty-pound plates to stop bullets from assault rifles, but, trying not to seem churlish, I accepted a ten-pound "presidential" version that might or might not stop a 9-mm pistol shot, shrapnel, or knife thrust in a bazaar. It still lies under my bed, unused.

I had no wish to be one of the embedded correspondents, and most of those missions had gone to correspondents from the U.S. side of the paper. In theory, the most glamorous place for me to cover the war would have been at Saddam Hussein's side in Baghdad. But I knew how difficult it would be, how dangerous, and how likely it was that my stories would be overwhelmed by those from the victorious American legions. I also still felt anger against the coming war and a strong determination not to be a casualty of it, especially since my wife was due to give birth in three months. Besides that, the *Journal* wasn't much of a newspaper for the long daily foreign news stories that could make a *New York Times* correspondent feel like he or she was making a difference in the world. I decided not to push fixer Samir for the Iraqi visa I had applied for.

Still, I would have to find somewhere useful to go to justify my salary and my claims to expertise. I considered Iran, Jordan, and Syria, but all seemed second-rate options. My real hope was to take a quiet ringside seat in Iraqi Kurdistan. It would win me an Iraqi dateline and the possibility of communicating some meaning. It would attract little danger, its administration worked, I knew many people there, and it had been relatively free and protected by Western military might for more than a decade. But Turkey had closed the border, traveling there through Iran was uncertain, and my application for a permit to go through Syria was going nowhere.

The war began to look imminent. For two months, I had been regularly calling up the chief of an Iraqi Kurdish office in Damascus, whom I had asked to organize my travel to northern Iraq. He was vague and kept telling me to call back in a couple of days. Now I felt more pressure and tried his mobile phone. He turned out to be traveling himself, in a far corner of Syria. He suggested I call his office manager. I tried once. No luck. I read a newspaper. I tried again. Still no answer.

I had a visa for Syria, but there was not much point going there if I couldn't travel on to Iraq. I couldn't stay in Turkey, since the *Journal* had already sent in someone to replace me. I rang Turkish Airlines and booked a seat on the plane to Jordan, where other lukewarm stories beckoned. My bags had been basically packed for a month, and the patience of the New York editors was not infinite. Perhaps I'd have to accept my fate and make arrangements to go to Baghdad. One more try to Lokman in the Kurdish office. Finally someone picked up the phone in Damascus.

"Oh, no, Mr. Lokman, he's not here. He's in the toilet. Can you call back?"

"Okay."

"Or wait a minute. Yes. Who are you? What's that? Mr. Q? Q Bob? Okay. Wait a minute."

I waited for several minutes.

"Q Montagi Carol Bob?"

"Yes, Hugh Montague Garle Pope."

"Yes, Bob. We got your permission two weeks ago. Write down the number."

The line was scratchy, but by hit and miss I put together that it was Permission No. 1202 of February 26, 2003. I was off to the war, as safely as I could manage.

Success as a foreign correspondent requires a high level of organization in travel—a Lord's Prayer of things to take along, a knack for not being robbed or getting sick, an ear for inner voices about how long a particular place is worthwhile, and an ability to tell taxi drivers to slow down. Above all, it means having ways out as well as ways in. This last weighed on my mind as I headed for Iraqi Kurdistan. After the Gulf War in 1991, several of my friends had only just escaped on foot over dangerous mountain passes as Saddam's armies stormed back into the north. At least four colleagues lost their lives. Going in through Syria meant I could make a rapid move out through Syria if need be.

I now needed to get there as quickly as possible and reckoned I could take a shortcut across northeastern Syria if I entered at a remote crossing point in southeastern Turkey. I flew to Diyarbakır, a city two hours' drive from the border post, and asked the man who was my driver during the Gulf War to meet me. Hajji had been old twelve years before, but now he was elderly. His hand wobbled on the wheel, but I felt comfortable with him since his speed rarely exceeded fifty miles an hour. The spirit of the times had reached my hotel. A television van was parked outside, its satellite dish pointed at the sky. An American TV crew that had been traveling grumpily in business class ahead of me marshaled a bellboy to unload their twenty cases of gear. Such scenes always give a reporter a feeling of being-aliveness, of an adventure under way, of friends old and new.

I soon chanced on an Istanbul neighbor, Doug Vogt, a famed cameraman for America's ABC News. He introduced me to his reporter, a smart New Yorker, their South African soundman, and a Canadian reporter from the *Toronto Star*. For once, everybody was on the same wavelength. We had a snug dinner together drinking beer at our masters' expense, second-guessing international statesmen, condemning U.S. policy, marveling at the insensitivity of editors, agreeing that the war would create an utter mess in Iraq, and blaming Israel. We felt as though we'd regained a purpose in life, and the waiters were thrilled at the energy of our presence. It reminded me of the Gulf War, when Turkey's tourism crashed and the car rental agencies sent all their Suzuki beach holiday jeeps east to Diyarbakır for us to go explore Iraqi Kurdistan. Still, danger lurked behind the buzz. Doug was nearly killed near Baghdad three years later, when a roadside bomb smashed shrapnel into his brain.

Because Turkey had closed its border with Iraq long before, a Syrian visa and Permission No. 1202 meant that I, alone among these journalists, could advance to Iraq. The next morning I loaded Hajji's car with luggage that seemed worthy of an expedition to Africa—my satellite phone equipment and accessories alone filled a whole suitcase. It was very different from the days when I'd set off to some action in Lebanon wondering if I'd remembered my notebook and pen. But I'd organized things well. I topped up with a last few thousand dollars at a bank, managing in the end to secrete $17,000 in cash about my person. Four border posts and another speedboat crossing of the Tigris later, I was ensconced in a comfortable hotel room in the Iraqi Kurdish town of Dohuk, enjoying a good dinner, CNN on TV, and all modern conveniences including globe-shaped metal lights the size of basketballs beside my bed.

I felt both smug and a little guilty. In the aftermath of September 11, too, I had spent the most luxurious week of my life commenting on events from the beach-front Ritz-Carlton Hotel in Dubai. My colleagues embedded with U.S. forces were in genuine discomfort. One pair of reporters were so determined to reach Iraq that they risked days of hair-raising perils to be smuggled through the mountain mine-fields and machine-gun nests on the Turkey-Iraq border. On the other hand, for the next seven weeks, I had the choice of hotel rooms whose only sin was eccentricity. One was like living in a white wedding cake and served softish porn twenty-four hours a day on its in-house television channel. Another was a bridal suite meant for newlyweds high in the mountains, with a mattress liberally stained with virgins' blood to prove it. I was glad I was not in a military camp in the Arabian desert. But now I did have to deal with one nagging worry. I was not on the mainstream news beat. What would I have to write about?

In the old days, just getting to a dateline was half the battle, and the other half being able to call back to say, "I got there. Here's what I saw." Now editors had already seen so much on television they thought they knew it all. Both the *Journal* and the *New York Times* had had reporters working Iraqi Kurdistan for weeks already. The main locations for the story were in ground zero Baghdad, or with the massing armies in the Persian Gulf, or in Washington's corridors of power. Nobody expected any decisive military action on the northern front, and they were right. We were secondary and felt it.

Furthermore, to win a *Journal* editor's heart I had to find a conceptual scoop and then illustrate it through a main character or institution facing a dramatic junction never written about before in this way. I had to supply a novelist's clarity about people's intentions, failures, and sense of mission. This was an uphill battle when writing for the American public. Middle Easterners rarely had that American talent to communicate their life story and future goals in the first ten minutes of an acquaintance. In fact, most people spent a lifetime trying to hide any such personal information. It could take weeks to establish any real level of trust.

Indeed, the whole concept of a life goal was somewhat irrelevant to people who couldn't be sure who'd be ruling their country next week, whose families made such demands of loyalty that individual freedom was a filmy dream, and whose chance of selling out and moving to the next city to start all over again was virtually nil. On top of that was the whole tradition of fighting not to lose face. This meant never admitting fault, even at the cost of a life of lying and cheating. "Samir! You're quite wrong, again," I protested once to my Baghdadi driver and fixer, who prided himself on his bravado, his political incorrectness, and his ability to pretend not to mind the way I teased him. "Why can't you apologize, just for once?"

"Mr. Q! Don't they teach you anything at your *inglizi* spy school? If we show weakness for one minute, just one minute, in this country we will be crushed!"

These Middle Eastern facts of life were all iron balls chained to our mission to fit stories into the worldview of American editors and readers. Not only could readers not really imagine the dreary limits of life outside the world's richest country, but they could also really engage—or so we were led to believe by editors—only with stories that implied a plan to change the world, to carve out a personal dream, and to surmount some great obstacle that lay in the way to success. Hence American correspondents' understandable tendency to stick to writing about Americans abroad, or those who have converted to American values in some way.

As I started my first day's work in Iraq in March 2003, I sat glumly looking over the crowded breakfast room of the Jiyan Hotel in Dohuk. The coffee was too strong and too sludgily black, and I knew its effect would hang in my head like a dark cloud for the rest of the day. Fellow correspondents chatted cheerfully, looking forward to another day of using long lenses to film Iraqis moving about behind their lines. Huddles of local notables compared notes to make sure they survived the excitement. In a corner I spotted one of Saddam's former nasties, an ex–military intelligence boss who'd whitewashed himself by going over early to the Washington-backed "opposition." Sensibly, he'd brought a couple of heavies with him to watch his back. I later met one of the ex-general's cohorts, a white-haired retired brigadier in the Iraqi opposition who wanted America to prosecute the war "Saddam's way. Kill a million of them!" Whatever new Iraq was on the way, I began to see, it would have many elements of the old.

The cynicism I had enjoyed in Diyarbakır about the war turned out not to be fashionable here, where much was made of the rhetoric of bringing democracy to a liberated Iraq. But watching the former intimate of Saddam Hussein made me realize that I had to try, for instance, to tell readers what Iraq's dictatorial ideology of Baathism was like and how hard it would be eradicate. Perhaps I even realized how hard it would be to run the country without it. But this was still just an idea. First I had to shake off my first-day insecurities, one of those uphill days of getting accredited, jumping in and out of four-wheel-drive jeeps with men with assault rifles, greeting party officials in villa after villa, picking up guides, and sorting out drivers.

I was impressed by Dohuk. When I first came to the town in 1991, it had been looted and wrecked in the Gulf War fighting and shops protected their meager wares with the cloth of parachutes from Western aid drops. Now everything looked clean and prosperous, with new suburbs of grandiose villas sprouting up and everything painted in bright colors. The shops in one district had their metal shutters and walls painted a hot, shocking pink—all of them. Looking around I realized that there was another quarter painted a deep blue and another was in the process of becoming canary yellow.

"That's democracy," said my new driver, watching with approval my appraisal of his hometown. "In the old days Saddam told us how to make things look. Now we do it ourselves."

Filled with this pink glow of democracy I lunched at the Dunya restaurant on Dohuk's main street, an establishment overflowing with real and plastic plants. War might be on its way, but here was a feast in the Iraqi style, the table stocked to the edges with innumerable dishes including two varieties of soup, thickly textured chickpea paste, a succulent tangle of fresh thyme in olive oil, fierce pickled peppers, a slippery mash of aubergine and garlic, fresh warm bread, and hillocks of charcoal-roasted chickens, lamb kebabs, and beefsteaks. Quite replete, I found a Mercedes to whisk me on to the main city of Iraqi Kurdistan, Arbil. The journey that in 1991 took six perilous hours could now be done in under three, the driver boasted as I settled in to sleep off lunch. I found out why when I woke and looked around.

"Where are we? Aren't you taking me to Arbil?"

"Of course I am. This is the new shortcut. Look up there," said the driver.

Figures were walking along the ridge between foxholes. The Iraqi lines! I couldn't see the whites of the conscripts' eyes, but it was an easy rifle shot.

"You'll get me killed! We're in Saddam's zone, aren't we? What are you doing?" I protested.

"We're in no-man's-land. It's quite safe."

The jolt woke me from my stupor. Another sense of vulnerability arose as I checked into an Arbil hotel, a professional one this time. Here all the well-established reporters were chasing their leads, telephoning editors, and swapping deliberately misleading versions of what they were up to with a war-is-coming gleam in their eyes. I needed to get a grip on the "story." The next morning I forced myself out to the bazaar. I would do ten substantial but random interviews with ordinary people. Perhaps that way I could pick up the flow.

Arbil's covered market was difficult to love, some parts of it old, others strung out between the 1980s concrete buildings that dominated the city of one million people. Still, stopping the car and plunging into a covered passageway already made me feel better. No vehicles could penetrate here, and people's humanity expanded. I wandered through the street of spice shops. Sacks in front of the shops overflowed with henna, cumin, dried mountain herbs, and finely chopped red and black peppers. The familiar heavy mix of scents reassured me, and I chose to talk first to an old shopkeeper in an immaculate dark suit of Kurdish traditional dress, baggy trousers, thickly wound cummerbund, and long-sleeved tunic. He had kept his spice stall unchanged from the old days, a big archway in the wall bisected by a worn wooden platform, where he could sit cross-legged and reach everything on the shelves behind him. Easy questions first.

"What's happened to the roof?" I asked. Long thin poles of sunlight punched through the spice-laden air from a patch of corrugated iron roughly covering a hole in the infrastructure between the buildings. The shopkeeper's eyes rose up.

"The souk roof fell down in 1973, 1974. We paid the municipality fifty dinars each back then to fix it."

"Saddam's time?"

I left the comment hanging but got only silence in return.

"What do you think of having a war to take out his government?"

"I'm against Saddam. But I'm also against a war to remove him."

I moved on to the street of tailors. Chatting my way down the little hole-in-the-wall shops, a young tailor also said he opposed both Saddam and the war. Then a tailor's customer, a Kurdish gentleman of seventy-five, said he had been in the Iraqi expeditionary force that fought in Palestine in 1948. For him, all war was bad, especially the coming one, since it was an invasion of the Iraqi nation, the Iraqi state, indeed, an insult to the president. He sat there in satisfaction in his fine navy blue Kurdish suit and tightly wound turban.

"So you support Saddam Hussein?" I asked in astonishment—after all, a half dozen people were listening in, and being anti-Saddam was the main platform of the Iraqi Kurdish leadership.

"Yes!" he bravely declared.

That set the tailor opposite into paroxysms of wanting to talk, so I went over to him. He turned down his small radio playing the U.S. Voice of America's Kurdish service and told me that he wanted Saddam to be blasted out of Baghdad as soon as possible—by nuclear bomb if necessary.

In the alleys with shops selling gold, all the traders were very much against a war disrupting their business again. They made money from steady turnover, not speculation. Ladders of horizontal rods in the glass fronts were half filled with gold bangles, a barometer that indicated a higher level of prosperity than the empty displays of ten years before.

In the end, only one person supported Saddam, but seven opposed the war. In this supposedly gung-ho, pro-Western part of Iraq, only three of my ten random interview subjects were in favor of the U.S. invasion. I also felt that I was not as welcome as I had been in the past. When I next returned to the bazaar a year later, when the allied military victory was turning sour, this relative coolness was pronounced. Superficially, the shops seemed even more prosperous. Most people remained polite, but more than ever declined to answer my questions. There was a new edginess, a kind of cold hostility.

I turned for an explanation from Sagvan Murad. I had hired this young researcher from Dohuk for the duration of the war to be my fixer and Kurdish translator, and he was back with me to look at its aftermath.

"Why do they seem angry? Or am I imagining things?" I asked.

"You're right. They didn't want the war but went along with it because the West promised that everything would get fixed afterward. Now they can see that it is actually going to get worse. And they blame the West."

During the weeks in north Iraq waiting for the U.S. invasion, I was determined to spend my time writing stories that spelled out the difficulties ahead. Half a year before I'd tried to show this from an economic perspective with a story from a southern fishing town and shipyard. By painstakingly listing percentages and systems, I'd detailed how Iraq's economy ran on a complex web of subsidies, private enterprise, and political management that was deep, cultural, and, if broken, nearly impossible to reproduce. The front-page editor had congratulated me on "putting a human face on life under Saddam's regime." What I'd actually been proud of was slipping in a last line from the young shipyard manager: "The Americans can try to take all this over. But I think they'd have a hard time making it work."

In one last effort to persuade America it was biting off more than it could chew, I focused my main effort in those preinvasion weeks on producing a story that would show the political challenges of running occupied Iraq. It would have to illustrate the depth and tenacity of Iraq's strain of Middle Eastern authoritarianism. Iraqis called it the Baathist mentality, named for the Baath Party, Saddam Hussein's vehicle for coming to power and staying there. According to the Iraqi Kurdish minister of education, this mentality was so tyrannical that it had to be confronted from the bottom up, starting with domestic violence, near-ritual humiliations of schoolchildren, militaristic teacher-student relations, and the way vast offices could tempt senior officials into authoritarian tendencies—including, he said, himself.

The Iraqis were sick, whether they knew it or not. An Iraqi villager had once screamed at me, "Saddam is God!"

As I wrote the story, I also wanted to note in passing the way the Baath Party's strength was also linked to the Arab-Israeli conflict. The rise of the Baathist ideology of national-socialist absolutism in the Middle East stemmed directly from the Arab reaction to its failure against Israel since 1948. The popular sense of solidarity with Palestine was still the central and most successful ideological pillar of Baathist regimes in Iraq and Syria. Indeed, the need for unity in the struggle against Israel and its backer, the United States, gave all nearby Middle Eastern regimes their main justification for curtailing freedoms and retaining a monopoly on power. Therefore, in the eyes of Middle Eastern populations, unquestioning U.S. backing of Israel delegitimized any U.S. criticism of Baathist and other dictatorial methods. As we worked up the story, however, the front-page editor didn't agree. Suggesting I delete anything Palestine-related, he noted, "Seems like the Wahhabis in Saudi Arabia would have said much the same thing, no???" Or farther on: "This doesn't seem illuminating about Baathism . . . sounds like lots of other things we've read about Arab sentiment and antipathy to West in Iraq."

When my story on the longevity of Iraqi Baathism appeared, not even a passing mention survived of the key Israeli role. Indeed, by the time it was published, the war was in its third week. No matter, perhaps. Even at that stage, rigorously developed State Department plans for the postwar period sensibly called for keeping the Baath Party largely intact. My report noted this, adding that whatever one thought of the Baath Party's 1.5 million members, "It was the skilled force needed to keep the country running." In the event, the new American administration of Iraq disbanded the Baath Party and most other state institutions. While we debated historical perspectives, it had never occurred to any of us that the U.S. government would not follow even its own advice.

16. STOP FIRING! THIS IS A MILITARY SITUATION

One Step Behind the War with the Kurds

"He fled, God disgrace him!" is better than
"He died, God have mercy upon him."
—ARABIC PROVERB

When in Iraqi Kurdistan, I always felt an escapist relief when I caught up with my old acquaintance Hussein Sinjari. Sinjari never failed to make me laugh, even now there was a war coming. He appeared to be extravagantly supportive of the invasion, but nobody could be sure, because he always balanced any statement with a contrarian opposite. He was a bundle of paradoxes that could not be untangled, an inseparable pair of Spanish exclamation marks, one right way up, the other upside down. He was utterly committed to democracy and to his feudal privileges, to his Kurdishness and to his Iraqiness, to cheerfully fondling foreign women and to declaring his love for his wife.

I first met Sinjari, a high-born Iraqi Kurd, during the refugee emergency after the Gulf War in 1991. He was in a mud hut, squatting incongruously in a finely cut baggy Kurdish costume, working with an Iraqi Kurd guerrilla leader who had come back home from a stint as a secondhand car salesman in New Jersey. After that we had met sporadically in Iraqi Kurdistan and even at conferences in Paris. Now, twelve years later, he was installed in Arbil, the Iraqi Kurdish capital. He had rebranded his well-appointed house as the Iraq Institute of Democracy to attract foreign funding and to act as a base to publish an English-language alternative to the dreadful *Iraq Today* newspaper in Baghdad.

"Arbil! Arbil! Hugh, what are you doing here? It is a desert!" he commiserated with me after I'd walked past his ineffectual Kalashnikov-armed guard in a small blockhouse by his gate. "Don't you miss wine bars? Pubs? Chinese restaurants?"

I was more than satisfied with our daily feasts at the best restaurants of Kurdistan, even if the menu rarely changed. My colleagues were making do with much more basic provision elsewhere, not to mention the people of Iraq to our south, nervously waiting to go through yet another war. Sinjari wanted to chase away all such local concerns. He sat me down among his guests, mostly his relatives from the Iraqi-controlled region of Sinjar. He introduced a UN employee, a doctor, a businessman, a government minister's private secretary, and a building contractor.

"Nush! Nush!" Sinjari ordered us all, topping up our glasses with arak distilled from dates by the Iraqi General Chemicals Co. "Drink up!"

We did. Sinjari was irresistible, joking about how Kurds criticized him for his insistence on being different, right down to his democracy group, which was named in honor of Iraq.

"They said, 'Hussein, what is this Iraq? You should make it Kurdistan!' So I told them, 'You can keep your feudal lord and your tribe, and your little village, Arbil!'"

Of course, Sinjari himself was a Kurdish feudal lord and had been in the Iraqi Kurdistan government, a minister of tourism in a land with no tourists. He called his servant to bring out more of the dinner, as excellent as advertised: warm whole chickpeas in stock, wild asparagus root in yogurt and garlic, tomato and cucumber salads, big Egyptian beans, and then the main meal: tomatoes, aubergines, vine leaves, and zucchini stuffed with rice and minced lamb.

We began to talk about the philosophy of the war. Sinjari loved the dramatic plans for democratizing the Middle East being talked about in Washington. He jumped up and began to pace the vast reception room.

"Hugh, what we need here is a revolutionary reformation in the way the Muslim world thinks about itself!" he announced. "Don't quote me on that. They'll kill me!"

"Who should I quote, then?"

"The common man, the common man!" Sinjari insisted.

Apparently, this common Iraqi man now followed the new neoconservative American orthodoxy, believing that Islam was fascism, that the Prophet Muhammad was a militaristic role model for Saddam Hussein, and that the Koran was full of oppressive lies.

"You don't really believe that!" I parried. "And tanks don't bring democracy; educating the common man does! Around here that will take decades and decades!"

Sinjari clapped his hands and cried out the name of another servant. A face appeared at one of the outside doors. The gardener sheepishly slipped off his shoes, stepped inside, and waited patiently to learn his master's will. The door behind him led out onto a neat front lawn, one of Iraq's omnipresent British colonial survivals, along with soup tureens in hotels, electrical plugs with thick rectangular prongs, sponge cakes with round holes in the middle, a national passion for custard, a much-abused idea of punctuality as "British time," and blue bottles of gripe water for babies, complete with Victorian-era labels.

"Our leaders should be servants of the people. Servants! That's what Mullah Mustafa said, and that's why his is the only picture I have on my wall."

I looked up at the wall above him. I couldn't see a picture of the legendary late Kurdish leader, father of the current leader Masoud Barzani. I did see a lovingly inscribed piece of calligraphy that spelled out a quotation from the supposedly scorned Koran: "We all die, even if we live in the most splendid towers."

"What do you want to know from the common man?" Sinjari asked grandly, looking around his table of boon companions.

I suggested that the gardener might tell us if he cared for Ahmed Chalabi, an Iraqi opposition leader who had done so much to charm neoconservative Washington into thinking that it was a great idea to oust Saddam Hussein. I'd met Chalabi frequently since our first tête-à-tête banquet in his palatial house in Iraqi Kurdistan a decade before, when he lived high on U.S. clandestine funds in return for the supply of polished but dodgy intelligence. He was brave and brilliant, and had helped the Kurds in the past, but he had also been convicted of major bank fraud. Like a confidence trickster, he knew exactly how to make his interlocutors love him by telling them what they wanted to hear. He could see straight through my foibles and easily charmed me as well. I knew not to trust him, but his logic was so sweetly rational that it was hard to expose him. While talking of a new democratic Iraq, I supposed he also wanted to reclaim the Chalabi family's pre-1958 revolution estates and political fortunes.

Sinjari's gardener felt conflicted too, but the horizon of his dilemma was altogether closer to hand. Everyone watched him as he shifted uncomfortably from one sock to the other.

"Tell them, tell them! Tell them about Ahmed Chalabi!"

Sinjari patted my knee expectantly.

"Tell them that Chalabi is a cheat! That he owes huge bills in the Arbil bazaar!"

The gardener nodded, still looking down. Sinjari dismissed him with fulsome thanks. He fled gratefully.

"And the nationalism of the Kurdish leaders!" Sinjari continued as he strutted up and down in his old-fashioned British double-breasted suit, finished with a big white handkerchief in the breast pocket and very un-British thick white socks peeping out at the bottom. "Take my cousin Sami, stirring up cheap populism. Masoud Barzani too. I hate Kurdish nationalism, any kind of nationalism."

He didn't actually criticize Masoud, however. Iraq's Kurds mostly had a milder variant of the Middle Eastern habit of dictatorship and radicalized opposition. Masoud's father, the late Mullah Mustafa Barzani, was the founder of the Iraqi Kurdish nationalist struggle, and, as Sinjari had suggested, it was his picture as much as that of any living leader that kept watch over offices in Iraqi Kurdistan. The image always seemed too informal for proper tyranny. He wore the Iraqi Kurdish uniform, with a thick cummerbund that comfortably accommodated his belly, a wooden swagger stick, and a dagger. You could see his white vest at his neck, and an amused smile played around his half-open mouth as if half protesting that he didn't want his photo taken again. As for cousin Sami, he was one of the more intellectually rigorous and interesting people I knew in the Iraqi Kurdish leadership. An apparently Arab al-Qaeda suicide bomber was to kill him in a bloodbath in Arbil three years later.

Before I could defend Sami, however, Sinjari was already off on another tack, the new policy paradox then perplexing the Iraqi Kurds: They were becoming dependent on the Americans, who might save the Kurds, but this meant accepting the Americans' allies, the Turks, who might want to crush them.

"Let the Turks come and occupy us! Are we going to stop them or fight them? How can we resist?" Sinjari postured, seizing both my lapels and putting his face absurdly close to mine. "Let the Americans come to Iraq. They will be our liberators!'

"No, no, no!" I pleaded. "Don't you see that it will just create another Lebanon! I was there, I saw it—militia fiefdoms, foreign meddling, more violence! And everyone with any sense will leave, probably including you!"

My satellite phone rang. It was a U.S. cable television station. I excused myself and stepped outside on the lawn where the little aerial could see the satellites hovering high overhead. The signal locked in. I performed my part. But I could make no connection with the interviewer in his busy American studio.

"Hugh," the interviewer finally asked, "if you were in charge of the American effort to explain the position, if you had all the resources you wanted, what would you do to convince people that the U.S. has come to liberate, not to occupy?"

I was knocked off guard. The *Journal* had given me all the resources I could ever want to explain to Americans about Iraq, and I'd used them to try to convince people why occupation would never be seen as liberation. But as the sincerity of the interviewer's question showed, I had completely failed. I couldn't trot out glib words, or hide my anger at the war in the words of other people, "Iraqi Kurds say this . . ." or "A gold merchant I met today said that . . ."

Instead, I stumbled into an explanation of how liberation by the United States clashed with Iraqi perceptions of U.S. responsibility for twelve years of sanctions, about Iraqi fears that a U.S. invasion meant they would face the same fate as the dispossessed Palestinians. The interviewer quickly brought the conversation to an anticlimactic end. *Click*. I looked up at the star-studded sky over Sinjari's garden, listening to the U.S. bombers droning high overhead.

At that moment, Sinjari burst out of the big windows leading into the garden, mobile phone in hand. His English-speaking wife was calling from Brussels. The line kept dropping, and he would then swear darkly. But his line was altogether more effective than mine.

"Okay, my darling!" he shouted, entranced by his new rhetorical flow and gesturing toward me as if to include me in it too. "Yes, my lovey love. Okay, my lovely love. Bye-bye! I love you, my darling lovely lovey love."

Sinjari promised to help me in my quest to inform our readers about the Iraqi Kurds through a profile of their historic leaders, the Barzani clan. So a couple of afternoons later, I joined him at home for a glass of mint tea and table tennis. He had patience for only five bad rallies with his overspongy bats. Then we headed off to learn more about the Barzanis in Salahuddin, twenty-five miles to the north. On the way he pointed out the landmarks of the advance of the Barzani family. Every time he wanted to make a point about Kurdish self-government, he would rhetorically ask questions of Ali, his chauffeur.

"Ali, is it true or is it not true that you are a representative of the people?"

"Yes, it is true, my lord."

"Do you live in poverty and squalor?"

Ali knew his part. "Yes indeed, sire. I am not even able to buy a refrigerator."

"And what is this suburb that we are passing through called?"

"Dollarawa, sire!"

"You see, Hugh? This is what money has done to the party."

In this suburb, "Dollarville," Iraqi Kurdistan's well-connected elite, profiting royally from the region's building boom and status as a U.S.-protected smuggling crossroads between Turkey, Iran, Syria, and government-controlled Iraq, were putting up minimansions fronted with cut stone and polished marble. They chose the quasi-Baathist style of the core Arab countries, whose dominant feature is two tall columns on each side of the garage gate that support a high, flying roof over the whole front of the house. Immense effort goes into the beautification of the street façade. Then the sides are left an ugly, half-finished concrete, waiting for the next house to be built next door.

We passed the palace built on the edge of Arbil by a former right-hand man of Saddam, and, on TV appearances, his most loathsome flatterer in chief. It is on a large plot of land, and since the Iraqi Kurds took over in 1991, it has been used off and on by their leaders. Currently it was occupied by the Kurdistan Democratic Party of Masoud Barzani, universally known "Brother Masoud," whose yellow flag flew over western Iraqi Kurdistan. The other main leader was Jalal Talabani, universally known as "Uncle Jalal," head of the Patriotic Union of Kurdistan, whose green flag flew over the eastern half. The division dated back to a shift in cold war alliances in 1975. The United States and the shah's Iran had secretly supported the Iraqi Kurds against Baghdad in the 1960s and early 1970s, but had in 1975 made peace with Baghdad and abandoned the Iraqi Kurds to their fate. When an exhausted Mullah Mustafa gave up and led the Barzanis into exile, the opportunistic Uncle Jalal led an idealistic faction that wanted to fight on to the bitter end. Oddly, Brother Masoud told me that he had agreed with Uncle Jalal's stand in principle but could not possibly have gone against his father.

Now the United States was again protecting the Iraqi Kurds in order to weaken Baghdad. This could only paper over old quarrels and other differences, with Brother Masoud's westerly fiefdom seeming more conservative and rural with a predominance of speakers of the *kurmanji* dialect of Kurdish, while Uncle Jalal's easterly towns seemed more liberal and populated by speakers of the *surani* dialect. Sinjari had spent long years as a guerrilla fighter in his youth and had switched sides a couple of times between Brother Masoud's "Party" and Uncle Jalal's "Union." He now described himself as independent, that is, financed by do-good democracy institutes in the United States and Britain.

"When I was living there with Uncle Jalal, I had a small room, it was very modest. There was just a small fence around it," Sinjari said, as we passed a new high concrete wall with guard posts. "Now look at it. Brother Masoud made it a palace. And he even built a private road to his office. Isn't that right, Ali?"

"What's that, sire?

"A private road. Tell the reporter, Ali, can you use that road?"

"No, sire. If they see you on it, they chase you away."

Sinjari might criticize the Iraqi Kurdish leaders, and indeed, after one of his public outbursts, they had for four months suspended his pension as a retired minister. But the administration had made him the gift of a car and kept his place on the payroll, worth five normal workers' salaries.

We passed groups of Friday holiday picnickers gathered on the wide grass verges of the dual carriageway north, sitting around the saplings planted to replace trees cut down in the great fuel crises of the early 1990s. Beside the road were boys with stacks of boxes of bananas. Sinjari lit up with righteous anger again.

"Bananas! You see! They are only on this side of the road, for the officials going home from town. Only they can afford them!"

"Surely they are being sold to the people going out for picnics?" I asked.

"Ali! Tell him! When was the last time you ate bananas? I mean, apart from what we eat at my home?"

Ali made a show of thinking.

"I don't know, sire, but, by God, I think it was one and a half years ago!"

"And were you not a party member, and have you not now left?"

Ali had clearly done the right thing and resigned.

We soon started the steep switchback climb up to Salahuddin. The first grand houses of the new elite of the Barzani faction peeped over the brows of the hills. Sinjari was getting worked up, with some reason. After all, Salahuddin had been part of his ministerial portfolio for tourism. The whole town, he told me, was built on Iraqi state land as a place for the population to cool off. Now it was basically a Barzani gated community. Brother Masoud's headquarters were in an old hotel here. His son's intelligence organization's base was in a new palace nearby. This was a strategic choice, an outpost on the first line of hills before the great mountains of Kurdistan rising behind it. History repeatedly showed that front lines and alliances could change Kurdistan with lightning speed. Clearly, the Iraqi Kurdish guerrillas knew they had no hope of defending their current chief city of Arbil on the plain from any sustained or organized Iraqi Arab attack. They could make a stand here, or flee to the rugged fastnesses behind.

"This is a green zone! I told them. You can't build here! But they don't listen. Ali, tell the journalist! Was this not once the property of the people! Did you not come here to holiday?"

"Yes, sir, we could come here all the time."

"And now?"

Ali shrugged theatrically and lifted up his gear-lever hand in supplication to the gods of the rich and educated.

We were going to visit Jirjis, the eighty-year-old biographer of the Barzanis, who had been tempted home from Switzerland to a house built especially for him. Sinjari knew Jirjis well because Jirjis was also his newspaper's chief editorial writer. Servants ushered us into the gloom of his large stone villa and then through a corridor to a dimly lit study with drawn curtains. Pools of light illuminated a desk piled high with books and papers. Jirjis was an Assyrian Christian of considerable dignity. His cranium was low and his eyebrows ruggedly prominent, making him look like a wise, elderly tortoise.

"Tell him that you've heard that he is the best literary stylist in Arabic in northern Iraq," Sinjari hissed as we went in.

I happily passed on the pleasure of this flattery to someone who'd clearly been through much. We started to talk about the Barzani family.

"You should read my books, it's all in there," said Jirjis.

"It's so much better to hear it from you," I said, my heart sinking at the prospect of having to dig through many pages of impenetrably stylistic Arabic.

"I don't do interviews. I am tired. So tired," he replied, with a deep, resonant weariness.

Instead, he invited me to inspect the 1970s piece of paper on which Saddam Hussein, then deputy leader of Iraq, had spared his life from a death sentence. I was expecting a spiky, self-important scribble. Instead, Saddam's signature was a line of modest, circular loops above a thick line and subsquiggle. There was, if anything, something schoolgirlish about it. Saddam had let Jirjis live, but I felt like an actor in a film reaching the Great Wise Man at the end of a long quest, only to have the Great Wise Man expire before divulging the Secret.

"Come around again!" Sinjari said when we got back to town. "It'll be truffle season soon, we'll eat like kings! We can play Ping-Pong too!"

One reason I felt warm toward Iraqi Kurds was that they recognized what foreign correspondents had done to put them on the political map. On the main ring road of Arbil, for instance, two bronze statues stand to colleagues who died covering the Kurds, a touching tribute in a region that usually treats reporters with fear and scorn. This was despite our cruel nonchalance in the early 1980s, when we paid little attention to the Kurdish cause. In this we followed the lead of Western governments like the United States, which allowed only junior diplomats to chat informally with Kurdish envoys in cafés well away from the State Department in Washington. To be fair, we also rarely saw representatives of the "world's largest nation without a state," a people who today number about twenty-five million split between the mountainous borders of Turkey, Iraq, Iran, and Syria. They were too remote, too rural, too unmodernized, and too invisible to us.

I had stayed with Kurds in southeastern Turkey in the early 1980s and so knew something of their side of the story. One village still glows in my memory as an example of the pristine, premodern Middle East, a stone-built hamlet on the slopes of Mount Nemrut that was three hours' walk from the nearest road. Its winding beaten earth alleys were spotlessly clean. Our host's house was notable for its freshly whitewashed walls, the flowing lines of its adobe interior surfaces, its smoothly sculpted fireplaces, and its gorgeous orange-red flat-woven kilim rugs. Old wooden plows and hay forks hung decoratively on outside walls. I also remember their reaction when my companion, the French orientalist Jean-Pierre Thieck, began trying to tease out from the men sitting around the edge of the village hall some information about the military coup regime in Turkey. They retreated into silence behind a wall of hand-rolled cigarette smoke. Only later did I learn that tens of thousands of Turkish Kurds were at that very moment being crushed into Turkish jails and forbidden to speak Kurdish even with their illiterate visiting mothers. Untold thousands were tortured and many were killed.

A few years later I was in Beirut covering the Lebanese conflict, Arab-Israeli ructions, and the Iran-Iraq War. I didn't know that the Iraqi Kurds were being

Iraqi Kurdish leader Masoud Barzani *(right)* sits with an Iranian army officer in Northern Iraq. 1985. *(Hugh Pope)*

steadily destroyed by their president, Saddam Hussein. The United States and the West said little about this vicious campaign. We occasionally found messages from Kurdish organizations on our telex machine, begging us to pay attention to their plight. But the details of deaths and bombings always seemed melodramatic and unbelievable. We had no framework to fit any Kurdish story into, either in our own heads or in the parameters of everyday international news. I puzzled over these cries from beyond the horizon, realizing that I could think of nobody even to ask for more detail. There might have been academics in Europe, but even a local phone call in those days typically involved waiting half a minute for the dial tone, sometimes much longer, and long-distance calls rarely got through easily. Then some "urgent" local news would come in and once again we would give up on the Kurds.

I first reached Iraqi Kurdistan in 1985 in an aging Iranian army helicopter. The Iran-Iraq War was in full swing and I was the Reuters correspondent in Tehran. When our group of reporters landed in the middle of a mixed mountain camp of Iraqi Kurdish guerrillas and Iranian soldiers, none of us had a clue that the shy, turbaned, baggy-trousered guerrilla sitting cross-legged on a carpet in a mud hut was Masoud Barzani. Indeed, only one or two of us had heard his name before or knew that he was the Iraqi Kurdish leader. Years later, Barzani told me that he had no idea that the Iranians were bringing reporters that day. Stuck on the other fronts of its war against Iraq, Iran wanted to taunt Saddam Hussein by exposing its alliance with his domestic foes. Our stories can only have worsened the grisly violence against the Iraqi Kurds, in which Saddam used chemical weapons, razed some forty-five hundred Kurdish villages, and killed 180,000 people, including three dozen members of Barzani's own extended family.

The United States was discreetly backing Saddam at the time. In 1988, when these attacks forced tens of thousands of Kurds to flee over the Turkish and Iranian borders, their plight could no longer be ignored. I formally asked American diplomats what they knew about persistent but confused reports by refugees of the use of chemical weapons. Repeatedly and resolutely, the diplomats denied any such Iraqi wrongdoing. Still trusting then that Western governments represented a fuller knowledge and some higher good, I accepted the denials.

The Kurds had a tough struggle against this invisibility. Even in Tehran, where the Iraqi Kurds' representative, Hoshyar Zebari, later foreign minister of Iraq, would roll up to my Reuters office in his stylish Range Rover for another jolly and irreverent chat, I usually couldn't think up ways to write anything about them. The Iraqi Kurds finally erupted into months of massive media consciousness in the refugee crisis after the Gulf War in 1991, but it subsided again soon enough. In the mid-1990s, an editor at the *Los Angeles Times* warned me in all seriousness, "Hugh, don't put the word 'Kurd' in the slug [the top computer catchline] if you want us to look at the piece for publication. To us, it guarantees that we won't understand the story."

Still, I kept going, as did many others. Perhaps we were led on by the Kurds' freer thinking, which made them more fun than other Middle Eastern peoples; or their marginal vulnerability, which caused them to treat outside parties who could help them with an exaggerated and flattering respect; or because they worked so hard to keep their journalistic visitors safe; or simply because we were drawn in by their charm.

In the mid-1990s, guided by Jonathan Randal, an inexhaustible *Washington Post* veteran, I rushed ahead of a whirlwind twist in inter-Kurdish feuding to reach Uncle Jalal in his mountain headquarters. Brother Masoud's raiders were racing toward his command center. Uncle Jalal was on his primitive satellite telephone, trying to beg for Washington's help. After a long wait, he got a brush-off from a junior desk officer whose only substantial question was to ask him how he was.

"I am not well!" Uncle Jalal roared, breaking for once his habit of saying whatever he felt the person he was speaking to wanted to hear.

Despite the emergency, Uncle Jalal and his wife, Hero, invited Randal and me to have dinner with them in a corner of their kitchen and then stay over in their guest room. The next day, after we had all slipped off, Brother Masoud's guerrillas would capture the headquarters, loot it, and race back to where they had come from. The Middle East is full of sudden shifts of fortune. Ten years later, Jalal Talabani was the president of Iraq, and Masoud Barzani was president of an autonomous, recognized Iraqi Kurdistan federal region, and both appeared the best of friends again.

This was achieved, of course, thanks to new U.S. support. Absent such a colonial or other protector, a credible army is indispensable, and I had my doubts about the Kurds' chances on this front. Kurdish soldiers are called peshmergas, those-who-face-death, but I knew they could be as flighty as me when it came to avoiding real trouble. Checking out peshmergas on parade as we all prepared for the Iraq war in 2003, I saw that the folkloric old baggy trousers, cummerbunds, and turbans of a decade before had gone. All now wore new uniforms of Western camouflage pattern. Eight companies of fifty men stood before me on their camp's rocky, beaten-dirt football field, fronted by a band of two drummers, a trombonist, a clarinetist, and a bugler. This last let out a strangled screech, the sergeant major raised his fine parade-ground baton, and the men went through paces that had survived from British colonial times. I had learned exactly the same steps when I played the tuba in my school's 1970s cadet force band. Their boots made a *carrr-UNCH* sound as they came down on the gravel. As they passed an informal reviewing stand, each unit in turn did an eyes-right and all shouted "KURDISTAN!" Their berets, however, were all slightly different shades of red. Footwear was sometimes boots, but also leather walking shoes, and occasionally sneakers too.

"Congratulations on your parade!" I told the commander, an immaculately uniformed and impressive-looking peshmerga veteran. "What is the parachute on the shoulder patches?"

"The parachute is to show that these men are from the special forces!" the commander replied spiritedly.

It was all a charade. Everyone knew the Kurds barely had any armored vehicles, let alone anything that could fly. In parallel with the civilizational collapse of Iraq, the peshmergas were no longer the well-educated, ideological force they had been in the heyday of the fight against Saddam's cruel injustice to the Kurds. Security companies in post-2003 Iraq actually stopped hiring peshmergas because they were illiterate. A lack of basic education prevented them from remembering even basic skills, such as stripping down any weapon more sophisticated than their old Kalashnikov rifles.

The peshmergas were great at surviving on tea and dried bread high in the mountain fastnesses of Kurdistan, picking off the troops from the plains with snipers and raids. But these peshmergas could not quickly overcome their chief characteristic on the lowland battlefields, the entirely rational choice of headlong flight whenever disciplined troops marched up against them. Brave and hardy when defending their mountain villages, they had little experience of discipline or statehood. As we spoke in his headquarters just before the new war broke out, Masoud Barzani was still struggling with himself as he tried to organize a regular government.

"I met a group of engineers and told them, 'I know how to blow up bridges, not how to build them,'" he said. "I met lawyers and said, 'I know how to break laws, but not how to make them.'"

I pointed out the irony that the Iraqi Kurds were once again working with the United States, which had let them down badly not only in 1975. In 1991, when Washington called on the Kurds to rebel after the Gulf War, it let Saddam crush them before saving them from a refugee disaster. The Kurds would always be partially beholden to some great or regional power, although no country could stop them from turning to a higher bidder whenever that suited them better. Even when under U.S. protection in 1996, Brother Masoud was capable of doing a quick and dirty deal with Saddam Hussein to get even with his then rival, Uncle Jalal.

"My father always used to say that without American support, it would be hard for the Kurds to achieve anything of value," he said. Once again, he cheerfully concluded, the Iraqi Kurds were ready to "give the Americans a try."

Black March clouds were piling up high in the evening sky over Arbil three days before the invasion of Iraq began. Immense thunderclaps made my flimsy hotel room shake. All television news channels were broadcasting the diplomatic endgame live. Deadlines loomed and expired, last-minute initiatives bloomed and failed. Correspondents talked of an atmosphere of gloom descending on New York, of a failure to reach consensus, of anger, and of war.

I was in the angry camp, my mind still focused on the war lust in the grins of U.S. Secretary of Defense Donald Rumsfeld and Chief of Staff General Tommy Franks, photographed as they watched the preparatory American military exercises in the Persian Gulf. On the TV, another point of no return was reached when the British ambassador to the UN, Sir Jeremy Greenstock, addressed the world's media after entirely failing to convince the Security Council that the international community should back the U.S.-led war.

"We reserve the right . . ." he intoned.

What right? I thought. Who exactly was "we"? What the world thought didn't matter. A couple of years later, I met Sir Jeremy at a fancy London conference. For once I managed to ask him what was on my mind when we came shoulder to shoulder in a corridor.

"How could you do it? How could you do it, when the British, above all people, must have known that it was impossible to win a war in Iraq?"

Sir Jeremy looked at me with apparent sincerity. He had already told newspapers that the British government of Tony Blair had somehow joined the United States against Iraq without actually having wanted to go to war.

"We really thought, we really thought that we could stop it, right up to the last minute," he said to me.

I was left speechless. My old sense of shame resurfaced—at Britain's historic carving up of the Middle East into unwieldy countries doomed to quarrel, at how the *Wall Street Journal*'s opinion pages recklessly sought war against Iraq, and now at my own country's new display of self-defeating conduct. I had not turned against my own kind, but in Arbil, I did despair. When I heard the news of the first casualties, a dozen British killed in a helicopter crash in the Gulf, I wept for the first time in years.

The next morning, I woke up feeling more practical. A war was really on the way, and I had a responsibility to keep my little group of driver, fixer, and myself well supplied. The trouble was, every Iraqi Kurd had woken up with the same idea. My driver returned from the market with the news that there was no more bottled water and that tinned goods were disappearing. A man appeared on the roof a few

A line of Iraqi Kurdish refugees from among the five hundred thousand who fled over the border mountains into Turkey after the Gulf War. The United States had urged them to rise up against President Saddam Hussein but then did nothing to stop Iraqi forces from crushing their rebellion. Media coverage of the emergency triggered U.S.-led intervention that allowed the refugees to return to an internationally protected Iraqi Kurdistan. 1991. *(Hugh Pope)*

buildings away, pointlessly swaddling his water tank with plastic sheeting against a chemical weapons attack. By the afternoon, half the shops were shut. Public offices emptied. On roundabouts at the main ring road, tent makers worked round the clock to sell temporary refuges for an average week's salary. Main roads to the mountainous north were jammed with cars and pickup trucks piled with people and their bundles of belongings. More would-be passengers stood about at taxi stands with their luggage, seeking transport out of the city. We were, after all, only a few miles from what might become a second northern front between Saddam Hussein's Iraqi forces and those who would overthrow him. Kurds near the front line were moving north to Arbil, Kurds in Arbil were moving north to Diyana, and Kurds in Diyana were moving into the slopes leading to the borders of Turkey and Iran. One Kurdish newspaper headline punned on the old Kurdish saying about having no friends but the mountains: THE MOUNTAINS ARE OUR GAS MASK.

Mass psychosis is a powerful force. I'd chosen northern Iraq for the war because I was convinced there would be no fighting here, but I too began to wonder if I should run away. Before I had time to make up my mind, my driver came to inform me that he had already decided to flee.

"I have to look after my family," he said, only slightly hangdog as he betrayed me. "It's just a precaution."

So I stayed. I was still supplying a few lines to the *Journal*'s daily output of grand war stories, so I went over to ask for an overview from a Kurdish government minister, Nimr Katcho. The building was almost empty and I was shown straight into his freezing office, where he sat in his coat.

"What can we say to the people? Sit tight? Can we put a policeman on every house?" Katcho said. "We have no gas masks, no medicines. We cannot guarantee anybody's safety, so we think it's best to let people do what they think best in their own time."

The editor of Hussein Sinjari's newspaper had described it to me as "a sixth sense for survival, a kind of genetic programming that tells us when it's time to flee." In other words, it was every person for himself. I didn't want to run away completely— although on the one day I did go to look at the front line, I got so nervous at the near complete lack of peshmergas that I staged a panicky retreat to the Turkish border—but I felt that perhaps I should have a new strategy. Usually, I operated on my own, partly because the stories required by the *Journal* were unique in nature. In the current confusion, I thought I should try to team up with someone.

Turning up for dinner on the evening that war had become inevitable, I found the usual mix of correspondents in Arbil's Tower Restaurant. There were old friends and regulars from previous trouble spots, with whom I generally sat. There was a good-looking young set that had seen their first real action in Afghanistan the year before, some of whom proved it by wearing flat Afghan caps and getting stoned. War excitement made that dinner unusually raucous, helped by the fact that the Tower Hotel was one of the few that served alcohol. Over meat kebabs and greasy vegetarian pastas, I heard snatches of conversation about "getting a good Pajero" or cameramen's talk of bribing their way through the front lines.

Most of my international colleagues believed, rightly, that the critical events in the north would be a struggle to control the mixed city and province of Kirkuk. Kurds, Arabs, and another ethnic group known as the Turcomans all believed this oil-rich prize to be their birthright, or even, in the case of the Kurds, the "Kurdish Jerusalem." I reckoned that events there could indeed be chaotic and bloody, and made no complaint when a younger colleague from the *Journal* seized the story as her own. One of the twenty-something "Afghans," Catherine Philp of the London *Times,* also had a colleague covering the Kirkuk section of the front and needed another story line to follow. A veteran of shortages and hair-raising scrapes in the Hindu Kush, she had a car, a driver, fuel, a generator, and satellite gadgets galore. Although intimidated by her ambition to do the war properly, I tried to persuade her that she should join forces with me by sharing part of my secret.

"Imagine," I said. "I know some Kurdish guerrillas we can trust, who will let us witness their liberation of a small northern Iraqi town! Then we can write about reunions, settlings of accounts, the future of the Kurdish region . . ."

I did not mention my real secret, the hope that this process would be entirely peaceful. Even so, a shadow of suspicion crossed Philp's face, suggesting that she realized that my proposal involved decidedly nonmainstream news. She underlined that her priority was to get to Mosul when it was liberated. Remembering the tensions I'd seen in that conservative Arab-majority city the year before, I murmured something ambivalent. Nevertheless, we agreed that we would set off together in a day or two. I still had a couple of things to sort out. Communications was top of the list.

I long prided myself on always being able to deliver a story, even if it wasn't the story my editors had been hoping for. There was little I hadn't tried. I had sent hand-typed stories by post and by fax. I had tried Morse code in the African bush. In Beirut, I learned to memorize stories as I wrote them because power cuts were so frequent, forcing me to retype the whole text into the computer several times. I had used a "pigeon" during a communications blackout in Tehran, surreptitiously handing an envelope with my story to a traveler on an international flight. In Tajikistan, I had typed out a story on a telex with a QWERTY brain but a Cyrillic face, a job so confusing that I had to hide the keyboard with a strip of cardboard and still ended up with a two-day headache. In other tight corners of Africa and Central Asia I had telexed stories by radio and later satellite. I had dismantled public telephones and taken apart hotel rooms to find live telephone wires for my crocodile clips. I had whistled long and hard into suction cup connectors to telephone handsets, trying and failing to start up the squelch of a computer connection. I'd dictated copy on the first $15-a-minute satellite phones to a talented blind transcriber at the *Los Angeles Times*. And I had put a nail in the coffin of a service called Iridium by revealing in the pages of the *Journal* its drawbacks in the 1999 Kosovo War. The signal cut out each time one of the ring of circling satellites dropped over the mountain, causing one TV correspondent to throw his brick-sized handset into a river.

Each conflict had brought a new device into its own, and this was the War of the Thuraya. Every correspondent had one of the new satellite phones. I believe that the "Afghans" slept with them, and they certainly spent the whole day plugged into them like horses in harness. Like its predecessors, it had its quirks, chiefly that it always had to have a clear line of sight southward. Most mornings would see me taking my Thuraya for a walk down the street like a pet so that it could wake up, see two satellites at once, figure out where I was, and let me start making calls. Hotels got used to profiting from correspondents who insisted on south-facing rooms. In restaurants, the Thurayas, like the drivers, got their own little corner where they could keep in touch. I often found myself crouched at the end of uninsulated corridors, frozen and waiting for the results of the Thuraya's painfully slow interactions with the head office's superfast computers. New York being New York, editors could never truly imagine what we went through to read their messages. Or what it meant on that night the war started when, shifting awkwardly from knee to stiff knee, I knocked my little Thuraya handset off a window ledge onto the ground. A tiny plastic hook that locked the computer cable in place snapped cleanly off. I would now have to hold it in place to keep the connection alive while talking. It was impossible to do this, however, while typing on the computer keyboard.

I had no real hope that I could replace the cable in Arbil, even though the isolated Iraqi Kurds were savvy about their communications. In one Internet café I'd sat next to a young man escaping reality with chat screens open to four American housewives at the same time. The Kurds had also managed to set up a basic but useful cell phone service. One telephone shop in Arbil dealt in Thuraya equipment. I reached it just as they finished clearing their entire stock off the shelves.

"There's going to be a war, and that means looting," the dealer said, grumpily chasing an armless street urchin out of his shop.

"You don't have one of these, do you?" I said, holding out my crippled but still operational cable.

"Hmm. No."

"Can't we solder it in some way?"

"We can try . . ."

Knowing that I was doing the wrong thing, I opened up the plug. An astonishing number of miniature wires burst out. It never worked again. Only a week later did I find a solution in another town, spending $400 on a docking station and 350 feet of heavy coaxial cables, dwarfing the one-pound handset.

Another key requirement to cover a war is a map, and in this respect, Iraqi Kurdistan was again impossible. I had bought a big aerial map of the region from the world's grandest map shop, Stanford Maps in London's Covent Garden, but it showed few names of towns and was no help in the delicate business of driving without hitting the Iraqi army front line. Another popular map published in Tehran was detailed, but I found it hard to read the flowery Persian calligraphy of the names or see exactly where they referred to. A Kurdish journalist friend offered me a map of greater Kurdistan instead. The map claimed most of the Middle East as Kurdish, and, unhelpfully for me, erased the borders of the states and front lines that currently divided the Kurds. In the end, I spent 30 cents on a letter-paper-sized bootleg photocopy of a United Nations aid agency map, which showed where all the front lines were and hot spots were likely to be.

In Arbil, meanwhile, tensions were rising. Iraqi Kurds were arming themselves against looters and hotels were operating with half their staff. When we were eventually ready to head west to join up with my Kurdish guerrilla friends, Philp and I piled our bags into her car. Her driver came uncertainly around to open the passenger door, or rather to stand by it with his hands folded in front of him. I recognized the beaten look in his lowered head and eyes.

"I've talked to my mother," he told Philp. "She's ill. I have to go to her."

The Middle Eastern mother is indeed an all-powerful figure. Whatever is said about other abuses of women's rights, even the most Westernized of Middle Eastern men often still call Mom every day, and pay for it dearly if they don't. Since the Middle Eastern man's wife may not get the same level of attention and respect, she too locks on to the relationship with her sons, spoiling them, celebrating them, loving them. And so the pattern repeats through each new generation. I could see the driver was torn. Philp was paying him a lot of money, which he could earn nowhere else. But compared to his mother, money didn't have a chance.

We felt we could delay no longer, and after a few hours found a substitute driver ready to accept a small fortune to take us west to Dohuk. The frontline skirmishing we had seen up until now was about to turn into the real conflict. If and when the Kurds started to move forward on our northern front, I hoped we would tag along with my group of Kurdish guerrillas to witness the new era. Its leader was a friend of Murad, my fixer, who woke me with polite knocking on my hotel door the next morning.

"Hugh! Wake up! Didn't you hear? The war has started!"

He had spent all night up at his village near the Iraqi front lines a few miles south of Dohuk. I switched on the television. A volley of missiles had hit Baghdad,

250 miles to the south, where the Pentagon thought Saddam Hussein might be hiding. Even though President Bush's unequivocal ultimatum had already expired, the TV reporters still talked about how the attack was a "surprise" and this "wasn't the real war."

I looked out the window at the pink district of Dohuk. Almost all shops were closed. A few cars still headed out of town between the rain-washed, flat-roofed concrete buildings.

"Should we join our friends yet?" I asked.

"No, no. It'll be a few more days before anything happens in the north," Murad reassured me.

My plan for a quiet war was working. While Philp toured the front lines, I spent my time in my hotel room typing up notes and fine-tuning my features about what I believed were the grave problems awaiting Iraq. My attempts to hustle these onto the *Journal*'s production line in New York were often unsuccessful, as editors were far more excited about news from the troops and politicians. On the television, tank-mounted cameras were beginning to plow through the desert in the new live reality-show version of warfare. In tones of shock, presenters talked of reports of Iraqi resistance. A little port south of Basra called Umm Qasr was, apparently, proving particularly hard to capture completely.

By now, Philp understood the implications of my lack of enthusiasm for trips to the front, my hiring of my own car, and of the way I seemed to have adopted the Iraqi Kurds' beloved "ten minutes"—a period of time that could last anything from an hour to a thorough reassessment of the whole situation the following day. My promise of moving south with Kurdish guerrillas seemed empty, due to the mysterious disappearance of Murad's friend, their leader. The last straw for her was one of my rare expeditions, to see an encampment of fleeing Kurds on the spring-greened slopes above Dohuk.

Instead of finding despair, we'd joined a big party. First we walked around tents made of old parachutes from the 1991 refugee aid drops, then sophisticated little houses of branches and plastic. One family of the voluntarily displaced had rigged up a small generator for their hut, and the children were being entertained by cartoon videos. Then we drove farther up the mountain into a small, perfectly formed stone village bursting with people. The inhabitants of this hamlet, Jaman, had fled an Iraqi army offensive in 1961, had fled when the Iraqis burned the village in 1963, had fled in 1988 when it was dynamited and bulldozed into the ground, and had fled from their new homes nearby in 1991 when Iraqi troops briefly surged back into Iraqi Kurdistan after the Gulf War. In 1994, Jaman had been rebuilt in the original stone, on its idyllic plateau overlooking the mountains. Many of its inhabitants now lived in nearby Dohuk, but, with the current excitements, everyone had fled up into the mountains again. In one house, sixty members of an extended family were sleeping in three rooms. In the little streets, girls clustered in doorways, resplendent in scarlet and green velvets, topped by long sequined gowns, giggling at the foreigners. Their mothers tended cauldrons of spinach and meat. People talked of the coincidence that today was Nowruz, the March 21 festival of the spring equinox that is marked almost as a national day by the Kurds. Ashes from the symbolically cleansing fires they had leaped through the night before still smoldered on the hill behind.

I loved it and lingered. But this wasn't the war that Philp needed to tell her editors about. Between the campsite and the village, she told me she would need more topical copy. The tone of her parting was friendly but familiar from editors through the years, subtly warning me to get on with the news at hand. I felt a pang as she took back her two jerry cans of fuel from my car. The war had just begun, fuel was unavailable in Dohuk, and I now had only thirty liters in my car's tank. I would have to trust to fate and the thousands of dollars still concealed about my person.

It was on one of these early days of the war that my telephone rang with a call from an unusual quarter. He introduced himself as being from the *Journal*'s opinion pages.

"Hello there," I replied, astonished. Not once during the whole past year had the *Journal*'s opinion pages contacted the newspaper's main Iraq correspondent.

"Hugh, I know we haven't seen eye to eye on things . . ."

"We've never even so much as talked about anything!"

"But I wanted to ask. This resistance, this fighting back, you know, in Umm Qasr. Why are they fighting?"

I said I thought resistance to a foreign invasion was a natural response, even if one opposed one's own regime. Our conversation was not a long one.

There was still nothing much to say on the northern front when the news came in that a suicide bomber had killed Paul Moran, a fine Australian photographer working as a television cameraman. He had been a friendly acquaintance in the 1990s, and his wife had given birth six weeks before to their first baby, a daughter. In my Dohuk hotel I sat with CNN correspondents Jane Arraf and James Martone, both Arabic speakers like myself. This was therapy of a sort.

"Couldn't we have done more to head off this war?" I said. "I wish I had simply flown to New York and demanded to see the opinion-page people."

"It would have made no difference," Arraf reassured me. "I had a meeting with the editor at CNN and tried to spell out the realities of the Israeli-Palestinian conflict. He listened for a minute or two, but when I challenged anything fundamental, I could see his attention drifting off."

At least we could laugh over a family—Murad's uncle's, in fact—in whose ancestral cave overlooking the front lines Arraf had found a toddler whose parents, very much in favor of the war, had named him after the U.S. vice president. His mother ran after him shouting "Dickcheney! Dickcheney!" That did make it to CNN.

A year later, I went to see the gurus of the *Wall Street Journal*. Over a congenial whisky with the then managing editor, Paul Steiger, I raised the issue of Israel and Palestine and relived Arraf's drifting attention experience exactly. The ins and outs of Arab or Muslim grievances weren't interesting to someone living in New York. I felt like I'd raised a subject not mentioned in polite society. Indeed, the prizewinning photographer Reza told me he reckoned that criticism of Israel triggered the same twitch of angst on Americans' faces that he remembered from prerevolutionary Iran, when it would afflict Iranians if the conversation drifted to an area of interest to the secret police.

I then made an appointment with the opinion-page editor, Paul Gigot. The opinion page's floor was very different from the open-plan *Journal* newsroom, being a cozy, ivory tower of a place where the floor had a carpet and people talked in hushed voices. Gigot was charming and gentlemanly. We could easily agree on things like the great corruption of the UN "oil-for-food" program that had kept Iraq on life support since 1996; we could not agree on what was to my mind the greater policy corruption that led the United States to impose sanctions on the country in the first place. It was the old problem. Whatever the flaws of their governments, I sympathized with the people of the Middle East with whom I had lived, eaten, chatted, and slept as a guest; their main contact with Middle Easterners were right-wing Israelis or exiles, who painted an often bitter, politicized, and unrepresentative picture of the region. I gamely tried to make the case that the United States had to change its blank-check policy to Israel. It should see that a traumatized and dictatorial Middle East would be unable to cope with any hurried attempts at democratization. Gigot gamely offered to consider printing commentaries of mine if I saw fit to write them. I noticed, however, that he seemed uncomfortable, perhaps even nervous, as if someone had warned him that I was mentally unstable.

"Please take me into your team, here in New York," I was to suggest hopelessly as my time ran out. "At least when you discuss the region you'll have someone who's lived in many of the countries there."

"Thanks for the offer, Hugh," Gigot replied, "but we're kind of homogeneous here."

Back in northern Iraq, Paul Moran's death was just the first of several media casualties. Bored of Dohuk, I drove east to Suleymani, where BBC correspondent Jim

Muir, an old pal, alarmed me with his account of a day he spent probing a section of the front lines just abandoned by the Iraqis. He'd done this because there was a rumor that from a nearby hillock, TV camera lenses might be able to give a presenter a backdrop of the fabled city of Kirkuk.

"The peshmergas on the front line told everybody not to go too far forward, but we insisted. Then they said, just go in two or three cars, not the ten you have. The journalists all wanted to stay independently powered. So we all went in a long convoy over the ridge and toward the next one. A few minutes later, the first Iraqi shell exploded, just fifty to a hundred yards away!" Muir explained.

Somehow they all made it back safely. I felt torn. I knew Muir lived and breathed for reporting the cutting edge of war fronts, and he was one of the most reliable newscasters of them all. To do that required risking one's life from time to time. I reminded myself that most people get killed in car accidents. *Newsweek*'s careful Tom Masland, for instance, would survive this war and dozens of other danger spots and be killed in New York two years later by the wing mirror of a passing SUV. I went back to discussing the unusual Indian food we were eating with Kaveh Golestan, a genial, bearded Iranian then working with Jim as a BBC cameraman. I was in awe: He'd won the Pulitzer Prize for his photographs of the Iranian Revolution.

The next morning, the breakfast room buzzed with news of a new media casualty. Gaby Rado, a leading foreign affairs reporter for Britain's Channel 4 news, had been found on the pavement outside his hotel. He had inexplicably fallen off the flat roof at eight thirty A.M., perhaps, I thought, while trying to get his satellite phone to start up. Eric Bigala of France's *Le Figaro* later told me that he'd found him after he'd landed on his head and had blood bubbling out of his mouth and ears. If that hadn't killed him, the crude scooping up of his body to take him to the hospital probably did so. A rumor that it was suicide, almost certainly false, made the Kurdish corps of translators and drivers shake their heads in amazement. For all the Middle East's troubles, taking one's own life is rare.

Three evenings after my dinner in Suleymani, the screen of my Thuraya woke up with a text message bearing the news that Jim Muir's BBC team had met with disaster. Kaveh Golestan had trodden on a land mine and died. Muir's British producer had lost the heel of his foot. Muir had survived unscathed but was in shock. It happened after they had once again probed toward the front lines, and Muir had allowed a peshmerga guard to overrule his better instincts about where it was safe to stop the car to record a stand-up in front of the camera. The next morning Muir sat at his table in the breakfast room, weeping inconsolably and blaming himself. But the team had done nothing much different from previous days. As for Kaveh, he had loved living on the cusp of change. At a roadside picnic on the day he died, he told Muir, "When I'm in situations like these, I feel I am me."

Most reporters remained hungry to see action. When a battle broke out between peshmergas and the Iraqis on the front line near Arbil, a contingent of thirty to fifty correspondents went to forward foxholes to watch. I too heard the distant roar of U.S. warplanes and a mysterious thump of bombs. I had acquired binoculars to keep me far from trouble and used them to watch a column of black smoke rising from a ridge to the south of the city. Chatting with my colleagues afterward, it turned out that the Iraqi army withdrew from a frontline village; the peshmergas rushed forward to take it over; the Iraqis mortared them; the U.S. Special Forces called in air support; the planes kept missing their targets; the Iraqis then started circling around the back of the peshmergas; the U.S. warplanes finally managed to drive them back; the Iraqis shelled the whole peshmerga front line in frustration; finally, one shell sailed over the journalists and killed a villager as he was heading home for the night.

I was reluctant to be negative. I feared I was alienating people with my comments about the pointlessness of it all. But I couldn't resist.

"If you want to be on the front line, why don't you join the army?"

"But I was in the army!" countered Fritz, a Dutch photographer. Indeed, he had been in a tank regiment and specialized in plane spotting. He kept the other journalists up to date with cries of "Tomcat! Hornet! Air effect bomb!"

Everyone dispatched long graphic accounts. Over breakfast the next morning, Damien McElroy of the London *Telegraph* relished the chaos of the situation. Early on the day of the battle, he recalled, a burst of machine-gun fire from somewhere prompted the easily scared peshmergas to jump up and start loosing off their Kalashnikovs in every direction. Their allies in the U.S. Special Forces group, manning a foxhole over the road, became exasperated. They sent out runners to calm the peshmergas and prevent unnecessary casualties before the arrival of the warplanes. One of the Americans' shouts spoke volumes about the paradox of the peshmergas, that even when engaging their weapons in battle, they could be a wartime liability to their better-trained allies: "Stop firing! Stop firing! This is a military situation!!"

Other colleagues chimed in with what they'd seen. Part of me envied their excitement and the satisfaction and recognition they were winning.

"After my last story, my editor called up and told me, 'I love you,'" said Aart Heering, a Dutch correspondent, a happy smile on his cartoon-chubby cheeks. "But I suppose it's only because he knows I want to leave."

We all laughed. Still, I couldn't forget the face of the Frenchman Eric Bigala when he came back from the "military situation" battle. He literally ran into me as he rushed into the hotel lobby at midnight, with dust on his clothes and bang-bang adrenaline in his eyes. He was talking nineteen to the dozen about being in a foxhole two hundred yards in front of everyone else, of it being amazing from beginning to end, and of shells landing five hundred yards away.

"It was the first time I see a full battle and understand it," he blabbered. "My editors told me it was the first full battle story about the war that they had had!"

"Eric! What are you doing? What difference does it make if you saw it? You're married! You need to live!" I began to shout at him, shaking his shoulders. He and his wife were neighbors and friends from Istanbul. I don't think he even felt me.

Two days later, in another peshmerga push forward on the front, a U.S. warplane bombed the wrong convoy and killed an Iraqi Kurd translator for the BBC. Within minutes, BBC correspondent John Simpson was on the air, bleeding from a deafened ear. It was a crazy perversion of news, but it was one the editors and audience wanted. One of the only scenes outsiders would remember of the northern front of the Iraq war is that of Simpson, visibly scratched and with half his trousers shot away, doing his stand-up in front of a burning Toyota Land Cruiser, filmed through a camera lens bright with a fat red spot of real blood.

In the first five years of the Iraq War, 136 reporters would die in Iraq, more than 20 of them foreigners. Journalism was becoming more dangerous in other ways. Correspondents were not just taking survival courses, they were arming themselves. A few days later I watched grainy CNN images of reporter Brent Sadler daring himself deeper into a no-man's-land on the road to Tikrit in the Sunni Arab heartland. As his vehicle bravely nosed around deserted army bases, slick anchormen in Kuwait and Qatar egged him on with "extraordinary's," "amazing's," and other I-love-you talk. In return, Sadler understandably indulged in plenty of ecstatic "in-my-twenty-years-of-war-zones-around-the-world-I-have-never's." And then . . . surprise, someone in Tikrit emerged to start shooting at the intruding vehicle. Gunfire! Now it was utterly perfect TV.

But it was also perfect real-time spying. The map coordinates he was publicly reading from his satellite telephone had clear military applications. And, watching with horrified fascination, traditionalists like me were shocked to see CNN's ex–British Special Air Service security guards then fire back, apparently horizontally, in other words, to kill. CNN later defended itself in general by saying that Saddam's minister had threatened to assassinate its correspondents, and indeed evidence did emerge that an assassination team was sent. What the world saw, however, was that journalists were not just well-intentioned observers. Some of us were now participants.

17. THE YEZIDI HERESY

An Alternative Approach to Military Liberation

We rejoiced at the rising Nile, then it drowned us.
—EGYPTIAN PROVERB

A good introduction is an invaluable asset. My fixer, Sagvan Murad, was a young and active member of an ancient religious community called the Yezidis. They numbered about half a million people in Iraq, the bulk of them living south of the front line and under Saddam Hussein's government control. Murad told me that community leaders on the side that was free, liberated, and developing since 1991, had organized a plan for a smooth takeover of the Saddam-controlled areas. It was his boss in a Yezidi cultural center, a part-time guerrilla chief, who had invited us to accompany them south when Saddam's control collapsed. This offer of open access to whatever awaited these Yezidis presented what I thought was my best bet for an original story about the northern front of the Iraq War. Here was something that might go right, as opposed to what I felt to be the great wrong of Operation Iraqi Freedom. Yezidis might seem obscure, but they were as Iraqi as Kurds, Sunnis, Shias, Assyrians, Marsh Arabs, Sabaeans, and all the other subgroups that made up the country's twenty-five million people. After all, if the war was on behalf of human rights and democratic freedoms, the Yezidis were the kind of issue it should have been all about.

The Yezidis had princes, castles, fortune-tellers, and an unusual religion. A subgroup of the Kurds—in their eyes, they were the original Kurds—their ancient faith was, to say the least, notably different from any of the surrounding patchwork of religious cultures. Indeed, Yezidi priests were so secretive that their exact doctrines were a mystery even to most of their adherents. Since they were Kurds, not orthodox Muslims—possibly not Muslim at all—they had been subjected to plenty of discrimination, or, as the Yezidis put it, "seventy-two genocides," which put them high on the scale of oppression, even in the Middle East's competitive arena. Muslims and others even put out the scandalous rumor that Yezidis worshipped the devil, which was entirely untrue.

As he halfheartedly agreed to my war strategy by satellite telephone, the long-suffering Bill Spindle added the warning that my story would have to be very strong to make it to the front page. I knew I faced a great challenge. Like the rest of the Kurds, the Yezidis were part of the solution, not the problem. They were marginal and inherently unnewsworthy. Still, whatever my story about the Yezidi northern front lacked in confrontational punch, I reckoned I would be able to make up in telling details about one alternative, peaceful method of taking over a chunk of Saddam Hussein's Iraq.

Early on, Murad had introduced me to the leader of the "free" Yezidis, Prince Kamuran, a nephew of the overall prince who lived in the Saddam-controlled areas. Prince Kamuran dressed the part, wearing a splendid baggy costume in fine stripes and a pale red-and-white head scarf. He had invited me to stay at his palace in the village of Baadra, from where, he said, I could see the lights of Mosul at night or, when the war started, the smoke of high explosives from any bombing by day.

While waiting for our part of the front to become active, I took the prince up on his invitation. My first sight of Baadra seemed to justify the whole journey. In a valley I saw the metal tanks and cinder-block huts of one of the principal smuggling routes for petrol between the government areas and free Iraqi Kurdistan—still open for business, despite the war, the Nowruz holiday, and the fact that night was falling. A steady stream of donkeys was arriving from the hill between us and the Saddam-ruled area with hard plastic jerry cans of fuel strapped to their saddles. We pulled up and soon the driver was sucking on hoses and juggling containers to fill our car. I then bought a whole blue barrel of benzene—fifty-five gallons—and sent it down to Dohuk by pickup truck. It cost me just $85, and now I had my own private gas station.

"Thanks very much," I told Rashid, the cheery Yezidi seller, as he pocketed my money in his baggy khaki pants. He soon brought me back to earth.

"What are you Westerners doing here?" he wanted to know. "Why are you messing around with our people, killing again? Why don't you stay at home?"

I said I agreed with his sentiments entirely, and drove on to the prince's palace. On a bluff with its back to Baadra, it overlooked the government-held valley that led to Mosul. It was neither particularly grand nor humble, a one-story, thick-walled structure built around a square courtyard with some trees and the obligatory little

English lawn. Prince Kamuran was waiting in the corner of his reception room, next to his Thuraya perched precariously on a windowsill. He greeted us with practiced and roguish ease. Iraqi arak appeared for me, as did some whisky for Murad and Turkish beer for the driver. On the wall was an erratic array of pictures: his princely father, a Yezidi holy peacock, and Richard Nabb, the legendary American colonel whose careful pushes forward did so much to make Iraqi Kurdistan a feasible zone in 1991. There was also his father's ancient-looking sword, its scabbard tied together with a ragged strip of cloth and its handle bound with dirty string. We sat on an assortment of stuffed armchairs and stools lined up around the edge of the room, which was dominated at one end by a grainy television screen.

Servants arrived with fruit, Pringles and, in the end, two plates of mushy, well-seasoned chicken-and-vegetable stew.

"We always used to kill a lamb for visitors, but then we realized you never ate it," the prince joked, zapping through the channels of his television.

It was true that such Middle Eastern lambs could turn out to be tough, smelly old sheep, but I kept my counsel.

"When I went to Italy, you know, it was the first time I saw men with flat tummies, without big bellies like we have. You Westerners taught us to eat light. No cholesterol molesterol!"

Our unpromising conversation faltered and crashed as live news streamed onto the screen of the first big U.S. bombing of Baghdad, 240 miles to the south. We all rushed up to the roof, expecting explosions when the U.S. planes and missiles reached the city of Mosul, whose lights glowed silently on the horizon to the southwest. A few antiaircraft shells lofted into the air. We began to get cold in the open. The prince had a better idea.

"This is no good. Let's go and watch it on TV."

The bombardment of Baghdad didn't satisfy my host, however.

"You have to bomb the whole of Iraq to bits before there will be any collapse in the armed forces. Saddam's terror machine cannot be derailed by anything else!" the prince declared.

Annihilation of the enemy might be the house rule in Mesopotamia, but I couldn't agree it would do much good. I was sure many innocent people were getting killed and injured in the hail of destruction raining down on the Iraqi capital. In faraway America, a retired U.S. general doing analysis for CNN declared that "it really is a symphony that has to be orchestrated by a conductor." When Secretary of Defense Rumsfeld appeared to talk about how carefully targets had been chosen, the prince laughed in scornful protest.

"You can't fight Saddam like that," he scoffed, and switched to al-Jazeera.

The prince didn't like al-Jazeera's anti-U.S. politics, but he did prefer the local perspective. At the height of the bombing, the Qatari satellite channel just let us watch the massive mushroom clouds billowing up into the Baghdad night sky, underlit by new and continuing explosions. I felt sick. It looked like Armageddon.

"Well, here's the war to disarm Iraq of its weapons of mass destruction," the al-Jazeera correspondent said. Then he added with finely tuned sarcasm, "Clearly, the weapons you are seeing being used tonight are not those of mass destruction."

I retired to an uneasy sleep under a thick, heavy, cotton-packed duvet. I woke up to take stock of my palace quarters: a thin carpet, a blanket over the unwashed window, a rickety plywood cupboard, hooks to hang clothes on, and, in a nod to the prince's British tastes, an iron bedstead with sagging springs under the thin mattress. The morning news on television was now nonstop war fever. Back on the roof, I scanned the entirely peaceful front lines below me. The hours ticked by. It was hard to know what to do in this town of about one thousand flat-roofed, mud-brick houses. Apart from watching TV, my only distraction was trying to work out the protocol when the prince's wife emerged from her private harem in a voluminous purple gown to enjoy a cigarette in the courtyard.

"Baadra is also famous for something else, you know," Murad suggested. "There's a fortune-teller here who's famous throughout Iraqi Kurdistan."

It was an idea, at least. On the way we toured the old castle of the great Yezidi princes, in ruins and abandoned behind its high walls. Our guide, Saeed, another offspring of the Yezidi princely dynasty, took particular pride in showing the unassuming room where, in 1913, rivals in a struggle for the princedom had smuggled themselves into the citadel dressed as women and had bludgeoned the old prince to death. Despite his tatty leather jacket, Saeed was also a peshmerga officer who in 1991 had engineered the capture of the government's vast yellow Foreign Legion–style fort overlooking the town. This had brought Baadra into "free" Iraqi Kurdistan. It had been, he boasted, a bloodless advance with ten men, after which the Iraqi soldiers were allowed to walk home with their luggage. Like the primary school next to the prince's palace, the fort was now overflowing with peshmergas. If the order came to chase a fleeing Iraqi enemy, I supposed they might move forward. Once again, Murad promised that we had been assured of a place in the vanguard.

A short walk away down the ridge, the fortune-teller, Shammu, sat cross-legged on a thin cushion on a worn-out floor covering in his gloomy, flat-roofed house. Thick dark glasses covered his eyes and a colored map of the signs of the zodiac hung above his turbaned head. Large-scale maps of the world torn from newspapers and some sparkly women's dress material covered parts of the mud wall. The roof was held up by round poplar beams, and I could see stones from the mud roof pushing through the interwoven branches above. A former road-building contractor, Shammu had found his current calling after being exiled for his Communist

Yezidi fortune-teller Shammu of Baadra *(right)* points up to his star map to read my horoscope before the Iraq War starts. My fixer, Sagvan Murad *(left)*, notes down Shammu's predictions, inaccurate in my case. He correctly forecast, however, that Saddam Hussein would be successfully ousted, and that this would not solve America's problems in the Middle East. 2003. *(Hugh Pope)*

leanings and sentenced to build highways in Iraq's western desert. Almost in passing, Murad whispered that his wife had been shot dead by the Baathists in 1981.

The ex-engineer certainly had a scientific approach. He checked me in as his 10,519th consultation. Many of his star charts had been neatly precalculated in a child's notebook. He knew how to please by giving me positive prospects for wealth, sexual performance, openness, courage, and prescience. I was beginning to doubt the value of the exercise when my ears pricked up.

"Next year, you will win a prize."

Such talk gladdens any hardworking journalist's heart. I slipped him a couple of bars of Turkish chocolate, and soon it became "the big prize." Months later, I duly applied to a modest competition for foreign correspondents, in which I told myself that I had a chance of recognition for my efforts to warn America of the dangers of the Iraq War. The prize givers didn't acknowledge the entry. Similarly not as predicted, my child born two months later was a girl, not a boy. I received no great sum of money. I had no "heavy" social life. And instead of being offered a great new job after September, the futility I felt covering the Iraq War made me entirely lose my appetite for writing about the Middle East for the *Wall Street Journal*. Some eighteen months later I left the paper to build a house on a remote Turkish mountainside.

Clearly I was wrong to hope for much from the little backwater of Baadra. Perhaps the flaws in Shammu's predictions derived from an alphanumerical calculation based on my name, which has no standard Arabic spelling, and that of my mother, which once again made everyone worry. In any event, he hedged each prediction with an invocation of the divine.

"Your color is red. Your day is Tuesday. Your metal is gold. Your number is nine. And God only knows."

"How can you be a Communist and say these things?" I asked politely.

"That bit about God is tough for me to say, but if I didn't, they'd run me out of the village as an unbeliever! It's the same with my mustache. I want to shave it off, but nobody can accept that. They say it's a symbol of manhood, of being a Yezidi."

"As a Marxist, I suppose you don't accept business from the prince, then."

"Yes, I am very opposed to him on political grounds. But he pays handsomely for his horoscope. The schoolmaster comes by too. And our local holy man."

He saved his best line, though, for when I returned later to check something he'd said.

"I knew you'd be back."

I also did what many of his supplicants had done, it seemed: I asked what the stars had in store for Saddam Hussein. For this he extracted a loose-leaf page closely filled with calculations.

"He will die on April fifteenth, or disappear, believed to have been killed. The West will overthrow the regime of Saddam Hussein," he said. "But, like Osama, his renown will haunt the West for years. Saddamism and bin Ladenism will be strong. From May twentieth, a new Middle East will start being built. There will be two and a half years of chaos in Iraq. Then a new character will arrive who will lead the country into evil. The United States will win a tactical victory but will have many troubles that will lead to the collapse of the American Empire."

Not much surprising in that—Saddam's name, perhaps, having the proper Arabic astrological equivalent. What perplexed me, though, was the reaction of colleagues and interviewees over the next few weeks. I had become used to talking little at dinners and get-togethers. I had no daring escapades to boast of from the front lines and my antiwar commentaries were unfashionable. But whenever I let slip that I had the details of Saddam's horoscope, everyone fell silent, gathered close, and hung on my every word. I was clearly working in the wrong sector of the prediction business.

Perhaps it was partly my status as a *Journal* correspondent that was dignifying the fortune-teller's words, even if I was joking. American newspaper readers were also, I felt, beginning to distinguish between the message they received and the messenger. Due to the careful way that mainstream newspapers framed their reporting about Iraq, paradoxically done partly in order to make readers read the stories, Americans seemed to be losing trust in our traditional, objective prose. Circulation figures were sagging, but the *Journal* was determined to stay high-minded. Publisher Peter Kann once told me and a group of trainees that, since many subscribers were retired people, we should just imagine we were writing for our parents.

Yet readers still seemed to believe in us reporters on the ground, provided that we were legitimized by representing traditional media institutions. My colleague Farnaz Fassihi experienced this after the war, when she wrote a gloomy assessment of the situation in Baghdad in an e-mail to friends. The substance contained little that she had not written in the pages of the *Journal*. But precisely because Americans perceived it as the real opinion of a credible correspondent, rather than a newspaper-processed authorized version, the letter whizzed around the Internet and within days became famous as a more real truth.

There was good reason for Americans to believe that *Journal* reporters knew what they were talking about. I never attempted a major story for the paper before I'd filled a notebook or two with interviews. In the past weeks, I'd made sure I did that for the Yezidis too, especially since it was a good way to keep myself occupied away from the front. On the seventh day of the war, for instance, I tracked down a young Hungarian doctoral student in Dohuk and spent the day discussing her thesis, "Gnostic Elements in Yezidi Mythology." From the beginning I knew that Eszter Spät and I shared the same mad stamina for digging up the obscure paradoxes that are the warp and weft of the Middle East. The building blocks of early Christian theology, all of which developed in this general area of northern Syria and western Iraq, were as toys in her hands. According to her, Yezidism had incorporated a good deal from these pre-Islamic times. When our discussion turned to whether or not the sum of Yezidism could even be said to be older than today's Judaism, I invited her to continue our conversation over lunch.

Then Jon Hemmings from Reuters pitched up at the next table and the present imposed itself. He had just come from a hilltop lookout on the front a few miles to the south. He had watched U.S. bombs rip up a village in the plains below, where several rows of Iraqi army barracks stood. He'd filmed this on his digital pocket camera. We played the recording of the rising columns of smoke again and again, somehow disbelieving the reality of the small puffs appearing on the back of his palm-sized machine. At five P.M., al-Jazeera reported an Iraqi claim that fifty local villagers had died in the attack. After the war, Spät visited the bomb craters, saw that they were around military targets, and heard of no civilians killed. In any event, real fighting was clearly imminent on the northern front.

Murad had been phoning our Yezidi guerrilla contacts regularly to make sure they didn't make their move to take over the Saddam-ruled areas without us. Nevertheless, in the confusion of those days, they did so. Not being with them as they crept or charged through the lines was another strike against the likelihood that my story would make it to the front page. But, as I was now practiced at telling myself, I was no photographer needing to be on the scene. I wouldn't give up. I could follow in their footsteps and piece the story together.

On the way, Murad and I paid a call on the mecca of the Yezidis, the shrine of Sheikh Adi at Lalish, whose fluted, conical spires are tucked into an idyllic mountain valley near Prince Kamuran's village of Baadra. I made the halt because Tahsin Beg, Prince of All the Yezidis of the World, had sent word that he would receive us at the shrine. We parked and passed through a low, narrow corridor in a stone wall, headed up some steps, took off our shoes, and found him holding court behind a colonnade. Yezidi men sporting long mustaches with a parting in the middle sat on the thin cushions around the walls. His armed guards milled about the courtyard with all kinds of weaponry strapped to their chests.

Tahsin Beg—Beg is a title, the equivalent of Sir in Ottoman times—had inherited his position as a child an extraordinary sixty years before. One result was that he received only a primary school education. Another was that he yearned for freedom, not just from Saddam but from his communal duties. Indeed, while talking to him, I got the impression he had been happiest during a seven-year stint of exile in London's Kensington High Street, mostly living alone and washing his own dishes. He now sat in state on a green armchair whose sides had split and from which sheets of cardboard were poking out. His dark gray robes were the worse for wear, and his 1970s black Rado watch, with a wide gold rim, was wearing out around the bracelet. His English had become rusty from disuse.

"I am not quite free yet. I can't be without bodyguards here. I hope when Iraq becomes a democracy that I won't need them anymore. All our life has been fighting, fighting, fighting. There have been no good times since the revolution against the king in 1958," he said wistfully. "When my people get freedom, maybe I'll get freedom too."

At this moment three of my correspondent colleagues arrived. Luckily they were the three I got on with best, and none worked for American media. But my heart sank at yet another strike against my plan. So much for my hopes of being able to craft an exclusive Yezidi narrative from the northern front.

"Ask me any questions!" commanded Tahsin Beg.

"Some conservative Muslims say you worship the devil," said the *Daily Tele-graph*'s Damien McElroy. "What do you say to that?"

I was shocked at the bluntness of this question. I knew from Murad and Spät that the Yezidis revere a benign angel they call Azazil, or the Peacock King, and that they get upset that outsiders, notably Muslims, keep identifying him as the devil. As a result, the word for Satan was actually banned by Yezidis. My other Yezidi princely friend, Tahsin Beg's nephew Kamuran in Baadra, would refer to him only as "so-and-so." Tahsin Beg, however, was used to dealing with the question.

"He's not devil, no, sorry, he's very different from devil. The devil is nothing to do with us," he said. "We just believe in one God."

Murad and I then set off to join the newly liberated people of Ain Sifni, a town a few miles to the south. Crossing into no-man's-land sent a frisson down my spine. From the escarpments above us we were watched by the blank holes of the sand-bagged foxholes in the old Iraqi front line. Then came the old Iraqi checkpoint. Comprehensively rocketed and shot up, there was satisfyingly little left but smashed-up old slogans. The only one still legible was IRAQ IS FOR US ALL, AND LOOKING AFTER IT IS THE RESPONSIBILITY OF US ALL. The front wall of the Baath Party building was already rebranded for the militia that was its new master, the "Party" of Brother Masoud, which ran this part of Iraqi Kurdistan. In the main slogan above the front door, someone had crossed out the "Saddam" part of YES, YES, TO SADDAM and had spray-painted "the Party" in its place. Living in Middle Eastern countries can sometimes be like attending kindergarten for your whole life.

The "Party" and its U.S. backers had taken no chances with their takeover. The streets were still littered with debris from an eight-hour bombardment. Perhaps two dozen Iraqi army defenders died in the surroundings, mostly shot as they fled. But thanks to the preparations by the Yezidis, like establishing secret contacts with major figures in town, there had been minimal fighting. Kurdish guerrillas de-terred looting with checkpoints and guarded untouched districts of plush, empty houses once occupied by people close to the regime.

They were determined not to repeat the mistakes of the liberation of the north in 1991, which had been accompanied, as was now happening in the U.S.-controlled south, by widespread stripping of public buildings, reprisals, and disorder. Within four days of the liberation, engineers in hard hats could be seen climbing pylons to fix high-voltage cables snapped by bomb blasts. Elsewhere I met officials who were sorting out the records of telephone line subscriptions. Party officials sifted through documents from government buildings, some of them flattened in the bombing. Sitting cross-legged on thin cushions, making reassuring visits and holding long meetings, they quietly took up the reins of power.

We called on Khatto Baba Sheikh, the spiritual leader of the Yezidis. Seated at one end of a long rectangular reception room, he looked impressive: a long, finely combed black-and-gray beard, white robes, and a tightly wound turban. He offered me the seat of honor beside him at the head of the assembly. But he couldn't speak Arabic very well, and I didn't get much out of him as everyone bantered about one of the most unusual weeks in the history of the town.

Murad had a question. In proper fashion, he wanted to check with the religious leader whether he had any objection to his smaller community of Yezidis from free Iraqi Kurdistan going forward and proselytizing the much greater number who had been stuck under the regime of Saddam Hussein. One of his hesitations was that the much-oppressed Yezidis are highly reticent when it comes to revealing religious matters.

"As long as everything is done correctly, go ahead!" Baba Sheikh replied, grinning broadly through his great mustache. "We kept things secret because there was no freedom, we were living in a bad atmosphere . . . Now we want everyone to see what's going on in the world. Let them all buy satellite televisions. I'm going to buy one right now!"

One of those responsible for the previous lack of freedom was sitting uncomfortably on one edge of the majlis gathering in Baba Sheikh's reception room. Hazem Haydar was one of the 100 to 150 former Baath Party officials in the town and had taken refuge with the religious leader. I asked to see him on his own. In a guest room we sat on parallel iron bedsteads and chatted. His eyes, constantly seeking reassurance, showed that he could hardly believe his luck would last. He had not been killed. When he surrendered his gun, he had been given a receipt. It was in his native Kurdish, which he had never seen written down. Now for the first time in his life he was meeting a foreigner and using the musty English he'd learned at school and kept on life support by buying copies of Saddam's *Iraq Daily*. What could be next?

"Did you expect to survive?" I asked.

"Our kinsmen from the north have changed, with the help of Britain and America. We are with the change." He lowered his voice to complain about how Baathism had also changed under pressure from the West, dropping its secularist beginnings so that Saddam Hussein could claim to be a grand "Islamic" leader. "You know, Saddam closed all the restaurants and bars serving alcoholic drinks. That's one thing I can't wait to see open again."

We drove on through Ain Sifni. Shops were gradually reopening, and a few cars full of visitors or relatives cruised the streets like tourists from the already liberated areas to the north. It was sobering to see how Arabized this Kurdish town looked. There was not a single sign in Kurdish, as had now become the norm in Iraqi Kurdistan. It was uplifting, too, to see how quickly shopkeepers get fresh fruit and vegetables back onto their stalls after a conflict.

We passed by a school where many Iraqi army soldiers had been hiding for the last week before they ran away. Although the American pilots could see them there and circled overhead, they did not bomb them, which would certainly have killed plenty of civilians. Indeed, in the liberated areas that I toured, U.S. warplanes seemed mostly to have hit what they aimed at, flattening barracks and party buildings. The Foreign Legion–style forts were all left looking as though some giant had taken a huge bite out of each one, scattering crumbs of stones everywhere.

The trouble for U.S. policy was that this technical proficiency was not part of any overall plan to sort out the huge psychological and other dysfunctions of Iraqi state and society. Then there was the collateral damage. One fifteen-foot-deep crater in Ain Sifni was dug by a bomb dropped by an American pilot aiming at a Toyota pickup truck with a gun mounted on the back. The Toyota was now a pile of burned and twisted metal, the engine block lying dozens of yards away. The Baathist who had sought asylum in the Yezidi sheikh's home told me that a local Arab had been using it to shoot at the American planes. When the planes closed in to bomb, this man wisely hid behind a wall to save himself. But the explosion torched at least three cars, wrecked four or five houses, and sprayed shrapnel in a radius of fifty yards or more. It had ripped the living room wall off the nearest house, killing a man and blinding his wife. People milled about, poking and pulling at things.

"First they bomb us, then they come and take photographs of us," Murad overheard someone saying as we left the site.

Eventually I caught up with the guerrilla leader who had promised and failed to take me along with the first wave of liberators of Ain Sifni, Khayri Namo Sheikhani, a forty-five-year-old Yezidi activist from Dohuk.

"How come the takeover was such a mess elsewhere, and so smooth here?" I asked. Down the road in Mosul, there was already virtual anarchy despite a far greater U.S. presence.

"When we arrived, we knew who was who, we gathered people together straightaway. We told them to stay in their jobs, that we'd pay officials' salaries, and that they shouldn't steal public property," he said. "We're fortunate that we've already been living liberated lives nearby for twelve years. We can show them how to live this new, democratic life. In southern Iraq, they have no such thing. All they know is Saddam, religion, and now the U.S. military."

I drove with Sheikhani to the settlement of Babir, north of Mosul, abandoned by Iraqi troops and therefore liberated. Babir was one of Saddam's notorious "collective towns," where any Kurds who might support the never-ending Kurdish rebellions were resettled from their ancestral villages in the mountains. In theory, all Saddam's army had to do to control them was to park a tank at the end of each unpaved street on the grid.

We drove toward Babir in convoy on a smooth dirt track through fields of wheat. I sat cramped in the front cab of a Toyota pickup truck with Sheikhani's Kalashnikov jammed between my knees. Behind us, a pickup mounted with speakers used for wedding parties pumped out a song by the famous Turkish Kurd musician Sivan Perwer. Children playing outside the town were clearly ready to embrace the new order. As soon as they saw our little convoy they raced toward us, waving little flags on bamboo poles and sticks made of anything they could find in the yellow color of "the Party"—furnishing fabrics, sheets, tablecloths, and clothing. Through the loudspeakers, one of Sheikhani's men stirred them up with shouts of, "This is the day of freedom! This is the fruit of all the years of fighting!"

When we reached the town, Sheikhani and his lieutenants got out to greet the notables. The houses were all walled-off, one-story miniature compounds built of gray concrete blocks. In no order whatsoever, we advanced on foot, followed by the cars, into the town's main open space, a kind of dustbowl in the center. A few hundred people clamored around us. All were Yezidis. Sheikhani and Fariq Farouq, an official from "the Party," climbed onto the back of the truck. They were greeted by chaotic, frenzied shouting.

"Who won? Who won? Barzani is the winner!" the crowd chanted, on cue. "The Party is our leader and Masoud is our president!"

Sheikhani and Farouq looked on indulgently.

Sheikhani then began the first political speech that any of them had ever heard live in Kurdish. He told them that the Baath regime was finished and that Arab rule was history. He talked of the many sacrifices of the struggle.

Farouq from "the Party" took the microphone and thanked God that they were liberated, reminded them they had been persecuted for thirty-five years, pointed out that the Baath had lied to them saying they were Arabs, not Kurds, and told them that Masoud Barzani called the Yezidis the original Kurds. He named a famous Yezidi martyr for the cause. Rounds of hearty clapping greeted these sentiments. Then Farouq moved onto less familiar territory.

"Freedom should not be for some, but for all—Kurds, Arabs, Turcomans, Christians, Muslims. We are all Iraqis. We want to work together for this land. We are asking for democracy, brotherhood. Even the Arab people say, 'Long Live Barzani!'" he said.

The mention of Arabs earned him a sudden drop in applause.

"We will forgive those Baathists who didn't do evil. We have to respect them. We want the rule of law, human rights, the rights of minorities, which we have established in Kurdistan," Farouq said.

I checked what the man beside me, Edris, thought. No, he wasn't interested in cohabiting with Arabs. He saw them solely as oppressors who had robbed him of his land and who had occupied his village. His only priority was to rebuild the village and, if he had a political outlook at all, to live in free Kurdistan. Right now, he never wanted to see an Arab again.

I turned to the people around Edris to ask if a pluralistic future was really so impossible. But I could get no sense out of people who had been under so much stress and who had no educational equipment to articulate their new freedom and excitement. We jostled, we shouted, we joked and laughed about silly things. I asked them about the Yezidi *gerîvan,* the special white undershirt with a rounded neck cut open by a specially chosen relative, and half the men started unbuttoning their shirts to show me the thin fabric of the garment. I parried invitations for tea, dinner, to stay the night.

"Do you have a picture of Bush? I want to kiss it!" one man begged me.

"Give my love to Mr. Bush and . . . what is his name? What is his name? Mr. Blair!" shouted another into my ear.

"Thank you, thank you, thank you," shouted one man as I fought through the crowd to get back into the car.

Back in Dohuk, I watched the big-screen TV in the hotel lobby as it showed the live action from Baghdad's Paradise Square, right in front of the Palestine Hotel, where I always used to stay. I remembered how exactly a year before I'd seen them put a new statue of Saddam up on the new roundabout reservation, wrapped in sheets as one of his birthday presents. Now a U.S. soldier pulled a noose around the statue's neck. A U.S. armored vehicle took up the strain. It bent down, fell forward, bounced groggily, and was then dragged to the ground.

We were tuned to Abu Dhabi TV, and the announcer, a good Arab, was in shock at this show of disrespect.

"The body has come down, but the feet are firmly stuck in place. Let's see whether that is an omen for the future!" he declaimed.

Soon we were watching crazy kids dragging the head around for rides and hitting it with their shoes. The camera panned back to take in the whole square. The TV announcer was right about it not being so easy to extirpate all signs of Saddam. You couldn't see it on TV, but I knew that each one of those white columns around where the statue stood had the initials *S.H.* molded into its capital.

Baghdad was now swarming with embedded correspondents from the *Wall Street Journal.* I could go home. I had one last page to fill in my notebook. Bill Spindle, valiantly struggling to get my alternative narrative of the conquest onto the front page, suggested that the first paragraph would be livelier if the commander had some kind of Yezidi fetish that he took along with him to liberate the

Yezidi zone. I had long stopped resenting such requests. They always turned up something new. But it did mean more delays, and I began to suspect the worst for my story.

I caught up with Sheikhani and maneuvered toward the question on my editor's mind.

"Did you carry any Yezidi objects with you when you were on your way to liberate your compatriots?"

The former dermatologist spoke good English, but it took some time to explain the Western concept of lucky charms.

"No, I don't have anything like that," Sheikhani said.

"So you don't wear the *gerîvan?*" I asked, the only Yezidi thing I could think of.

"Oh, no, I never wear that." He laughed at such an absurd, anachronistic idea.

"Didn't you wish you had one that night when you walked over the mountain? It was pretty cold, wasn't it?"

"Not at all, it's spring. It was normal. Remember, I was a peshmerga for years."

I had another go. "So when you were a peshmerga, you never carried anything special with you at all?"

"I always used to carry a bag of medicines. I was the peshmerga doctor," he said. Aha.

"Did you take any medicines with you on your night march, then?

"Yes, I took a small bag of medicines, for old times' sake."

Phew.

A few days later, the *Journal's* front page passed on my report on the peaceful change of power in our corner of Iraq. Spindle explained that editors felt triumphant events elsewhere overshadowed the Yezidi angle. I was beyond arguing and could do nothing about what I suspected was the last flaw in my Yezidi tale: Although the U.S. invasion made the Yezidis' success possible, and U.S. warplanes were a critical backup for the takeover of Ain Sifni, no Americans were obviously involved in the narrative for readers to identify with. By then I was out of the country, not greatly proud of my achievements but pleased that the foreign pages had published my last report at length and delighted to have survived to see my family and friends again.

A few years later, Murad rose to somewhere miraculously appropriate for his high standard of traditional politeness, becoming acting head of protocol for President Jalal Talabani of Iraq, photographed behind the scenes of world summits with President Bush's arm draped around his shoulders or being kissed by Iranian President Ahmadinejad. The Yezidis' fate was less happy. They suffered along with other minorities like the Christians, and lots of ordinary Iraqis, as the United States dumped well-laid American plans for running the country. Sunni Muslim extremists used the chaos to engineer a steady campaign of murders of Yezidis. One of the worst was in April 2007, when, apparently in revenge for the Yezidis' stoning of a Yezidi girl betrothed to a Muslim boy, Muslim militants stopped a bus, pulled off twenty-two with identity cards identifying them as Yezidi, and shot them dead. Ethnic cleansing forced many Yezidi families to flee their homes. An al-Qaeda–style quadruple truck bombing in August 2007 killed another two hundred Yezidis in villages and small towns in my eccentric friend Hussein Sinjari's tribal district of Sinjar, a formerly Saddam-ruled area east of Mosul. Tahsin Beg went on to survive at least three attempts on his life.

18. THE GENERAL AND THE PROFESSOR

America Collides with History in Iraq

The camel is of one mind, the camel driver of another.
—ARAB PROVERB

I used to call them "plucky corporal" stories, tales of an unusual American, often a soldier, striding boldly forth to do good in some obscure corner of the Iraqi stage. These reports began to proliferate in the aftermath of the U.S. invasion in 2003. U.S. editors had soon tired of purely Iraqi concerns like power cuts, civilian casualties, or runaway lawlessness. Such local phenomena were no longer headline news. All of us in the field, therefore, honed to a fine art something that our news desks always loved: uplifting profiles of idealistic young Americans—or even better, Iraqis—struggling to evangelize the best of U.S. values like teaching basketball, saving lives, building schools, or just "making a difference."

I hadn't had much luck finding plucky corporals in northern Iraq during the war. When I heard that the first Americans had parachuted in, I drove into the mountains to have a look. It was my third encounter with a major U.S. expeditionary force entering a Middle East war, but I still felt the curiosity of a visitor checking out the new family moving into the neighborhood. A protective cordon of Kurdish pickups on the road was the first sign of the American camp. As if guarding a national treasure, the scruffy Kurdish peshmerga fighters would not let me go close. Instead I accepted their offer of a glass of tea, keeping the late afternoon chill at bay beside a fire made from the glowing trunk of a shrub oak. I shared a bar of chocolate and watched the Americans establish their perimeter checkpoint, overburdened, fatigued, and moving slowly about their tasks. Eventually the Kurds trusted me enough to let me go over to chat with them. I peeled off my outer clothing to dispel any suspicion that I might have a gun or bomb, and gingerly approached the platoon. The soldiers were defended by an impromptu berm bulldozed by the road, but it came up only to their knees. They were covered in mud and looked groggy. From several yards away, I called out a greeting.

"I'm a correspondent for the *Wall Street Journal*! How are you?!"

"Oh, jeez, the *Journal*! What are you doing here?" one responded cheerily.

"What have you done to the lousy stock market!" shouted another.

I moved closer. One had ripped his trouser leg. Another's kneecap protector, like skateboarders use, was hanging around his calf. I later learned they'd had to walk for hours because they'd been dropped in the wrong place. However, his rifle was amazing compared to the Kurds' Second World War, Russian-designed Kalashnikovs. With a laser target finder, night vision accessories, and a telescopic sight, it looked like a science fiction ray gun.

"My stocks went up when we attacked, it was great," a third wandered up to complain. "Then they took those prisoners of war and those mutual funds of mine went down the toilet."

"The *Journal*, huh?" said a fourth, suspending for a while his effort to make a sleeping bag out of his parachute. "I like to travel. Will you hire me after I've done my twenty?"

I asked if I could visit their commander, and they radioed my request to headquarters. A few minutes later came the reply: sorry, sir, negative. I'd have to leave any plucky corporal story to my fellow correspondents embedded with the unit. Still, I wondered what sort of understanding of Iraq they would be able to build up in their sealed-off world. At the weekend I passed the same "sky soldiers'" convoying south to Arbil, their eyes wary and wondering at all the Iraqi Kurdish families picnicking by the roadside. The last soldier I met wanted to know more, at least. A small shortwave radio was the carry-on luggage he'd chosen to take on his jump. I wrote out the BBC frequencies for him. I hope he learned more from it than I had from him.

So it was that when I started a new tour of Iraq reporting duty six months after the March 2003 invasion, I assumed I would gain no access to real plucky corporals. To describe the changes wrought by the American occupation, my first idea was to write about how events had affected the lives of two Iraqi professors of English literature whom I'd met exactly a year before in Mosul.

Driving through Mosul's nondescript streets of concrete houses on the way to the university, I remembered the crazed atmosphere of that visit. I had joined a government-sponsored group of international dignitaries who toured the town to watch the populace vote for Saddam Hussein in a referendum that won him a perfect 100 percent victory. We all sat through the Baathist governor's welcoming speech, a pompous oration about the referendum being a "great vow of loyalty" made by the people, who were "defiant soldiers ready to defend the immortal principles of the Arab Baath Socialist Party." What struck me as more remarkable were the excellent translations into English and French by academics from Mosul University, almost as if they were floating on the flow of words. It reminded me of my early days as a radio monitor, when, even listening to Baghdad Radio, I too could forget myself in the extraordinary power of Arabic rhetoric to make facts redundant, conjure up meaning from nothing, and camouflage intolerance with rampant grandiloquence.

As our propaganda tour progressed, I naturally gravitated to two of the professors, Mohammed and Daoud. I was touched by their warmth and excitement at talking English with an Englishman again. I was the first native speaker they had met in the decade since all foreigners left after the 1990 Iraqi invasion of Kuwait. As buses took us from referendum voting station to schoolyard to refreshment tent, the two professors kept losing themselves in never-ending banter and questions about how something should be best said in English. They were delighted that I could now be included in their well-practiced game—should the translation be described as spontaneous, impromptu, or simultaneous? Were the paper and plastic flowers fake, artificial, or imitation? This thesaurus therapy, it was clear, kept the two men sane and insulated from the collapse of their country around them.

"You have to be optimistic," Daoud had said.

"Or, should we say, look at the sunny side of life?" rejoined Mohammed, even though he'd whispered earlier that a U.S. warplane had dropped a bomb two hundred yards from his house on the edge of Mosul that very morning. He bid me farewell by saying, "Nice to see you. To see you, nice." I hadn't heard the banal catchphrase since the 1970s, when it was made briefly popular by an English television personality in the days that Mohammed had studied in Britain.

A year and a war later, I found their university campus. It was a desolate place, half desert, half modern concrete buildings. Even in its prime it had been quite different from the soft carved sandstone and green-lawned quadrangles that had nurtured me. When the U.S.-led invasion unlocked the decades of frustrations bottling up Iraqi society, looters had ripped apart the institution of which Mohammed and Daoud were so proud. I tracked down the English faculty and started asking about the two professors along corridors and in lecture halls that had been stripped bare. When I appeared triumphantly before them, they were astonished, and not a little suspicious. We sat down in Mohammed's office. Some tables were bureaucratic steel and Formica, but some cupboards belonged in an Oriental boudoir. He saw my quizzical appraisal.

"When things settled down a bit after the invasion, the social leaders in Mosul called on everyone to return the stolen furniture to the mosques. Quite a lot was handed in," apologized Mohammed. "Trouble is, nobody could work out what was originally where, so it got redistributed like this."

Their mental furniture was in a similar disarray. After we'd met during the referendum a year before, Mohammed had given up hope and used his superior Iraqi education to take up a teaching position in a backward valley of Yemen, where the government could pay him far more than his own once oil-rich country. Until the last minute, like me, he couldn't believe the United States would be so crazy as to invade Iraq. When it happened, he rushed back to look after his family in Mosul. Now he had put on weight and was struggling to answer my stream of questions.

Both men became alarmed as I spoke of using their stories to paint a portrait of Mosul before and after Saddam. They clearly craved to return to safe subjects like Shakespeare or romantic poetry or homonyms. I gave up my hope of making their struggle into all-Iraqi plucky corporal story. The threat from Saddam might have gone, but at that point he hadn't been found. Mohammed and Daoud still couldn't even say his name out loud. Daoud uncomfortably scratched his curly white halo of hair.

"When 'the man' was there, if you weren't involved in politics, nobody came to take you away," he said, an apologist not for Saddam but for the memory of what dignity had been afforded by his former life. "Even then, we could still talk about 'the man,' you know. What we talk about now is no different."

"There are Baathists who did horrible things and Baathists who were respectable people. It will take time to sort out. People are not used to chaos," said Mohammed.

The two men complained about rising prices and the kidnapping of girl students. Breakdowns were getting worse in the private neighborhood generators that lurked at the heart of the great cobwebs of wires which, since sanctions had hobbled normal infrastructure, gave private houses some electric power. Mostly, however, Mohammed and Daoud were scared by the rise of semieducated Islamist radicals who, they said, would kill them just for speaking their real thoughts. The subsequent years of killings and ethnic cleansing would prove how right they were to be concerned.

I asked about the gray sheets of metal now clamped to balconies on the jail-like women's dormitories on campus, but neither could decide whether it was to protect the women from dangerous male marauders or to shield them from marauding male eyes. Society was in deep self-defense, and it was hard to draw the line between religious conservatism and security fears. Ironically, such metal plates had previously barred the classroom windows that overlooked Saddam Hussein's local palace, built on a large tract of neighboring land seized from the university. The same palace was now used a base for the American troops in Mosul.

"It's worse, and it's not getting better," Mohammed said.

"Perhaps it's exaggerated," said Daoud. "But here, you know, things can happen in a jiffy."

When I started asking about the Americans, they clammed up completely. Instead, they sent me to meet the vice-chancellor of the university. I found him in his office. We chatted briefly, but he was busy and I was too depressed about my dashed illusion of common cause with the English professors to pay much attention.

Having failed to rustle up the Iraqis I wanted to tell me about the new purgatory of their country, I turned to the American forces. My news-gathering experience immediately changed gear. After a couple of phone calls, an efficient major arranged an appointment with their commander the next afternoon. My driver and I set off for Saddam's old palace near the university, on top of a hill overlooking a bend in the Tigris River. For several minutes we warily circled the concrete outer perimeter walls, searching for a way in. At last I spotted a way up from the sandy highway to an entrance protected by concrete blocks. I warned the driver to go very slowly. About fifty yards from where I judged the gate to the fort must be, I told him to stop. I got out and walked with my arms well out from my sides, rather like a cowboy in a Western ready to draw his six-shooter. Except here in Iraq this stance signaled the reverse, the absence of any finger on a trigger or on the pull cord of a suicide bomber's explosives-packed jacket.

"A reporter, huh? Always wanted to be one of them," the pleasantly lazy-voiced African-American soldier said as he put me through the usual motions: dig out my identity papers, listen to the telephone call being made to the boss, stand in the blazing sun for several minutes, then open my bag, show my cameras, and allow a curious flip through my notebooks, as if they too were potentially explosive.

Eventually I was allowed to walk on past dusty rows of Humvees, satellite dishes, and other clutter of the modern war machine. Emblazoned in prominent places were the division's catch name of "Screaming Eagles" and a bare-clawed mascot to match. I was ushered inside and given a printout of the biography of the man I had come to interview, U.S. Army Major General David H. Petraeus, as well as a history of the unit, the 101st Airborne Division—Air Assault. I sat down to read them on a chair near the nerve center of the HQ, the palace's air-conditioned main hall.

This war room was like a small theater set up on scaffolding. Under a cornice fresco that included an image of the former occupant—a swarthy Saddam Hussein, gazing calmly to a glorious future—two dozen officers sat on four tiers of long desks, watching their computer screens in the midday torpor. Their labors progressed before a giant, empty projection screen, which was topped with an unwieldy motto: WE ARE IN A RACE TO WIN OVER THE PEOPLE. WHAT HAVE YOU AND YOUR UNIT DONE TODAY TO CONTRIBUTE TO VICTORY? I sneaked a closer look at how the officers were setting about this. All were firing off salvos on a customized version of Microsoft's Outlook messaging system. Occasionally a big red message filled a screen, emblazoned TOP SECRET.

The summons to meet Petraeus arrived. His office was upstairs, in a bedroom doubtless meant for Saddam himself. The ceiling was hung with curvaceous waves of tentlike material. Huge armchairs filled one corner of the room. In a regal display of modesty, however, the general worked from two black plastic field campaign tables in another corner.

"I only use the armchairs to receive the sheikhs. I hate having to talk while trying to look at someone who's sitting alongside me," he said, answering my wandering eyes. "We try to be an army of liberation, not occupation. It's very hard to pull off, because the only way you can win respect is individually."

So I got the plastic chair right opposite him. Petraeus flattered me with the high beam of his attention. He knew that victory is the sum of many battles, and that one key front for him and his unit was their reputation back home. As a reporter for one of America's biggest newspapers, I was worth his time. Petraeus was suffused with all the energy, concentration, and attention to detail that has helped put the United States on top of the world. He even had a doctorate in international relations from Princeton University.

I'd already been in the city for days and knew that the atmosphere was edgy. A rash of bombings had hit shops selling alcohol, where I had crunched on broken glass and smelled the burned furnishings and half-combusted spirit. I had talked for hours with the frightened Christian community. I'd sat with the manager of one of the shuttered local movie theaters, all closed after a bomb attack that had killed two people. As my two academic friends had hinted, Mosul was spiraling down into sectarian killings and deeper poverty. I doubted that there was much an armed unit from distant America could do about it.

But Petraeus wanted to make sure that nobody could accuse him and his division of not trying. He subjected me to a full-frontal barrage to shake me out of my conviction that Mosul was doomed. For three hours I jotted down notes of his account of the 101st Airborne's achievements. My homemade shorthand could hardly keep up with him. The 101st had "leapfrogged" up Iraq, surprised by the way Baathist militiamen were "dug in and fought like hell." After taking over Mosul from the hands of an underpowered U.S. marine unit, Petraeus, in contrast to the Washington orthodoxy of the time, showed himself to be a leader who believed in "nation-building kind of stuff." The slogans defining the war room may not have been his strong point—A RIFLE IN ONE HAND AND A WRENCH OR RECONSTRUCTION

ROAD MAP IN THE OTHER was one—but he did have 250 aircraft, packing more strike power than many small nations. He also had a treasure chest filled with $26 million in cash seized from the previous regime, and liked an adage that its previous owners well understood: "Money is ammunition." Figures tripped off his tongue to show rising production of electricity, cement, oil, and asphalt. He later counted off some of a breathtaking five thousand projects undertaken in seven months.

"The Iraqis can do almost anything!" he said.

"But they were doing all this before the United States invaded. The reason there's no infrastructure is that America smashed the lot in the Gulf War in 1991 and then slapped on sanctions for twelve years," I protested.

Indeed, on an expedition to Baghdad during that same trip I managed to get a story published about the way the U.S. invasion had distorted a key part of any Middle Eastern economy. The price of cement was now eight times its prewar cost and the invasion had knocked out five-sixths of Iraqi production. Three-quarters of what was produced went into pouring concrete for airstrips, sprawling new army camps, and barricades rising up to sixteen feet high around every American outpost. Hardly any went to schools or reconstruction. Spindle and I had front-page hopes for the report, but it was more of a gloomy statement than a tale with rounded and uplifting characters, and it ended up on the inside. Nevertheless, the American mood had become questioning and I didn't have to pull any punches. Some sarcasm even made it to the second paragraph, from a man I found in a formerly middle-class suburb of concrete villas, hosing water into a circle of earth and straw to make an adobe mix of mud for a new roof. "America brought us freedom, sure," I quoted him as saying. "The freedom to go back to the Stone Age."

Petraeus would have none of such talk and compared this mission to his previous ones.

"The Iraqis have got infrastructure they could only dream of in Bosnia and Haiti!" he said.

As we continued to talk, however, I found Petraeus's nation-building image hard to square with his adoption of the army's corporate culture of toughness: "We are going out, seeking and killing bad guys every day," "Operations in the last two–three weeks seriously disrupted the bad-guy network," and, as if it underlined just how bad they were, "The only people who ever shot back were Uday and Qusay," the two sons of Saddam Hussein. They had been rubbed out in a 101st ambush on their safe house three months before. If he died fighting, it was a fleeting moment of honor in Uday's despicable career of rape, murder, and theft. I wasn't sure how to take Petraeus's description of the death of Qusay's fourteen-year-old son, however. The boy had been riddled with bullets as he tried to crawl out from under a bed, where he was hiding. The reason: He'd still been clutching a gun. Apparently he was pretty obese too.

"When we did the postmortem," Petraeus said with a strange kind of wonder in his voice, "we couldn't find an ounce of muscle on him."[1]

General Petraeus was no neoconservative ideologue, however, aiming to drive anti-American regimes out of the Middle East by brute force. The new civilian American administrator in Baghdad, L. Paul Bremer, had disbanded the Iraqi army and dismissed all manager-level Baath Party members. These decisions had disastrous consequences for the everyday running of the country, and Petraeus worked quietly to mitigate the trauma. He met with Baathist officials—Mosul was a Baath Party stronghold and legendarily home to one thousand retired generals—and turned the other cheek when they kept "wanting audiences to explain how I should do my job." He pragmatically ignored the Bush administration's characterization of neighboring Syria as part of an "axis of evil." He had opened up the Syrian border to the "freest trade there has ever been" and was busily swapping Iraqi oil for Syrian electricity. I listened later to a presentation he made in the war room for some visitors from Washington, all resplendent in the Iraq War fashion of navy blue blazers and desert boots, and he drove home the need for normalization with Syria by putting up on screen a big picture of the late Syrian president Hafez al-Assad.

The interview ended with the same abruptness as it had begun. Petraeus turned to the paperwork on his desk, leaving me to find my way downstairs. Deprived of the attention of this powerful man after three intense hours, I suddenly felt empty. I returned to the media room and asked if I could sit down for a few minutes. Lacking any better plan of action, and since the soldiers assumed that I was waiting for something from somewhere else in the hierarchy, I just stayed to see what happened.

Nobody can keep up appearances for long. Photographers know that even the most personal inhibitions fall away after a couple of days, even when people are living with lenses pointed at them in their homes. I became part of the media room furniture. The adulation some admitted to loving when they walked through U.S. airports in uniform was all very well, but here and now everyone was beyond bored. A sergeant who had previously been attentive sat with her feet up on a table and pettily made a more junior soldier fetch papers she could easily have got up and got herself. Two other soldiers surfed the Internet, looking for jobs back home. Everyone e-mailed. Occasionally one would strike up a desultory conversation with me. The job seekers were unhappy and worried about the effect of their absence on their families. One of the many women soldiers said she disliked being on permanent duty so much that she secretly slept in her civilian clothes in order to feel briefly normal. Another soldier remarked that it wasn't worth much being the conquerors of this palace and the rest of Iraq, since they weren't allowed to do anything for fear of

---

1. Interviews with the author, October 2003.

offending local Muslim sensitivities, not even enjoy a beer off duty on their own base. Her favorite escape was onto the roof of the palace, where she was reading through the base's collection of paperback novels for the second time.

As I sat in my own stone-cold-sober hotel room that evening, I mulled over something in my interview with Petraeus. He'd mentioned in passing that he was rehabilitating Mosul University to "win over the people." As he talked about it, I'd noticed a rare tone of perplexed frustration. Wondering if there was more to this, I went over to make a new appointment with the vice-chancellor, Jazeel Abd al-Jabbar al-Jomard. He agreed to see me right away. His share of the cupboards and desks returned by looters swirled with baroque woodwork that would have been at home in the Austrian Alps.

Jomard embarked on a lively but familiar account of the illegitimacy of the American invasion and the disaster that had befallen Mosul. We were just getting going on the iniquity of U.S. policy in the Middle East as a whole when an American major from the 101st popped his head around the door, in full combat gear, and called in a friendly greeting.

Mosul University vice-chancellor Jazeel Abd al-Jabbar al-Jomard *(right)* presses the 101st Airborne's Major Mike Shenk *(left)* to remove a lookout post from one of his faculty buildings. Shenk agreed. This empathetic approach to governance in Iraq reversed Jomard's former rejection of Americans, even if his suspicions remained strong about a pro-Israel bias. 2003. *(Hugh Pope)*

"It's all done!" he said.

"Thanks!" Jomard replied with a warm smile.

I later learned that the major had dropped off yet more cash to buy the university such items as office furniture, telephone exchanges, computers, air conditioners, refrigerators, and ceiling fans. Jomard rose to see the major out of the building. I followed them. The American officer registered the surprise on my face.

"He only lets us on campus because we're nice," he joked beside his jeep, neatly parked next to Jomard's in an otherwise empty parking lot.

Jomard quietly took the opportunity to persuade the major to remove two American lookouts posted on the engineering faculty building because the rector was "incandescent" with rage. The major promised to do what he could, even though American patrols had been attacked on the road below it.

"You see?" Jomard said after the major had driven off. "Whatever I think about the historical situation, I can't help liking them. I learned to see these people as my friends once I realized that, as individuals, they had nothing to do with U.S. policy, nothing to do with Zionists."

In other words, the American neoconservative thesis that anti-American attitudes were simply because "they hate us" did not apply here. What people like Jomard disliked was one-sided U.S. support for Israel. The psychological struggle between the short, portly Professor Jomard and the unit led by the lean, hungry General Petraeus went to the heart of one of the paradoxes of the U.S. occupation of Iraq: a willingness of some Iraqis to like the Americans themselves while nursing an unyielding suspicion of the United States. I called Spindle that evening to announce that I was sure I'd found our story. In Jomard, perhaps due to his years spent writing his doctorate in the Scottish University of St. Andrews, I'd also been lucky to meet someone who satisfied the exacting demands of personal openness vital to make the front-page editors happy.

Jomard's trust, I soon realized, could not have been easy for Petraeus to win. He had impeccable nationalist credentials. His prominent family had actively opposed British imperial rule, and, after the bloody coup that ousted the British-backed monarchy in 1958, Jomard's father was for six months the foreign minister in the first revolutionary nationalist government. His academic specialty was the history of the Christian Crusaders, their attempt to take over the Middle East, and their defeat in the twelfth century by Saladin, a Kurdish leader probably born not far from Mosul. For Iraqis and most Arabs, the century of crusader rule in the Holy Land nearly a millennium ago remains a misleading metaphor for today's Israel, feeding the fantasy that however disorganized the Arabs might be, Israel is condemned to be driven into the sea.

When the first U.S. marines arrived in Mosul, Jomard told me, he had been one of eighty civic leaders who had gone to the airport to meet them. Their mission was to ask the Americans to protect the city. So many looters had crowded onto the university campus that there were traffic jams of thieves. They even stole one of the university gates. But the marines weren't interested in helping. Jomard remembered that the officer sent out to talk to them was young, arrogant, and concerned only with the safety of his own troops. Then the reporters embedded with the unit came to ask them questions. Jomard, a Sunni Muslim, was shocked that they seemed interested in talking only to the Christian priests in their group.

"It was, like, the Arabs have to wait, the Muslims are the last ones to have a say," he said.

Jomard joined a group of Mosul judges who tried again the next day to appeal for American troops to get a grip on the city. They failed.

"It wasn't useful. The Americans seemed irritated by us," Jomard said, pushing his unfashionably big aviator glasses up against his eyebrows and rearranging a flop of his thin, light brown hair. "I felt like I was being confronted with a relic of the British occupation a century ago. I went home and never went back to them."

The scenes of chaos in Mosul merged in his mind with how he imagined the wars in Palestine as Israeli armies took control. Aside from unquestioning U.S. support for Israel, he ticked off reasons why no Iraqi should expect any good from Washington. There was U.S. strategic support of Saddam during the 1980s, when the Iraqi leader was in his murderous prime, just because Iraq was at war with Islamic Revolutionary Iran. He spoke of his deep resentment at the way the United States left Saddam Hussein in power after wrecking Iraq's entire infrastructure in the first Persian Gulf War in 1991. In the decade that followed, he pointed out, it was once again the United States that led the effort to impose crippling sanctions on the country.

"I swear that even Iraqi ants were affected by those sanctions," Jomard said. "Before, they used to stay in the garden of my house. Now they've even reached my bedroom, looking for things to eat."

Then the 101st Airborne arrived to relieve the overaggressive marines, who, as one of the 101st's colonels put it, sent back a fusillade of two thousand bullets if just one bullet came in over the base perimeter. General Petraeus rammed through a one-month plan to bring the city back to its senses, hold local elections, and form a Governing Council. He sent officers around to neighborhoods where houses were raided to explain why such actions were taken. He visited a respected Mosul-born Baathist defense minister when the man was in an American jail in Baghdad, and brought back a letter for his family. And while the Islamists were bombing Christian liquor stores, the Americans were picking up the drunks from the streets at night (mostly Muslims, by locals' accounts).

I attended a meeting of the Governing Council, where Petraeus, hunched like a predator in a side chair with a sheaf of notes, pounced on any hint of conflict to try to work forward to a compromise. In a discussion about raising money for schools, he even tried to inject a note of humor—"We're going to make cookies and sell them outside"—but nobody got the joke, let alone the idea of working out some self-sufficiency. As the new police chief told me, it was hard to build any sense of common work for the public good after the thirty-five-year monopoly of Saddam Hussein and the Baath Party. So, like any good leader of an impoverished Arab Muslim community, Petraeus fell back on the suggestion that the town organize another fund-raising trip to the oil-rich Gulf sheikhdoms.

When the new council first met, it elected Jomard as university vice-chancellor, without the professor's knowledge. Jomard initially refused the job, since he had publicly announced that he was boycotting the U.S.-backed group. His colleagues pressed him to accept the post. He remained reluctant.

"I told them it's very difficult to work with a foreign occupier," Jomard said. "But they played with my emotions, my sense of duty. For us, the looting and chaos in Mosul were a tragedy, spiritually and physically." Although he subsequently accepted the appointment, he kept his job teaching history, so he could leave the administrative post at any time. He also tried to maintain a psychological distance. "I told myself I would not be dealing with the invader. I would never be a collaborator."

But he began to discover a new face of the occupation. The American officer in charge of the university area passed by on a courtesy call. Jomard had personally tied up the remaining campus gates when there was nothing left for the looters to carry away, and he remarked that the university couldn't fix those that were hanging off their hinges. Before long, U.S. army engineers arrived to repair them. On the other hand, Jomard, who had grown up with rhetoric about Arab solidarity, had hoped for aid from the Arab world. But little materialized. Two Persian Gulf states sent gifts, but one included a TV crew that asked him to sing the praises of its generous prince.

"When they asked me to sit in front of a banner to do the interview, I had to refuse," Jomard said.

Wealthy local families gave about $50,000 to the university, hoping to get it back on track before exam time so that students wouldn't have wasted a year's study. The 101st Airborne channeled in nearly $1.4 million. Jomard was impressed by the military's efficient generosity, even though he knew that the money was originally Iraqi. It helped that the American officers accepted the professor's sometimes prickly behavior and made no demands for public expressions of gratitude. Working together behind the scenes, Petraeus and Jomard managed to sidestep the American-Iraqi administration's ban on all Baathists in public positions. Some thirty Baathist teachers had already left. But Jomard was able to keep another one hundred at their posts.

Even under Petraeus, the occupation was not all presentational polish. When I left a police training school in Mosul where I'd watched a graduation, my driver told me how the American soldiers at the gates had been amusing themselves: forcing the boys of the neighborhood to fight each other for prize money of a dollar per win. The Iraqi boys, sensibly enough, tried to fake the fighting. But the American soldiers, my driver told me, demanded their money's worth with viciously worded interventions as the scuffles progressed on the road in front of them: "Kick him in the ass! Kick him in the balls!"

On the other hand, I saw how Jomard found it hard to maintain an inflexible, suspicious hatred. I also began to understand the hero worship that affected some of my embedded colleagues when they worked alongside the best of the American officers. Petraeus's intelligent engagement made him a natural in achieving this effect. I also admired the officer whom Petraeus had put in charge of the university. Colonel Will Harrison, about my age at the time, forty-four, was not just enthusiastic and glamorous. He was able concurrently to run all higher education in Mosul, look after the needs of his brigade's two thousand men, repulse frequent attacks on his base at Mosul airport, command and organize the daily work of an air assault brigade with 134 helicopters and, on top of all that, pilot of one of the big twin-rotor Chinooks. I could count on the fingers of my two hands the number of weeks of training I'd had for anything since my undergraduate days. Yet Harrison and the colonels of the 101st Airborne had been in intensive training for decades and held advanced academic degrees.

Petraeus and the 101st could not, of course, count on winning over all Iraqis. Colonel Harrison may not have known that even outside his office, the Arabic writing part covered by a collage of "God Bless America" sent by Mrs. Schiller's Patriotic Kindergartens was a Koranic slogan painted by his predecessor at the old Iraqi air base: CONFRONT THEM [THE INFIDELS] WITH EVERY LAST OUNCE OF YOUR POWER. Such sentiments could quickly resurface. In the center of town, the biggest shopping mall was decorated with a new banner reading THE PROPHET AND HIS FOLLOWERS ARE TOUGH ON THE INFIDELS. Jomard told me that even he fell prey to a baseless rumor that swept through Mosul that the Americans were allowing in Israelis to buy up land in the city.

"I couldn't help myself. What causes fear is the size of America, the idea that we might just be a little part of a much bigger policy," he said. "I have no desire to find myself at my age like the Palestinians, suitcases in my hand and my family on the road."

As a historian, he had started keeping a day-to-day chronology of Mosul's experiences but had given up.

"It's all going too fast. There are too many tensions, fears, anxieties about the future. What will the coming days bring? Will things go backward? Can the Governing Council work? Will the U.S. stay or go? What is the Israeli role? Can I leave home safely today?" he said. "The problem is not the Americans but the new rules. Are we independent or not independent? What is my relationship with the Ministry of Education? Frankly, I don't even know the name of the current minister."

Indeed, Iraqis were probably right to fear that the new U.S.-backed Iraqi government might just pick up where the old one had left off. Below the surface of the new American order lurked Iraq's deep reflex of centralizing authoritarianism. The spokesman of the Governing Council formed by Petraeus took me aside to advocate harsh measures to establish their authority over Mosul's remaining Baathists and the criminals let out of jail as one of Saddam's last presidential gifts to Iraq.

"They've cut off the head of the snake, but the tail is still with us. We need a shirt of democracy cut to our size. Let there be a massacre, let us leave no stone upon a stone! We should get the old security people back in. They really know how to break fingers and get results. We need them especially for those Islamists. They are the dangerous ones. They have heads of stone. The Americans just don't understand."

"What?" I asked. "You just told me that you were tortured by Saddam's people, that you were condemned to death and only narrowly escaped!"

"Exactly!" the spokesman said with total conviction. "There should have been three stages to all this: an invasion, a mess, then democracy. The Americans didn't let us have a real mess. I want this chaos. Then I can find and torture and kill those people who tortured me."

In such a vicious atmosphere, and given the xenophobia among his fellow townsmen, Jomard was wise to hide the growing trust he felt for the Americans. He defended himself from a steady stream of threats by keeping a profile so modest that he drove an extravagantly dusty 1980 Datsun whose dashboard was stuck together with tape. I knew all about these pressures. Haqqi, my Iraqi fixer, kept his work with an American newspaper a secret and explained to those who found out that he was actually on an Iraqi resistance mission to brainwash and spy on the invaders. Haqqi soon fled Iraq for the United States, one more drop in the flood of talent leaving the country. I had little doubt that when the Americans eventually pulled out, most of the best and the brightest Iraqis who worked with them would have to leave too, just as thousands of the best-qualified Kurds fled Iraqi Kurdistan when America partially pulled back in 1996.

"One or two professors were spreading rumors that 'Jazeel, whom we thought was working for the interests of the people, is now shaking hands with the enemy,'" Jomard said. "But when I meet an American, I feel that I am shaking hands as a fellow human. I too believe the American occupation should end, but if they leave now, everyone will be killed on the streets, there'll be civil war. The biggest problem is not that the U.S. came, but that it's not willing to say that it is staying. That way, it can't get people, a constituency, properly behind it. People can't believe in the change. They don't know whether the U.S. is coming or going."

As I built up my article, I realized the presence of Americans in Iraq now made much easier my job of presenting the conflict between the Iraqi and U.S. world-views. The general could win the trust of his Iraqi counterparts as an admirable American (satisfying the "plucky corporal" requirement), but Iraqis could not actively support him because of antiforeigner sentiment, Koranic prejudices, and the history of U.S. policies. Along the way, I could list almost all the reasons why I thought the U.S. occupation of Iraq could not last long. The *Journal*'s editors improved and focused my story. For once, they agreed to leave in two of the three original references to the way U.S. room for maneuver was limited by Iraqi perceptions of U.S. support for Israel against the Palestinians. There was even a nuanced kicker at the end, in which Jomard voiced a hope, which I fervently shared, that the depth of America's sudden engagement with Iraq might one day bring a new U.S. assessment of the Arab world.

"They're asking us to say thanks to them. I hope that in future talk of gratitude won't be a one-way street," Jomard had told me one day as we motored around the campus. He did this reconnaissance twice daily to check that all was well, as if he couldn't believe the current stability would last. "We should remember that the crusaders took back not just spices but a different way of looking at life."

I basked in self-satisfaction when the front-page story appeared. My e-mail in-box filled with a dozen positive messages from readers, an unusually prolific reaction. One reader told me "it was great to get some real insight into how the other side feels," another that he felt Jomard was a "good man." But as I read through the rest of them, I felt bewildered. Readers thought I meant that the United States was on the right track.

"Your article provides hopeful news about the morass in Iraq," wrote a lawyer from New Hampshire. "It gives me hope!" added an executive in customer care. "Encouraging . . . I was beginning to waver on [my] stand that America should just pack its bags and leave Iraq . . . I will definitely forward this article to my friends," said another reader. "I appreciate an article that shows how we can truly be world leaders," said a fourth. "America's efforts in rebuilding Iraq are working, one institution, one university, one power plant, one oil field at a time. Witness your article," said a CEO from New York. "We need more positive news like this since we continue to spill our Treasure in Iraq," wrote a man from South Carolina. "However, I also must ask why the Arabs must live in such a state of conflict with the Jews."

I even received a message from General Petraeus himself, gracefully offering his thanks. "Believe it or not," the general typed, "your article made some of what we've gone through worthwhile all over again."

Tempting though it was to see a hint of skepticism here about the American project in Iraq—after all, he'd famously asked one of my embedded colleagues earlier in the war, "Tell me where this ends"—nothing was to dent Petraeus's unflinching and ambitious professionalism. After he got the twenty-one thousand men and women of the 101st Airborne back to their base in Fort Campbell, Kentucky, a few months later—less the sixty dead, and with five hundred wounded—Petraeus returned to help train the Iraqi army. He became a coarchitect of the "surge," which, reflecting the wisdom of Jomard's observation, settled the question of who would be boss in Iraq as long as U.S. troops were to be there. He then rose to command all U.S. troops in the Middle East, Afghanistan, and Central Asia.

In Mosul, the United States replaced the 101st Airborne with an underpowered unit less than one-half its size and with few financial resources. A year after my visit, insurgents briefly overran the city and assassinated the governor. The police force collapsed, army bases were emptied of weapons, and Sunni Muslims pulled out of the Governing Council. The ancient community of Christians came under massive pressure and a slow-motion ethnic cleansing deepened divisions between Kurdish and Arab quarters of the town. Five years later, electricity was still on only a couple of hours a day.

The 101st Airborne was certainly not responsible for this breakdown. The city could not avoid the fate of the rest of Iraq, and the blame for the mess and tens of thousands of dead lies squarely on those who ordered the invasion. In hindsight, too, my confusion over the readers' reactions has cleared. The *Journal*'s high reporting standards had served a purpose, despite my own intentions. Obsessed with the historical mistake of the invasion, I thought that my "plucky corporal" story would chiefly illustrate inevitable defeat. The readers who wrote in, however, had seen a side of reality whose force I had been reluctant to believe in. The 101st Airborne's efforts did illustrate America's extraordinary potential to redeem itself in the Middle East, if a new leader chooses to do so.

EPILOGUE

I believe and trust in those who love life,
not in those who claim that they understand it.
—ALI SALEM

Several Middle Eastern peoples independently retell a fable of how Satan shows a visitor to hell around a hall of boiling cauldrons, one for people of each nationality. Devils guard each bubbling vat, poking the tortured souls back in with a fiery pitchfork if they try to escape. The visitor finally comes to the cauldron designated for the country where the teller of the joke happens to come from—perhaps Turkey, perhaps Egypt, or perhaps Iran. Here the cauldron's victims are being boiled alive, as elsewhere, but there is no guard.

"Where's the devil guarding this one?" the visitor asks.

"Oh, we don't need one here," Satan replies. "It's simple. In the other cauldrons they help each other out. In this one, they pull each other back in."

In this book I have laid out my experiences of a life on the road in the Middle East, from its vivacious humor to its many cauldrons. Lying at the intersection of Asia, Europe, and Africa, home to the holy lands of the three great monotheistic faiths, the region has been turbulent with proxy battles and sweeping tides of conquest since the dawn of civilization. Today's Middle Easterners bear the burden of violence, failures, sanctions, and, for most local parties, defeats in fifteen major wars in this past century alone. Dozens of revolutions have interrupted their progress. They feel a wariness born of countless ill-conceived and deceitful foreign interventions, and the limitations imposed by poverty, overpopulation, religious conservatism, and dictatorship. The ability to rely on income from oil, natural gas, or foreign aid has cast a national torpor over some states. Many countries in the region have been hollowed out in the past half century by the disappearance of their original educated and entrepreneurial classes. The best minds have headed to safe harbor in the United States and Europe, where they have often flourished. Many have no desire to go back and are forever lost to the region.

The enduring social deficit has robbed the Middle East of its indigenous high culture, and attempts to establish more pluralist governments or democracy will take a long time. The region also lacks any natural supranational center, especially since the demise of Istanbul as capital of the Ottoman Empire in 1923. Attempts at unity—the Arab League since 1945, the 1958–61 United Arab Republic of Egypt and Syria, the Organization of the Islamic Conference since 1971, the Gulf Cooperation Council since 1981—have failed to rival the attraction and power of the European Union or the United States. This has in practice kept the Middle East a dysfunctional backyard of the world, not the self-standing region that many people both inside and outside the region imagine it to be.

The "Islamic world" does not offer a much more meaningful framework for the fifty-seven very diverse countries with Muslim majorities. Even the idea of the "Arab world," the twenty-two countries speaking mainly Arabic, promises more than it delivers. It too is an umbrella for great varieties of identities, religions, Muslim cultures, and ethnicities, making the idea of being an "Arab" hard to pin down. After all, Jews can also be Arabs. And Syrians, for instance, often volunteered to me that they hated Saudis as much as the Israelis, for quite different reasons.

This book has been my attempt to make all the connections I could among these states during my more than three decades in the Middle East's orbit. Early on, I often felt alienated by the unplanned concrete cities, uneducated masses, and injustice meted out by the region's own governments. These are of course not unique to the Middle East. Once well rooted in the languages and history, I was able to tune in to intense undercurrents of human contact, unpredictability, excitement, generosity, and spontaneity. It is a warmer world, and one that I immediately miss when visiting more Western countries. The Middle East became my educator and, in part, my home.

In early 2001, supposedly wise in the ways of the Middle East, I pooh-poohed my foreign editor, John Bussey, who pressed me to go to Pakistan to discover more about fundamentalists threatening to attack America. My "truth" was that they were a marginal and well-known element. I also thought their Islamist monomania distorted what most Muslims felt about Islam, and that any stories profiling them would feed the vicious circle in which Westerners thought that such fundamentalists represented the whole of Islam. As for the threat to America, I saw little new or surprising in it. I had seen American targets attacked by all kinds of people as long as I had been working in the Middle East and felt that predicting more of the same lacked dramatic punch. But on September 11, my editor found himself on the front line as he hunkered down in a doorway, clinging on for dear life after these same extremists brought down the World Trade Center right next to my newspaper's New York offices. Bussey was the one proved right, and it was my turn to be bewildered.

Perhaps there is a lie even in the confident, all-knowing tone we reporters use to frame the Middle Eastern events unfolding and sometimes exploding all around us. This tone is born of the transparency achieved by Western societies, and is demanded by editors often unaware of the polluted stream of unreliable data that leaves Middle Eastern societies so misinformed. Reporters cannot let on that the quality of information they work with is usually a fraction of that typical in other sections of the newspaper.

There also are editorial sins of omission, due partly to the pressures of lobbying groups and partly to the need to make stories more acceptable to American readers. Decades of incomplete reporting have opened up great gulfs between perception and reality. It is not surprising that regular readers of Middle East news reports feel baffled, despite the many years that have passed since the beginning of the Arab-Israeli conflict, Iran's Islamic Revolution, or turmoil in Afghanistan. For a long time, the mainstream press has been giving only part of the story.

Editors of the *New York Times* and the *Washington Post* have now apologized for playing down their own reporters' articles about prewar suspicions that Iraq probably had no weapons of mass destruction. This distorted perspective resulted from the difficulty of standing up against the gale-force wind of a U.S. executive fixated on going to war in Iraq. As someone who tried to write articles that challenged the logic of that invasion, I felt by turns futility, emasculation, depression, and even physically sick. Whistle-blowers were low level and the U.S. diplomats who resigned in protest against the plans of their government did not have eye-catchingly senior posts. Top officials seemed reluctant to stand up to a president who wanted only victorious news and might fire anybody who did not give it to him. I discovered this when I confronted a Middle Eastern affairs spokesman deep in the U.S. State Department.

"How can you accept this war? You know it can't work!" I said after setting aside my pen and notebook.

"I know. But if I resign, what good will it do? At least I can do *some* good where I am. If I go, some relative of Dick Cheney's will take my job, and it will only get worse."

Muffled by such political pressure and confused by the region's own lack of transparency, it is also not surprising that grand newspapers and TV shows find it hard to pin down other dynamics in play, like natural anarchy, the weight of history, and the perverse actions of powerful individuals. That's not to mention other drugs in the Middle Eastern bloodstream: the adrenaline rush of risk, the blanket comfort of the clan, the windfall income of corruption, the kick of bigotry, the loot from banditry, sweet revenge, and even sheer bloodlust.

How can Americans understand the level of passion a Palestinian from Gaza feels, if they hardly see bloody carnage on screen, let alone in real life? This distortion doesn't cut only one way. I once sat in a Palestinian West Bank café at the height of the Second Intifada uprising and noticed that the owner had given up on al-Jazeera television's passion-play coverage. The reason he'd switched over to a calmer network, he said, was that life was normal in their town most of the time, and he believed al-Jazeera, safely in the Persian Gulf, was exaggerating the intifada in support of its own agenda to keep the Arab street angry and glued to its screen.

Given the Middle East's history, it is understandably hard to believe that the region can save itself without outside help. Nevertheless, some peripheral states are making progress against the odds. Westernmost Turkey has attracted attention among Middle Eastern leaders and intellectuals with its economic dynamism, freely elected politicians, and negotiations to join the European Union. While the ideology of Middle East states is still mired in the dead ends of authoritarianism, nationalism, or Islamism, Turkey appears one step ahead with its combination of Muslim identity, nation-state, and modernization. At the southeastern end of the Middle East, some Persian Gulf states also set an example of how to play their cards well, attracting tourists, financiers, and functionality.

Defying the traditions of the uplifting ending, which so distorted our coverage of the region in U.S. media, I cannot pretend that I envision much dramatic political improvement soon in the heartlands of Iran, Iraq, Israel, and adjacent countries like Syria, Egypt, Jordan, and Lebanon. Of course, I hope Middle Eastern societies find a way to move beyond their xenophobia and their frustrated, angry rejection of change. But I see the primary responsibility being on Western countries, which have such huge advantages of military strength, economic power, and security at home. One key to what happens is unquestionably in the hand of the United States, the country that is best organized, is most deeply engaged in the region, and whose political support or military protection is often the invisible hand helping countries where things are going relatively well.

There are signs that U.S. attitudes may slowly be changing. President Barack Obama immediately set a good new tone. He gave his first televised interview from the White House to an Arabic-language channel, acknowledged mistakes, promised to listen, understood the interconnection of Middle Eastern problems, and offered a return to the (presumably more evenhanded) U.S. policies of twenty and thirty years ago. Later he publicly reached out to Tehran and recognized its regime, an important gesture for the region and the future of Iran, however unlikely it may be that the current group in power will think it possible to survive more open government and normalization of U.S. relations. He made his first major trip to Turkey, which, for all its flaws, has most successfully shown to the region that universal values of representative governance, secular laws, and a mixed market economy do work for Muslims too. This sensibly paced cycle continued with a speech in Cairo to another audience, the Arabs, offering them hope that his predecessor's ideological rigidity and readiness to use force was an aberration that was over, and that U.S. policy toward Israel/Palestine was in the hands of an empathetic leader who might address their basic sense of dispossession, discrimination, and powerlessness. Obama's outreach is supported by a new spirit in the American mainstream, evidenced by a film like *Body of Lies* in 2008. Actor Leonardo DiCaprio is seen speaking respectable Arabic, falling in love with a fairly credible Middle Easterner, explicitly challenging a claim that a dislike of the Middle East represents America, and ultimately rejecting his role as a U.S. spy in favor of reconnecting to life in the crowded bazaars.

Since this is my book, I will list a few ideas of what I think would help further. In Israel/Palestine, I believe real peace can come only when Israelis agree to fully share the country they have conquered with its native Palestinian inhabitants, that is, work toward a truly democratic, one-state solution. And the United States can win traction in other Middle Eastern states only if it acts evenhandedly in this and other regional disputes, and tries to hold everyone, including Israel, to agreed international standards of behavior. Likewise, Europeans should also stop crediting Israel with their automatic support, whatever it does. European Union states should shake off their nostalgia for a supposedly monocultural past and engage fully with Turkey as it negotiates to join the group. So far it is the best working model of Muslim-Western collaboration and of what even partial inclusion can achieve. For the same reasons, the United States should work to end its blood feud and engage with Iran, partly since that step above all would deprive authoritarian Iranian hardliners of their main domestic political prop. Western countries should review their harsh new visa policies, especially for students and businesspeople, since this is driving a new and self-defeating wedge between East and West.

More generally, the West should look skeptically at policies and analyses based on the perception that "Islam" is a monolith or the cause of "terror," or that the Middle East is a distinct unit that can be dealt with separately from everything else. The lines between East and West, if they were ever very meaningful, are increasingly blurred, with immigration, trade, business, and Internet communities forming an ever-thicker web of interrelationships. Western universities should continue to move the study of the region's history away from Oriental institutes and Middle East centers, as if the issues in play there are somehow aberrant and distinct from those in the rest of the world.

Such inclusive approaches, however, can find no support without personal experience or at least some context, which this book aims to help provide. I love the Middle East because I can still taste the fresh white sheep's cheese wrapped in mint leaves served on a terrace one spring morning in Lebanon's Bekaa Valley. Because I remember the cheerful, conspiratorial smile of the deposed president of former South Yemen as he chased after me down a staircase to give a departing present, a bushy armful of leaves of the mildly narcotic qat. And because I was privileged to sit with the late Mehmed Uzun amid the wealth and sophistication of Sweden and learn how he helped pioneer a Kurdish literary language for a people who did not yet have a homeland, let alone a modern novel.

Middle Eastern suspicions linger about the intentions of more powerful Western states. As I made the arguments for Turkey-Europe convergence on a Turkish TV show, a viewer's message soon popped up on a monitor: "Who do you think you are, Lawrence of Arabia?" When a 2008 exhibition of orientalist paintings was advertised in Istanbul by a portrait of Lawrence in Arab dress, the words "English spy" were soon scrawled over his robes, which, of course, he was in a way. Then someone ripped the poster open as if it had been bombed. Indeed, five years before, a suicide truck bomb had deafeningly ripped apart the nearby British Consulate-General. I lived up the street and saw the blast shoot high up into the sky, the same ugly column of debris and fumes that I had seen twenty years earlier at the U.S. embassy in Beirut. I felt so sick that I couldn't leave the house for hours. My local shopkeepers had no time for terrorists, but later they openly blamed me as a Westerner for the way the Christian West and its ally Israel had so messed up the Middle East that its widening fallout had now reached them and killed their neighbors.

Luckily, interaction between the West and the Middle East is not always brutal. The orientalist exhibition featuring the painting of Lawrence included a performance by Palestinian-British singer Reem Kelani in one of the city's leading venues, Babylon. By coincidence, I discovered she is married to a fellow member of my generation of British Arabists who studied in early 1980s in Damascus, Christopher Somes-Charlton. He told me how he had given up work as a banker to become Kelani's manager and help overcome what he said were barriers of prejudice and politics that constantly blocked her path to a bigger Western audience. Her music joyfully mixes Palestinian folk songs and piano and double bass blues, interlaced for this occasion with the Eastern European gypsy tunes of Turkish clarinettist Selim Sesler. With a foot-stamping rhythm she demanded the attention of her listeners for the suffering of her Middle Eastern people.

"My insistence on a Palestinian narrative makes it hard for me to get mainstream work in the UK," Kelani told me afterward as she signed her CDs for an enthusiastic Istanbul crowd, as receptive as any audience in Paris, London, or New York, and quite a bit younger. "But I insist on it. There's no way people can keep me quiet anymore."

ACKNOWLEDGMENTS

My Middle Eastern journeys began in earnest after my tutor at Oxford, Dr. John Gurney, accepted me to be his only full-time undergraduate student of Persian. I owe a great debt to him and also to his wife, Faraneh, for all that they did to introduce me to the subtleties of Iran and the region.

My reporting benefitted over the years from shared experiences with many colleagues and editors, including Jack Dabaghian, Julie Flint, Hala Jaber, Jack Redden, Claude Salhani, and David Zenian at United Press International; François Duriaud, Alistair Lyon, Alan Philps, Andrew Tarnowski, and Jonathan Wright at Reuters; Patrick Cockburn and Harvey Morris at the *Independent;* and the late Bill Montalbano at the *Los Angeles Times.* I was particularly influenced by my decade at the *Wall Street Journal.* Many thanks to the *Journal*'s foreign editor, John Bussey, for giving me my head to write and travel more or less where I liked, to editor Michael Williams for bringing out a better writer in me, and to Middle East supreme Bill Spindle for his patience and professionalism under unimaginable stress after September 11, 2001.

I learned much from the early example of David Hirst, Middle East correspondent of the *Guardian,* who showed me that truthfulness and levelheaded analysis are more valuable than sensationalism. Thanks too for encouragement, advice, or hospitality during the making of this book to Afshin Abtahi, Didem Akyel, Matthew Campbell, the Darwishah family, Philip Epstein, Olaf Farschid, Christina

Bache Fidan, Stephen Glain, Andrew Jeffreys, Francis Matthew, Damien McElroy, Sagvan Murad, Khaled Oweis, Mariane Pearl, General David Petraeus, Gail Pirkis, Frank Pope, Nicole Pope, Jonathan Randal, Charles Richards, Yigal Schleifer, Eszter Spät, Mohammad Zargham, the exemplary International Committee of the Red Cross, and my inspiring new colleagues at the International Crisis Group, especially Sabine Freizer and Joost Hiltermann. A special thank-you also to Mikael Molin, whose unusual insights and talent for connections strengthened the backbone of the narrative.

I would like to express my gratitude once again to all the hundreds of people I have spoken to or traveled with during the long gestation of this book, and, in several cases, to those who checked relevant chapters. I beg forgiveness if there have been oversights. A Middle Eastern carpet weaver traditionally slips in a wrong knot just to make sure that there is no suspicion of trespassing on God's prerogative of perfection, but any foreign correspondent knows that flawlessness in reporting remains an aspiration as much as a vital goal.

The preparation of this book took many years. It would doubtless have been even longer in the making without the instant faith and support shown by my publisher, Thomas Dunne. Many thanks to his excellent team of editors, notably Rob Kirkpatrick and Margaret Smith, for taking the book smoothly through to publication. Cynthia Merman's deft touch and fine tuning made the text sing. Mike Shand, honorary secretary of the Society of Cartographers in Britain, produced an exacting map on short notice. Thanks as well to Farley Chase of Waxman Literary Agency for shepherding the book forward.

Finally, *Dining with al-Qaeda* would not have taken its current shape without the frankness, editing skill, and novelist's eye of my wife, Jessica Lutz, a former reporter who displayed her cool judgment in a number of tough Middle Eastern corners that we visited together. Above all, however, this book is dedicated to my parents, Maurice and Johanna Pope. Besides introducing me to the Middle East, they taught me to aim for values that proved essential to survive it in one piece—honesty, stamina, and moral scruple.

INDEX

Italic page references denote illustrations.

Ain al-Helweh, Beirut, 20
Ain Sifni, Iraq, 280, 282
Ajami, Fouad, 63
Akol Akol, Albino, 161, 162, 165, 167
al-, *many personal names beginning with.*
    See next element of name
al-Aqsa Mosque (Jerusalem), 50, 58
Alawite Muslims, 3
Albania, 102
Albright, Madeleine, 224
alcoholic drinks, prohibited in Islam, 97,
    292
al-Dumari (The Lamplighter) magazine,
    202–7, 208
Aleppo, Syria, 1–4, 7, 9–10, 194, 209
    troubles in (1980), 3–4
Alexandretta, Turkey, 4–6
Algeria, 143, 211
    independence from France, 194
Ali, Sherif (pretender to Iraq throne), 216
Ali (a chauffeur), 253
al-Jazeera television, 138, 230, 274–75,
    278, 306
al-Jazzar Mosque, 57
al-Qaeda, 61, 114, 125, 136, 140, 147–48,
    151–54, 174, 184–85
    bombings of American embassies, 61,
        184–85
    computers of, bought by the *Wall Street
        Journal,* 174
    disavowed by Saudis, 125
    fight against, 114
    murders of Westerners, 140, 151–54
    origin of, 136
    reporting on, 151
    training camp in Afghanistan, 147–48
American Colony Hotel, Jerusalem, 63
American Israel Public Affairs Committee
    (AIPAC), 53
Americans
    believers in individual opportunity and
        volition, 222, 244
    believers in own good intentions, 42, 44
    identified with Israelis, 42, 44, 135, 238,
        296–97
    in Lebanon, in 1980s, 41–46
    spies, 31

American troops in Iraq, 287–88, 291–302
    author's visit to, 291–95
    boredom felt by, 294–95
Amnesty International, 139
amputations, judicial, 182
Anatolia, conservative social attitudes in, 93
Anderson, Terry, 48
Angawi, Sami, 120–26, 129–31
Ankara, Turkey, 17
anti-Americanism
    ignored in dispatches of reporters to
        Western media, 42, 233
    U.S. support for Israel as cause, 135, 238,
        296–97
Anti-Lebanon Mountains, 29
Apache helicopters, 25
apostasy, 118
Arab Advertising Institute, 206
Arabian Peninsula, tribes of, 123
Arabic language
    author's interpreting work in, 16
    author speaks only, while in Israel, 57,
        59–60
    author's studies of, 1–2, 7, 11, 30, 59, 87,
        133, 171
    God speaks, 134
    rhetorical power of, 289
    Western students of, 34
Arab-Israeli conflict
    attempts to make peace, opposed by
        Islamists, 137
    linkage to anti-Americanism, 248
    reporting on, 50, 60–67
    warped values displayed in, 103
    See also Israeli-Palestinian conflict
Arab League, 304
Arab Legion, 5
Arab nationalism, 200
Arabness
    of Israel, partly due to immigration of
        Jews from Middle East, 60
    as trait shared by Jews to some extent, 54
Arabs
    as conquerors, 81
    of Iraq, 283–84
    moral tradition of, 94
    writers, 63

American embassy, 34
Soviet embassy, 36–37
Damascus Sheraton Hotel, 16–17
Damascus Spring, 200, 202, 208
Daoud (a professor at Mosul University),
289–91
Darfur, Sudan, 157
Darwish, Mahmoud, 61
Davis, Peter, 23–24
deaths, in news stories, relative importance
of, on an ethnic basis, 45, 53
"Death to America!" slogan, not meant
literally, 72, 75–76
de-development, 225
democracy
difficult to introduce into Middle East,
193
not liked, 202
depleted uranium, 223, 227
Der Spiegel magazine, 107, 109
Desert Fox bombardments, 234
desert mentality, to own no more than you
can carry, 126
devil worshippers, 273, 280
diaspora populations, lobbying groups of, 53
DiCaprio, Leonardo, 307
Dickcheney (name of a Kurdish baby), 268
Dinka tribesmen, 158, 161, *167*
Diriya, Saudi Arabia, 122–23
Diyarbakir, Turkey, 242
dogs, unusual to have as pets in Muslim
lands, 88
Dohuk, Iraq, 243, 244–45, 265, 282, 284
"Dollarawa," Kurdistan, 253
Dome of the Rock, Jerusalem, 58, 61
Douglas, Leigh, 48
Douri, Izzat Ibrahim al-, 221
driving, not allowed to women in Saudi
Arabia, 95–97
drug use
execution for, 147
in Iran, 83
Druze, 19
Dubai, 172, 216
sheik of, 210–11
Duriaud, François, 158, 168
Durrani, Tehmina, 187

eating, with the right hand, 6
Economist, The, 16, 85
Edris (a Yezidi), 283–84
Egypt, 35, 86–87, 91, 171–72, 193, 210, 211,
307
American aid to, 37
author's first journalism job in, 13–15
damage to culture, after revolution against
King Farouk, 193
dynastic rule of, 211
favored by U.S., 135, 210
Obama's reaching out to, 307
peace with Israel, 35
women in, 91
Egyptian Gazette, 13–16
spoof stories inserted by author, 15
elections, 186, 192
England
class system, 186
high culture of, 171
schooling, compared to Saudi, 128
See also Britain
English language, mastery of, by educated
Middle Easterners, 171
Esam (a Saudi), 130
Europeans, interested in Middle Eastern men,
8–9
European Union, 307
executions, public, 39–40

facts
"hang-ups" about, shouldn't get in
the way, 25
in reporting and writing books, 25–27
Fadi (a student), 103
Faisal, Abu, 148–49
Faisal, Prince Turki al-, 137, 146, 174, 185,
215
Faisaliyeh, mosque of the, Mecca, 133
famine, in the Sudan, 156–63
somewhat a myth, 169
Farouk, King, 193
Farouq, Fariq, 283
Farzat, Ali, 203–4, 206–7
Fassihi, Farnaz, 278
Fatah, 35
Faw peninsula, Iraq, 106–11

female circumcision, 91
Fertile Crescent, 4
fez, 209
filth and rubbish in public, not being
    responsible for, 88
Financial Times, 157
First World War, 29
Fisk, Robert, 11, 16, 21–25, 26, 55
Flint, Julie, 20
foreign correspondents, 16
    habits of successful, 242–43
Fox News, 52
France, 93
Franks, Tommy, 260
freedom, in Iraq, meaning freedom to kill,
    234
French
    in Lebanon, in 1980s, 41–42, 45
    in Middle East, 40
    spies, 31
Friday
    day of obligatory prayer, 89–90
    day of rest, 74
Fritz (a photographer), 270

Galpin, Richard, 176
Garang, John, 162
Gardner, Amanda, 153
Gardner, Frank, 153
Gaza
    Israeli settlements withdrawn from (2005),
        51, 64
    Israel's complete control of, an open-air
        prison, 64–65
    reporting from, 64–65, 306
general strikes, by shopkeepers, 3
gerîvan (Yezidi clothing item), 284
Gezira club, Cairo, 87
Ghadafi, Muammar al-, 48, 211
Ghamdi, Ahmed al-, 146
Ghamdi, Hamza al-, 146
Gigot, Paul, 268
Gisele (at UPI, Beirut), 18–19
Glain, Stephen, 51, 60, 62–63, 198, 219,
    221
Glass, Charlie, 48
Glubb, John (Pasha), 5

God
    of Muslims, 81
    speaks Arabic, 81
Golan Heights, 35, 205
Gold, Dore, 62
Golden, Michael, 155
Golestan, Kaveh, 269
Goltz, Thomas, 239
government, predictability of,
    better than chaos, 177
gowns, Muslim, 140
Great Mosque (Mecca), seized by tribal
    ikhwan (1979), 125
Greek Americans, lobbyists, 53
Greek Orthodox priest, gay advance by, 7
Greeks
    in Sudan, 157
    in Turkey (Anatolia), 193
Green Line (in Beirut), 42, 43
Greenstock, Sir Jeremy, 260–61
Grenada, 44
ground-to-air missiles, 107
Gulf Cooperation Council, 304
Gulf War (1991)
    author's reporting in, 22, 218
    destruction of Iraq's infrastructure after,
        U.S. blamed for, 293, 297
    foreign correspondents' deaths in, 242
    looting, disorder, and reprisals, appearing
        after liberation, 280
    U.S. abandonment of Kurds,
        at conclusion of, 260

Ha'aretz newspaper, 53
Hadi, Dr. Ahlam Al-, 222–24, 226–27
hadith, as manual for living, 139
Hafez, Mohammad Shems al-Din, 70–83
    burial place of, the Hafeziyeh, 80, 81–83
    oracles (*fal*) to be found in work of, 74, 82
Haifa, Israel, 57
hajj (pilgrimage), 117–19
    money to be made from, 124
Hajji (a driver), 242–43
Hama, Syria, 200–202
    flattened by Baathist artillery, 201
Hamas (Palestine), 100, 103
Haqqi (a fixer), 300

Iran (*continued*)
Islamic revolution in, causing millions
to emigrate, 194
loyalty to, 100
native dress, 78
Obama's reaching out to, 307
original culture of, kept when it adopted
Islam, 81
reaching out to, 307
revolutionary ferments, coverage of, 69–70
sympathy for America after 9/11 disaster,
99
women in, 90, 92, 94
Iran-Iraq War, 76, 100–113, 114, 115
American support of Iraq during, 76, 102,
114, 115, 297
author's reporting during, 218, 257–58
causing millions to emigrate, 194
chemical warfare during, 240
commemorative exhibit of, 100–106,
112–13
news coverage of, 19, 85
spiritual bonding experienced by
warriors in, 112
stalemate in, 68
strain of, on Iran, 31
Iraq, 218–31
author's unauthorized visits to,
during wars, 218–19
chemical weapon use, 76
children suffering, 226
democratization of, 250
dictatorship in, 218
difficulty of governing it, after 2003
conquest, 247, 287–302
dismissal of Baathists and Iraqi army after
the Iraq War, 294
economy of, 247
environmental unhealthiness of, 225
exodus of best-educated people from,
from 1990s to present, 194
fragmented society of, 237
marshes, 107
monarchy overthrown, 193, 210, 218
newspapers in, 14
potential for success after Hussein, 238
propaganda, 234

sanctions against, hardship caused by,
223–27, 233–34, 268
societal breakdown in, after the Iraq War,
290–91
women in, 91
Iraq Daily newspaper, 281
Iraqi News Agency, 19
Iraq Institute of Democracy, 249
Iraqis
American misunderstanding of, 31
fearfulness of, 218, 222
suspiciousness of the West, 233
views about liberation by Americans,
252–53
Iraq Today newspaper, 249
Iraq War (2003), 232–302
American troops in, 287–88, 291–302
author's reportng of, 218–19, 287–302
decision to invade, 232, 239
eve of, 260–65
fleeing from, 262, 266–67
Iraqi resistance in, 267
looting, disorder, and reprisals, appearing
after liberation, 280, 289
newspapers' justification of, 26, 62, 235
northern front, 243, 272
start of, 265–67
supported by American hard-liner
opinion-makers, 235
supported by Israel hard-liners, 62
unstoppability of, 260–61
warnings beforehand of the likely
consequence of invasion, 233–34,
237–39, 247
Ireland, 91
Iridium, 264
Islam
converting to, 118
different everywhere, 81, 91
founding of, 118–19
perceived as monolithic, 134–35, 307
relations with Christianity and Judaism,
134
warlike nature of, claimed, 134
Islamabad, Pakistan, 173
Islamic Emirate of Afghanistan, 173. *See also*
Afghanistan

Islamic fundamentalism, 79, 80, 181
Islamic Jihad (Lebanon), 48
Islamic law, 119, 134
Islamic punishments, 181–82
Islamic Republic (newspaper), 69
Islamic Republic News Agency (INRA)
    (Iran), 19, 45, 71, 111
Islamic Republic of Iran, 68. *See also* Iran
Islamic Revolution (Iran), 12, 31, 102
    reviving the spirit of, 104
Islamic Revolutionary Guards Corps (Iran),
    100, 103, 104
Islamic world
    too large a concept to be meaningful, 304
    unity of, goal, 119
Islamist fundamentalism, underestimated,
    304–5
Islamist radicals (Iraq), 300
    killings by, 290
Islamists
    author's discussion with one who debates
        killing him, 140–43
    dissidents in Saudi Arabia, 136–39
    supported by Iran, 102–3
    in Syria, 3
Ismaili (Muslims), 123
Israel, 18–20, 30, 41, 51–67, 103, 114–15,
    205, 210, 267–68, 307
    Americans' automatic support for, 51–54,
        307
    Arab-Israel coexistence in, 62, 66
    Arab states that make peace with, 210
    army, in Lebanon, in 1980s, 41
    author's bias against, 54–60
    creation of State of, 30
    criticism of, 53
    expansion into Palestinian
        territories, 51
    hard treatment of Palestinians, 54
    invasion of Lebanon (1982), 18–20
    Lebanon border crossing, 56
    Muslim world's hatred of, 103, 205
    prosperity of, 56
    right-wingers in, 53
    sins of, according to Khameini, 114–15
    a typical Middle Eastern state, 59
    Israeli Arabs, attitudes of, 62

Israeli-Palestinian conflict
    incomprehension of American editors,
        267–68
    one-state solution for, 307
    See also Arab-Israeli conflict
Israelis
    Arabness of, 60
    entrepreneurs, investing in Eastern
        Europe, 65
Istanbul, 49, 172
    former Muslim center, 304
    Topkapi Palace, 84
Istanbul Museum of Modern Art, 193
Italians, in Lebanon, in 1980s, 41

Jalalabad, Afghanistan, 175
Jaman, Iraq, 266
Jaquemet, Stéphane, 159, 165
Jeddah, Saudi Arabia, 94, 95, 118, 119, 129,
    136
    urban sculpture in, *122*
Jeddah Economic Forum, 97–98
Jerusalem
    Arab-Israeli dividing lines in, 63
    history and symbolism of, 58–59
    sealed off from West Bank, 61
Jerusalem syndrome, 58
Jewish-Americans, lobbyists, 53
Jewishness, 54
Jews
    Koran's injunctions against, 133
    worldwide, not represented solely by Israel,
        54
jihad, 143
jihadists, 143–48
Jirgis (a writer), 255–56
Jomard, Jazeel Abd al-Jabbar al-, 295–301,
    295
Jordan, 5, 12, 135
    favored by U.S., 210
    modernization of, 211–14
journalism
    Americans' loss of trust in, 278
    emotion in, 26
    ethics of, 26
    harmonized views in (groupthink), 27
    made-up and embellished details in, 21–27

Spät, Eszter, 278–79
Special Forces (American), 22
Spindle, Bill, 60–61, 65–66, 70–73, 112,
    206, 208, 234, 237, 273, 284–85, 293,
    296
spying, 28–32
    author accused of, 30–32
    author propositioned for, but declines,
        28, 31–32
    by British, 29–30
    by foreign powers in the Middle East, 34
Stahl, Lesley, 224
Stanford Maps, 265
Stark, Freya, 5
Star of David, 103
starving children, appeal of, 163
states, predictability of, better than chaos,
    177
Steiger, Paul, 268
Stockholm syndrome, 38
stockings, women's, 184
stone throwing at Satan, 118–19
Sudan, 156–69
    division of, between Muslim North and
        Christian/animist South, 156
    famine in, 156–69
    weak government of, 169
Sudan News Agency, 166
Sudan People's Liberation Army (SPLA),
    159–69
suicide, rarity of, in Middle East (aside from
    suicide bombers), 269
suicide bombings
    graffito depicting, 65
    invention of, 40
    in Iraq, 286
    motivation for, 146
    pictures of, in a "terrorist exhibition,"
        102–3
    in Turkey, 308
    of U.S. embassies in East Africa, 184–85
Suleyman, Colonel (Syrian), 209–10
Suleymani, Iraq, 268
Sunni Muslims
    history of, 105
    in Iran, 80
    Iraqi extremists, 285–86, 302

in Lebanon, 40
in Syria, 3
survivor's guilt, 168
Swiss, the, 166
Syria, 1–10, 17, 32–37, 38, 41, 55, 91, 194,
    196–217
    in axis of evil, 294
    civil liberties in, 203
    crossing the border into, 196–98
    damage to culture, with revolution, 194
    dictatorship in, 38, 55
    dynastic rule of, 211
    economy, 202
    ethnic mosaic of, 209
    human rights in, 207
    Intelligence service (mukhabarat), 208–10
    in Lebanon, in 1980s, 41
    Ministry of Information, 17
    Palestinian refugees in, 32–33
    political parties, 205
    union with Libya, 14
    women in, 91
Syriac Orthodox Christians, 209

tabloids, infotainment reporting by, 26
Tahsin Beg, 279–80, 286
Tajiks, 177
Talabani, Hero, 258
Talabani, Jalal, 254, 258–59, 260, 285
Taliban, 106, 172–85, 176
    appearance of, 179
    drive against modernity, 176
    fight against, 76, 114
Tani, General Ghazai Dara al-, 220
Tanzania, U.S. embassy bombing (1998),
    184
taqiyyeh, 77
Tehran, Iran, 80, 99–100, 198
Tehran Times, 31
Tel Aviv, 59, 60
television
    images of Palestinian suffering on, 145
    Saudi, 98, 130
Temple Mount, Jerusalem, 58
terrorism
    condemned by an Iranian diplomat, 104
    a loaded word in news stories, 113

resentment of, by some Saudis, 129
Saud alliance with, 214
Waldman, Peter, 62, 237–39
Wall Street Journal
  American troops' greeting to, 288
  audience of, many retired, news catered to
    reading habits of, 278
  author hired by, to cover Middle East,
    49–50
  author reporting to, 22, 219, 243
  author's interview with a missionary not
    printed, 149–50
  Chinese wall separating editorial from
    op-ed pages, 62–63
  coverage of Middle East, 49–50, 60–63
  editorial changes distorting stories,
    112–13
  and the execution of Danny Pearl, 151–52
  front-page A-heds in, 151
  journalist ethics of, 26
  letters to the editor, 53
  making a case for invading Iraq, 235, 261
  opinion pages of, 62, 235, 267, 268
  a reporter getting on front page of, 72–73,
    112–13
  reporting from Afghanistan, 172
  reporting from Baghdad, 284
  reporting from Israel, watering down of
    news, 63–64
  reporting from Saudi Arabia, 131
  view of Israeli-Palestinian conflict, 268
waqf, author called a, 9
war
  excitement of, 11
  romanticism of, in Middle Eastern films, 8
war on terror, 99
  called a "crusade," 238
war reporters
  death-cheating addiction of, 239
  deaths of, 109, 110, 268–69, 271
  embedded, 241
  hungry to see action, 268–71
  as participants in fighting, 271
  taking courses in battlefield safety, 240
Washington Post, 111
  apologies for not challenging the premises
    of the Iraq War, 305

Wau, Sudan, 157–69
Wazir Akbar Khan, Kabul, 176
Weekly Standard, 235
Western lifestyle, sought by some Saudis, 128
Western Wall, Jerusalem, 58
whippings, 182
whistleblowers, 305
Wilder, David, 64
Wilders, Geert, 134
wine, 72
  prohibited in Islam, 77
"Wipe out Israel" slogan, not meant literally,
    71
wives, multiple, allowed to Muslims but
    uncommon, 85–86
Wolfowitz, Paul, 238
women in Muslim society, 84–98
  absent in public space, in Middle East, 8
  anonymous sex and propositioning of men
    by, 92
  behavior of, in private, 86
  education of, 95
  honor killings of, 91
  men's assumed lust for, 93
  oppression of, 181, 182–84
  oversight of, by male family members, 89,
    91–92, 94–95
  professionals and businesswomen, 92–94,
    95, 96–98
  restrictions on, in public, 8, 87
  schooling forbidden to, in Afghanistan,
    183–84
  segregation of living quarters, 85
  traditional dress of, 85, 90, 91, 93–94, 96,
    182–84
World Trade Center destruction (2001),
    65–66, 126, 145, 305
World War II, spell of, 11
worship, of buildings, considered wrong,
    121–23
Wright, Jonathan, 26, 45, 48
writing, factuality in, rather than exciting
    embellishments, 25–27
Wurzelbacher, Joe "the Plumber," 51–52

Yahyazadeh, Shabnam, 104–5
Yarmuk refugee camp, Syria, 32–33